D1460361

Theatrical Costume

PERFORMING ARTS INFORMATION GUIDE SERIES

Series Editor: Louis A. Rachow, Librarian, The Walter Hampden-Edwin Booth Theatre Collection and Memorial Library, New York

Also in this series:

ACTORS AND ACTING—*Edited by Stephen M. Archer**

AMERICAN AND ENGLISH POPULAR ENTERTAINMENT—*Edited by Don B. Wilmeth*

THE AMERICAN STAGE TO WORLD WAR I—*Edited by Don B. Wilmeth*

THE AMERICAN STAGE FROM WORLD WAR I TO THE 1970S—*Edited by Don B. Wilmeth**

BUSINESS OF THE THEATRE, FILMS, AND BROADCASTING—*Edited by J. Kline Hobbs**

GUIDE TO DANCE IN FILM—*Edited by David Parker and Esther Siegel*

LAW OF THE THEATRE, FILMS, AND BROADCASTING—*Edited by Daniel Jon Strehl**

PERFORMING ARTS RESEARCH—*Edited by Marion K. Whalon*

STAGE SCENERY, MACHINERY, AND LIGHTING—*Edited by Richard Stoddard*

THEATRE AND CINEMA ARCHITECTURE—*Edited by Richard Stoddard*

*in preparation

The above series is part of the
GALE INFORMATION GUIDE LIBRARY

The Library consists of a number of separate series of guides covering major areas in the social sciences, humanities, and current affairs.

General Editor: Paul Wasserman, Professor and former Dean, School of Library and Information Services, University of Maryland

Managing Editor: Denise Allard Adzigian, Gale Research Company

Theatrical Costume.

A GUIDE TO INFORMATION SOURCES

Volume 6 in the Performing Arts Information Guide Series

Jackson Kesler

Associate Professor of Communication and Theatre
Western Kentucky University
Bowling Green

Gale Research Company
Book Tower, Detroit, Michigan 48226

PN
2067
K47

Library of Congress Cataloging in Publication Data

Kesler, Jackson.
    Theatrical costume.

    (Performing arts information guide series ; v. 6)
(Gale information guide library)
    Includes indexes.
    1. Costume—Bibliography. I. Title.
Z5691.K47   [PN2067]   016.792'026   79-22881
ISBN 0-8103-1455-X

VITA

Jackson Kesler studied at Randolph-Macon College (B.A., 1959), George Peabody College (M.A., 1960) and the University of Texas at Austin (Ph.D., 1968). He has taught on the faculty of the University of Texas (1968) and the University of Georgia (1968-76). Presently he is associate professor of communication and theatre at Western Kentucky University, Bowling Green, where he designs costumes for university productions and teaches a full complement of courses in the area of costuming. He has served as designer for over eighty productions of theatre, opera, ballet, and outdoor dramas. He has published articles in THEATRE CRAFTS, SOUTHERN THEATRE and other professional journals. He is a member of the Costume Society of Great Britain and other organizations.

CONTENTS

Preface   ix

Chapter 1. Reference Works   1
   A. Bibliographies   1
   B. Dictionaries, Encyclopedias, and Glossaries   4
   C. Sourcebooks and Guidebooks   8

Chapter 2. Theatrical Costume   13
   A. Western Theatrical Costume   13
   B. Theatrical Costume of the East   23
   C. Costume for the Dance   25
   D. Costume for the Cinema   31

Chapter 3. Historical Costume   33
   A. General Works   33
       1. Pre-Twentieth-Century Costume   33
       2. Twentieth-Century Costume   45
   B. Costume by Geographical Areas   48
       1. Costume of Africa   48
       2. Costume of the Americas   51
           a. North America   51
           b. North American Indians   57
           c. Central and South America   61
       3. Costume of the Ancient World   65
       4. Costume of the British   68
           a. England   68
           b. British Isles, Australia, and South Africa   76
       5. Costume of Eastern Europe, The Near East, and
           Russia   79
       6. Costume of the Orient   85
       7. Costume of Scandinavia   90
       8. Costume of Western and Southern Europe   94
           a. General Works   94
           b. France   96
           c. Germany, Austria, and Switzerland   98
           d. Italy   99

Contents

        e. Netherlands 101
        f. Spain and Portugal 102

Chapter 4. Accoutrements and Special Categories of Costume....... 107
    A. Accessories 107
    B. Dance Wear 113
    C. Fashion Plates and Silhouettes 114
    D. Footwear.................................. 115
    E. Headwear 117
    F. Jewelry................................... 119
    G. Juvenile Costume 125
    H. Makeup and Hairstyles 127
    I. Masks 133
    J. Men's Wear 137
    K. Militaria 139
    L. Occupational Costume Including Academic and
                Ecclesiastical Costume.................... 158
    M. Regalia, Coronation Costume, and Heraldry............ 163
    N. Special Occasion: Births, Deaths, and Marriages 169
    O. Costume for Sports............................ 171
    P. Underclothes and Foundation Garments................ 173

Chapter 5. Theatrical and Historical Movement and Dance 177

Chapter 6. Manners, Modes, and Customs 189

Chapter 7. Selected Illustrated Social History 199

Chapter 8. Costume Design............................. 209

Chapter 9. Ornamentation and Symbols 217

Chapter 10. Costume Construction Techniques and Pattern
             Sources.............................. 221

Chapter 11. Textile History and Conservation 239

Chapter 12. Textile Decoration: Dyeing, Painting, and
             Printing............................. 247

Chapter 13. Fashion Designers and the Fashion World........... 251

Chapter 14. Theory and Psychology of Fashion and Costume 255

Author Index 261

Title Index 277

Subject Index 301

PREFACE

The principal purpose of this publication is to provide for costume designers, primarily, a practical, utilitarian listing, mostly of English-title books in the field in more recent years. Unfortunately, the newest such publication of significant length and scope has been the 1957 supplement to Monro and Cook's COSTUME INDEX (see entry 17). Other reference and bibliographical studies since then have been restricted in length or scope or devoted to special interest areas; all are listed in chapter 1. Attention in this volume, however, has been given mainly to publications issued since 1957, generally omitting numbers from previous bibliographies, the exception being when an earlier publication retains a position of prominence in an area. A broad definition of the subject of theatrical costume has been taken, with the inclusion of several important areas related to costuming that have not been previously included in bibliographical studies. All annotations and entries have been made with the basic principle in mind of that particular volume's potential value to a working costume designer. Also, no attempt has been made to distinguish among the many levels of design, for example, children's theatre or professional theatre.

The procedure for the study has been chosen to provide a practical, usable bibliography, as opposed to a comprehensive volume. Most foreign-language publications have been omitted with the exception of those unique in an area or those with outstanding illustrative content. The entries in this bibliography are generally to be found without excessive difficulty in most libraries or through their lending facilities. All volumes have been personally examined by the author for content prior to inclusion. The books are located mainly in the libraries of the following institutions: Western Kentucky University; the University of Texas at Austin; Nashville University Center; University of Georgia; The Costume Institute, Metropolitan Museum of Art; The Fashion Institute of Technology; and Tulsa University. Because of the paucity of costume-related periodical information, such has not been included. With the exception of the bulletins of the costume societies of Great Britain and America, no periodical is devoted exclusively to the field. Occasional articles on costume are to be found in various publications as listed in ULRICH'S INTERNATIONAL

Preface

PERIODICALS DIRECTORY: A CLASSIFIED GUIDE TO CURRENT PERI-
ODICALS, FOREIGN AND DOMESTIC (17th ed., 1977-78) and/or
GUIDE TO REFERENCE BOOKS (9th ed., 1976), compiled by Eugene P.
Sheehy.

Three unpublished doctoral dissertations are of particular interest to students of theatrical costuming in the American professional stage. These
are Genevieve Richardson, "The Costuming on the American Stage, 1751-
1901: A Study of Major Developments in Wardrobe Practice and Costume
Style," University of Illinois, 1953; Janet Loring, "Costuming on the New
York Stage from 1895 to 1915 with Particular Emphasis on Charles Frohman's
Companies," State University of Iowa, 1960; and Josephine Paterek, "A
Survey of Costuming of the New York Commercial Stage: 1914-1934," 3
vols., University of Minnesota, 1961.

The organization of the material as presented in the table of contents is
straightforward and practical. Notations of cross-references are listed at
the beginning of each section. Because of the overlapping of the areas
of theatrical costuming and the various approaches to them, the reader
should note the necessity of referring to general as well as specific subject areas. The main determinant of the placement of a title within a
particular section has been its major emphasis and/or value. The primary
concern has been topical subject material rather than nationalistic concerns; for example, a book on particular African hairstyles was placed in
the section on makeup and hairstyles as opposed to the section on African costume. In such cases, cross-referencing from the primary to the
secondary area is necessary.

The author gratefully acknowledges a grant from the Faculty Research Committee of Western Kentucky University. Special gratitude is expressed to
numerous individuals and libraries, particularly Mrs. Jane Combs of the
Hoblitzelle Theatre Arts Collection, the University of Texas at Austin;
Mr. Gordon Stone, Librarian of the Costume Institute of the Metropolitan
Museum of Art; and Mr. Robert Turek and the entire Reference and Technical Services Staff of the Helm-Cravens Library, Western Kentucky University. Particular gratitude is expressed to my wife Betty for her unfail-
ing assistance and to my family for their support and patience.

Chapter 1
REFERENCE WORKS

A. BIBLIOGRAPHIES

1 American Educational Theatre Association. THEATRE ARTS PUBLICA-
TIONS AVAILABLE IN THE UNITED STATES, 1947-1952: A FIVE YEAR
BIBLIOGRAPHY. Edited by William W. Melnitz. Dubuque, Iowa: 1959.

> Sources of unannotated entries on costume, entries 1028-1194.

2 _____. THEATRE ARTS PUBLICATIONS AVAILABLE IN THE UNITED
STATES, 1953-1957: A FIVE YEAR BIBLIOGRAPHY. Edited by Roger
M. Busfield, Jr. Evanston, Ill.: 1964.

> Sources on costuming in unannotated bibliographic entries 2007-
> 2100.

3 Anthony, Pegaret, and Arnold, Janet. COSTUME: A GENERAL BIBLI-
OGRAPHY. London: Victoria and Albert Museum, 1974.

> Selected bibliography of more recent publications arranged by
> subject headings covering most areas of costuming.

4 Baker, Blanch M. DRAMATIC BIBLIOGRAPHY: AN ANNOTATED LIST
OF BOOKS ON THE HISTORY AND CRITICISM OF THE DRAMA AND
STAGE AND ON THE ALLIED ARTS OF THE THEATRE. 1933. Reprint.
New York: Benjamin Blom, 1968.

> Somewhat dated; entries in section on costume valuable for
> older sources.

5 _____. THEATRE AND ALLIED ARTS: A GUIDE TO BOOKS DEALING
WITH THE HISTORY, CRITICISM AND TEACHING OF THE DRAMA AND
THEATRE AND RELATED ARTS AND CRAFTS. New York: H.W. Wilson
Co., 1952. Reprint. New York: Benjamin Blom, 1967.

> Section on costume sources.

Reference Works

6 Burston, W.H., and Green, C.W., eds. HANDBOOK FOR HISTORY
TEACHERS. London: Methuen and Co., 1962.

Useful guide to books on social history as well as books on
costume.

7 Colas, Rene. BIBLIOGRAPHIE GENERALE DU COSTUME ET DE LA
MODE: DESCRIPTION DES SUITES, RECUEILS, SERIES, REVUES ET
LIVRES FRANCAIS ET ETRANGERS RELATIFS AU COSTUME CIVIL, MILI-
TAIRE ET RELIGIEUX, AUX MODES, AUX COIFFURES ET AUX DIVERS
ACCESSOIRES DE L'HABILLEMENT, AVEC UNE TABLE METHODIQUE ET
UN INDEX ALPHABETIQUE. 2 vols. 1933. Reprint. New York:
Hacker Art Books, 1969.

Extensive listing of sources in all languages.

8 COSTUME: A LIST OF BOOKS. Detroit: Detroit Public Library, 1928.

Dated bibliography, containing some entries not found elsewhere.

9 Eicher, Joanna Bubolz. AFRICAN DRESS: A SELECT AND ANNOTATED
BIBLIOGRAPHY OF SUBSAHARAN COUNTRIES. East Lansing: Michigan
State University Press, 1969.

Bibliography of 1,025 entries arranged by country; most extensive bibliography in the area.

10 Filene, Adele. "Bibliography on Costume." New York: Costume Society of America, 1975. Mimeographed.

Eighteen-page listing of recent publications and reprints, with
some annotations and a guide to specific areas within costuming to which the entry most pertains; list of publishers.

11 Hiler, Hilaire, and Hiler, Meyer. BIBLIOGRAPHY OF COSTUME: A
DICTIONARY CATALOG OF ABOUT EIGHT THOUSAND BOOKS AND
PERIODICALS. New York: H.W. Wilson Co., 1939.

Somewhat dated but quite extensive listing.

12 Hunter, Frederick J. DRAMA BIBLIOGRAPHY: A SHORT-TITLED GUIDE
TO EXTENDED READING IN DRAMATIC ART FOR THE ENGLISH-SPEAK-
ING AUDIENCE AND STUDENTS IN THEATRE. Boston: G.K. Hall and
Co., 1971.

Two sections of unannotated entries: "Costume: Construction
and Design" and "Costume: History of Dress."

13 Laver, James. THE LITERATURE OF FASHION. London: Cambridge University Press, 1947.

Exhibition catalog with 251 entries, mostly annotated, of costume sources.

14 Levy, June Rosine. AFRICAN TRADITIONAL GARB OF THE NATIVE TRIBES OF SOUTHERN AFRICA. Johannesburg: University of Witwatersrand, 1972.

Bibliography of 252 annotations of sources on all facets of the subject including dress, physical adornment, hairstyles, and accessories.

15 Lipperheide, Franz Joseph freiherr von. KATALOG DER FREIHERRLICH VON LIPPERHEIDE'SCHEN KOSTUMEBIBLIOTHEK. 2 vols. 1896-1905. Reprint. New York: Hacker Art Books, 1963.

Main source of extensive listings of costume materials in the nineteenth century.

16 Meyers, Charles L. BIBLIOGRAPHY OF COLONIAL COSTUME COMPILED FOR THE SOCIETY OF COLONIAL WARS IN THE STATE OF NEW JERSEY. New York: Society of Colonial Wars in the State of New Jersey, 1923.

Somewhat dated but arranged by author according to library depository; covers years 1600 to 1775 with sections on Shakespeare and Elizabethan festivals and pageants.

17 Monro, Isabel, and Cook, Dorothy E., eds. COSTUME INDEX: A SUBJECT INDEX TO PLATES AND ILLUSTRATED TEXT. New York: H.W. Wilson Co., 1937. Supplement, 1957.

Includes list of costume books.

18 A READING AND REFERENCE LIST ON COSTUME, ARRANGED ALPHABETICALLY. Brooklyn: Brooklyn Public Library, 1932.

Published in COSTUME DESIGN AND ILLUSTRATION by Traphagen (entry 1454); lists sources of late nineteenth and early twentieth century costume with useful arrangement and entries.

19 Snowden, James. EUROPEAN FOLK DRESS: A BIBLIOGRAPHY. London: Costume Society, 1973.

Five-hundred fifty-five entries of information on national and regional dress plus peasant, burgher, festival, and dance costume in European countries.

20 Stephenson, Lois, and Stephenson, Richard. A HISTORY AND ANNO-
TATED BIBLIOGRAPHY OF SKATING COSTUME. Meriden, Conn.: Bay-
berry Hill Press, 1970.

Unique book with 166 bibliographic annotations and 28 plates
illustrating historical skating costume from 1680 to present;
historical survey in text.

21 THE WESTERN RESERVE HISTORICAL SOCIETY: THE CHARLES G. KING
COLLECTION OF BOOKS ON COSTUME. Cleveland: Western Reserve
Historical Society, 1914.

Over one hundred annotations in this bibliography of older
books on costume.

B. DICTIONARIES, ENCYCLOPEDIAS, AND GLOSSARIES

22 American Fabrics Magazine. ENCYCLOPEDIA OF TEXTILES: AN ILLUS-
TRATED AND AUTHORITATIVE SOURCE BOOK ON TEXTILES, PRESENT-
ING A COMPLETE AND PRACTICAL COVERAGE OF THE ENTIRE FIELD--
ITS HISTORY AND ORIGINS, ITS ART AND DESIGN, ITS NATURAL
AND MAN-MADE FIBERS, ITS MANUFACTURING AND FINISHING
PROCESSES, COLOR AND DYES, TEXTILE PRINTING, SPECIALTY END
USES. PLUS A COMPREHENSIVE DICTIONARY OF TEXTILE TERMS.
2d ed. Englewood Cliffs, N.J.: Prentice-Hall, 1972.

Lengthy subtitle indicative of comprehensiveness of volume;
dictionary of textile terms useful.

23 Baker, William Henry. A DICTIONARY OF MEN'S WEAR. Cleveland:
Britton Printing Co., 1908.

Unillustrated and quite dated but valuable source for late
nineteenth century men's fashions, including military, trade,
civil and livery dress.

24 Birmingham, Frederic A. ESQUIRE FASHION GUIDE FOR ALL OCCA-
SIONS. New York: Harper and Brothers, 1957.

Valuable glossary of male fashion words and meanings.

25 Calasibetta, Charlotte Mankey. FAIRCHILD'S DICTIONARY OF FASHION.
New York: Fairchild Publications, 1975.

Dictionary primarily of modern fashion terms but with some
historical information, drawings, and photographs.

26 Carbone, Linda. DICTIONARY OF SEWING TERMINOLOGY. New
York: Arco Publishing Co., 1977.

Comprehensive dictionary composed of concise and authoritative definitions of sewing and garment construction terms with
drawings and equivalency charts.

27 Carman, W.Y. A DICTIONARY OF MILITARY UNIFORMS. New York:
Charles Scribner's Sons, 1977.

More than fifteen hundred entries, definitions and descriptions,
and illustrations of garments, badges, decorations, headdresses,
and accessories for most countries; valuable reference source;
numerous black-and-white and some colored illustrations.

28 Caulfield, S.F.A., and Saward, B.C. THE DICTIONARY OF NEEDLE-
WORK: AN ENCYCLOPEDIA OF ARTISTIC, PLAIN AND FANCY NEED-
LEWORK. 1885. Reprint. London: Paul Hamlyn, 1972.

Complete dictionary with illustrations of many decorative
motifs, techniques, patterns, and designs of great use to costumers.

29 Clarke, Mary, and Vaughan, David. THE ENCYCLOPEDIA OF DANCE
AND BALLET. New York: G.P. Putnam's Sons, 1977.

Useful reference of dance and movement terms, with brief section on design and numerous black-and-white photographs of
costumed performers.

30 Cox, James Stevens. AN ILLUSTRATED DICTIONARY OF HAIRDRESS-
ING AND WIGMAKING: CONTAINING WORDS, TERMS, AND
PHRASES (CURRENT AND OBSOLETE), DIALECTAL, FOREIGN, AND
TECHNICAL, USED IN BRITAIN AND AMERICA PERTAINING TO THE
CRAFTS OF HAIRDRESSING AND WIGMAKING: ALSO WORDS DE-
RIVED FROM THESE CRAFTS HAVING A WIDER USE: BUT EXCLUDING,
WITH SOME NECESSARY EXCEPTIONS, MEDICAL, CHEMICAL AND
SCIENTIFIC TERMS. London: Hairdressers' Technical Council, 1966.

Extensive dictionary with 664 monochrome illustrations covering every facet of the subject.

31 Cunnington, C. Willett, et al. A DICTIONARY OF ENGLISH COS-
TUME 900-1900. London: Adam and Charles Black, 1960.

Complete dictionary of costume items including date of introduction and discontinuance; sexual preference of wearer; glossary of materials; section of obsolete color names; 303 line
illustrations in text by Cecil Everitt and Phillis Cunnington.

32 Downs, Harold, ed. THEATRE AND STAGE: AN ENCYCLOPEDIC GUIDE
TO THE PERFORMANCE OF ALL AMATEUR DRAMATIC, OPERATIC AND
THEATRICAL WORK. 2 vols. London: New Era Publishing Co., 1951.

"Historic Stage Costuming" entry in volume 1 by Nevil Truman; historical survey with drawings and some color paintings; material on ecclesiastical costume.

33 Fairholt, F.W. A GLOSSARY OF COSTUME IN ENGLAND TO THE END OF THE EIGHTEENTH CENTURY. 1885. Reprint. West Yorkshire, Engl.: EP Publishing Co., 1976.

Dictionary section from volume 2 of author's COSTUME IN ENGLAND; numerous line drawings and contemporary literary quotes with entries.

34 Franklyn, Julian, and Tanner, John. AN ENCYCLOPAEDIC DICTIONARY OF HERALDRY. Oxford, Engl.: Pergamon Press, 1969.

Glossary of terms with useful line drawings and illustrations for designers working in this area.

35 Ironside, Janey. A FASHION ALPHABET. London: Michael Joseph, 1968.

A dictionary primarily of post-1940 fashion terms and words arranged in sections covering each aspect of the fashion scene, for example, "Silhouettes and Looks," "Accessories"; glossary of materials and textiles; line drawings.

36 Klein, Ruth. LEXIKON DER MODE: DREI JAHRTAUSENDE EUROPA-EISCHER KOSTUEMKUNDE. Baden-Baden, Germany: Woldemar Klein Verlag, 1950.

Extensive historical survey of European costume in dictionary format; text in German.

37 Kybalova, Ludmila, et al. THE PICTORIAL ENCYCLOPEDIA OF FASHION. Translated by Claudia Rosoux. New York: Crown Publishers, 1968.

Numerous reproductions of primary pictorial material arranged in a topical order with descriptive notes; index.

38 Leloir, Maurice. DICTIONNAIRE DE COSTUME ET DE SES ACCESSOIRES DES ARMES ET DES ETOFFES DES ORIGINES A NOS JOURS. Paris: Librairie Grund, 1951.

Though text in French, extensive number of excellent drawings and illustrations.

39 Marks, Stephen S., ed. FAIRCHILD'S DICTIONARY OF TEXTILES. New York: Fairchild Publications, 1959.

No illustrations but useful for explanations of types of textiles.

40 Mason, Anita. AN ILLUSTRATED DICTIONARY OF JEWELLERY. New York: Harper and Row, 1974.

Clear selected line drawings for entries covering terms in area of jewelry.

41 Osborne, Harold, ed. THE OXFORD COMPANION TO THE DECORA-TIVE ARTS. Oxford, Engl.: Oxford University Press, 1975.

General reference with illustrated sections on costume and related subjects.

42 Picken, Mary Brooks. THE FASHION DICTIONARY: FABRIC, SEWING AND APPAREL AS EXPRESSED IN THE LANGUAGE OF FASHION. New York: Funk and Wagnalls Co., 1973.

Usable reference source with entries applicable to historical and theatrical costume.

43 _____. THE LANGUAGE OF FASHION: A DICTIONARY AND DI-GEST OF FABRIC, SEWING, AND DRESS. New York: Funk and Wagnalls Co., 1939.

Extensive dictionary and pronunciation guide of many costume terms, historical and modern, accompanied by line drawings.

44 Planche, James Robinson. A CYCLOPAEDIA OF COSTUME: OR, DIC-TIONARY OF DRESS, INCLUDING NOTICES OF CONTEMPORANEOUS FASHIONS ON THE CONTINENT, AND A GENERAL CHRONOLOGI-CAL HISTORY OF THE COSTUMES OF THE PRINCIPAL COUNTRIES OF EUROPE, FROM THE COMMENCEMENT OF THE CHRISTIAN ERA TO THE ACCESSION OF GEORGE III. 2 vols. London: Chatto and Windus, 1876-79.

Older source with dictionary in volume 1; quite useful for volume's thoroughness, accuracy, and illustrations.

45 Quick, John. ARTISTS' AND ILLUSTRATORS' ENCYCLOPEDIA. 2d ed. New York: McGraw-Hill Book Co., 1977.

Numerous illustrations with descriptions of wide range of artistic materials and methods, most of which are applicable to costume designers.

46 Schoeffler, O.E., and Gale, William. ESQUIRE'S ENCYCLOPEDIA OF 20TH CENTURY MEN'S FASHIONS. New York: McGraw-Hill Book Co., 1973.

Complete coverage of the entire area of male attire and acces-sories, well-illustrated with glossary, lists of menswear designers, and fabric information; index.

47 Shover, Edna Mann. ART IN COSTUME DESIGN: PRACTICAL SUGGES-
TIONS FOR THOSE INTERESTED IN ART, SEWING, HISTORY, AND
LITERATURE. Springfield, Mass.: Milton Bradley Co., 1929.

Dictionary arrangement of costume styles, terms, artistic motifs,
and items from various historical periods.

48 SIBYLLES MODELEXIKON: ABC DER MODE. Berlin: Verlag fur die
Frau, 1968.

Brief dictionary in German of fashion terms.

49 Stafford, Maureen, and Ware, Dore. AN ILLUSTRATED DICTIONARY
OF ORNAMENT. New York: St. Martin's Press, 1974.

Well-presented material in dictionary form of value to costume
designer.

50 Uden, Grant. A DICTIONARY OF CHIVALRY. New York: Thomas Y.
Crowell Co., 1968.

Entries of costume and armor terms, with descriptive notes and
many secondary-source drawings, some in color.

51 Wilcox, R. Turner. THE DICTIONARY OF COSTUME. New York:
Charles Scribner's Sons, 1969.

Dictionary arrangement of terms pertaining primarily to historic
costuming, with many line drawings.

52 Wingate, Isabel B. FAIRCHILD'S DICTIONARY OF TEXTILES. New
York: Fairchild Publications, 1967.

Listing and definitions of textile terminology; no illustrations.

C. SOURCEBOOKS AND GUIDEBOOKS

53 Arnold, Janet. A HANDBOOK OF COSTUME. New York: Macmillan
Co., 1973.

Introduction to major phases of costume: history, design and
construction; primary-source materials; technical information;
costume conservation and storage; bibliography; and guide to
costume collections in the British Isles.

54 Bennett, H., and Witt, C. 18TH CENTURY WOMEN'S COSTUME AT
BLAISE CASTLE HOUSE. Bristol, Engl.: Bristol City Art Gallery, 1972.

Detailed catalog and numerous illustrations of costumes and
accessories at Blaise Castle.

55 Bowman, Ned Allen. HANDBOOK OF TECHNICAL PRACTICE FOR THE PERFORMING ARTS: NED A. BOWMAN'S INTERGALACTIC SERIAL SHOP COOKBOOK. Wilkinsburg, Pa.: Scenographic Media, 1972.

Guidebook to use of modern media in areas of scenery, lighting, costume design, and makeup.

56 Boyd, Margaret A. THE MAIL-ORDER CRAFTS CATALOGUE. Radnor, Pa.: Chilton Book Co., 1975.

Comprehensive listing of over sixteen hundred outlets for craft materials; valuable source for designers.

57 Bullard, Daphne. CATALOGUE OF THE COSTUME COLLECTION: PART I, EIGHTEENTH CENTURY; PART II, 1800-30. Borough of Worthing, Engl.: Worthing Museum, 1964.

Guidebooks of over two hundred items in the costume collection, each listed with descriptive notes; black-and-white photographs; line drawings; and one pattern for an outer and a foundation garment and accessories.

58 Colin, Paul, and Lippman, Deborah. CRAFT SOURCES: THE ULTIMATE CATALOG FOR CRAFTSPEOPLE. New York: M. Evans and Co., 1975.

Guidebook with sections on all major craft areas; each section with instruction sources, bibliography, suppliers, brief glossaries, periodicals, and other pertinent information.

59 De La Iglesia, Maria Elena. THE NEW CATALOGUE OF CATALOGUES: THE COMPLETE GUIDE TO WORLD-WIDE SHOPPING BY MAIL. New York: Random House, 1975.

Extensive listing of sources of suppliers throughout the world.

60 Dunham, Lydia Roberts. COSTUME COLLECTION, DENVER ART MUSEUM. Denver: Denver Art Museum, 1962.

Photographs and description of forty-eight examples of costume from the collection, arranged historically.

61 Ginsburg, Madeleine. VICTORIA AND ALBERT MUSEUM: THE COSTUME COURT WITH NOTES ON RELATED MATERIAL ELSEWHERE IN THE MUSEUM. 3d ed. London: Victoria and Albert Museum, 1971.

Guidebook to facilities at Victoria and Albert Museum for observation and study of costumes and costume history; basic reading list.

62 Glassman, Judith. NATIONAL GUIDE TO CRAFT SUPPLIES. New York: Van Nostrand Reinhold Co., 1975.

Sourcebook for items often needed and not readily available, for example, beads, feathers, Indian craft, and shells; lists of bookstores, organizations, museums, periodicals, fairs; bibliography and index.

63 _____. NEW YORK GUIDE TO CRAFT SUPPLIES. New York: Workman Publishing Co., 1971.

Listing of supply sources of hard-to-find materials useful to costumers, for example, beads, stones, leather, unusual fabrics, trims, and notions.

64 Hoggett, Chris. STAGE CRAFTS. New York: St. Martin's Press, 1976.

Extensively illustrated sourcebook of basic procedures in theatre, including many in costume; arms and armor, accessories, makeup and masks; glossary; lists of materials and suppliers.

65 Huenefeld, Irene Pennington. INTERNATIONAL DIRECTORY OF HISTORICAL CLOTHING. Metuchen, N.J.: Scarecrow Press, 1967.

Listing of sources in Canada, United States, and Europe, of authentic clothing collections.

66 Lambert, Eleanor. WORLD OF FASHION: PEOPLE, PLACES, RESOURCES. New York: R.R. Bowker Co., 1976.

Guidebook organized by geographical areas of whole industry of fashion and costume, including information on designers, editors, organizations, awards, costume archives, and publications.

67 Lubell, Cecil, ed. TEXTILE COLLECTIONS OF THE WORLD: AN ILLUSTRATED GUIDE TO TEXTILE COLLECTIONS. 2 vols. New York: Van Nostrand Reinhold Co., 1976.

Valuable sourcebooks with many illustrations of costumes; volume 1: UNITED STATES AND CANADA, and volume 2: UNITED KINGDOM AND IRELAND; presentation of many basic design themes adaptable to modern textiles; 118 color plates.

68 Simon, Bernard, ed. SIMON'S DIRECTORY OF THEATRICAL MATERIALS, SERVICES, INFORMATION. 5th ed. New York: Package Publicity, 1975.

Indispensable sourcebook of theatrical materials and services, many useful to costume designers.

69 Victoria and Albert Museum. GUIDE TO THE COLLECTION OF COSTUMES. London: 1924.

Thirty-four monochrome photographs of historical costume and accessories of all types and periods in the collection.

70 Wadsworth Atheneum. THE SCULPTURE OF STYLE. Hartford, Conn.: 1964.

Review of the costumes in the museum's collection dating from 1815 to 1929.

71 Wlock, Violet. THE COLLECTION OF COSTUMES. York, Engl.: Castle Museum, 1949.

Guide to the collection of the museum with monochrome photographs of fourteen examples of period costume.

72 Zechlin, Ruth. COMPLETE BOOK OF HANDCRAFTS. 2d ed. Newton Centre, Mass.: Charles T. Branford Co., 1967.

Sourcebook for a number of crafts and techniques useful in costuming.

Chapter 2
THEATRICAL COSTUME

A. WESTERN THEATRICAL COSTUME

See also 272, 596

73 Applebaum, Stanley, ed. SCENES FROM THE NINETEENTH CENTURY
   STAGE IN ADVERTISING WOODCUTS. New York: Dover Publications,
   1977.

   Reproductions of 234 illustrations, most of which contain costumed performers; valuable for popular depictions of costume
   during the century.

74 Barbier, George. VINGT-CINQ COSTUMES POUR LE THEATRE. Paris:
   C. Bloch and Meynial, 1927.

   Beautifully colored reproductions of designer's costume plates
   for selected theatrical and dance productions including CASA-
   NOVA, LYSISTRATA, and others.

75 Beaumont, Cyril W. THE HISTORY OF HARLEQUIN. 1926. Reprint.
   New York: Benjamin Blom, 1967.

   Interesting text but most valuable for pictorial illustrations of
   development of the Harlequin character, his costumes, masks,
   props, and even movements from the reproduction of a period
   choreography for the character; valuable for designers working
   in the commedia dell'arte style.

76 Bell, John. DRAMATIC CHARACTER PLATES FOR BELL'S EDITION OF
   SHAKESPEARE'S PLAYS, 1775-1776. London: Cornmarket Press, 1969.

   Facsimile publication of thirty-six engravings of full-length portraits of eighteenth-century costumed actors and actresses in
   Shakespearian roles.

77 Boegel, Jozsek, and Janosa, Lajos, eds. SCENOGRAPHIA HUNGARICA [Hungarian scenography]. Budapest: Corvina Press, 1973.

English text with 131 reproductions (some in color) of stage and costume designs by Hungarian designers.

78 Boehn, Max von. DAS BUHNENKOSTUM IN ALTERTUM, MITTELALTER UND NEUZEIT. Berlin: Bruno, 1921.

German text but extensive collection of illustrations showing history of stage costume from ancient to modern times; of importance to theatrical costume designers.

79 Brooke, Iris. COSTUME IN GREEK CLASSIC DRAMA. New York: Theatre Arts Books, 1962.

Presentation of all available detail of theatrical costume during the period, with line drawings based on primary sources and also on the general style; inclusion of specific textual references from the dramas.

80 Buell, William Ackerman. THE HAMLETS OF THE THEATRE. New York: Astor-Honor, 1968.

Survey of descriptions and depictions of famous Hamlets from Burbage to Burton; valuable for theatrical costume designers dealing with this character.

81 Burdick, Elizabeth B., et al., eds. CONTEMPORARY STAGE DESIGN, U.S.A. New York: International Theatre Institute of the United States, 1974.

Collection of both costume and scenic designs chosen from a comprehensive exhibition of designs for every type of theatrical presentation in the United States.

82 Cabasino, Salvatore. IL FIGURINO NEL TEATRO ITALIANO CONTEMPORANEO [Pictures from contemporary Italian theatre]. Rome: Danesi in Via Margutta, 1945.

Collection of numerous costume designs from productions, historical and contemporary, from the modern Italian theatre.

83 Cooper, Douglas. PICASSO THEATRE. New York: Harry N. Abrams, 1967.

Survey of artist's work for the theatre with over five hundred reproductions, some colored, of his designs for both costume and scenery.

84 COSTUMES IN SHAKESPEARE'S PLAY OF THE WINTER'S TALE, 1856. London: Cornmarket Press, 1970.

Facsimile reprint of illustrations of costumes used in the Charles Kean production of the drama.

85 Damase, Jacques. LES FOLIES DU MUSIC-HALL: A HISTORY OF THE MUSIC HALL IN PARIS FROM 1914 TO THE PRESENT DAY. London: Anthony Blond, 1970.

Pictorial record of costumed performers in this specialized aspect of theatre.

86 Disher, M. Willson. CLOWNS AND PANTOMIMES. 1925. Reprint. New York: Benjamin Blom, 1968.

Excellent and interesting text with numerous illustrations of costumed performers in theatrical presentations as opposed to clowns in the circus aspect of entertainment.

87 Duchartre, Pierre Louis. THE ITALIAN COMEDY: THE IMPROVISATION SCENARIOS, LIVES, ATTRIBUTES, PORTRAITS, AND MASKS OF THE ILLUSTRIOUS CHARACTERS OF THE COMMEDIA DELL'ARTE. Translated by Randolph T. Weaver. London: George G. Harrap and Co., 1929.

Somewhat older book but valuable for its richness of illustrative material and textual coverage of the subject; one of the major works in the area.

88 Fulop-Miller, Rene, and Gregor, Joseph. THE RUSSIAN THEATRE: ITS CHARACTER AND HISTORY WITH ESPECIAL REFERENCE TO THE REVOLUTIONARY PERIOD. Translated by Paul England. 1930. Reprint. New York: Benjamin Blom, 1968.

Excellent text with 405 monochrome illustrations, many of which are of costume designs or costumed actors; bibliographical footnotes; not extensively documented, but useful book in area.

89 Genauer, Emily. CHAGALL AT THE "MET." New York: Tudor Publishing Co., 1971.

Brilliant color reproductions of artist's scenic and costume designs for the Metropolitan Opera.

90 Hainaux, Rene. STAGE DESIGN THROUGHOUT THE WORLD SINCE 1935. New York: George G. Harrap and Co., 1975.

91 _____. STAGE DESIGN THROUGHOUT THE WORLD SINCE 1950. New York: Theatre Arts Books, 1964.

92 _____. STAGE DESIGN THROUGHOUT THE WORLD SINCE 1960. New York: Theatre Arts Books, 1973.

93 _____. STAGE DESIGN THROUGHOUT THE WORLD 1970-75. New York: Theatre Arts Books, 1976.

Extensive pictorial surveys of theatrical design, costume and scenic, during the specified period; some color plates; captions in English and French; bibliographies and indexes.

94 Hartman, Rudolf, ed. OPERA. Translated by Arnold J. Pomerans. New York: William Morrow, and Co., 1977.

General introduction to historical operatic stage design of the European theatre; discussion of the areas, problems, techniques, and methods of opera production; treatment of production aspects of twelve major operas, e.g. DON GIOVANNI, FIDELIO, THE TALES OF HOFFMAN and THE WOMAN WITHOUT A SHADOW, by major world opera companies, with excellent illustrative material (some in color) of costumes and scenery.

95 Hibbert, Christopher. GILBERT AND SULLIVAN AND THEIR VICTORIAN WORLD. New York: American Heritage Publishing Company, 1976.

Description of each opera with 280 historical illustrations (24 plates in color), many of costumed performers; excellent source for costumers of Gilbert and Sullivan.

96 Holmes, M.R. STAGE COSTUMES AND ACCESSORIES IN THE LONDON MUSEUM. London: Her Majesty's Stationery Office, 1968.

Exhibition catalog containing twenty-eight black-and-white and one color photograph of costumes worn by famous actors from Grimaldi to Irving; useful in study of historical theatrical costume.

97 Jones, Inigo. DESIGNS BY INIGO JONES FOR MASQUES AND PLAYS AT COURT: A DESCRIPTIVE CATALOGUE OF DRAWINGS FOR SCENERY AND COSTUMES MAINLY IN THE COLLECTION OF HIS GRACE THE DUKE OF DEVONSHIRE, K.G. 1924. Reprint. New York: Russell and Russell, 1966.

Fifty selected monochrome plates from the extensive collection showing various scenery and costume designs by Jones; introduction and notes by Percy Simpson and C.F. Bell.

98 Kahan, Gerald. JACQUES CALLOT: ARTIST OF THE THEATRE. Athens: University of Georgia Press, 1976.

Ninety-two monochrome plates of the artist's work showing costumed actors in commedia dell'arte, festivals, and court theatre.

99 Kelly, Francis M. SHAKESPEARIAN COSTUME FOR STAGE AND SCREEN. Revised by Alan Mansfield. London: Adam and Charles Black, 1970.

General historical survey of subject originally published in 1938; specific sections of costume considerations for each Shakespearian play; eight monochrome period portraits and numerous line drawings; bibliography.

100 Komisarjevsky, Theodore. THE COSTUME OF THE THEATRE. 1932. Reprint. New York: Benjamin Blom, 1968.

Excellent textual historical survey from earliest to modern times of stage costume; forty-two primary-source illustrations; major work in the area.

101 Komisarjevsky, Theodore, and Simonson, Lee. SETTINGS AND COS-TUMES OF THE MODERN STAGE. 1933. Reprint. New York: Benjamin Blom, 1966.

Brief textual introductory material with a number of photographs of productions in the first quarter of the twentieth century; arranged by country.

102 Lamb, Ruth S. THE WORLD OF ROMANIAN THEATRE. Claremont, Calif.: Ocelot Press, 1976.

Specialized study; historical survey with many production photographs, including many of costumed performers.

103 Laver, James. COSTUME IN THE THEATRE. New York: Hill and Wang, 1964.

Historical survey of theatrical costume, with particular attention to stage costume for the dance and opera; 174 illustrations and photographs; bibliography; major work.

104 _____. DRAMA: ITS COSTUME AND DECOR. London: Studio Publications, 1951.

Authoritative survey of history of theatrical costume and scenic design from ancient times to the present with selected illustrative materials; important source for costumers.

105 Linthicum, M. Channing. COSTUME IN THE DRAMA OF SHAKESPEARE AND HIS CONTEMPORARIES. New York: Russell and Russell, 1963.

Brief survey of period colors; discussion of costume textiles
and garments; earliest date of use in England of costume items
in plays by Elizabethan dramatists; definitions with quotations
from primary period sources of each color, textile, and garment; twenty plates of costume garments and accessories; bibliography and index; major work.

106 Mander, Raymond. HAMLET THROUGH THE AGES: A PICTORIAL REC-
ORD FROM 1790. London: Rockliff, 1952.

Numerous (250) photographs of various productions showing
many approaches to costuming for the drama.

107 _____. THEATRICAL COMPANION TO SHAW: A PICTORIAL RECORD
OF THE FIRST PERFORMANCES OF THE PLAYS OF GEORGE BERNARD
SHAW. New York: Pitman, 1955.

Numerous excellent photographs of costumed actors in pre-
mieres of Shaw's plays.

108 Mander, Raymond, and Mitchenson, Joe. MUSICAL COMEDY: A
STORY IN PICTURES. New York: Taplinger Publishing Co., 1970.

Two hundred thirty photographs, primarily of costumed performers in productions from 1893 to 1970.

109 _____. PANTOMIME: A STORY IN PICTURES. New York: Taplinger Publishing Co., 1973.

Textual survey of pantomime from the Romans through John
Rich to the present, with extensive pictorial material (249 pho-
tographs); inclusion of George Bernard Shaw's "The Story of
Pantomime."

110 _____. A PICTURE HISTORY OF THE BRITISH THEATRE. New York:
Macmillan Co., 1957.

Survey of the English stage with 538 illustrations and photographs well presenting the practices of theatrical costuming.

111 _____. REVUE: A STORY IN PICTURES. London: Peter Davies, 1971.

Numerous (225) photographs of performers in specialized theatrical form.

112 Maresova, Sylva, ed. CZECH STAGE COSTUMES. Prague: Theatre
Institute, 1972.

Collection of numerous monochrome photographs of costume
plates by Czech designers.

113 Marshall, Herbert. THE PICTORIAL HISTORY OF THE RUSSIAN THE-
ATRE. New York: Crown Publishers, 1977.

Overview of subject from the Middle Ages to the present,
with many illustrations of costume designs and costumed performers; valuable source in an area having little pictorial material.

114 MAX REINHARDT: SEIN THEATER IN BILDERN. Hannover, Germany:
Friedrich Verlag, 1968.

German text but comprehensive collection of photographs of
costumed actors in Reinhardt's productions; valuable for illustrations of famous director's use of costume in productions.

115 Mellencamp, Emma Hirsch. RENAISSANCE CLASSICAL COSTUME,
1450-1515. Ann Arbor, Mich.: University Microfilms, 1956.

Scholarly treatment of subject in an often overlooked but important period; poor reproduction of illustrative materials in
this particular copy.

116 Messel, Oliver. STAGE DESIGNS AND COSTUMES BY OLIVER MESSEL.
Introduction by James Laver. London: John Lane the Bodley Head
Limited, 1933.

Eight color illustrations and sixty-four black-and-white drawings and photographs of this British designer's costumes, masks,
and decors for ten productions.

117 Molinari, Cesare. THEATRE THROUGH THE AGES. Translated by Colin
Hamer. New York: McGraw-Hill Book Co., 1975.

Example of a historical theatre book in which the excellence,
extensiveness, color reproduction of illustrations, and textual
material are of great value to theatrical costumer; bibliography.

118 Montgomery, Elizabeth, et al. [Motley]. DESIGNING AND MAKING
STAGE COSTUMES. New York: Watson-Guptill Publications, 1964.

Introduction to broad range of costume materials, without adequate depth of coverage in this volume; valuable for numerous
examples of authors' and other designers' renderings for various
roles; color and black-and-white illustrations; bibliography and
index.

119 Moussinac, Leon. THE NEW MOVEMENT IN THE THEATRE: A SURVEY
OF RECENT DEVELOPMENTS IN EUROPE AND AMERICA. 1932. Reprint. New York: Benjamin Blom, 1967.

Reprint of excellent pictorial survey of scenic and costume
designs of the early twentieth century.

120 Newton, Stella Mary. RENAISSANCE THEATRE COSTUME AND THE
SENSE OF THE HISTORIC PAST. New York: Theatre Arts Books, 1975.

Unique and quite valuable study of the theatre and its costume
in the fifteenth and sixteenth centuries; well illustrated with
primary-source material; extensive bibliography and index.

121 Nicoll, Allardyce. THE WORLD OF HARLEQUIN: A CRITICAL STUDY
OF THE COMMEDIA DELL'ARTE. Cambridge: Cambridge University
Press, 1963.

Critical and historical detailed study with extensive (130) pictorial survey of the costumed characters and the genre generally; bibliography; important source.

122 Oreglia, Giacomo. THE COMMEDIA DELL'ARTE. Translated by Lovett
F. Edwards. New York: Hill and Wang, 1968.

Historical survey of the development of this theatrical form
from beginnings to the present, with copious illustrations of
costumes and masks; bibliography and index.

123 Orgel, Stephen, and Strong, Roy. INIGO JONES: THE THEATRE OF
THE STUART COURT: INCLUDING THE COMPLETE DESIGNS FOR PRO-
DUCTIONS AT COURT FOR THE MOST PART IN THE COLLECTION OF
THE DUKE OF DEVONSHIRE TOGETHER WITH THEIR TEXTS AND HIS-
TORICAL DOCUMENTATION. 2 vols. Berkeley and Los Angeles:
University of California Press, 1973.

Definitive edition of Jones's designs, costume and scenic; invaluable source.

124 Parmelin, Helene. CINQ PEINTRES ET LE THEATRE: DECORS ET COS-
TUMES DE LEGER, COUTAUD, GISCHIA, LABISSE, ET PIGNON. Paris:
Editions Cercle d'Art, 1956.

French text but excellent reproductions, many in color, of a
large number of costume designs by the five painters in the
title.

125 Prideaux, Tom. WORLD THEATRE IN PICTURES FROM ANCIENT TIMES
TO MODERN BROADWAY. New York: Greenberg Publisher, 1953.

Pictorial review of contemporary productions of historical as
well as modern plays; many illustrations of costumed actors.

126 Rischbieter, Henning. ART AND THE STAGE IN THE 20TH CENTURY: PAINTERS AND SCULPTORS WORK FOR THE THEATRE. New York: New York Graphic Society, 1968.

Excellent, extensive collection of photographs, some colored, of modern theatrical design, scenic and costume, with many designers' concepts and approaches, for example, Klee, Calder, and Kandinsky; extensive notes, index, and documentation; interesting and valuable source.

127 Sheringham, George, and Laver, James. DESIGN IN THE THEATRE. London: Studio Publications, 1927.

Reproductions of many original costume designs for the theatre of the day.

128 Sheringham, George, and Morrison, R. Boyd. ROBES OF THESPIS: COSTUME DESIGNS BY MODERN ARTISTS. London: Ernest Benn, 1928.

Somewhat dated, but excellent color reproductions of costume designs for varying genres during the first quarter of the twentieth century: dramatic, revue, operatic, and ballet; good source.

129 Spencer, Charles. CECIL BEATON STAGE AND FILM DESIGNS. London: Academy Editions; New York: St. Martin's Press, 1975.

Retrospective survey of famous designer's works; many excellent color and monochrome illustrations, especially those of original design and then the completed costume; listing of productions designed by Beaton; bibliography.

130 _____ . ERTE. New York: Clarkson N. Potter, 1970.

Biographical survey of important modern designer, with particular emphasis on his theatrical designs; extensively illustrated with 183 color and black-and-white plates; bibliography.

131 Strong, Roy. FESTIVAL DESIGNS BY INIGO JONES: AN EXHIBITION OF DRAWINGS FOR SCENERY AND COSTUMES FOR THE COURT MASQUES OF JAMES I AND CHARLES I. London: Victoria and Albert Museum, 1969.

Exhibition catalog containing many reproductions of Jones's costume designs, some in color.

132 _____ . SPLENDOR AT COURT: RENAISSANCE SPECTACLE AND THE THEATRE OF POWER. Boston: Houghton Mifflin Co., 1973.

Outstandingly illustrated volume surveying the Renaissance festival which combined the talents of many artists, musicians, composers, poets, dramatists, designers, architects, and engineers for more than two centuries beginning in the sixteenth; treatment of the reflection of rulers as god-like heroes in such splendors as ballets, water fetes, triumphal entries, and tournaments; sixteen pages in color; two hundred black-and-white photographs; genealogical trees; information index.

133 Tirtoff, Romain de [Erte]. THINGS I REMEMBER: AN AUTOBIOGRAPHY. New York: New York Times Book Co., 1975.

Designer's personal account of his fascinating career as both fashion and theatrical designer; major emphasis upon his costume designing; useful chronological table listing his major designs from 1913 to 1975; examples of theatrical costume designs in color; index.

134 Troster, Frantisek. COSTUME ON THE STAGE: A BOOK OF COSTUME DESIGNS. Prague: Artia, 1962.

A designer's collection of his goals, analyses, and renderings of costumes for thirty-one dramas of wide range in style and period; usually a minimum of eight designs from such productions as AIDA, LYSISTRATA, LE CID, SCHOOL FOR SCANDAL, THREE SISTERS, and OF MICE AND MEN.

135 Webster, Thomas B.L., and Trendall, Arthur Dale. ILLUSTRATIONS OF GREEK DRAMA. London: Phaidon, 1971.

Richly illustrated exclusively with primary sources of all aspects of the Greek drama including costuming; illustrations of costumed actors in all genres of Greek drama.

136 Weintraub, Stanley. AUBREY BEARDSLEY: IMP OF THE PERVERSE. University Park: Pennsylvania State University Press, 1976.

Biographical study with numerous examples of the designer's work.

137 Zeh, Gisela. DAS BAYREUTHER BUEHNENKOSTEUM. Munich: Prestel Verlag, 1973.

German text but very large number of original designs of costumes in color and over four hundred illustrations and photographs of costumed performers for the important productions at Bayreuth, particularly of the Wagnerian operas.

B. THEATRICAL COSTUME OF THE EAST

See also 536, 563, 565, 841

138 Ando, Tsuro. BUNRAKU: THE PUPPET THEATRE. Translated by Don Kenny. New York: Walker-Weatherhill, 1970.

Full textual treatment of subject with 173 illustrations, some in color, of costumed puppets, musicians, and operators in this unique form of theatre.

139 Arlington, Lewis C. THE CHINESE DRAMA FROM THE EARLIEST TIMES UNTIL TODAY: A PANORAMIC STUDY OF THE ART IN CHINA, TRACING ITS ORIGIN AND DESCRIBING ITS ACTORS (IN BOTH MALE AND FEMALE ROLES): THEIR COSTUMES AND MAKE-UP, SUPERSTITIONS AND STAGE SLANG: THE ACCOMPANYING MUSIC AND MUSICAL INSTRUMENTS: CONCLUDING WITH SYNOPSES OF THIRTY CHINESE PLAYS. 1930. Reprint. New York: Benjamin Blom, 1966.

Comprehensive study of subject, with chapters on theatrical costumes, headwear, facial hairstyles, footwear, and makeup; extremely large number of paintings and drawings, some in color, of costumes, accessories, and makeup; bibliography; major study.

140 CHINESE OPERA COSTUMES. Taipei: Teng Chang-Kuo Publisher, n.d.

One hundred twenty colored, very detailed plates of costumes and accessories, with brief notes of each in English; very useful source.

141 Ernst, Earle. THE KABUKI THEATRE. Oxford, Engl.: Oxford University Press, 1956.

Complete examination of the subject, with much costume information and fifty-six plates, many of performers in traditional theatrical garb; bibliography.

142 Gargi, Balwant. FOLK THEATRE OF INDIA. Seattle: University of Washington Press, 1966.

Survey of folk theatre from the beginning, with chapters on various forms; Jatra, Nautanki, Bhavai, Chhau, and others; numerous black-and-white photographs; detailed descriptions of costumes for each form; glossary and index.

143 _____. THEATRE IN INDIA. New York: Theatre Arts Books, 1962.

Survey in first section of book of traditional theatrical forms; epics; Sanskrit drama; classical and folk dance; and puppet,

23

Theatrical Costume

pageant, and folk theatre. Treatment of modern theatre in
second section of book; detailed descriptions of costume and
its uses for each form; fifty-one photographs; bibliography and
index.

144 Gunji, Masakatsu. BUYO: THE CLASSICAL DANCE. Translated by
Don Kenny. New York: Walker-Weatherhill, 1970.

Good textual descriptive and explanatory material with 153
illustrations, some colored, of costumed performers.

145 Kawatake, Shigetoshi. KABUKI: JAPANESE DRAMA. Tokyo: Foreign
Affairs Association of Japan, 1958.

Concise textual description of costumes, with some selected
illustrations.

146 Mackerras, Colin. THE CHINESE THEATRE IN MODERN TIMES: FROM
1840 TO THE PRESENT DAY. Amherst: University of Massachusetts
Press, 1975.

Emphasis on textual survey but with thirty-five monochrome
illustrations of historical developments in costume, masks, and
accessories; bibliography and index.

147 Nakamura, Yasuo. NOH: THE CLASSICAL THEATRE. Translated by
Don Kenny. New York: Walker-Weatherhill, 1971.

Many (163) illustrations; textual discussions of subject, including chapters on masks, costumes, and stage movement.

148 Pe-Chin, Chang. CHINESE OPERA AND PAINTED FACE. Taipei: Mei
Ya Publications, 1969.

Folio edition; analysis of the more important facets of Chinese
opera: its origin, the painted face and its evolution; bril-
liantly colored designs for the painted faces for all characters
of the art form; best study of the topic.

149 Scott, Adolphe Clarence. THE CLASSICAL THEATRE OF CHINA. London: Allen and Unwin, 1957.

Brief historical survey followed by chapters on the actors and
the plays, with descriptive commentary and line drawings of
the costumes.

150 Shaver, Ruth M. KABUKI COSTUME. Rutland, Vt.: Charles E. Tuttle
Co., 1966.

Excellent authoritative survey of every aspect of Kabuki and
Isho costume including historical background, armor and battle

costume, patterns and colors, accessories, hairstyles, and makeup; helpful illustrations in color and black-and-white and line drawings (252) by Soma Akira and Ota Gako; glossary, bibliography, subject index, and index of actors, plays, and roles; major study.

151 Snow, Lois Wheeler. CHINA ON STAGE: AN AMERICAN ACTRESS IN THE PEOPLE'S REPUBLIC. New York: Random House, 1972.

No specific information on theatrical costume as such but good descriptions and photographs of modern Chinese theatrical activities.

152 Togi, Masataro. GAGAKU: COURT MUSIC AND DANCE. Translated by Don Kenny. New York: Walker-Weatherhill, 1971.

Two hundred twenty photographs, some in color, on the subject; chapter on the costumes and masks for this performing art.

153 Toita, Yasuji. KABUKI: THE POPULAR THEATRE. Translated by Don Kenny. New York: Walker-Weatherhill, 1970.

Valuable source with excellent, succinct text and numerous (181) illustrations, some colored, of costumed actors; good description of the development and practices of this style of theatre.

154 Yoshinobu, Tokugawa. THE TOKUGAWA COLLECTION: NO ROBES AND MASKS. New York: Japan Society, 1977.

Exhibition catalog of great value to costumer for color photographs and text.

155 Zung, Cecilia Sieu-Ling. SECRETS OF THE CHINESE DRAMA: A COMPLETE EXPLANATORY GUIDE TO ACTIONS AND SYMBOLS AS SEEN IN THE PERFORMANCE OF CHINESE DRAMAS. 1937. Reprint. New York: Benjamin Blom, 1964.

Comprehensive treatment of the subject, with a chapter on theatrical costume plus 240 illustrations; synopses of fifty Chinese plays.

C. COSTUME FOR THE DANCE

156 Alexandre, Arsene. THE DECORATIVE ART OF LEON BAKST. Translated by Harry Melville. 1913. Reprint. New York: Benjamin Blom, 1971.

Notes on the ballets by Jean Cocteau; survey of designer's
work with scenery and costumes for the dance; seventy-seven
plates of Bakst's designs, with some reproduced in color.

157 Anderson, Jack. DANCE. New York: Newsweek Books, 1974.

Historical survey of the popular appeal of the art and history
of dance with excellent illustrations and photographs, many
in color, of costumed dancers; index.

158 Anthony, Gordon. THE SADLER'S WELLS BALLET: CAMERA STUDIES.
Introduction by Eveleigh Leith. London: Geoffrey Bles, 1942.

Performance record of selected ballets by the famous dance
company; forty-seven monochrome photographs, all of which
include costumed dancers in featured roles.

159 BAKST. New York: Rizzoli, 1977.

Brief introduction to life and work of the famous designer for
the dance, with forty-eight selected plates (41 in color) of
which forty-four depict costume designs from throughout his
career.

160 Bakst, Leon. THE DESIGNS OF LEON BAKST FOR THE SLEEPING PRIN-
CESS. 1922. Reprint. New York: Banjamin Blom, 1971.

Complete costume and scenery designs for the ballet--unfortun-
ately not in color; nevertheless, a very helpful record.

161 Beaumont, Cyril William. BALLET DESIGN PAST AND PRESENT. New
York: Studio Publications; London: Studio, 1946.

Evolution of scenic and costume design for the ballet from the
Italian Renaissance to the present; vast pictorial collection arranged historically by designers, with brief textual descriptions;
combination and extension of earlier works, FIVE CENTURIES
OF BALLET and DESIGN FOR THE BALLET.

162 _____. DESIGN FOR THE BALLET. New York: Studio Publications;
London: Studio, 1937.

Collection of representative designs and photographs of scenery
and costumes for ballet from 1920 to 1935; some color illustrations.

163 _____. FIVE CENTURIES OF BALLET DESIGN. New York: Studio
Publications; London: Studio, n.d.

Brief textual overview of extensive compilation of illustrations, some in color, of ballet designs, primarily of costumes from about 1580 to 1921, with brief descriptive notes.

164 Bland, Alexander. THE NUREYEV IMAGE. New York: New York Times Book Co., 1976.

Biographical and artistic study of the dancer Nureyev, with photographs of the majority of his leading roles as performed in costume.

165 Buckle, Richard. IN SEARCH OF DIAGHILEV. London: Sidgwick and Jackson, 1955.

Outline of author's preparation of catalog for Diaghilev Exhibition in 1955; retrospective presentation of primary examples of designer's total theatrical and dance design production including sketches, designs, and photographs.

166 _____. MODERN BALLET DESIGN: A PICTURE-BOOK WITH NOTES. London: Adam and Charles Black, 1955.

Many photographs and illustrations (207) of thirty-nine English and French designers' work for the ballet from the period 1945-55, with notations and descriptions of both costumes and scenery.

167 Clark, Mary, and Crisp, Clement. BALLET: AN ILLUSTRATED HISTORY. New York: Universe Books, 1973.

Presentation of pictorial survey of costumed dancers from beginning of formalization of performed dance to the present, with 253 monochrome illustrations; bibliography.

168 _____. DESIGN FOR BALLET. New York: Hawthorn Books, 1978.

Extensive survey of costume and scenic design from the Renaissance spectacle to the present ballet, with excellent text and numerous (300 black-and-white and 35 color) plates; bibliography; major work.

169 COSTUMES AND CURTAINS FROM THE DIAGHILEV AND DE BASIL BALLETS. New York: Viking Press, 1972.

Extensively illustrated (some in color) catalog of the Sotheby sale of the original costumes and curtains from the Diaghilev Ballet as later acquired and used until 1951 by Colonel de Basil and the de Basil Ballet; careful description of each item in the sale and photographs of many, for example, costumes and curtains by Bakst, Benois, Chanel, Matisse, and Picasso; index.

170 Crisp, Clement, and Thorpe, Edward. THE COLORFUL WORLD OF
BALLET. London: Octopus Books, 1978.

Survey of the foundations of ballet, the romantics and the
classics, Diaghilev and modern dance, and ballet since the
1930s; with numerous color illustrations and photographs of
costumed dancers; guide to classical ballet steps; index; helpful source.

171 Demidov, Alexander. THE RUSSIAN BALLET PAST AND PRESENT. Translated by Guy Daniels. Garden City, N.Y.: Doubleday and Co., 1977.

Historical survey with 146 excellent monochrome primary-
source photographs of costumed dancers; informative and interesting text.

172 DIAGHILEV AND RUSSIAN STAGE DESIGNERS: A LOAN EXHIBITION
OF STAGE AND COSTUME DESIGNS FROM THE COLLECTION OF MR.
AND MRS. LOBANOV-ROSTOVSKY. Washington, D.C.: International
Exhibitions Foundation, 1972.

Essay, "Watercolors by 36 Artists of the Diaghilev Era," by
John E. Bowlt; catalog with textual notes and 110 monochrome
reproductions of scenic and costume designs from Diaghilev
and his contemporaries; Andreenko, Bakst, Benois, Larionov,
and Tchekhonine, among many; brief biographies of the designers; selected bibliography.

173 Doeser, Linda. BALLET AND DANCE. New York: St. Martin's Press,
1977.

Descriptions of world's leading dance companies and information on choreographers, dancers, repertoire, and training pro-
grams, among other information; quite numerous black-and-
white photographs of costumed dancers.

174 Dominic, Zoe, and Gilbert, John Selwyn. FREDERICK ASHTON: A
CHOREOGRAPHER AND HIS BALLETS. Chicago: Henry Regnery Co.,
1971.

Pictorial biography of famous choreographer's ballets, illustrated with excellent photographs (256) of performances.

175 Hurry, Leslie. SETTINGS AND COSTUMES FOR SADLER'S WELLS BAL-
LETS: HAMLET (1942), LE LAC DES CYGNES AND THE OLD VIC HAM-
LET (1944). Introduction by Cyril Beaumont. London: Ariel Books on
the Arts, 1946.

Fifty monochrome plates for documentation of production scenery and costumes for the three ballets mentioned in the title.

176 Johnson, Alfred Edwin. THE RUSSIAN BALLET. London: Constable
and Co., 1913.

Dated source, but valuable for descriptive material included
in survey of notable Russian ballets; line drawings and color
illustrations of leading-costumed dancers.

177 Kirstein, Lincoln. MOVEMENT AND METAPHOR: FOUR CENTURIES
OF BALLET. New York: Frederick A. Praeger, 1970.

Extensive amount of primary-source material demonstrating vis-
ually the developments in ballet and theatrical dance costume
in the last four hundred years.

178 _____. THE NEW YORK CITY BALLET: New York: Alfred A. Knopf,
1973.

Retrospective pictorial survey of the ballets produced by this
company with monochrome and a few color photographs by
George Platt-Lynes and Martha Swope of principal costumed
dancers; bibliography.

179 Kochno, Boris. DIAGHILEV AND THE BALLETS RUSSES. Translated by
Adrienne Foulke. New York: Harper and Row Publishers, 1970.

Individual treatment of each of the company's ballets, with
photographs of dancers, settings, and many original costume
plates, reproduced in color by such designers and artists as
Bakst, Picasso, and Utrillo.

180 Levinson, Andre. BAKST: THE STORY OF THE ARTIST'S LIFE. 1923.
Reprint. New York: Benjamin Blom, 1971.

Primarily a biographical study with descriptions and reproductions of sixty-eight of designer's plates, the majority being of
costumes.

181 Oxenham, Andrew, and Crabb, Michael. DANCE TODAY IN CANADA.
Toronto: Simon and Pierre, 1977.

Introduction to Canadian dance with general background and
over 150 pages of excellent black-and-white photographs of
dancers and productions, providing illustrations of the full
range of variety of Canadian dance; listing of major companies.

182 Payne, Charles. AMERICAN BALLET THEATRE. New York: Alfred A.
Knopf, 1978.

Historical survey, decade by decade, from the 1940s to the
present, with photographic record of the company, dancers,

and productions; many photographs in color; complete list of productions, 1940–77, with full personnel listing.

183 Philp, Richard, and Whitney, Mary. DANSEUR: THE MALE IN BAL-LET. New York: McGraw-Hill Book Co., 1977.

Historical survey and contemporary analysis of the function and status of the male dancer, with approximately 250 black-and-white photographs of costumed dancers, historical as well as modern.

184 Reade, Brian. BALLET DESIGNS AND ILLUSTRATIONS, 1581-1940. London: Her Majesty's Stationery Office, 1967.

Collection of 173 costume and scenic designs for ballet with historic and descriptive notes for each plate; valuable for sense of historical development in ballet costuming.

185 RUSSIAN STAGE AND COSTUME DESIGNS FOR THE BALLET, OPERA AND THEATRE: A LOAN EXHIBITION FROM THE LOBANOV-ROSTOV-SKY, OENSLAGER AND RIABOV COLLECTIONS. Washington, D.C.: International Exhibitions Foundation, 1967.

Brief notes on Russian designers and artists and the rebirth of theatrical arts, with 111 monochrome reproductions of stage and costume plates by such designers as Bakst, Benois, Exter, and Zak, plus many others.

186 Spencer, Charles. LEON BAKST. New York: St. Martin's Press; London: Academy Editions, 1973.

Critical and biographical study with 226 illustrations, many in color, of the designer's work, including many of theatrical and dance costumes.

187 _____. THE WORLD OF SERGE DIAGHILEV. Chicago: Henry Reg-nery Co., 1974.

Reproductions of designer's costume plates and production pho-tographs of costumed dancers in this biographical study; addi-tional contributions by Philip Dyer and Martin Battersby; bib-liography and index.

188 Winter, Marian Hannah. THE PRE-ROMANTIC BALLET. Brooklyn: Dance Horizons, 1975.

Many excellent primary-source illustrations of costumed dancers within a survey of theatrical dance from mid–seventeenth cen-tury until about 1820; bibliography and index.

D. COSTUME FOR THE CINEMA

See also 272

189 Chierichetti, David. HOLLYWOOD COSTUME DESIGN. New York: Harmony Books, 1976.

Arranged by major studios; presentation of numerous examples of designs and costumes for film; more concentration on emergence of costume designers in the formative years of movie industry; excellent color photographs and reproductions of costume plates; filmography and index.

190 Leese, Elizabeth. COSTUME DESIGN IN THE MOVIES. New York: Frederick Ungar Publishing Co., 1977.

Brief introduction with historical background; section on couture and the screen relationship; major portion of volume with biographical and professional resumes of major costume designers for the movies, with numerous illustrations, some in color, of designs and completed costumes, usually shown on actresses or actors; list of Oscar winners and SFTA (Society for Film and Television Arts) members in appendix.

191 McConathy, Dale, and Vreeland, Diana. HOLLYWOOD COSTUME DESIGN: GLAMOUR, GLITTER, ROMANCE. New York: Harry N. Abrams, 1976.

Decade-by-decade review of most outstanding costume designs, with seventy-nine color and fifty monochrome photographs of costumes mainly from the Metropolitan Museum's exhibition, "Romantic and Glamorous Hollywood Design," with informative text plus descriptive notes on each costume; biographical notes on each of the designers; glossary, bibliography, and index.

192 ROMANTIC AND GLAMOROUS HOLLYWOOD DESIGN. New York: Metropolitan Museum of Art, 1974.

Exhibition catalog for a survey of costume design for the cinema sponsored by the Costume Institute; numerous photographs of costumed performers; brief biographical sketches of the designers included in the exhibition.

193 Sharaff, Irene. BROADWAY AND HOLLYWOOD: COSTUMES DESIGNED BY IRENE SHARAFF. New York: Van Nostrand Reinhold Co., 1976.

Informative account of author's experiences, insights, and life as a theatrical and cinematic costume designer, with reproductions of many of her original plates and photographs of the completed costume as it appeared on screen; listing of all of the productions that she designed; index.

Chapter 3
HISTORICAL COSTUME

A. GENERAL WORKS

1. Pre-Twentieth-Century Costume

See also 1450, 1517, 1533, 1581

194 Allen, Agnes. THE STORY OF CLOTHES. New York: Roy Publishers, 1958.

Clear and basic textual history of the development of costume from prehistory to the modern day, with a few line drawings for illustrations.

195 Aretz, Gertrude. THE ELEGANT WOMAN FROM THE ROCOCO PERIOD TO MODERN TIMES. London: George G. Harrap and Co., 1932.

Somewhat dated historical survey of female dress and modes as epitomized in the lives of such women as Mme. de Pompadour, Marie-Antoinette, and Lola Montez and their influences upon fashion; numerous illustrations, some in color; very interesting and informative approach to costume history.

196 Barfoot, Audrey. DISCOVERING COSTUME. London: University of London Press, 1959.

Condensed volume of historical costume from 460 to 1929, with drawings by the author.

197 Barsis, Max. THE COMMON MAN THROUGH THE CENTURIES: A BOOK OF COSTUME DRAWINGS. New York: Frederick Ungar Publishing Co., 1973.

Redrawings of primary sources of the common man and his costume from the period of the ancients through the eighteenth century; textual comment and explanation for each drawing; illustration of wide range of types, countries, and periods of costumes; also a guide to the pictures.

198 Barton, Lucy. HISTORIC COSTUME FOR THE STAGE. New ed. Boston: Walter H. Baker Co., 1961.

Somewhat dated but unsurpassed as the most complete historical survey of costume for the serious period designer; information on general background of each of the designated nineteen costume periods plus sections on colors, motifs, famous personalities, accessories, special fashions, construction notes, and a reading list, plus more; discussion of costume, covering each sex and dealing with anatomical areas, for example, sleeves, legs, headwear; detailed line drawings for each costume period; index and bibliography.

199 Batterberry, Michael, and Batterberry, Ariane. MIRROR MIRROR: A SOCIAL HISTORY OF FASHION. New York: Holt, Rinehart and Winston, 1977.

Well-illustrated general survey of historical fashion with emphasis on the relationship between costume and social history; index and bibliography.

200 Beaton, Cecil. FASHION: AN ANTHOLOGY. London: Victoria and Albert Museum, 1971.

Exhibition catalog for collection of garments most admired by Beaton from the museum, with twenty-one plates of historical dresses.

201 Bernstein, Aline. MASTERPIECES OF WOMEN'S COSTUME OF THE 18TH AND 19TH CENTURIES. New York: Crown Publishers, 1959.

Thirty-two color paintings of period costumes by the author, with descriptions in great detail and accompanying plates of appropriate accessories; selected patterns; excellent source.

202 Bigelow, Marybelle S. FASHION IN HISTORY: APPAREL IN THE WESTERN WORLD. Minneapolis: Burgess Publishing Co., 1970.

Majority of book devoted to condensed historical survey, accompanied with drawings often incomplete and sketchy; remaining sections deal briefly with fashion design and illustration.

203 Boehn, Max von. MODES AND MANNERS. 4 vols in 2. Translated by Joan Joshua. 1932. Reprint. New York: Benjamin Blom, 1971.

Coverage in volume 1 from decline of ancient world to Renaissance and the sixteenth century; coverage in volume 2 of the seventeenth and eighteenth centuries; comprehensive survey of fashions and manners, with chapters on such areas as general conditions, social life, the arts, and domestic life, always with the costume and fashion as the main focus; extremely large number of well-chosen half-tone primary-source illustrations; very valuable source.

204 Boehn, Max von, and Fischel, Max. MODES AND MANNERS OF THE NINETEENTH CENTURY AS REPRESENTED IN THE PICTURES AND EN-GRAVINGS OF THE TIME. 4 vols in 2. Translated by M. Edwards. 1909. Rev. enl. ed. 1927. Reprint. New York: Benjamin Blom, 1970.

Numerous primary-source half-tone illustrations in support of survey of fashions and manners from 1790 to 1914; attention to every facet and aspect of the century and its effect upon costume and behavior; extremely valuable source.

205 Boucher, Francois. A HISTORY OF COSTUME IN THE WEST. London: Thames and Hudson, 1967.

Also entitled 20,000 YEARS OF FASHION; very important history of costume because of the large number (352 color and 798 black-and-white) and quality of the plates, all of which are primary-source material; complete text divided into countries, with special sections when needed, for example, theatrical costume and children's fashions; glossary, index, and bibliography.

206 Bradfield, Nancy. COSTUME IN DETAIL: WOMEN'S DRESS, 1730-1930. Boston: Plays, 1968.

Historical survey divided into five sections, with a general description of female costume followed by detailed drawings of dresses from almost each year, showing proper foundation and underwear garments; details of inner construction; also accessories and decorative motifs.

207 Bradley, Carolyn Gertrude. WESTERN WORLD COSTUME: AN OUT-LINE HISTORY. New York: Appleton-Century-Crofts, 1954.

Survey of the development of historical costume divided generally by centuries and presented in outline form with redrawings, chronology, and glossary for each century.

208 Bradshaw, Angela. WORLD COSTUMES. London: Adam and Charles Black, 1961.

Coverage of traditional national dress of seventy-seven countries from Albania to Yugoslavia; extended sections on ancient costume and English costume; drawings of accessories and decorative motifs; sixteen color plates and 142 pages of line drawings.

209 Braun and Schneider Publishers. HISTORIC COSTUME IN PICTURES. 1907. Reprint. New York: Dover Publications, 1975.

Republication of 1907 edition of COSTUMES OF ALL NA-TIONS from original plates of Braun and Schneider Publishers issued between 1861 and 1900; illustrations of more than 1,450 costumed figures of many nations, social levels, and occupations; excellent pictorial source.

210 Braun-Ronsdorf, Margarete. MIRROR OF FASHION: A HISTORY OF EUROPEAN COSTUME, 1789-1929. Translated by Oliver Coburn. New York: McGraw-Hill Book Co., 1964.

Twenty-eight primary-source, color plates, plus 415 mono-chrome primary-source illustrations in addition to succinct text; index and bibliography.

211 Broby-Johansen, R. BODY AND CLOTHES: AN ILLUSTRATED HISTORY OF COSTUME: New York: Reinhold Book Corp., 1968.

Well illustrated with drawings, diagrams, and primary-source material; survey of dress, beginning with primitive peoples and including some unusual costumes such as Mesopotamian wrap, Arab haik, Indian sari, feather poncho, and Eskimo skin garments.

212 Brooke, Iris. DRESS AND UNDRESS: THE RESTORATION AND EIGH-TEENTH CENTURY. London: Methuen and Co., 1958.

Detailed historical survey of formal (dress) and informal (un-dress) attire of the period, with numerous drawings by the au-thor; attention to accessories, undergarments, motifs, and construction diagrams.

213 Bruhn, Wolfgang, and Tilke, Max. A PICTORIAL HISTORY OF COS-TUME: A SURVEY OF COSTUME OF ALL PERIODS AND PEOPLES FROM ANTIQUITY TO MODERN TIMES INCLUDING NATIONAL COSTUME IN EUROPE AND NON-EUROPEAN COUNTRIES. New York: Frederick A. Praeger, 1965.

Two hundred plates, mostly in color, drawn and painted by Tilke of around four thousand examples of total costumes, ac-cessories, hairstyles, and decorative motifs with a description of each costume by Bruhn; valuable for costume depiction of many overlooked areas and minor categories, for example, monastic orders, Russia, Poland, Portugal, and Algeria.

214 Burris-Meyer, Elizabeth. THIS IS FASHION. New York: Harper and Brothers, 1943.

Material in individual chapters on historical survey in the areas of silhouette, color, accessories, fabrics, cosmetics, and coiffure; older source.

215 Button, Jeanne, and Sbarge, Stephen. A HISTORY OF COSTUME: IN SLIDES, NOTES AND COMMENTARIES. New York: Theatre Arts Slides Presentations, 1975.

Unique source; collection of twelve hundred slides of primary-source materials illustrating the history of costume from the Egyptian period to the 1930s, with accompanying notes and commentary to supplement the slides.

216 Cassin-Scott, Jack. COSTUME AND FASHION IN COLOR, 1760-1920. New York: Macmillan Co., 1971.

History of costume and fashion from 1760 to 1920, divided in-to historical periods with a special section of children's cos-tume; drawings and ninety-six paintings by the author with de-scriptive notes; glossary, index, and bibliography.

217 Coleman, Elizabeth Ann. CHANGING FASHIONS, 1800-1970. Brooklyn: Brooklyn Museum, 1972.

Exhibition catalog with thirty-five excellent photographs of period dresses on mannequins with accessories and with brief descriptive notes.

218 Contini, Mila. FASHION FROM ANCIENT EGYPT TO THE PRESENT DAY. Edited by James Laver. New York: Odyssey Press, 1965.

Historical survey of costume with greatest value in the number and excellence of the primary-source illustrations, many in color, but unfortunately not specifically dated; best in treat-ment of the nineteenth and twentieth centuries; index.

219 Crawford, M.D.C. ONE WORLD OF FASHION. 3d ed. Revised and edited by Beatrice Zelin and Josephine Ellis Watkins. New York: Fair-child Publications, 1967.

Ninety plates of numerous line drawings of historic fashion, with greater emphasis on the period since 1945.

220 D'Assailly, Gisele. AGES OF ELEGANCE: FIVE THOUSAND YEARS OF FASHION AND FRIVOLITY. New York: Hachette, 1968.

Handsome volume with excellent illustrations, mostly in color, for survey of fashion from Mesopotamian kaunakes to the mod-ern miniskirt; strongest in treating and picturing the Empire period of costume; brief bibliography.

221 Davenport, Milia. THE BOOK OF COSTUME. 2 vols. in 1. New York: Crown Publishers, 1948.

Most detailed study devoted specifically to historic costume with all of its accompanying elements: accessories, ornament, hairstyles, and so forth; chronological arrangement with further breakdown by countries; almost three thousand illustrations in black and white; index.

222 Dorner, Jane. FASHION: THE CHANGING SHAPE OF FASHION THROUGH THE YEARS. London: Octopus Books, 1974.

Concentration on fashion development from 1700 to the present, with color and black-and-white primary-source illustrations; chapters on female shapes, adornment, sports attire, dandies, American influences, and couture; brief bibliography and index.

223 Evans, Mary. COSTUME THROUGH THE AGES. 1930. Reprint. Philadelphia: J.B. Lippincott Co., 1950.

Survey in part 1 of historic development of dress of the ancients; French, English, and American colonists; survey in part 2 of national costume in Europe, Northern Africa, Asia, and the Americas; 210 primary-source illustrations in black and white; index and bibliography.

224 Fabre, Maurice. HISTORY OF FASHION. Translated by Joan White. London: Leisure Arts, 1966.

Condensed general survey of fashion, with selected illustrations.

225 Fletcher, Marion. FEMALE COSTUME IN THE 19TH CENTURY. Melbourne: Oxford University Press, 1966.

Brief, simply written historical survey with eighteen black-and-white photographs of examples of dresses, coats, and accessories; brief bibliography.

226 _____. LADY OF FASHION, 1800-1935. Victoria, Australia: National Gallery of Victoria, n.d.

Exhibition catalog of Schofield Collection of costumes and accessories, some of Australian origin; complete listing and brief descriptions of 367 items; brief decade-by-decade survey of changes in fashion with selected illustrations, some in color.

227 GALLERY OF FASHION 1790-1822 FROM PLATES BY HEIDELOFF AND ACKERMANN. New York: B.T. Batsford, 1949.

Reproductions of fifteen color plates, with notes by Doris
Langley Moore.

228 Garland, Madge, and Black, J. Anderson. A HISTORY OF FASHION.
New York: William Morrow and Co., 1975.

Handsome volume of historical costume, containing only primary-source illustrations and totally in color, with textual
material; glossary; guide to costume collections; index; and
bibliography.

229 Gernsheim, Alison. FASHION AND REALITY, 1840-1914. London:
Farber and Farber, 1963.

Costume history of a selected era with illustrations based entirely upon period photographs; emphasis on the discrepancy
between the ideal of the fashion plates and the actuality of
the dress practices as seen in the period photographs; index
and bibliography.

230 Giafferri, Paul Louis Victor de. THE HISTORY OF THE FEMININE COS-
TUME OF THE WORLD FROM THE YEAR 5318 B.C. TO OUR CENTURY.
New York: Foreign Publications, 1926-27.

Twenty parts in two portfolios with each part containing eight
pages of text and ten color plates covering such areas as
China-Japan, Egypt, Assyria, Persia, India, Greece, Rome,
Britain and Europe, and the three Americas.

231 Gilbert, John. NATIONAL COSTUMES OF THE WORLD. London:
Paul Hamlyn, 1972.

Brief introduction followed by condensed textual descriptions
and detailed color paintings by Gwen Green of selected national costumes arranged by continents or subcontinents; bibliography.

232 Gorsline, Douglas. WHAT PEOPLE WORE: A VISUAL HISTORY OF
DRESS FROM ANCIENT TIMES TO TWENTIETH-CENTURY AMERICA.
New York: Viking Press, 1952.

Brief text for historically arranged costume drawings by the
author; valuable section on American costume, including many
native types, for example, plainsfolk, cowboys, and rivermen;
sources given for all drawings.

233 GREAT COSTUMES 1550-1950: A PICTURE BOOK. Boston: Museum of
Fine Arts, 1963.

Exhibition catalog containing twenty-four color photographs of
costumes within the four-hundred-year period; additional monochrome photographs in the survey.

Historical Costume

234 Green, Ruth M. COSTUME AND FASHION IN COLOUR, 1550-1760. London: Blandford Press, 1975.

Devised and illustrated with line drawings and color plates by Jack Cassin-Scott, with descriptive notes and general historical information on costume.

235 Hansen, Henny Harald. COSTUMES AND STYLE. New York: E.P. Dutton and Co., 1956.

Pictorial survey of 685 color examples of historic costumes based on works by anonymous and known artists; brief descriptions of costume periods; brief bibliography and index.

236 Hartnell, Norman. ROYAL COURTS OF FASHION. London: Cassell, 1971.

Beginning with the Tudors and extending to the demise of most royal courts in 1919, a survey of influence of royalty upon the fashions of the day; section of color portraits of royal personages plus many more monochrome illustrations; bibliography and index.

237 Kahlenberg, Mary Hunt. FABRIC AND FASHION: TWENTY YEARS OF COSTUME COUNCIL GIFTS. Los Angeles: Los Angeles County Museum, 1974.

Exhibition catalog of thirty-two excellent photographs of period costumes and textiles dating from ancient Egypt to 1947.

238 Kelly, Francis M., and Schwabe, Randolph. A SHORT HISTORY OF COSTUME AND ARMOUR. 2 vols. 1931. Reprint. New York: Arco Publishing Co., 1973.

Volume 1, 1066-1485; volume 2, 1485-1800; inclusion of topic of armor within fairly standard costume history survey, with many line drawings and primary illustrations.

239 Kemper, Rachel H. WORLD OF CULTURE SERIES: COSTUME. Edited by Kathleen Berger and Ned Bayrd. New York: Newsweek Books, 1977.

Handsome volume of history of costume from cave paintings to fashion magazines with over 160 illustrations, many in color.

240 Koehler, Carl. A HISTORY OF COSTUME. Edited and augmented by Emma von Sichart. Translated by Alexander K. Dallas. 1928. Reprint. New York: Dover Publications, 1963.

Quite useful survey of costuming from the ancients to 1870; inclusion of material on costumes of some countries often overlooked: Netherlands, Spain, Germany; many primary-source illustrations and monochrome photographs; large number of patterns which are readily usable and not to be found elsewhere; index and bibliography; excellent source.

241 Laver, James. THE ARTS OF MAN: COSTUME. London: Cassell, 1963.

Condensed treatment of a historical survey of costume, with excellent illustrations; but not author's most noteworthy volume.

242 _____. A CONCISE HISTORY OF COSTUME. London: Thames and Hudson, 1969.

Background chapter on the beginnings of costume with nine successive chapters of direct, succinct survey of costume from Greeks to 1960 with 314 illustrations (58 in color); selected bibliography and index; very useful book for quick reference.

243 _____. COSTUME. London: B.T. Batsford, 1956.

Simplified history of costume from 1000 to 1910 for younger readers; numerous drawings of costume and accessories.

244 _____. TASTE AND FASHION FROM THE FRENCH REVOLUTION UNTIL TO-DAY. New York: George G. Harrap and Co., 1937.

Sociohistorical survey of costume in the first half of book, with discussions in the remainder, of separate costume items, generally in a historical manner: corsets, colors, sport attire, and male garments, among others.

245 Laver, James, and Klepper, Erhard. COSTUME THROUGH THE AGES. New York: Simon and Schuster, 1963.

Brief introduction by Laver plus over one thousand drawings by Klepper of historical costumes from the classical period to 1930; all drawings based on historical sources but grouped very closely together on a page.

246 Lester, Katherine Morris, and Kerr, Rose Netzorg. HISTORIC COSTUME: A RESUME OF STYLE AND FASHION FROM REMOTE TIMES TO THE NINETEEN-SIXTIES. Peoria, Ill.: Charles A. Bennett Co., 1967.

Mostly black-and-white drawings in support of a brief historical survey of fashion.

247 Ley, Sandra. FASHION FOR EVERYONE: THE STORY OF READY-TO-WEAR 1870'S-1970'S. New York: Charles Scribner's Sons, 1975.

Interesting decade-by-decade survey of ready-made fashions with excellent primary illustrations; not a costume book as such but presentation of much costume history incidentally.

248 Lister, Margot. COSTUME: AN ILLUSTRATED SURVEY FROM ANCIENT TIMES TO THE TWENTIETH CENTURY. London: Herbert Jenkins, 1967.

Large number of drawings and descriptions of a typical male and female costume from selected intervals within each century.

249 _____. STAGE COSTUME. London: Herbert Jenkins, 1954.

Very condensed and simplified survey of historic costume, with scant illustrative materials; of some use perhaps for younger readers.

250 Louden, Adelaide Bolton, and Louden, Norman P. HISTORIC COSTUMES THROUGH THE AGES: A PORTFOLIO OF TWENTY PLATES IN COLOR, REPRESENTATIVE COSTUMES, HISTORIC ORNAMENT, ANNOTATIONS. Philadelphia: H.C. Perleberg Co., 1936.

Short, simplified historical survey.

251 Mallath, Regine. HISTORIC COSTUME DESIGNS: 100 DRAWINGS FROM ANCIENT EGYPTIANS TO THE PRESENT DAY. Chicago: Carter Publications, 1960.

Collection of one hundred (6 colored) of the author's drawings and paintings of historical costume, each based on primary sources, with descriptive notes.

252 Metropolitan Museum of Art. EXHIBITION OF VICTORIAN AND EDWARDIAN DRESSES. New York: 1939.

Brief introduction in exhibition catalog containing sixty monochrome photographs of dresses from 1837 to 1907; photographs not available elsewhere.

253 Moore, Doris Langley. THE WOMAN IN FASHION. London: B.T. Batsford, 1949.

Series of 108 photographs of period fashions, presented chronologically with commentary and descriptive notes.

254 Payne, Blanche. HISTORY OF COSTUME FROM THE ANCIENT EGYPTIANS TO THE TWENTIETH CENTURY. New York: Harper and Row, Publishers, 1965.

Rather thorough survey of costume, generally divided by centuries and separated into discussion of male and female dress;
564 photographs and line drawings by Elizabeth Curtis, none
in color; section of pattern drafts of high quality; bibliography
and index.

255 Pringle, Patrick. FASHION. London: Thomas Nelson and Sons, 1972.

Brief survey in booklet form.

256 Selbie, Robert. THE ANATOMY OF COSTUME. New York: Crescent
Books, 1977.

Condensed historical survey in text, with paintings by Victor
Ambrus, generally of a typical male and female during the
respective periods, with assorted other sketches and paintings
of accessories and decorative features.

257 Sichel, Marion. COSTUME REFERENCE. 6 vols. Boston: Plays, 1977.

Volume 1: ROMAN BRITAIN AND THE MIDDLE AGES; volume 2: TUDORS AND ELIZABETHANS; volume 3: JACO-
BEAN, STUART AND RESTORATION; volume 4: THE EIGH-
TEENTH CENTURY; volume 5: THE REGENCY; volume 6:
THE VICTORIANS; general historical survey plus detailed descriptions of male and female costume, with author's redrawings of primary sources; glossary and selected bibliography for
each volume; much repetition of material available elsewhere.

258 Squire, Geoffrey. DRESS AND SOCIETY 1560-1970. New York: Viking Press, 1974.

Historical presentation of fashionable European dress as an es-
sential manifestation of changing patterns in thought and be-
lief; very weak on the last century; bibliography and index.

259 Squire, Geoffrey, and Baynes, Pauline. THE OBSERVER'S BOOK OF
EUROPEAN COSTUME. London: Frederick Warne, 1975.

General handbook of survey of historical fashion from the first
century to 1900, with line drawings and brief glossary.

260 Sronkova, Olga. FASHIONS THROUGH THE CENTURIES: RENAISSANCE,
BAROQUE, AND ROCOCO. Translated by T. Gottheiner. London:
Spring Books, 1959.

Numerous primary illustrations in support of textual survey of
Western European costume.

Historical Costume

261 Stavridi, Margaret. HISTORY OF COSTUME. 4 vols. Boston: Plays, 1970.

> Volume 1: B.C.-A.D. 1500; volume 2: 1500-1600; volume 3: 1600-1800; volume 4: THE NINETEENTH CENTURY; brief descriptive commentary for each of twenty color paintings by Faith Jaques in each volume in the series.

262 Vertes, Marcel. ART AND FASHION. New York: Studio Publications, 1944.

> Twenty color plates of famous artists' depictions of historical costume.

263 Walkup, Fairfax Proudfit. DRESSING THE PART: A HISTORY OF COS-TUME FOR THE THEATRE. New York: Appleton-Century-Crofts, 1950.

> Survey of historical fashion divided by cultures and/or centuries, from the Egyptians to the twentieth century; line drawings of completely costumed figures; vague pattern shapes; condensation of background materials for each section; many sketches of individual garments and accessories; list of playwrights and plays by period; index and bibliography.

264 Wilcox, R. Turner. FOLK AND FESTIVAL COSTUME OF THE WORLD. New York: Charles Scribner's Sons, 1965.

> Descriptive notations for the 111 plates of drawings of costume from every major country from Afghanistan to Yugoslavia; illustrations of accessories and motifs.

265 _____. THE MODE IN COSTUME. New York: Charles Scribner's Sons, 1948.

> Historical survey from Egypt to the modern day, with concise descriptive commentary by the author on line drawings of costumes, accessories, and motifs.

266 Wilkerson, Marjorie. CLOTHES. London: B.T. Batsford, 1970.

> General introduction to subject of historical clothing, with sixty-seven illustrations.

267 Yarwood, Doreen. EUROPEAN COSTUME: 4000 YEARS OF FASHION. New York: Larousse and Co., 1975.

> Historical overview of European costume in a condensed arrangement with line drawings of prototype costumes and accessories presented by country within periods, for example, baroque, rococo; glossary, index, and bibliography.

268 Young, Agnes Brooks. RECURRING CYCLES OF FASHION 1760-1937.
New York: Cooper Square Publishers, 1966.

Historical survey of women's fashions in terms of fixed cycli-
cal and predictable patterns of shapes: bustle, bell, and tube;
diagrams and primary materials in support of concept.

2. Twentieth-Century Costume

See also 440, 449, 466, 467, chapter 13

269 Battersby, Martin. THE DECORATIVE THIRTIES: New York: Walker
and Co., 1971.

Coverage of the entire range of decorative arts in the decade
of the 1930s, with a chapter devoted to fashion; excellent for
feeling of the period and illustrations of the design elements,
especially in costume and fashion.

270 _____. THE DECORATIVE TWENTIES. New York: Walker and Co.,
1969.

Overview of artistic trends of entire decade of the 1920s, with
a chapter on fashion, costume, and accessories, with a number
of illustrations, some in color.

271 Carter, Ernestine. THE CHANGING WORLD OF FASHION, 1900 TO
THE PRESENT. New York: G.P. Putnam's Sons, 1977.

Well-documented and illustrated history of female dress during
the period.

272 _____. 20TH CENTURY FASHION: A SCRAPBOOK--1900 TO TODAY.
London: Eyre Methuen, 1975.

Decade-by-decade survey of female fashion since 1900, with
152 monochrome plates; chapters on special influences, for
example, the wars, sports, and Chanel; inclusion of some theatrical and cinema designs.

273 Dorner, Jane. FASHION IN THE FORTIES AND FIFTIES. London: Ian
Allan, 1975.

Careful examination and generously illustrated overview of
fashion and clothing during these two decades; attention to
male clothing, often a neglected area.

274 _____. FASHION IN THE TWENTIES AND THIRTIES. London: Ian
Allan, 1973.

Survey of female fashion and accessories during the period, with primary illustrative materials: designs, photographs, and advertisements.

275 Ewing, Elizabeth. HISTORY OF TWENTIETH CENTURY FASHION. London: B.T. Batsford, 1974.

Interesting coverage of subject, with 252 photographs and illustrations of most aspects of female fashion and costume during the period.

276 Garland, Madge. FASHION. Middlesex, Engl.: Penguin Books, 1962.

Emphasis on fashion and haute couture, but also presents a large variety of pictorial material from the 1950s and early 1960s.

277 Ginsburg, Madeleine. FASHION: AN ANTHOLOGY BY CECIL BEATON: London: Victoria and Albert Museum, 1971.

Catalog for exhibition of 447 twentieth-century fashions admired most by Beaton from Costume Court; many black-and-white photographs and line drawings plus descriptive notes and brief biographical sketches of represented designers.

278 Gold, Annalee. 75 YEARS OF FASHION. New York: Fairchild Publications, 1975.

Numerous line drawings only; historical survey of female attire beginning in 1900, divided into types of garments with a decade-by-decade sampler of accessories.

279 Howell, Georgina. IN VOGUE: SIX DECADES OF FASHION. New York: Allen Lane, 1976.

Survey of coverage of fashion from the pages and pictures of VOGUE MAGAZINE from 1916 to 1975, with descriptive text and notes; representation of highest style of fashion during the period.

280 Laver, James. WOMEN'S DRESS IN THE JAZZ AGE. London: Hamish Hamilton, 1964.

Detailed survey of fashion in the 1920s, with numerous primary-source illustrations.

281 Lessing, Alice, et al. SIXTY YEARS OF FASHION. New York: Fairchild Publications, 1963.

Brief textual and pictorial survey of general fashion from 1900 to 1960, with sections on dresses and coats, millinery, furs, and leisure and sportswear.

282 MODES DES ANNEES FOLLES, 1919-1929. Paris: Musee du costume de la ville de Paris, 1970.

Exhibition catalog with sixteen monochrome plates of fashions and accessories from the period.

283 Peacock, John. FASHION SKETCHBOOK: 1920-1960. New York: Avon, 1977.

No commentary, but a treatment of fashion in each of the four decades in numerous (120) two-color sketches with descriptive notations; covers all types of day, evening, and special occasion dress, foundation wear, and accessories; fairly comprehensive and informative study.

284 Robinson, Julian. FASHION IN THE FORTIES. London: Academy Editions; New York: St. Martin's Press, 1976.

Historical survey in detailed text of the effects of the war on 1940s fashion and the postwar revolution in female fashions; large number of primary-source illustrations, some in color.

285 _____. THE GOLDEN AGE OF STYLE. New York: Harcourt Brace Jovanovich, 1976.

History of artistic trends in female fashion from 1901 to 1939, illustrated almost entirely with color plates of works by famous designers supplemented with a few photographs; excellent pictorial review.

286 Scottish Arts Council. FASHION, 1900-1939: A SCOTTISH ARTS COUN· CIL EXHIBITION WITH THE SUPPORT OF THE VICTORIA AND ALBERT MUSEUM. London: Idea Books, 1975.

Exhibition catalog containing excellent and numerous photographs, some in color, of selected fashions and accessories during the period; chapters on fashion in general; fashion photography; fashion illustration; textiles; and the relationship of costume with the other arts of the period; notes and descriptions of items in the exhibition; very helpful source of the period.

287 Torrens, Deborah. FASHION ILLUSTRATED: A REVIEW OF WOMEN'S DRESS 1920-1950. New York: Hawthorn Books, 1975.

Year-by-year arrangement of extensive amount of primary illustrative materials, many colored; informative text with discussion of trends in each decade for an overall survey; section of a few basic patterns from the period; useful source.

B. COSTUME BY GEOGRAPHICAL AREAS

1. Costume of Africa

See also 837, 867, 884, 1501

288 Abbate, Francesco. AFRICAN ART AND OCEANIC ART. New York: Octopus Books, 1972.

No commentary on costume as such, but many excellent photographs of statuary and masks helpful to costumer.

289 Bernolles, Jacques. PERMANENCE DE LA PARURE ET DU MASQUE AFRICAINS. Paris: G.P. Maisonneuve et Larose, 1966.

Text in French, but many helpful drawings of African costume, hairstyles, accessories, masks, and decorative motifs easily adaptable to costuming for the theatre.

290 Broster, Joan. AFRICAN ELEGANCE. New York: Purnell, 1973.

Over 150 photographs, some in color, by Alice Mertens, of African native costume; one of few books dealing with costume in more specific detail.

291 Cole, Herbert. AFRICAN ARTS OF TRANSFORMATION. Santa Barbara: Art Galleries, University of California, 1970.

Discussion and illustration of dress for ceremonies and rituals, including headwear and masks.

292 Fagg, William Buller, ed. THE LIVING ARTS OF NIGERIA. New York: Macmillan Co., 1971.

Excellent study of the panorama of Nigerian life, with section on costumes and crafts; color drawings and photographs; useful, extensive study.

293 Gardi, Rene. AFRICAN CRAFTS AND CRAFTSMEN. New York: Van Nostrand Reinhold Co., 1969.

Close connection between crafts and costumes in African cultures; many color photographs of costumes, decorative motifs, and accessories.

294 _____. INDIGENOUS AFRICAN ARCHITECTURE. Translated by Sigrid MacRae. New York: Van Nostrand Reinhold Co., 1973.

Though an architectural study, many excellent color photographs of costumed people in native garb.

295 Gorer, Geoffrey. AFRICAN DANCES. New York: W.W. Norton and Co., 1962.

Discussion of body adornment, tattooing, and costume, with photographs of special costume as it pertains to African dances.

296 Haskins, Sam. AFRICAN IMAGE. New York: Madison Square Press, 1967.

Not specifically on costume, but has notes and monochrome photographs of costume incidentally in text.

297 Huntingtonford, G.W.B. THE GALLA OF ETHIOPIA: THE KINGDOMS OF KAFA AND JANIERO. London: International African Institute, 1955.

Inclusion within broader text of descriptions of hairstyles, ornaments, and costumes.

298 Jefferson, Louise E. THE DECORATIVE ARTS OF AFRICA. New York: Viking Press, 1973.

Broad study which includes many photographs and descriptions of costumes, accessories, and ornamentation.

299 Kyerematen, A.A.Y. PANOPLY OF GHANA. London: Longmans, Green and Co., 1964.

Specialized study including photographs and descriptions of the royal Ghanan swords and gold ornaments.

300 Leirie, Michel, and Delange, Jacqueline. AFRICAN ART. Translated by Michael Ross. New York: Golden Press, 1968.

Extremely well illustrated survey of the topic, with a chapter entitled "Arts of the Body," including costume, makeup, hairstyles, masks, and accessories; helpful source.

301 NIGERIA IN COSTUME. 5th ed. N.p.: Shell Co. of Nigeria, 1975.

Forty-eight detailed color paintings with descriptive notes of varieties of Nigerian native dress.

302 Nordquist, Barbara, et al. CREATIVE WEST AFRICAN FASHION. Plainfield, N.J.: Textile Book Service, 1973.

Guide to constructing and decorating in the style of West African fashions through clearly presented diagrams, patterns, instructions, and photographs.

303 Paulme, Denise, and Brosse, Jacques. PARURES AFRICAINES. New
York: Hachette, 1956.

> French text, but numerous excellent photographs, many in
> color, of African costume and decoration.

304 Ricciardi, Mirella. VANISHING AFRICA. Rev. ed. New York: Holt,
Rinehart, and Winston, 1974.

> Information on costume incidental in this photographic study
> of the continent, its peoples, and their lives.

305 Riefenstahl, Leni. THE LAST OF THE NUBA. New York: Harper and
Row, Publishers, 1973.

> Presentation of the Nuba tribe, its people, customs, and cos-
> tumes in excellent photographic study.

306 _____. THE PEOPLE OF KAU. New York: Harper and Row, Publishers,
1976.

> Photographic essay format with visual record of the people,
> costumes, and customs; excellent section on body adornment.

307 Sieber, Roy. AFRICAN TEXTILES AND DECORATIVE ARTS. New York:
Museum of Modern Art, 1972.

> Exhibition catalog with numerous illustrations, many in color,
> of costume masks, motifs, textiles, jewelry, and other acces-
> sories; helpful section on musical instruments; bibliography.

308 Tyrrell, Barbara Harcourt. TRIBAL PEOPLES OF SOUTHERN AFRICA.
Capetown: Books of Africa, 1968.

> Illustrations and information on costume and ornamentation of
> southern African peoples.

309 Wassing, Rene S. AFRICAN ART: ITS BACKGROUND AND TRADITIONS.
New York: Harry N. Abrams, 1968.

> Excellent text, with 24 color and 120 monochrome plates of
> examples of African costumes, masks, fetishes, and accessories.

310 Willett, Frank. AFRICAN ART: AN INTRODUCTION. New York:
Frederick A. Praeger, 1971.

> Many photographs of costume, motifs, and accessories in this
> book not specifically on costume but helpful nevertheless.

2. Costume of the Americas

a. NORTH AMERICA

See also 1494, 1506

311 AMERICAN MAIL ORDER FASHIONS, 1880-1900. Scotia, N.Y.: Americana Review, 1961.

Booklet, with illustrations, of selected fashions and accessories from catalogs and magazines of the period; descriptions and prices included in the advertisements.

312 Blum, Stella, ed. VICTORIAN FASHIONS AND COSTUMES FROM HARPER'S BAZAAR, 1867-1898. New York: Dover Publications, 1974.

Over one thousand primary-source illustrations in vivid expression of the panorama of the total feminine attire of the late Victorian era in the United States.

313 Brett, K.B. WOMEN'S COSTUME IN EARLY ONTARIO. Toronto: Royal Ontario Museum, 1966.

Booklet of sixteen selected photographs of costumes and accessories of the region, with a condensed historical survey of the subject from the period 1784-1867.

314 _____. WOMEN'S COSTUME IN ONTARIO, 1867-1907. Toronto: Royal Ontario Museum, 1966.

Booklet of twenty-one selected monochrome photographs of fashions and accessories, with condensed historical notes in the text; suggested reading list.

315 CITY OF NEW YORK GOLDEN ANNIVERSARY OF FASHION, 1898-1948. New York: Mayor's Committee for the Commemoration of the Golden Anniversary of the City of New York, 1948.

Brief history of fashion and the fashion industry in New York, with a number of historic illustrations and advertisements; excellent for fashions of the mid- and late-1940s.

316 Collard, Eileen. CLOTHING IN ENGLISH CANADA: CIRCA 1867 TO 1907. Burlington, Ont.: 1975.

Separate coverage in text and many primary-source illustrations of women's clothing and underclothing and men's clothing and underclothing from 1867 to 1907; reproductions of period tailors' patterns and layouts; bibliography.

317 ____. EARLY CLOTHING IN SOUTHERN ONTARIO. Burlington, Ont.: Mississauga, 1969.

Booklet with condensed coverage of clothing from 1784 to 1967; redrawings of period fashion plates, individual garments and accessories; one pattern; short section on underclothing; suggested reading list.

318 Collins, Henry B., et al. THE FAR NORTH: 2000 YEARS OF AMERI-CAN ESKIMO AND INDIAN ART. Bloomington: Indiana University Press, 1977.

Originally published in 1973 as an exhibition catalog for the National Gallery of Art; chapters on Eskimo, Athabaskan, and Tlingit art, with numerous black-and-white and fifteen color plates of costumes, masks, and accessories, with complete descriptive notes and measurements; reading list.

319 Denlinger, Donald M., and Warner, James A. THE GENTLE PEOPLE: A PORTRAIT OF THE AMISH. Soudersburg, Pa.: Mill Bridge Museum, 1969.

Pictorial study of the Amish people, their lives and their daily routines; many excellent photographs of the people.

320 Dines, Glen. SUN, SAND AND STEEL: COSTUMES AND EQUIPMENT OF THE SPANISH-MEXICAN SOUTHWEST. New York: G.P. Putnam's Sons, 1972.

Coverage of the years from 1540 to 1850 with concise text and numerous drawings; material on costumes of explorers, priests, landers, rancheros, soldiers, and civilians, plus section on the respective flags of the region; glossary; excellent source for the area.

321 Earle, Alice Morse. TWO CENTURIES OF COSTUME IN AMERICA, 1620-1820. 2 vols. 1903. Reprint. New York: Dover Publications, 1970.

Older source, but extremely useful and usable; coverage of costume items rather than historical survey; chapters on every phase with novel topics included, such as dress of the Quaker, riding attire, bridal dress, mourning clothing, and fashion dolls; excellent selection of illustrative materials, all primary-source; inclusion of large amount of period documentation from diaries, letters, quotes, and so forth; index.

322 Espinosa, Carmen. SHAWLS, CRINOLINES, FILIGREE: THE DRESS AND ADORNMENT OF THE WOMEN OF NEW MEXICO, 1739 TO 1900. El Paso: Texas Western Press, 1970.

Brief introduction to the history of dress of the area, followed by chapters on separate items of apparel and accessories with numerous illustrations and photographs, some in color; available in English or Spanish; bibliography.

323 FASHIONS OF THE SEVENTIES, STYLE, CUT AND CONSTRUCTION, 1870-1879. Toronto: Costume Society of Ontario, 1972.

Ten monochrome illustrations and five chapters ("Women's Status," "Ladies' Underwear," "Period Patterns," "Gentlemen's Dress," and "Fashion Chronology") on Canadian fashion of the decade.

324 Fennelly, Catherine. COUNTRY GARB IN EARLY NEW ENGLAND: COSTUMES AT OLD STURBRIDGE VILLAGE. Sturbridge, Mass.: Old Sturbridge Village Publications, 1966.

Brief account of rural or regional dress in New England from 1775 to 1840, with extensive illustrations and chapters on farmers' frocks, gowns, and home weaving for clothing.

325 Fife, Austin, et al., eds. FORMS UPON THE FRONTIER: FOLKLIFE AND FOLK ARTS IN THE UNITED STATES. Logan: Utah State University Press, 1969.

Collection of essays with illustrations on various phases of folk culture, with a chapter entitled "Sectarian Costume Research in the United States," by Don Yoder.

326 Gehret, Ellen J. RURAL PENNSYLVANIA CLOTHING: BEING A STUDY OF THE WEARING APPAREL OF THE GERMAN AND ENGLISH INHABITANTS IN THE LATE 18TH AND EARLY 19TH CENTURY. York, Pa.: Shumway Press, 1973.

Profusely illustrated text containing selected patterns and detailed descriptions of rural Eastern clothing.

327 Gummere, Amelia Mott. THE QUAKER: A STUDY IN COSTUME. 1901. Reprint. New York: Benjamin Blom, 1968.

Based largely on primary documents, accounts, diaries, and so forth; full treatment of all facets of Quaker attire, including hats and bonnets, hairstyles, and female dress, with illustrations and line drawings.

328 Haire, Frances Hamilton. THE AMERICAN COSTUME BOOK. New York: A.S. Barnes and Co., 1937.

Somewhat general descriptions of dress characteristics of various American types, for example, Plains Indians, homesteaders, and cowboys; also survey of costume of each century through the nineteenth, with a color painting of a typical male and female.

329 Hassrick, Peter. THE WAY WEST: ART OF FRONTIER AMERICA. New York: Harry N. Abrams, 1977.

Not a costume book as such, but a full pictorial survey (233 illustrations with 103 in full color) of the frontier, its inhabitants and life, as seen by photographers and artists; presented chronologically with an index.

330 Hicks, Marjorie. CLOTHING FOR LADIES AND GENTLEMEN OF HIGHER AND LOWER STANDING: A WORKING PAMPHLET TO AID THE IMITATORS OF NEW ENGLAND CITIZENS OF THE EIGHTEENTH CENTURY. Washington, D.C.: Government Printing Office, 1976.

Brief introduction, with treatment of women's and men's clothing composed of a few basic patterns; line drawings, basic descriptions of garments and accessories; sections on specialized clothing, fabrics, and primary-source information; bibliography.

331 Horan, James D. THE GREAT AMERICAN WEST: A PICTORIAL HISTORY FROM CORONADO TO THE LAST FRONTIER. New York: Crown Publishers, 1959.

Extremely well illustrated survey of wide-ranging scope, valuable to costumer for information and picturization of western types, cowboys, frontiersmen, scouts, Indians.

332 Hostetler, John A. AMISH LIFE. Scottdale, Pa.: Herald Press, 1952.

Brief survey of social life, customs, and dress of the Amish people, with primary-source illustrations.

333 _____. MENNONITE LIFE. Rev. ed. Scottdale, Pa.: Herald Press, 1954.

Brief survey of Mennonite people, their customs, and dress, with primary-source illustrations.

334 Jacopetti, Alexandra. NATIVE FUN AND FLASH: AN EMERGING FOLK ART. San Francisco: Scrimshaw Press, 1974.

Excellent color photographs of costumes, accessories, and decorative motifs currently popular in the San Francisco culture area; useful for modern plays within this milieu.

335 Kerr, Rose Netzorg. 100 YEARS OF COSTUMES IN AMERICA. Worcester, Mass.: Davis Press, 1951.

Brief descriptive notes for author's drawings of selected historical costumes in America.

336 Kidwell, Claudia A., and Christman, Margaret C. SUITING EVERYONE: THE DEMOCRATIZATION OF CLOTHING IN AMERICA. Washington, D.C.: Smithsonian Institution Press, 1974.

History of garment manufacturing industry in the United States, with numerous primary illustrations and photographs of great value to any costumer dealing with an American play set within the last 150 years.

337 Klapthor, Margaret Brown. THE FIRST LADIES HALL. Washington, D.C.: Smithsonian Institution Press, 1965.

Booklet with photographs of costumes and selected accessories of the First Ladies as displayed in the Smithsonian Institution.

338 Kunciov, Robert, ed. MR. GODEY'S LADIES: BEING A MOSAIC OF FASHIONS AND FANCIES. New York: Bonanza Books, 1971.

Presentation of the entire range of nineteenth-century American female attire and accessories, from illustrations from the magazine, with reproductions of fifteen of its famous fashion plates.

339 McClellan, Elisabeth. HISTORY OF AMERICAN COSTUME, 1607-1870. 1904. Reprint. New York: Tudor Publishing Co., 1969.

Part 1 covers the seventeenth century in respect to the colonies and geographical areas; part 2 covers each decade by male and female costume; over 750 monochrome reproductions of primary source material; separate chapters on Quaker, clergy, military, Shaker, children's, and sporting dress; glossary for each volume; very valuable source.

340 McCracken, Harold. THE AMERICAN COWBOY. Garden City, N.Y.: Doubleday and Co., 1973.

Topic covered in interesting text, plus numerous paintings, drawings, and photographs, some in color.

341 Mackey, Margaret Gilbert, and Sooy, Louise Pickney. EARLY CALIFORNIA COSTUMES AND HISTORIC FLAGS OF CALIFORNIA. Stanford, Calif.: Stanford University Press, 1949.

Clear and concise treatments with line drawings covering lower and upper classes, Indians, clerical, military, and occupational costumes; bibliography.

342 Milbern, Gwendolyn. SHAKER CLOTHING. Lebanon, Ohio: Warren County Historical Society, n.d.

Concise treatment of specialized topic, with nine line drawings.

343 Mills, Betty J. FLASHES OF FASHION: 1830-1972. Lubbock: West Texas Museum Association, 1973.

Brief visual guide to clothing of the American women of the last 140 years, as seen in color photographs and descriptive notes of ninety-five costumes on models arranged by functional categories: boudoir, business, wedding, day, sportswear, graduation, ball and festival gowns, among others; bibliography.

344 MODESTY TO MOD: DRESS AND UNDRESS IN CANADA, 1780-1967. Toronto: Royal Ontario Museum, 1967.

Catalog of one hundred items in an exhibition; background treatment of clothing in the country with numerous excellent photographs, many in color, of assorted types of clothing: work, day, wedding, and sport; section of patterns.

345 Schroeder, Joseph J., Jr., ed. THE WONDERFUL WORLD OF LADIES' FASHION, 1850-1920. Northfield, Ill.: Digest Books, 1971.

Compilation of primary material forming an illustrated history of the evolution of women's fashions; coverage of a broad range of the female world: education, manners, and pastimes, in addition to fashion in all respects; bibliography.

346 Sellner, Eudora. AMERICAN COSTUMES: 150 YEARS OF STYLE IN AMERICA, 1775-1925. Worcester, Mass.: Davis Press, 1925.

Forty-eight drawings with notations of color and descriptive notes of fashionable American costumes.

347 Severa, Joan. THE GLASS OF FASHION, 1830-1930. Rochester, N.Y.: Rochester Museum and Science Center and the Margaret Woodbury Strong Museum, 1974.

Exhibition catalog with decade-by-decade survey of American fashion, with brief historical notes and photographs, four in color, of garments and accessories from the museum and in selected fashion miniature dolls by Evelyn Green.

348 Trahey, Jane, ed. 100 YEARS OF THE AMERICAN FEMALE FROM HARPER'S BAZAAR. New York: Random House, 1967.

American fashion as seen through the pages of the well-known magazine; interesting source.

349 Truett, Randle Bond. THE FIRST LADIES IN FASHION. New York: Hastings House, 1970.

Monochrome photographs and brief descriptions of the gowns of the First Ladies exhibited in the Smithsonian Institution, from Martha Washington to Patricia Nixon; fashion notes by Philip Robertson.

350 Tyler, Ron. THE COWBOY. New York: William Morrow and Co., 1975.

Photographic study of the modern cowboy.

351 Warwick, Edward, et al. EARLY AMERICAN DRESS: THE COLONIAL AND REVOLUTIONARY PERIODS. New York: Benjamin Blom, 1965.

Extremely valuable source for the period; coverage arranged by geographical areas with further division into male and female costume, chronologically if necessary; special chapters on children and frontier life; section on seamen's dress; most valuable section of ninety-six plates of primary-source material; many line drawings in the text; bibliography and index; chart of chronology of the illustrations.

352 Wilcox, R. Turner. FIVE CENTURIES OF AMERICAN COSTUME. London: Adam and Charles Black, 1963.

Historical survey beginning with the Vikings, covering early Indian settlers, tracing the colonists up to modern times, with many drawings by the author; great attention to military costume; one chapter on children's dress; bibliography.

353 Worrell, Estelle Ansley. EARLY AMERICAN COSTUME. Harrisburg, Pa.: Stackpole Books, 1975.

Coverage of historical American costumes from 1580 to 1850; 238 drawings by the author with descriptive notes; twelve color plates generally unimaginative; first chapter on designing for the theatre and last chapter on constructing costumes-- all very simple and very basic; section of vague, unscaled pattern drawings.

b. NORTH AMERICAN INDIANS

See also 318, 328, 329, 331, 341, 352, 737, 878, 885

354 Appleton, Leroy H. AMERICAN INDIAN DESIGN AND DECORATION. New York: Dover Publications, 1971.

Descriptions and illustrations of many Indian designs and ornamentation motifs.

355 _____. INDIAN ART OF THE AMERICAS. New York: Charles Scribner's Sons, 1950.

Extensive text and numerous drawings of Indian ornamentation, accessories, masks, costumes, and textiles.

356 Bahti, Tom. AN INTRODUCTION TO SOUTHWESTERN INDIAN ARTS AND CRAFTS. Flagstaff, Ariz.: KC Publications, 1964.

Illustrations of Indian decorative motifs and arts, costumes, and accessories indigenous to the area.

357 Collier, John. PATTERNS AND CEREMONIALS OF THE INDIANS OF THE SOUTHWEST. New York: E.P. Dutton Co., 1949.

Excellent text with over one hundred drawings by Ida Moskowitz, showing costumes, accessories, and manners of various southwestern tribes.

358 Conn, Richard. ROBES OF WHITE SHELL AND SUNRISE: PERSONAL DECORATIVE ARTS OF THE NATIVE AMERICAN. Denver: Denver Art Museum, 1974.

Exhibition catalog with many excellent black-and-white and color photographs, some patterns, and complete descriptive notations.

359 Dickason, Olive Patricia. INDIAN ARTS IN CANADA. Ottawa, Ont.: Information Canada, 1973.

Excellent photographs, some in color, decorative motifs, and accessories; not a costume text as such.

360 Dockstader, Frederick J. INDIAN ART IN AMERICA: THE ARTS AND CRAFTS OF THE NORTH AMERICAN INDIAN. Greenwich, Conn.: New York Graphic Society, 1961.

Very thorough study with interesting text and extensive color illustration of costumes, accessories, masks, and motifs; bibliography.

361 Douglas, Frederic H., and D'Harnoncourt, Rene. INDIAN ART OF THE UNITED STATES. 2d ed. New York: Museum of Modern Art, 1949.

Excellent textual and illustrative coverage of the subject.

362 Ewers, John Canfield. BLACKFEET CRAFTS. Edited by Willard W. Beatty. Lawrence, Kans.: Haskell Institute, 1945.

Brief booklet; somewhat dated; coverage and illustration of Blackfeet decorative motifs, costumes, and accessories; specialized study with bibliography of selected readings on the topic.

363 Fundabunk, Emma Lila. SOUTHEASTERN INDIANS: LIFE PORTRAITS: A CATALOG OF PICTURES, 1564-1860. Luverne, Ala.: 1958. Reprint. Metuchen, N.J.: Scarecrow Reprint Corp., 1969.

Valuable reprint because of its being the only collection of illustrations and descriptive materials of costumes of the Indian tribes of the Southeast: Creeks, Cherokees, Seminoles, and others.

364 Hofsinde, Robert. INDIAN COSTUMES. New York: William Morrow and Co., 1968.

Brief but succinct descriptions of costumes of major Indian tribes in the United States; useful for overview of major costume differences among the major tribes.

365 Horan, James D. THE McKENNEY-HALL PORTRAIT GALLERY OF AMERICAN INDIANS. New York: Crown Publishers, 1972.

Excellent source; compilation of full-dress portraits of 120 Indian chiefs, taken upon the occasion of the chiefs' visits to Washington, D.C., in the first half of the nineteenth century.

366 Hunt, W. Ben, and Burshears, J.F. "Buck." AMERICAN INDIAN BEADWORK. New York: Bruce Publishing Co.; London: Collier-Macmillan, 1951.

Full coverage of historical beadwork, processes and looms, and color plates of motifs; section of illustrations of miscellaneous beadwork articles, including costume items and accessories.

367 INTRODUCTION TO AMERICAN INDIAN ART. New York: Exposition of Indian Tribal Arts, 1931.

Dated; series of essays on aspects of the subject, including costume and accessories; many illustrations.

368 Josephy, Alvin M., Jr., ed. THE AMERICAN HERITAGE BOOK OF INDIANS. New York: American Heritage Publishing Co., 1961.

Broad survey of the development of Indians from the beginning to the present; excellent primary illustrations in black and white and color; deals with Indians from all regions; index.

369 Koch, Ronald P. DRESS CLOTHING OF THE PLAINS INDIANS. Norman: University of Oklahoma Press, 1977.

> Well-documented and illustrated (9 color plates and 65 black-and-white figures) survey of distinctive tribal traditions of costumes, cut, color, decoration, hair and headdress, footwear, and accessories; some patterns and construction diagrams; excellent source.

370 'KSAN: BREADTH OF OUR GRANDFATHERS. Ottawa: National Museum, 1972.

> Exhibition catalog with seventy-eight monochrome plates of regalia and masks of Indians of British Columbia.

371 Lyford, Carrie Alberta. THE CRAFTS OF THE OJIBEWA (CHIPPEWA). Edited by Willard W. Beatty. Phoenix: Phoenix Indian School, 1943.

> Published under the auspices of the U.S. Office of Indian Affairs; coverage in text and illustrations of tribal costume, crafts, and adornment; specialized study; bibliography.

372 _____. IROQUOIS CRAFTS. Edited by Willard W. Beatty. Washington, D.C.: U.S. Department of the Interior, Bureau of Indian Affairs, 1957.

> Survey of costume, among other crafts of the Iroquois tribe, with selected illustrations, maps, and bibliography.

373 _____. QUILL AND BEADWORK OF THE WESTERN SIOUX. Edited by Willard W. Beatty. Lawrence, Kans.: Haskell Institute, 1940.

> Illustration through photographs and drawings of the subject, with material on tribal costume, accessories, decorative motifs, and adornment; bibliography.

374 Mason, Bernard S. THE BOOK OF INDIAN-CRAFTS AND COSTUMES. New York: Ronald Press, 1946.

> Basic book of construction and design of Indian costumes and accessories, with numerous photographs, drawings, and diagrams; useful source.

375 Roediger, Virginia M. CEREMONIAL COSTUMES OF THE PUEBLO INDIANS: THEIR EVOLUTION, FABRICATION AND SIGNIFICANCE IN THE PRAYER DRAMA. Berkeley and Los Angeles: University of California Press, 1941.

> Specialized but useful study with forty color plates and line drawings.

376 Stirling, Matthew W. NATIONAL GEOGRAPHIC ON INDIANS OF THE AMERICAS: A COLOR-ILLUSTRATED RECORD. Washington, D.C.: National Geographic, 1955.

Excellent coverage and text of daily life of Indians; useful source.

377 Thompson, Judy. PRELIMINARY STUDY OF TRADITIONAL KUTCHIN CLOTHING IN MUSEUMS. Ottawa, Ont.: National Museum, 1972.

Fifty-five drawings and photographs of costume of northwestern Indians.

378 Underhill, Ruth Murray. PUEBLO CRAFTS. Edited by Willard W. Beatty. Phoenix: Phoenix Indian School, 1945.

Textual survey with illustrations and maps of indigenous Pueblo costumes, accessories, and decorative motifs, with a list of sources for further reading.

379 Whiteford, Andrew Hunter. A GOLDEN GUIDE: NORTH AMERICAN INDIAN ARTS. Edited by Herbert S. Zim. Racine, Wis.: Western Publishing Co., 1970.

Booklet format for condensed survey of arts of Indians in such areas as pottery, textiles, decorations, shellwork, featherwork, and costumes, with numerous illustrations; index; quick reference.

380 Wissler, Clark. INDIAN COSTUMES IN THE UNITED STATES. New York: American Museum of Natural History, 1931.

Somewhat dated but helpful booklet of drawings, patterns, primary-source illustrations, and other materials.

c. CENTRAL AND SOUTH AMERICA

See also 320, 322, 761, 883

381 Adrian, Rupert. MEXICAN COSTUMES AND CUSTOMS. Pasadena, Calif.: Norman H. Kamps, 1946.

Twelve color lithographs by Norman H. Kamps of scenes of Mexican costumes and customs from various regions, with descriptive notes.

382 Alberu de Villava, Helena. FOLK DANCES AND MEXICAN COSTUMES. Guadalajara, Mexico: Jalisco, 1965.

Seven color paintings of regional Mexican costumes, with descriptions of the costumes and the dances for which the costumes are used.

383 Benitez, Jose R. EL TRAJE Y EL ADORNO EN MEXICO, 1500-1910 [Clothing and adornment in Mexico, 1500-1910]. Guadalajara, Mexico: Imprenta Universitaria, 1946.

Spanish text, but numerous excellent photographs in this historical survey of costumes and accessories in Mexico.

384 Briggs, Frederico Guilherme. LEMBRANAC DO BRASIL [The Brasillian souvenir: A selection of the most peculiar costumes of the Brazils]. Rio de Janeiro: Sedegra, 1970.

Coverage in Portuguese text of the history of Ludwig and Briggs Lithographers, whose prints represent the typical Brazilian costumes of the late 1830s and early 1840s; thirty detailed, color reproductions of the original lithographs, with English titles.

385 Carrillo y Gariel, Abelardo. EL TRAJE EN LA NUEVA ESPANA [Clothing in New Spain]. Mexico: Instituto Nacional de Antropologia e Historia, 1959.

Spanish text; 189 monochrome plates of costumes of all types.

386 _____. INDUMENTARIA COLONIAL [Colonial costume]. Mexico: Ediciones de Arte, 1949.

Small volume available in Spanish, English, French, or Italian, containing over fifty monochrome illustrations of historical Mexican costume, primarily of the upper-class level of society.

387 Cordry, Donald Bush, and Cordry, Dorothy M. COSTUMES AND TEXTILES OF THE AZTEC INDIANS OF THE CUETZALAN REGION, PUEBLA, MEXICO. Los Angeles: Southwest Museum, 1940.

Eleven plates and twenty-two drawings, with complete descriptions of men's and women's dress described separately, including such topics as hairdressing, headwear, footwear, and accessories.

388 _____. MEXICAN INDIAN COSTUMES. Austin: University of Texas Press, 1968.

Panorama of contemporary Mexican Indian life through numerous photographs of excellent content and quality; valuable source for depiction of everyday costume.

389 Covarrubias, Luis. MEXICAN NATIVE COSTUMES. Mexico: Fisch-grund, n.d.

Condensed discussion of native dress in fourteen regions of Mexico, illustrated with a color plate from each of the areas, for example, Oaxaca, Puebla, Chiapas, and Yucatan; helpful directions as to the construction and decoration of the costume.

390 De Palavecion, Maria Delia Millan. VESTIMENTA ARGENTINA [Argen-tine costume]. Buenos Aires: Marcus Victor Durruty, 1961.

Unique study and presentation of pictorial sources of Argen-tine costume and textiles.

391 Doerner, Gerd. FOLK ART OF MEXICO. Translated by Gladys Wheel-house. New York: A.S. Barnes and Co., 1962.

Explanatory text with considerable information on costumes, accessories, decorative motifs, and textiles, with numerous photographs.

392 Du Solier, Wilfrido. ANCIENT MEXICAN COSTUME. Translated by W. Du Solier and John G. Roberts. Mexico: Ediciones Mexicanas, 1950.

Thirty-two color plates and numerous drawings and diagrams of costumes and accessories of all levels, from priest to peasant; excellent source.

393 Enciso, Jorge. DESIGN MOTIFS OF ANCIENT MEXICO. New York: Dover Publications, 1953.

Reproductions of examples helpful to designers, presented in clear line drawings.

394 Goodman, Frances Schaill. THE EMBROIDERY OF MEXICO AND GUATE-MALA. New York: Charles Scribner's Sons, 1976.

Recent study with vivid color plates of traditional costume sketches presented as a portion of the survey of needlework techniques and motifs.

395 Halouze, Edouard. COSTUMES OF SOUTH AMERICA. New York: French and European Publications, 1941.

Portfolio of forty color paintings of male and female costumes from all South American countries, with complete descriptive notes, plus eight plates of various accessories; very useful source.

396 Hopper, Janice H., ed. and trans. INDIANS OF BRAZIL IN THE
TWENTIETH CENTURY. Washington, D.C.: Institute for Cross-Cultural
Research, 1967.

A socioeconomic cultural study containing some color illustrative material of native costumes, accessories, manners, and
customs; maps and bibliographies.

397 Juliao, Carlos. RISCOS ILLUMINADOS DE FIGURINHOS DE BRANCOS
E NEGROS DOS UZOS DO RIO DE JANEIRO E SERRO DO FRIO [II-
luminated sketches of the apparel of blacks and whites of Rio de Janerio
and Serro do Frio]. Rio de Janeiro: Livraria Sao Jose, 1960.

Forty-eight handsome color plates, mostly multifigured, of native Brazilian costume from these two geographical regions of
the country.

398 Linati, Claudio. TRAJES CIVILES, MILITARES Y RELIGIOSOS DE MEXI-
CO (1828) [Civilian, military and religious costume of Mexico (1828)].
Mexico: Imprenta Universitaria, 1956.

Spanish text with fifty-six color plates of Mexican civil, military, and religious costumes of the early nineteenth century.

399 Merida, Carlos. MEXICAN COSTUME. Chicago: Pocahontas Press,
1941.

Twenty-five color plates by the author of various regional costumes of Mexico, with brief descriptive notes for each and
with particular attention to decorative detail and motif.

400 Osborne, Lilly de Jongh. INDIAN CRAFTS OF GUATEMALA AND EL
SALVADOR. Norman: University of Oklahoma Press, 1965.

Large section devoted to costume with color and black-and-
white illustrations.

401 Reyes, Roman B. ORIGIN AND HISTORY OF "LA POLLERA." Panama:
La Academia, 1954.

Thorough, interesting, and well-illustrated discussion of the
development and current status of the traditional Panamanian
dress; text in Spanish and English.

402 Silvester, Hans. THE ROUTE OF THE INCAS. New York: Viking Press,
1976.

Recent study with brilliant color photographic record of the
peoples of the Inca area.

403 Spicer, Dorothy Gladys. LATIN AMERICAN COSTUMES. New York: Hyperion Press, 1941.

Descriptions of the costumes of each Central and South American country; many shown in color plates, designed by Jolanda Bartas; folio edition.

404 Torres Mendez, Ramon. CUADROS DE COSTUMBRES [Depictions of costumes]. Columbia: Banco Cafetero, n.d.

Illustrations of various customs, including costumes, of the country, presented in painted plates and line drawings.

405 TRAJES TIPICOS DE GUATEMALA [Typical costumes of Guatemala]. Guatemala: Impresor El Faro, 1971.

Twelve plates of native costumes of the country.

406 Valdiosera, Ramon, and Echeverria, Salvador. TWELVE MEXICAN NATIVE COSTUMES. Translated by Ruth Poyo. Mexico: Fischgrund, n.d.

General introduction to regional Mexican costumes; with twelve paintings and descriptions.

407 Wood, Josephine, and Osborne, Lilly de Jongh. INDIAN COSTUMES OF GUATEMALA. Graz, Austria: Akademische Druck, 1966.

Sixty color paintings of full costume, plus line drawings; descriptive notations for each plate.

408 Zarate, Dora P., and Zarate, Manuel F. LA POLLERA PANAMENA [The pollera dress of Panama]. Panama: Universidad de Panama, 1966.

Pictures, patterns, and diagrams of the traditional dress of the country.

409 Zimmern, Nathalie. INTRODUCTION TO PERUVIAN COSTUME. Brooklyn: Brooklyn Museum, 1949.

General survey; map and twenty-four illustrations of garments, textiles, motifs, and accessories.

3. Costume of the Ancient World

See also 574, 583, 584, 752, 774, 776, 780, 781, 787, 791, 797

410 ANCIENT GREEK DRESS. Baltimore: Walters Art Gallery, 1945.

Brief picture pamphlet of museum's primary sources of Greek dress.

411 Bonfante, Larissa. ETRUSCAN DRESS. Baltimore: Johns Hopkins Press, 1975.

Thorough and scholarly treatment of subject with 164 monochrome illustrations; chapters on fabrics, patterns, basic garments, footwear, hairstyles, and foreign influences; index and bibliography.

412 Bossert, Helmuth T. FOLK ART OF ASIA, AFRICA AND THE AMERICAS. New York: Frederick A. Praeger, 1964.

Combined edition of Bossert's FOLK ART OF PRIMITIVE PEOPLES and DECORATIVE ART OF ASIA AND EGYPT: eighty color plates with notes of native art as seen in textiles, ornamentation, accessories, and costumes; helpful source for extensiveness of illustrative material.

413 Broholm, Hans Christian, and Hald, Margrete. COSTUMES OF THE BRONZE AGE IN DENMARK. Oxford, Engl.: Oxford University Press, 1940.

Scholarly study of early Danish costumes and textiles based on excavations from the Bronze Age; five plates of garments, accessories, and textiles.

414 Fol, Alexander, and Marazov, Ivan. THRACE AND THE THRACIANS. New York: St. Martin's Press, 1977.

Pictorial social history with extensive section on Thracian art, providing many examples of costumes and accessories of the ancient people; illustrations.

415 Gullberg, Elsa, and Astroem, Paul. STUDIES IN MEDITERRANEAN ARCHAEOLOGY: THE THREAD OF ARIADNE: A STUDY OF ANCIENT GREEK DRESS. Goeteborg, Sweden: Lund, 1970.

Technical, scholarly study of early Greek costume by a textile historian and an archaeologist, with primary-source illustrations.

416 Hiler, Hilaire. FROM NUDITY TO RAIMENT: AN INTRODUCTION TO THE STUDY OF COSTUME. London: W. and G. Foyle, 1929.

Dated, but standard work on the development of prehistoric and primitive costume throughout the world; with numerous monochrome illustrations, some in color; maps and bibliography.

417 Hope, Thomas. COSTUMES OF THE GREEKS AND ROMANS. 1812. Reprint. New York: Dover Publications, 1962.

Formerly entitled COSTUME OF THE ANCIENTS; three-hundred line drawings with over seven-hundred figures of the entire range of classical costume from garments, footwear, militaria, headwear, and so forth, plus a brief historical survey of costume of the period generally.

418 Houston, Mary G., and Hornblower, Florence S. ANCIENT EGYPTIAN, ASSYRIAN AND PERSIAN COSTUMES AND DECORATIONS. London: Adam and Charles Black, 1920.

Concise textual study; sixty basic costume diagrams and scaled patterns; twenty-five illustrations; bibliography.

419 _____. ANCIENT GREEK, ROMAN AND BYZANTINE COSTUME AND DECORATI ON. 2d ed. London: Adam and Charles Black, 1947.

Survey of costume from the Aegean period to the Byzantines, with numerous line drawings, diagrams, and patterns; separate chapters on costume and ornament of each culture; color plates; bibliography.

420 Johnson, Marie, ed. ANCIENT GREEK DRESS: A NEW ILLUSTRATED EDITION COMBINING GREEK DRESS BY ETHEL ABRAHAMS AND CHAPTERS ON GREEK DRESS BY LADY EVANS. Chicago: Argonaut, 1964.

Authoritative guide to the subject though somewhat dated (1908); chapters in the Abrahams section on ornamentation, hair, accessories, and footwear in addition to costume; primary-source illustrations; selected patterns; index and bibliography.

421 Laver, James. COSTUME IN ANTIQUITY. New York: Clarkson N. Potter, 1964.

Series of 480 illustrations by Erhard Klepper encompassing the whole range of ancient costumes from the Egyptians to the Byzantines; brief historical introduction.

422 Lutz, Henry F. TEXTILES AND COSTUMES AMONG THE PEOPLES OF THE ANCIENT NEAR EAST. New York: G.E. Stechert and Co., 1923.

Dated source with many monochrome plates and line drawings for survey of ancient Egyptian, Assyrian, Babylonian, and Hittite costume; chapter on the technical aspects, such as spinning, weaving, and dyeing.

423 Madhloom, T.A. THE CHRONOLOGY OF NEO-ASSYRIAN ART. London: Athlone, 1970.

Illustrations and information on the entire range of Assyrian and Babylonian costume, among other topics within the cultures.

424 Wilson, Lillian M. THE CLOTHING OF THE ANCIENT ROMANS. Baltimore: Johns Hopkins Press, 1939.

> Authoritative coverage of the subject with thorough textual discussion and illustration of every facet including materials, dyes, manufacture, adornments, types of garments, children's dress, bridal costume and female attire; patterns; primary-source illustration and modern reconstructions on live models; excellent source.

425 _____. THE ROMAN TOGA. Baltimore: Johns Hopkins Press, 1924.

> Exhaustive study of the subject, with historical background, construction notes, patterns, and suggestions for modern use; seventy-five primary-source illustrations, drawings, patterns, and modern reconstructions on live models; index and bibliography.

4. Costume of the British

a. ENGLAND

See also 1174, 1478, 1479

426 Ashdown, Emily Jessie. BRITISH COSTUME DURING XIX CENTURIES, CIVIL AND ECCLESIASTICAL. London: Thomas Nelson and Sons, n.d.

> Major emphasis on historical survey of civil costume from early Britons to reign of George III, with much less attention to ecclesiastical dress in earlier periods; numerous drawings and monochrome primary source material; somewhat dated source.

427 Barfoot, Audrey. EVERYDAY COSTUME IN BRITAIN FROM THE EARLIEST TIMES TO 1900. London: B.T. Batsford, 1961.

> Condensed survey of common attire, with drawings; chapter on the national costumes of the United Kingdom and Eire; index and bibliography.

428 Bradfield, Nancy. HISTORICAL COSTUMES OF ENGLAND FROM THE ELEVENTH TO THE TWENTIETH CENTURY. New York: Barnes and Noble, 1971.

> Historical development of English dress, arranged by monarchs, with condensed historical descriptions and line drawings by the author.

429 Brooke, Iris. ENGLISH COSTUME IN THE AGE OF ELIZABETH: THE SIXTEENTH CENTURY. 2d ed. London: Adam and Charles Black, 1963.

Decade-by-decade arrangement of a historical survey of costumes, with forty-eight color drawings and paintings by the author.

430 _____. ENGLISH COSTUME OF THE EARLY MIDDLE AGES: THE TENTH TO THE THIRTEENTH CENTURIES. London: Adam and Charles Black, 1956.

Durable survey of costume and accessories from the Anglo-Saxon period to 1300, with text and forty illustrations by the author (8 in color) of fully dressed figures.

431 _____. ENGLISH COSTUME OF THE LATER MIDDLE AGES: THE FOURTEENTH AND FIFTEENTH CENTURIES. London: Adam and Charles Black, 1956.

Descriptions by the author of her forty-eight color paintings and her drawings of various costumed figures representative of the period.

432 _____. ENGLISH COSTUME OF THE SEVENTEENTH CENTURY. 2d ed. London: Adam and Charles Black, 1964.

Guidebook with general descriptions of costumes and accessories of the period, with forty (8 in color) of the author's drawings and paintings.

433 _____. A HISTORY OF ENGLISH COSTUME. 4th ed. London: Methuen and Co., 1972.

Basic general historical survey beginning with the Norman Conquest and ending with the present; numerous drawings and paintings by the author, with descriptions.

434 Brooke, Iris, and Laver, James. ENGLISH COSTUME FROM THE FOURTEENTH THROUGH THE NINETEENTH CENTURY. New York: Macmillan Co., 1937.

General survey of costume history with illustrations, some colored, by Brooke and with commentary shared by both Laver and Brooke.

435 Buck, Anne M. VICTORIAN COSTUME AND COSTUME ACCESSORIES. New York: Thomas Nelson and Sons, 1961.

Excellent chapter on the broad range of the subject, with fifty-one photographic plates and twenty-nine figures, covering the period from 1837 to 1900.

436 Clinch, George. ENGLISH COSTUME: FROM THE PREHISTORIC
TIMES TO THE END OF THE 18TH CENTURY. 1909. Reprint. Totowa,
N.J.: Rowman and Littlefield, 1975.

Somewhat dated historical survey with period source illustrations and attention to specific areas, for example, military,
ecclesiastical, monastic, academic, and legal.

437 Cooke, Patricia Gerrard. ENGLISH COSTUME: ITS HISTORY AND ITS
DESIGN. Liverpool: Gallery Press, 1968.

Simplified, condensed treatment of historic English costume
and aids to costume design, with numerous line drawings.

438 The Costume Society. HIGH VICTORIAN COSTUME, 1860-1890. London: Victoria and Albert Museum, 1969.

Collection of miscellaneous articles on costume and related
subjects of the period: clothing manufacture, pictorial sources,
cut and construction, wedding dresses, lace, and foundation
garments; many illustrations and photographs.

439 Cunnington, C. Willett. ENGLISH WOMEN'S CLOTHING IN THE
NINETEENTH CENTURY. London: Faber and Faber, 1937.

Decade-by-decade arrangement of encyclopedic information
and numerous line drawings, primary illustrative material and
several color photographs; glossaries of materials and fabrics,
technical terms, obsolete color names; chronological table;
museum guide; index and bibliography; very helpful source.

440 _____. ENGLISH WOMEN'S CLOTHING IN THE PRESENT CENTURY.
London: Faber and Faber, 1952.

Textual coverage from year to year of the changes in dress,
materials, colors and costs; over seven hundred illustrations in
monochrome and line drawings, including fashion designs and
plates and contemporary photographs of day dresses, evening
dresses, underclothes, sport attire, headwear and hairstyle,
and accessories; glossary of textiles; sources and index.

441 Cunnington, C. Willett, and Cunnington, Phillis E. HANDBOOK OF
ENGLISH COSTUME IN THE EIGHTEENTH CENTURY. 2d ed. London:
Faber and Faber, 1957.

Example of the excellence of the Cunningtons' scholarship and
thoroughness (see items 442-46, as well as 439-40 and 447-48);
illustrations by Barbara Phillipson and Phillis Cunnington; divisions of discussion of men and women in two periods: 1700-
1750 and 1750-1800; glossary of materials; prices of materials;
sources and index.

442 _____. HANDBOOK OF ENGLISH COSTUME IN THE NINETEENTH CENTURY. 3d ed. London: Faber and Faber, 1970.

Distinguished for its completeness of text and illustration of all facets of male and female dress of the century; decade-by-decade survey; illustrations by Phillis Cunnington and Cecil Everitt; overview of the century; glossary of materials; sources and index.

443 _____. HANDBOOK OF ENGLISH COSTUME IN THE SEVENTEENTH CENTURY. 3d ed. London: Faber and Faber, 1972.

Guidebook with great authority and extensive illustrations by Barbara Phillipson and Phillis Cunnington to the male and female fashions of the century; divisions of discussion into fifty-year periods; glossary; sources and index.

444 _____. HANDBOOK OF ENGLISH COSTUME IN THE SIXTEENTH CENTURY. 2d ed. London: Faber and Faber, 1970.

Reference book to this important century of costume for the theatre; general introduction to the period; discussion of male and female costume in two periods: 1500-1545 and 1545-1600; chapters on decoration, working-class clothing, children's garments; glossary of materials; illustrations by Barbara Phillipson; sources and index.

445 _____. HANDBOOK OF ENGLISH MEDIEVAL COSTUME. 2d ed. London: Faber and Faber, 1969.

Authoritative survey of men's and women's costumes from the ninth through the fifteenth centuries, with many drawings and illustrations by Barbara Phillipson and Catherine Lucas; sections of children's costume and working clothing; glossary, sources, and index.

446 _____. A PICTURE HISTORY OF ENGLISH COSTUME. New York: Macmillan Co., 1960.

Four hundred forty-one monochrome primary-source illustrations of English costume from 1370 to 1948, with brief descriptive notes arranged by centuries; handy reference.

447 Cunnington, Phillis E. COSTUMES OF THE NINETEENTH CENTURY. Boston: Plays, 1970.

Published in England under the title YOUR BOOK OF NINE-TEENTH CENTURY COSTUME; a simplified version of materials found in HANDBOOK OF ENGLISH COSTUME IN THE NINE-TEENTH CENTURY (see item 442).

448 _____. MEDIEVAL AND TUDOR COSTUME. Boston: Plays, 1969.

Detailed account of clothing worn by English men, women, and children from 1066 to 1603; arranged by centuries; many illustrations and drawings from primary sources; index and sources.

449 Edwards, Anne. THE QUEEN'S CLOTHES. London: Express, 1976.

Excellent visual record of modern fashions for royalty as seen in the clothing of Queen Elizabeth II.

450 Fairholt, F.W. COSTUME IN ENGLAND: A HISTORY OF DRESS TO THE END OF THE EIGHTEENTH CENTURY. 2 vols. 1885. Reprint. Detroit: Singing Tree Press, 1968.

Historical survey in volume 1, with more than seven hundred engravings of costumes, accessories, and decorative motifs.

451 Fraser, Antonia, ed. THE LIVES OF THE KINGS AND QUEENS OF ENGLAND. New York: Alfred A. Knopf Co., 1975.

Panorama of English fashion throughout English history as seen in this very well illustrated record of the monarchs and the people around them.

452 Gibbs-Smith, Charles J. THE FASHIONABLE LADY IN THE 19TH CENTURY. London: Her Majesty's Stationery Office, 1960.

Based on the collection of costume in the Victoria and Albert Museum; brief summary of major costume changes in the century, with line drawings; reproduction in main body of the volume of 219 primary-source illustrations of female costume arranged in five-year periods, with each dominant silhouette; short bibliography of books and periodicals; major pictorial study of female dress in the nineteenth century.

453 Gibson, Mary. PERIOD COSTUME. Salisbury, Engl.: Salisbury and South Wiltshire Museum, 1974.

Survey of a framework of fashion from the eighteenth century to the present, with illustrations from the costume collection of the museum; brief sections on children's costume, smocks, textiles, and costume dolls; ten monochrome photographs; brief bibliography.

454 Halls, Zillah. WOMEN'S COSTUME, 1750-1800. London: Her Majesty's Stationery Office, 1972.

Continuation of study in entry 455; over twenty photographs of period costume and accessories, with brief historical commentary.

455 _____. WOMEN'S COSTUME, 1600-1750. London: Her Majesty's Stationery Office, 1969.

Catalog of costumes and accessories in the London Museum, with a brief textual history and over twenty black-and-white photographs of costumes; two patterns.

456 Holden, Angus. ELEGANT MODES IN THE NINETEENTH CENTURY FROM HIGH WAIST TO BUSTLE. London: George Allen and Unwin, 1935.

Succinctly written descriptions of the changes in shape in female costume; twelve color plates.

457 Houston, Mary G. MEDIEVAL COSTUME IN ENGLAND AND FRANCE: THE 13TH, 14TH, AND 15TH CENTURIES. London: Adam and Charles Black, 1939.

Complete discussion of construction, ornamentation, and style of costumes of each of the three centuries in the study; coverage of regal, ecclesiastical, civilian, armor, and academic costumes in the period; 8 color plates and 350 figures in pen and ink in the text; patterns for basic garments; glossary of medieval terms for costume; bibliography; major source for the period.

458 Inder, P.M. COSTUME IN PICTURES. Exeter, Engl.: Royal Albert Museum, 1972.

Twenty monochrome photographs with descriptive notes of selected English garments, foundations, underwear, and men's wear from the Royal Albert Museum's Costume Collection.

459 LaMar, Virginia. ENGLISH DRESS IN THE AGE OF SHAKESPEARE. Charlottesville: University of Virginia Press, 1958.

Condensed but informative survey with twenty-two primary-source illustrative plates of costume items.

460 Laver, James. COSTUME ILLUSTRATION: THE NINETEENTH CENTURY. London: Victoria and Albert Museum, 1947.

Brief introduction to costume of the century; one hundred primary-source illustrations of men's and women's costumes throughout the century; excellent source for fully attired figures from the period.

461 _____. COSTUME ILLUSTRATION: THE SEVENTEENTH AND EIGHTEENTH CENTURIES. London: His Majesty's Stationery Office, 1951.

Brief overview to collection of ninety-six primary-source illustrations of male and female costumes from the specified centuries, with notes on the sources of the illustrations; excellent
visual material.

462 _____. COSTUME OF THE WESTERN WORLD: EARLY TUDOR. New
York: Harper and Brothers, 1951.

Historical descriptions of the costume of the period, followed
by fifty-two plates (4 in color) of primary-source illustrations
of costumes.

463 _____. ENGLISH COSTUME OF THE EIGHTEENTH CENTURY. Illustrated by Iris Brooke. London: Adam and Charles Black, 1958.

Descriptions by Laver of Brooke's paintings in color and line
drawings of costume.

464 _____. ENGLISH COSTUME OF THE NINETEENTH CENTURY. Illustrated by Iris Brooke. London: Adam and Charles Black, 1929.

Continuation of format of entry 463, with forty-two illustrations, twelve in color.

465 _____. VICTORIANA. New York: Hawthorn Books, 1967.

Several chapters and many illustrations, some in color, on
costume and fashion accessories, for example, fashion plates,
fans, and jewelry of the Victorian period; good source for the
decorative arts of the period.

466 Manchester Art Galleries. THE GALLERY OF ENGLISH COSTUME PIC-
TURE BOOK. 8 vols. Manchester: 1949-63.

Six of the volumes deal with women's costume from the eighteenth century to 1930: volume 1: A BRIEF VIEW (1949);
volume 2: WOMEN'S COSTUME IN THE 18TH CENTURY
(1954); volume 3: WOMEN'S COSTUME 1800-1835 (1951);
volume 4: WOMEN'S COSTUME 1835-1870 (1951); volume 5:
WOMEN'S COSTUME 1870-1900 (1953); volume 6: WOMEN'S
COSTUME 1900-1930 (1956). Twenty monochrome photographs
of costumes and accessories from the collection of the museum,
with general introductory notes and specific descriptive com-
ments in each volume of the series.

467 Mansfield, Alan, and Cunnington, Phillis E. HANDBOOK OF ENGLISH
COSTUME IN THE TWENTIETH CENTURY, 1900-1950. Illustrated by
Valerie Mansfield. London: Faber and Faber, 1973.

Female dress coverage by decades and male dress coverage in twenty-five-year periods; encyclopedic treatment of all aspects of modern costume, with many line drawings; one color plate; appendixes on clothes rationing and the purchasing power of the pound sterling from 1900 to 1971; glossary of terms; index and bibliography; invaluable source for costumers.

468 Moncrieff, M.C. Scott. KINGS AND QUEENS OF ENGLAND. London: Blandford Press, 1966.

Reflection of English costume through the monarchs in a condensed survey from 1042 to the present, with numerous drawings and thirty-two color plates.

469 Morse, H.K. ELIZABETHAN PAGEANTRY: A PICTORIAL SURVEY OF COSTUME AND ITS COMMENTATORS FROM C. 1560-1620. London: Studio, 1934.

Excellent collection of primary-source illustration and commentary of court fashion in the style and spirit of the late Renaissance, including ecclesiastical, academic, ceremonial, and military costume; glossary, bibliography and index; excellent pictorial source.

470 Ormond, Richard. THE FACE OF MONARCHY: BRITISH ROYALTY PORTRAYED. New York: E.P. Dutton Co., 1977.

Not a costume book as such but a valuable collection of photographs and portraits (177) of the royalty of England from the medieval period to modern times; excellent pictorial overview of fashion as seen in the monarchs.

471 Reynolds, Graham. COSTUME OF THE WESTERN WORLD: ELIZABETHAN AND JACOBEAN. New York: Harper and Brothers, 1951.

Historical description of costume of the period with fifty-six plates, some in color, of typical examples.

472 Settle, Alison. ENGLISH FASHION. London: Collins, 1948.

Condensed survey of dress from the Anglo-Saxon period to modern day, with eight color plates and twenty-three monochrome illustrations of primary-source material.

473 Strong, Roy. PORTRAITS OF QUEEN ELIZABETH I. Oxford, Engl.: Clarendon Press, 1963.

Panorama of Elizabethan life and costume as shown through the Queen's portraits; twenty-two plates, some in color.

474 Strong, Roy, and Oman, Julia Trevelyan. ELIZABETH I.R.: HER FACE
AND COSTUMES. New York: Stein and Day Publishers, 1971.

> Interesting, condensed text but very informative treatment,
> with numerous illustrations in color and black-and-white of a
> specific subject which applies generally to the entire Elizabe-
> than period.

475 Strutt, Joseph. A COMPLETE VIEW OF THE DRESS AND HABITS OF
THE PEOPLE OF ENGLAND: FROM THE ESTABLISHMENT OF THE
SAXONS IN BRITAIN TO THE PRESENT TIME TO WHICH IS PREFIXED
AN INTRODUCTION CONTAINING A GENERAL DESCRIPTION OF THE
ANCIENT HABITS IN USE AMONG MANKIND, FROM THE EARLIEST
PERIOD OF TIME TO THE CONCLUSION OF THE SEVENTH CENTURY.
2 vols. Explanatory and critical notes by J.R. Planche. 1842. Reprint.
London: Tabard Press, 1970.

> Dated source but accurate picture of early costume, and use-
> ful for quotations from manuscript sources.

476 Wark, R. ISAAC CRUIKSHANK'S DRAWINGS FOR DROLLS. San Ma-
rino, Calif.: Huntington Library, 1968.

> Many (114) drawings containing good examples of eighteenth-
> century costumed men and women.

477 Yarwood, Doreen. ENGLISH COSTUME FROM THE SECOND CENTURY
B.C. TO 1967. 3d ed. London: B.T. Batsford, 1967.

> Historical survey without any new contributions; a few color
> primary-source plates but mainly line drawings.

478 _____. OUTLINE OF ENGLISH COSTUME. Boston: Plays, 1967.

> Very condensed survey of costume in England beginning in the
> year 1000; accompanied by drawings of basic costumes with
> selected accessories and the outstanding architectural feature
> of each respective period.

b. BRITISH ISLES, AUSTRALIA, AND SOUTH AFRICA

See also 427

479 Anthony, Ilid. COSTUMES OF THE WELSH PEOPLE. Cardiff: National
Museum of Wales, 1975.

> Survey of changes in dress of the Welsh people from the eigh-
> teenth to the twentieth centuries, with photographs of garments
> and accessories from the museum's collection of costumes.

480 Bain, Robert. CLANS AND TARTANS OF SCOTLAND. Enlarged and reedited by Margaret O. Macdougall. London: Collins, 1968.

Introductory material on Scottish dress followed by color illustrations of 133 family and clan tartans, with a brief history, the crested badge, and motto of each; also regimental tartans, heraldic terms, and a glossary of Gaelic personal and placenames; very complete treatment of subject.

481 Blake, Lois. WELSH FOLK DANCE AND COSTUME. 2d ed. Llangollen, North Wales: Gwynn Publishers, 1954.

Brief treatment of both dance and dress of Wales, with good description and illustration.

482 Campbell, Lord Archibald. HIGHLAND DRESS, ARMS AND ORNAMENTS. 1899. Reprint. London: Dawsons of Pall Mall, 1969.

Reprint of 1899 publication; dated, but full text with seventy-two illustrations.

483 Collie, George. HIGHLAND DRESS: WITH COLOR PLATES FROM McIAN'S THE CLANS OF THE SCOTTISH HIGHLANDS. London: Penguin Books, 1949.

Brief historical account and notes on twenty-four color plates of both male and female Scottish attire from the mid-sixteenth to the mid-nineteenth centuries; further reading list.

484 Crookshank, Anne. IRISH PORTRAITS, 1660-1860. London: Paul Mellon Foundation for British Art, 1969.

Exhibition catalog dealing mainly with artists and artistic concerns but valuable to costumer for numerous monochrome reproductions of Irish portraits, miniatures, and bronzes.

485 Dunbar, John Telfer. HISTORY OF HIGHLAND DRESS: A DEFINITIVE STUDY OF THE HISTORY OF SCOTTISH COSTUME AND TARTAN, BOTH CIVIL AND MILITARY, INCLUDING WEAPONS: WITH AN APPENDIX ON EARLY SCOTTISH DYES BY ANNETTE KOK. Philadelphia: Dufour Editions, 1964.

Exhaustive textual study but with only forty-eight plates, some in color; bibliography.

486 Ellis, M. PICTURE BOOK NO. 1: WELSH COSTUME AND CUSTOMS. Cardiff: National Library of Wales, 1951.

Treatment of Welsh traditional and regional dress, with fourteen monochrome, six color plates, and additional line drawings throughout the text.

487 Etheridge, Ken. WELSH COSTUME. 2d ed. Ammanford, Wales: 1959.

Brief illustrated survey of Welsh costume.

488 Flower, C. DUCK AND CABBAGE TREE: A PICTORIAL HISTORY OF CLOTHES IN AUSTRALIA, 1788-1914. Sydney: Angus and Robertson, 1968.

Unique study; excellent text and extensive collection of primary-source materials illustrating historical survey of Australian costume.

489 Fox, Lilla M. COSTUMES AND CUSTOMS OF THE BRITISH ISLES. Boston: Plays, 1974.

Distinctive examples of occupational and ceremonial dress of current British celebrations and rituals, plus regional costume of Wales, Scotland, and Ireland.

490 Grange, Richard M.D. SHORT HISTORY OF THE SCOTTISH DRESS. New York: Macmillan Co., 1966.

Extensively illustrated treatment of the subject.

491 Hesketh, Christian. TARTANS. New York: Octopus Books, 1972.

Well-illustrated account of the development of tartans as used by men, women, and children in clothing from the beginnings to the present; excellent and extraordinary color plates.

492 Innes, Thomas. THE CLANS, SEPTS, AND REGIMENTS OF THE SCOTTISH HIGHLANDS. 8th ed. Revised by Frank Adam. London: Johnston and Bacon, 1970.

Comprehensive treatment of the history, structure, cultural significance, insignia, and heraldry of clans, with seventeen monochrome illustrations and color plates of 112 tartans.

493 McClintock, H.F. OLD HIGHLAND DRESS AND TARTANS WITH A CHAPTER ON TARTANS BY J. TELFER DUNBAR. 2d ed. Dundalk, Ireland: Dundalgan Press, 1949.

Short volume with nineteen monochrome primary-source plates plus condensed but basic survey of the topic.

494 _____. OLD IRISH AND HIGHLAND DRESS AND THAT OF THE ISLE OF MAN WITH CHAPTER ON PRE-NORMAN DRESS AS DESCRIBED IN EARLY IRISH LITERATURE BY F. SHAW AND ON EARLY TARTANS BY J. TELFER DUNBAR. 2d ed. Dundalk, Ireland: Dundalgan Press, 1950.

Historical survey of the subject with fifty-six plates, some colored.

495 Maxwell, Stuart, and Hutchinson, Robin. SCOTTISH COSTUME, 1550-1850. Philadelphia: Dufour Editions, 1959.

Four color plates and twenty-four drawings on the subject, with chapters on general costume, plus additional materials on weapons, highland dress, and jewelry.

496 Scarlett, James D. TARTANS OF SCOTLAND. New York: Hastings House, 1972.

Brief survey with value in the seventy-eight color plates of tartan designs.

497 Telford, Alexander Alan. YESTERDAY'S DRESS: A HISTORY OF COSTUME IN SOUTH AFRICA. London: Purnell, 1972.

Historical survey dating from 1488 to 1890s, with many drawings, some in color, by the author; unique study.

498 Wilson, Anne. WOMEN'S CLOTHING IN THE 19TH CENTURY. Ulster, Ireland: Ulster Museum, n.d.

Brief introduction to general costume history with twelve photographs of historical Irish costume from 1800 to 1897.

5. Costume of Eastern Europe, The Near East, and Russia

See also 756, 773

499 Alyoshina, T.A., et al., comps. HISTORY OF RUSSIAN COSTUME FROM THE ELEVENTH TO THE TWENTIETH CENTURY. New York: Metropolitan Museum of Art in cooperation with the Ministry of Culture of the USSR, ca. 1976.

Exhibition catalog of descriptions of 513 displays with photographs, some in excellent color, of fifty-six examples from the exhibition; an introductory discussion of three phases of the subject: Russian costume from the eleventh to the seventeenth centuries; folk costume from the eighteenth to the early twentieth centuries; and urban costume from the eighteenth to the early twentieth centuries.

500 Argenti, Philip O. THE COSTUMES OF CHIOS: THEIR DEVELOPMENT FROM THE XVTH TO THE XXTH CENTURY. London: B.T. Batsford, 1953.

Historical survey of men's and women's costume separately,
plus chapters on special topics, with 121 plates, the majority
in color, and numerous line drawings.

501 Banateanu, T., et al. FOLK COSTUMES: WOVEN TEXTILES AND
EMBROIDERIES OF RUMANIA. Bucharest, Romania: State Publishing
House, 1958.

Valuable book of 433 monochrome and 55 color illustrations
of Romanian folk costume arranged by regions, with textual
descriptions and background information.

502 Bogatyrev, Petr G. THE FUNCTIONS OF FOLK COSTUME IN MORA-
VIAN SLOVAKIA. Translated by Richard G. Crum. The Hague, Netherlands: Mouton, 1971.

Treatment of various uses served by costume, for example, religious, nationalistic, and erotic, with eleven drawings of garments and accessories; bibliography.

503 Chalif, Louis Harvey. RUSSIAN FESTIVALS AND COSTUMES FOR
PAGEANTS AND DANCES. New York: Chalif Russian School of Dancing, 1921.

Dated source with survey of costume, art, home life, and
special occasions, containing many monochrome photographs of
all areas of Russian costume and accessories.

504 Chotek, Karel. POPULAR CULTURE AND COSTUME IN CZECHO-
SLOVAKIA. Prague, Czechoslovakia: Novina, 1937.

Summaries in French, English, and German.

505 De Quincey, Thomas. TOILETTE OF THE HEBREW LADY: EXHIBITED
IN SIX SCENES. 1828. Reprint. Hartford, Conn.: Edward Valentine
Mitchell Co., 1926.

Dated source but somewhat unique in the area for its description of the garments and accessories of a Hebrew lady.

506 Enachescu-Cantemire, Alexandrina. POPULAR ROUMANIAN DRESS.
Craiova, Romania: Scrisul Romanesc, 1939.

Best source on the subject, with 140 color paintings of national
Romanian costume.

507 THE FEMALE PORTRAIT IN RUSSIAN ART: 12TH--EARLY 20TH CENTUR-
IES. Leningrad: Aurora Art Publishers, 1974.

Excellent guide to fashionable Russian female dress and style as shown in many color plates; valuable pictorial source.

508 Fox, Lilla M. FOLK COSTUME OF EASTERN EUROPE. Boston: Plays, 1977.

Inclusion of the folk costume of the countries of Yugoslavia, Albania, Greece, Bulgaria, Romania, Hungary, Czechoslovakia, Poland, East Germany, and Russia; treatment of historical, social, and decorative aspects of the costume; many illustrations in color.

509 Gaborjan, Alice. HUNGARIAN PEASANT COSTUMES. Budapest: Corvina Press, 1969.

Sixteen color and thirty-two monochrome photographs, plus numerous line drawings; wide range of subjects, including such topics as accessories and ornamentation; excellent source.

510 Gervers-Molnar, Veronika. THE HUNGARIAN SZUR: AN ARCHAIC MANTLE OF EURASIAN ORIGIN. Toronto: Royal Ontario Museum, 1973.

Scholarly investigation with numerous illustrations, drawings, and patterns of variations of the basic garment so widespread in Europe and Asia.

511 Hoellrigl, Joseph. HISTORIC HUNGARIAN COSTUMES. Budapest: Officina, 1939.

Coverage of Hungarian costume of the sixteenth to the twentieth centuries, with thirty-two photographs of garments and accessories.

512 Holme, Charles. PEASANT ART IN RUSSIA. London: Studio, 1912.

Dated; not a costume study as such, but useful for its many illustrations of native Russian peasant dress as an art form.

513 Hubbard, Margaret, and Peck, Esther. NATIONAL COSTUMES OF THE SLAVIC PEOPLES. New York: Woman's Press, 1921.

Coverage of topic with line drawings and concise descriptions; interesting section on national holidays of the slavic region.

514 Hungarian Ethnographical Museum. HUNGARIAN DECORATIVE FOLK ART. Budapest: Corvina Press, 1954.

Survey of the subject containing a chapter on costume with excellent color and black-and-white photographs; useful source.

515 Lepage-Medvey. NATIONAL COSTUMES: AUSTRIA, HUNGARY, PO-
LAND, CZECHOSLOVAKIA. Translated by S.P. Skipworth. New
York: Hyperion Press, 1939.

Ten fully colored plates from each country showing the distinctive features of both men's and women's national costumes
from respective areas and regions within the country.

516 Markov, Jozef. THE SLOVAK NATIONAL DRESS THROUGH THE CEN-
TURIES. Translated by Hedda Vesela-Stranska. Prague, Czechoslovakia:
Artia, 1956.

Brief description of costume followed by 183 color and monochrome illustrations, with accompanying descriptive notes, of
all types and levels of dress from 1600 to about 1850; bibliography.

517 Mayer, L.A. MAMLUK COSTUME: A SURVEY. Geneva: Albert Kun-
dig, 1952.

Comprehensive work; survey of court and royal, military, civil,
and ecclesiastical costumes, with twenty monochrome plates;
valuable for understanding of general area of Islamic costume;
bibliography.

518 Onassis, Jacqueline, ed. IN THE RUSSIAN STYLE. New York: Viking
Press, 1976.

Extensive pictorial presentation, often in excellent color, of
the panorama of Russian milieu, especially the upper class,
arranged by rulers from Peter I (1682) to Alexander II (1882);
treatment also of the peasants as well as the royalty; illustrations of accessories and complementary decorative furnishings
and art objects; bibliography.

519 Oprescu, George. PEASANT ART IN ROMANIA. London: Studio,
1929.

Coverage of costume and dress, among other topics, with many
illustrations of garments and accessories.

520 Palotay, Gertrude de. HUNGARIAN FOLK COSTUMES. Budapest:
Officina, 1938.

Succinct textual descriptions with line drawings plus twelve
color paintings by George Konecsni of male and female folk
costume from different regions, for special occasions, for different occupations, and for pastimes.

521 Penzer, Norman H. THE HAREM: AN ACCOUNT OF THE INSTITU-
TION AS IT EXISTED IN THE PALACE OF THE TURKISH SULTANS WITH

A HISTORY OF THE GRAND SERAGLIO FROM ITS FOUNDATION TO MODERN TIMES. 1936. Reprint. London: Spring Books, 1965.

Unique, detailed study of subject; descriptions of costume worn by Turkish women of the Ottoman empire; many illustrations of the costumes, many in color; list of Turkish names for parts of dress.

522 Perlberg, H.C. HISTORICAL RUSSIAN COSTUMES XIV-XVII CENTURY WORN BY THE RUSSIAN IMPERIAL FAMILY AND THEIR GUESTS IN THE WINTER PALACE, ST. PETERSBURG, ON FEBRUARY 27, 1903. New York: H.C. Perlberg, 1923.

Portfolio of fifty monochrome photographs of costumes with identification, description, historical date, and wearer.

523 Rubens, Alfred. A HISTORY OF JEWISH COSTUME. New ed. New York: Crown Publishers, 1973.

Numerous color plates; complete tracing of Jewish attire from its origin during the biblical and talmudic periods and then its development in Jewries throughout the Eastern and Western worlds including rabbinical dress; special interest in appendix of extracts from Jewish sumptuary laws and dress regulations; glossary and bibliography.

524 RUSSIAN KOSTIUM, 1750-1917 [Russian costume, 1750-1817]. Moscow: Vsesoiuznoe Teatalnoe Obschchestro, 1965.

Very useful book; series of sections covering historic Russian costume; numerous monochrome reproductions of paintings showing all classes of costume and accessories; text in Russian but pictures clearly dated for ease in using them.

525 Sobic, Ierina. COSTUMES AND ORNAMENTS IN THE ETHNOGRAPHIC MUSEUM IN BELGRADE. Belgrade: Magazine Jugoslavija, 1956.

Brief introductory background to fifteen color photographs of complete national female costumes and close-ups of textiles and motifs, with rather complete descriptive notes on each costume.

526 Sotkova, Blazena. NATIONAL COSTUMES OF CZECHOSLOVAKIA. Prague, Czechoslovakia: Artia, n.d.

Extensive textual description of costume with 138 excellent photographs by Karel Smirous, many in color and many detailed close-ups, of all aspects of the subject, including regional characteristics of dress, accessories, motifs, special occasion attire, and ornamentation.

527 Tilke, Max. THE COSTUMES OF EASTERN EUROPE. New York: E. Weyhe, 1925.

Ninety-six color plates of costumes from Greece, Albania, Russia, and other eastern European countries and territories; several patterns and most costumes drawn in a flat manner for easy reproduction; some garments shown on people; valuable for representations not only of dress but of colors and decorative motifs.

528 Tuchelt, Klaus Franz. TURKISCHE GEWANDER UND OSMANISCHE GESELLSCHAFT IN ACHTZEHNTEN JAHRHUNDERT. Graz, Austria: Akademische Druck, 1966.

German text but valuable for over two hundred beautifully colored plates of historic Turkish costume during the eighteenth century.

529 Veleva, Maria. BULGARIAN NATIONAL ATTIRE. Sofia, Bulgaria: Science and Art [Nauka i izkustvo], 1950.

Section in English with general discussion and description plus sixty color paintings of national costumes and thirty-five illustrations of embroideries, motifs, and ornamentation.

530 VILLAGE ARTS OF ROMANIA. London: British Museum, 1971.

Exhibition catalog with a brief chapter on Romanian costume with thirty photographs, some in color, of national dress, accessories, and furnishings.

531 Viski, Karoly. HUNGARIAN PEASANT CUSTOMS. Budapest: George Vajna and Co., 1937.

Thirty-two illustrations of customs including regional and national costume.

532 _____. POPULAR ARTS OF THE HUNGARIANS OF TRANSYLVANIA. Budapest: Popular Literary Society, n.d.

Introductory background material for 132 photographs and drawings, many showing regional costume and accessories.

533 Vlahovic, Mitar S. NATIONAL COSTUMES OF SERBIA. Belgrade: Magazine Jugoslavija, 1954.

Seventeen color paintings by Nikola Arsenovic executed in the nineteenth century, each accompanied by descriptive notes.

534 Zderciuc, Boris, et al. FOLK ART IN RUMANIA. Bucharest, Romania: Meridiana, 1964.

Excellent chapter on folk costume, with numerous photographs.

6. Costume of the Orient

See also 757, 844, 848, 875, 986

535 Ambrose, Kay. CLASSICAL DANCES AND COSTUMES OF INDIA. Introduction by Rom Gopal. Foreword by Arnold Haskel. London: Adam and Charles Black, 1965.

Many detailed drawings, illustrations, and photographs in support of an authoritative text; very valuable book for students of Indian costume and dance; index and bibliography.

536 Ayer, Jacqueline. ORIENTAL COSTUME. New York: Charles Scribner's Sons, 1974.

Handsome volume with an extensive collection of the author's drawings of ancient through modern oriental costume, with descriptive notes covering court, temple, theatrical, and village dress; diagrams for cutting and wrapping basic garments; also drawings of accessories and motifs; section on masks; very useful source.

537 Bhavnani, Enakshi. THE DANCE IN INDIA: THE ORIGIN AND HISTORY, FOUNDATIONS, THE ART AND SCIENCE OF THE DANCE IN INDIA--CLASSICAL, FOLK, AND TRIBAL. Bombay: Taraporevala Sons and Co., 1965.

Comprehensive treatment of the subject, with extensive illustrations of performers in costume; valuable to the dancer as well as to the costumer.

538 Bhushan, Jamila Brij. THE COSTUMES AND TEXTILES OF INDIA. Bombay: Taraporevala Sons and Co., 1958.

Interesting textual survey accompanied by many (1,079) photographs, drawings, and illustrations of all facets of ancient, Muslim, and modern Indian dress; other chapters on embroidery, dyeing and printing, weaving, and textiles; attention to textile patterns and decorative motifs; no patterns but clear line drawings for ease of construction; bibliography; very comprehensive and valuable source.

539 Blakeslee, Fred Gilbert. EASTERN COSTUME. Hollywood, Calif.: Warner Publishing Co., 1935.

Brief treatment with no illustrations of oriental costume.

540 Bustros, Evelyne, comp. LEBANESE AND SYRIAN COSTUMES. Beirut, Lebanon: Imprimerie Catholique, 1935?

Brief introductory statement translated by Evelyne Bustros from the original by B. Bustros; twenty-four color paintings by Georges Cyr of various types of regional costume including royalty, wedding, and civil dress.

541 Cammann, Schuyler. CHINA'S DRAGON ROBES. New York: Ronald Press, 1952.

Extensive study of the subject including the history, symbolism, and construction, with twenty monochrome plates of examples; glossary and index.

542 Capon, Edmund. CHINESE COURT ROBES IN THE VICTORIA AND AL-BERT. London: Victoria and Albert Museum, 1970.

Exploration of topic in the text, with twelve illustrations, mainly of robes.

543 Chandra, Moti. COSTUMES, TEXTILES, COSMETICS AND COIFFURE IN ANCIENT AND MEDIAEVAL INDIA. Edited by S.P. Gupta. Delhi: Oriental Publishers on behalf of the Indian Archaeological Society, 1973.

Lengthy, thorough treatment of specialized topic, with fourteen monochrome plates and numerous line drawings; bibliography.

544 Dar, Shiv Nath. COSTUMES OF INDIA AND PAKISTAN: A HISTORI-CAL AND CULTURAL STUDY. Bombay: Taraporevala Sons and Co., 1969.

Systematic presentation of much information regarding various forms of clothing and toilet practices of the respective peoples, with 142 illustrations (4 in color); treatment of regional, re-ligious, dance, common, noble, bridal, and occupational cos-tume; vocabulary, index, and bibliography; useful source.

545 Dongerkery, Kamala S. THE INDIAN SARI. New Delhi: Ministry of Commerce and Industry, n.d.

Thorough treatment of the basic Indian female garment, includ-ing wrapping techniques.

546 Fabri, Charles Louis. A HISTORY OF INDIAN DRESS. Calcutta: Orient Longmans, 1960.

Discussion of historical as well as modern Indian dress, with illustrative material; bibliography.

547 Fairservis, Walter A., Jr. COSTUMES OF THE EAST. Riverside, Conn.: Chatham Press, 1971.

> In association with the American Museum of Natural History; excellent photographs by Thomas Beiswenger and drawings by Jan Fairservis of garments and accessories; diagrams covering the costume of all areas of Asia from the Balkans, Iran, India, and Pakistan, Tibet, China, Japan and Korea, and Siberia, among others; attention to distinctive traits of costume from one area to another; index and bibliography; excellent source.

548 Fernald, Helen E. CHINESE COURT COSTUMES. Toronto: Royal Ontario Museum, 1946.

> Exhibition catalog with emphasis on costumes from the Ch'ing Dynasty (1644-1912), with forty-one plates (4 in color) and line drawings.

549 Flynn, Dorris. COSTUMES OF INDIA. Bombay: Oxford and IBH Publishing Co., 1971.

> Clear line drawings and color paintings with descriptive notes for regional, religious, traditional, and modern costumes; chapters on dance costume and ornamentation; glossary.

550 Gallois, Emile. COSTUMES JAPONAIS ET INDONESIENS. Paris: Henry Laurens, 1955.

> Portfolio of forty-eight plates by the author, showing Japanese and Indonesian costume in color and in full detail, with brief descriptive notes in French.

551 Ghurye, G.S. BHARATANATYA AND ITS COSTUME. Bombay: Popular Book Depot, 1958.

> Description and explanation of costume for particular Indian dance, with seven monochrome plates.

552 _____. INDIAN COSTUME. New York: Humanities Press, 1967.

> Excellent text of historical survey plus section of 412 monochrome illustrations showing the development of various garments, motifs, and accessories; useful source.

553 Gunsaulus, H.C. JAPANESE COSTUME. Chicago: Field Museum of Natural History, 1923.

> Brief descriptive essay on peasant, juvenile, and court costume, with eight monochrome illustrations.

Historical Costume

554 Hansen, Henny Harald. MONGOL COSTUMES. Copenhagen: Nordisk Forlag, 1950.

Specialized topic with complete descriptions, drawings, photographs, and some patterns to reproduce the costumes.

555 Hasimoto, Sumiko. JAPANESE ACCESSORIES. Tokyo: Japan Travel Bureau, 1962.

Condensed volume covering accessories unique to Japanese costume, for example, apparel, hair ornaments, headwear, and jewelry; all well illustrated and described.

556 Hawley, W.M., ed. CHINESE FOLK DESIGN: A COLLECTION OF CUT-PAPER DESIGNS USED FOR EMBROIDERY TOGETHER WITH 160 CHINESE ART SYMBOLS AND THEIR MEANINGS. Hollywood, Calif.: W.M. Hawley, 1949.

Useful for many suggested design motifs of value to costumer-designers working with Oriental costumes.

557 Hayashi, Tadaichi. JAPANESE WOMEN'S COSTUMES. Tokyo: Ie-no-hikari Association, 1960.

Descriptive notes in both Japanese and English, with 121 illustrations, some in color.

558 Hyobu, Mishimura, et al. TAGASODE: WHOSE SLEEVES . . . KIMONO FROM THE KANEBO COLLECTION. Tokyo: Japan Society, 1976.

Splendid color photographs of forty-three examples of beautiful kimonos from an exhibit from the Kanebo Collection; descriptive and historical notes; glossary.

559 Innes, R.A. COSTUMES OF UPPER BURMA AND THE SHAN STATES. Halifax, Nova Scotia: Halifax Museum, 1957.

Five photographs, drawings, and several patterns, plus descriptive text.

560 MALAYSIANS. Singapore: Malaya Publishing House, 1963.

Collection of fifty-one color paintings of costumed natives of Malaysia; publication sponsored by the Shell Company of the Federation of Malaya Ltd.

561 Minnich, Helen Benton. JAPANESE COSTUME, AND THE MAKERS OF ITS ELEGANT TRADITION. Rutland, Vt.: Charles E. Tuttle Co., 1963.

Excellent source for its thorough and broad survey of Japanese costume from the viewpoint of costume as a reflection of the society and cultural heritage of the country beginning with the Asuka period (A.D. 552); many excellent primary-source illustrations, some in color; very useful source.

562 Noma, Seiroku. JAPANESE COSTUME AND TEXTILE ARTS. New York: Weatherhill, 1974.

Discussion of kimono and kosode, with major emphasis on Noh and Kyogen costume development, types, colors, and motifs, followed by similar treatment of Kabuki costume, with 43 excellent color and 149 black-and-white illustrations of costumes.

563 Priest, Alan. COSTUMES FROM THE FORBIDDEN CITY. New York: Metropolitan Museum of Art, 1945.

Exhibition catalog with background material and fifty-six monochrome photographs of robes, religious and theatrical, and examples of textiles; somewhat dated.

564 Sahay, Sachidanand. INDIAN COSTUME, COIFFURE AND ORNAMENT. Columbia, Mo.: South Asia Books, 1975.

Extensive textual treatment of the subject, with thirty-six plates of primary-source material and numerous line drawings.

565 Scott, Adolph Clarence. CHINESE COSTUME IN TRANSITION. Singapore: Donald Moore Co., 1958.

Succinct treatment of costume of the Ch'ing dynasty and subsequent modern dress with a chapter on theatrical costume; many line drawings by the author.

566 Sheppard, Mubin. TAMAN INDERA: A ROYAL PLEASURE GROUND: MALAY DECORATIVE ARTS AND PASTIMES. Kuala Lumpur, Malaysia: Oxford University Press, 1972.

Illustrated survey of decorative arts of Malaya with no information, as such, on costume, but with many photographs and illustrations containing costumed subjects; bibliography.

567 Strathern, Andrew, and Strathern, Marilyn. SELF-DECORATION IN MOUNT HAGEN. Toronto: University of Toronto Press, 1971.

Extensive and scholarly study of adornment and costume of the peoples of New Guinea, with eighty-four monochrome and thirty-one color plates, plus drawings and diagrams.

568 Tilke, Max. ORIENTAL COSTUMES: THEIR DESIGNS AND COLORS. New York: Brentanos, 1924.

Many (128) color plates with brief descriptive notations of costume of oriental countries from Morocco to Japan; some patterns but all costumes pictured for very easy reproduction.

569 Vollmer, John E. IN THE PRESENCE OF THE DRAGON THRONE: CH'ING DYNASTY COSTUME (1644-1911) IN THE ROYAL ONTARIO MUSEUM. Toronto: Royal Ontario Museum, 1977.

Presentation of historical background; treatment of East Asian clothing traditions; Manchu garments; explanation of five colors of the universe and the symbolism of the emperor's robes; thirteen excellent color plates, numerous black-and-white photographs of robes, other garments, and accessories; seven patterns and line drawings of layouts; bibliography; major source.

7. Costume of Scandinavia

See also 413, 734

570 Andersen, Ellen. DANISH FOLK COSTUMES. Translated by Birthe Andersen. Copenhagen: Nordisk Forlag, 1948.

Introductory, descriptive text with eighteen photographs and drawings of folk costume; not nearly so useful as entry 571.

571 _____. FOLK COSTUMES IN DENMARK: PICTURES AND DESCRIPTIONS OF LOCAL DRESSES IN THE NATIONAL MUSEUM. Translated by Birthe Andersen. Copenhagen: Hassing, 1952.

Broad discussion with detailed descriptions and thirty-six excellent photographs, twelve in color, of costume covering the period from 1790 to 1910; survey of costume from various regions of Denmark and for such special functions as communions, weddings, festivals, funerals, and dances; explicit descriptions of both male and female as well as juvenile; inclusion in photographs of appropriate settings giving a suggestion of furnishings, architecture, and decorative styles and motifs; excellent source.

572 Arneberg, Halfdan. NORWEGIAN PEASANT ART. 2 vols. Oslo: Fabritius and Sonner, 1951.

Two volumes dealing with men's handicrafts and women's handicrafts; historical background plus illustrations, including costume, accessories, and decorative motifs.

573 Arno-Berg, Inga, and Hazelius-Berg, Gunnel. FOLK COSTUMES OF SWEDEN: A LIVING TRADITION. Translated by W.E. Ottercrans. Orebro, Sweden: Ljungforetagen AB, 1976.

Most comprehensive treatment of the subject; background in section 1, with subsequent chapters on festive dress; folk costume practices; state, church, and people's dress; and farmers' dress; coverage in section 2 of costume by region; the wearing, making, and care of folk costume in section 3; quite numerous photographs entirely in color; glossary, index, and bibliography; major work.

574 Brondsted, Johannes. THE VIKINGS: AN ILLUSTRATED HISTORY OF THE VIKINGS: THEIR VOYAGES, BATTLES, CUSTOMS AND DECORATIVE ARTS. Translated by Kalle Skov. Baltimore: Penguin Books, 1965.

Many illustrations in this book showing costumes of the Vikings, although not a costume book as such; bibliography.

575 Ekstrand, Gudrun. KARL X GUSTAVUS DRAEKTER, 166-1660 [The costumes of King Charles X Gustavus, 1622-1660]. Stockholm: Livrustkammaren, 1959.

Swedish text but summary in English; fifty-two monochrome plates of costumes and portraits of the king and his court during the period 1622-60; four pages of patterns.

576 Gjessing, Gjertrud, and Gjessing, Gutorm. LAPPEDRAKTEN [Costume of Lapland]. Oslo: Aschehoug, 1940.

English summary for description of costume in Lapland, with sixteen monochrome illustrations; bibliography.

577 Gudjonsson, Elsa E. THE NATIONAL COSTUME OF WOMEN IN ICELAND. Reykjavik: Iceland Review, 1967.

Offprint of a brief magazine article describing the national dress of women in the country; eleven illustrations, one in color.

578 HANDCRAFT IN SWEDEN. Stockholm: Victor Pettersons, 1951.

Swedish and English text, with illustrations of decorative motifs, costumes, and accessories.

579 Hauglid, Roar, et al. NATIVE ART OF NORWAY. Oslo: Dryers Forlag, 1965.

Coverage of the whole range of native arts and handcrafts in Norway, with a good chapter on costume with many color and black-and-white illustrations and concise text.

Historical Costume

580 Hazelius-Berg, Gunnel. MODEDRAEKTER FRAN 1600-1900 [Costume from 1600-1900]. Stockholm: Nordiska Museet, 1952.

Exhibition catalog of sixty-four monochrome plates of costume in the museum's collection; Swedish text with English summary.

581 Holme, Charles. PEASANT ART IN SWEDEN, LAPLAND AND ICELAND. New York: Studio, 1910.

Somewhat dated but excellent descriptions and illustrations, some in color, of regional and national costume, decorative motifs, and accessories.

582 Hougen, Bjorn. THE MIGRATION STYLE IN NORWAY. Oslo: A.W. Broggers, ca. 1936.

Sixty-five photographs of examples of ancient Norwegian jewelry.

583 Munksgaard, E. OLDTIDSDRAGTER [Ancient clothing]. Copenhagen: National Museum of Denmark, 1974.

Survey of ancient costume in Denmark during the Stone, Bronze, and Iron ages, with a summary and notes, in English, to illustrations.

584 Norlund, Poul. VIKING SETTLERS IN GREENLAND AND THEIR DESCENDANTS DURING FIVE HUNDRED YEARS. Copenhagen: Glydendal, 1961.

Considerable information and illustrative material on the early costume and accessories of the settlers of Greenland; index and bibliography.

585 Nylen, Anna-Maja. SWEDISH HANDCRAFT. Translated by Anne-Charlotte Hanes Harvey. New York: Van Nostrand Reinhold Co., 1977.

Extensive coverage of wide range of topics with some chapters relating to fashion and textiles; knitting, knotwork, lace, fabrics, weaving; 585 monochrome photographs and line drawings; 63 color plates, many of accessories and garments and/or containing costumed subjects; bibliography.

586 _____. SWEDISH PEASANT COSTUMES. Translated by Ingemar Tunander. Stockholm: Nordiska Museet, 1949.

Excellent survey of peasant costume and dress customs in various regions of Sweden, including sixty-five paintings of male and female costume with detailed descriptions; valuable source.

587 Plath, Iona. THE DECORATIVE ARTS OF SWEDEN. New York: Dover
Publications, 1966.

Well-illustrated survey with a chapter on textiles; examples of
clothing and accessories in connection with the decorative
arts throughout the book.

588 Primmer, Kathleen. SCANDINAVIAN PEASANT COSTUME. London:
Adam and Charles Black, 1939.

Older, general work with sixty-four pages of drawings and
paintings, eight in color, of peasant costumes and accessories
in the countries of Denmark, Greenland, Norway, Sweden,
Finland, and Lapland; notes by M.S. Primmer; bibliography.

589 Pylkkanen, Riitta. BAROKIN PUKUMUOTI SUOMESSA, 1620-1720
[Baroque costume in Finland, 1620-1720]. Helsinki: Weilin and Goos,
1970.

English summary for Finnish text of survey with 406 black-and-
white illustrations; map and bibliography.

590 _____. SAATYLAISPUKU SUOMESSA VANHEMMALLA VAASAAJALLA,
1550-1620 [The costume of the nobility and burghers in the early Vasa
period, 1550-1620]. Helsinki: Suomen Muinaismuistoyhdistyksen. 1955.

Finnish text with English summary of an outline of the costume
of the nobility, clergy, and burghers in the period 1550-1620.

591 Stewart, Janice S. THE FOLK ARTS OF NORWAY. 2d ed. New York:
Dover Publications, 1972.

General study of the area with a chapter on folk costume with
many illustrations, some in color; bibliography.

592 SWEDISH FOLK DANCES. Stockholm: Nordiska Museet, 1939.

Deals generally with dances of Sweden but contains forty-
three plates of native folk costume.

593 Traetteberg, Gunvor Ingstad. FOLK COSTUMES OF NORWAY. Oslo:
Dreyers Forlag, 1966.

Concise descriptions with thirty-four color and monochrome
photographs of many examples of regional dress and accessories.

594 Vilppula, Hilkka, et al. FOLK COSTUMES AND TEXTILES. Helsinki:
National Museum of Finland, n.d.

Succinct description and photographic and drawn depictions of
all phases of historical costume styles from various geographic

regions of Finland, with particular attention to textiles, motifs, and accessories.

8. Costume of Western and Southern Europe

a. GENERAL WORKS

See also 1526

595 Bossert, Helmuth T. FOLK ART OF EUROPE. New York: Frederick A. Praeger, 1964.

Coverage in part 1 of fabrics, rugs, and textiles, with forty color plates of motifs and decorations plus depictions of primary costume garments and accessories.

596 Brooke, Iris. WESTERN EUROPEAN COSTUME AND ITS RELATION TO THE THEATRE. 2 vols. 2d ed. New York: Theatre Arts Books, 1964.

Volume 1, thirteenth to seventeenth centuries; volume 2, seventeenth to nineteenth centuries; historical survey of costume of western European countries and its usage in contemporary theatrical activities from the medieval period to the nineteenth century; many line drawings and illustrations.

597 Fox, Lilla M. FOLK COSTUME OF SOUTHERN EUROPE. London: Chatto, Boyd, and Oliver, 1972.

Coverage of regional folk costume of Italy, Switzerland, Mediterranean ports and islands, Spain, and Portugal; descriptions of headdress, decoration, jewelry, and other accessories, many illustrations in color by the author.

598 _____. FOLK COSTUME OF WESTERN EUROPE. Boston: Plays, 1971.

Author's illustrations and drawings for descriptions of the national and regional folk costumes of ten western European countries: Great Britain, France, Belgium, the Netherlands, Western Germany, Denmark, Sweden, Norway, Finland, Lapland, details of embroidery, lace, buttonwork, jewelry, and headdresses.

599 Mann, Kathleen. PEASANT COSTUME IN EUROPE. London: Adam and Charles Black, 1950.

Presentation of typical examples of male and female peasant costume from fourteen European countries (France, Spain, Italy, Switzerland, British Isles, Holland, Germany, Denmark, Sweden, Finland, Russia, Poland, the Balkans, and Central

Europe), with 16 color plates and 125 line drawings not only
of complete costumes but also of motifs, accessories, and costume details.

600 Norris, Herbert. COSTUME AND FASHION: THE EVOLUTION OF
EUROPEAN DRESS THROUGH THE EARLIER AGES. 2 vols. London:
J.M. Dent and Sons, 1925.

Historical survey of all aspects of European costume, accessories, and motifs from the Celts through the fifteenth century;
drawings and color paintings; a few selected patterns; somewhat dated source.

601 Oakes, Alma, and Hill, Margot Hamilton. RURAL COSTUME: ITS
ORIGIN AND DEVELOPMENT IN WESTERN EUROPE AND THE BRITISH
ISLES. London: B.T. Batsford, 1970.

Historical survey with 378 line drawings of the development
of rural dress; divided into men's clothing and women's clothing and arranged by century; chapters on separate items of
rural costume: the cloak, the corset-bodice, the tunic or
smock-frock, footwear; additional chapters on rural costumes
in Great Britain and Ireland, and dyes used by rural people;
reprints of sumptuary laws in various European countries; listing of museums and libraries; index and bibliography; very
helpful source.

602 Sronkova, Olga. GOTHIC WOMAN'S FASHION. Prague, Czechoslovakia: Artia, 1954.

Survey of female medieval European fashion with numerous primary-source illustrations (153 in monochrome and 19 in color).

603 Stibbert, Frederic. CIVIL AND MILITARY CLOTHING IN EUROPE
FROM THE FIRST TO THE EIGHTEENTH CENTURY. Translated by John
V. Falconieri. Notes by Alfredo Lensi. 1914. Reprint. New York:
Benjamin Blom, 1968.

First English version of earlier Italian edition (also in 1914),
of 217 excellent costume plates by Stibbert, published posthu-
mously; coverage of costume in the engravings of all major
European countries arranged by century with identification,
date, and source; bibliography.

604 Wagner, Eduard, et al. MEDIEVAL COSTUME, ARMOUR AND WEAP-
ONS (1350-1450). Text by Zoroslava Drobna and Jan Durdik. Translated by Jean Layton. London: Paul Hamlyn, 1962.

Extremely large number of excellent drawings, many in color,
by Wagner of the whole range of European medieval costume
and armor.

b. FRANCE

See also 457, 1514

605 Blum, Andre. COSTUME OF THE WESTERN WORLD: EARLY BOURBON, 1590-1643. Translated by D.I. Wilson. London: George G. Harrap and Co., 1951.

Sixty plates (8 in color) of primary-source material for the costume during the period of the two kings, Henri IV (1589-1610) and Louis XIII (1610-43); general description of costume as well as notes on each of the illustrations; bibliography.

606 _____. COSTUME OF THE WESTERN WORLD: THE LAST VALOIS, 1515-1590. Edited by James Laver. Translated by D.I. Wilson. London: George G. Harrap and Co., 1951.

Seventy-one plates (8 in color) of primary-source material on costume, arranged by each of the Valois kings from Francis I (1515-57) through Henri II (1547-59), Charles IX (1560-74), and finally Henri III (1574-89); brief general description of costume as well as brief notes on each illustration; bibliography.

607 Braun-Ronsdorf, Margarete. DES MERVEILLEUSES AUX GARCONNES HISTORIE DE L'ELEGANCE EN EUROPE DE 1789 A 1929. Paris: Editions des Deux-Modes, 1963.

Primary emphasis upon French fashions and costume; text in French but 415 monochrome and 28 color plates of primary material; each plate dated.

608 Connat, Madeline. MODES, 1785-1789. Paris: Paris Etching Society, 1951.

Folio collection of fourteen female and male costumes in excellent color, with descriptive notes in French.

609 COSTUMES FRANCAIS DU XVIII SIECLE. Paris: Musee Carnavalet, 1955.

Exhibition catalog with thirty-two monochrome photographs of complete eighteenth-century French male and female costumes and selected accessories.

610 D'Allemagne, Henry Rene. LES ACCESSORIES DU COSTUME ET DU MOBILIER. 1928. Reprint. New York: Hacker Art Books, 1970.

French text but very large number of illustrations of French costume.

611 Evans, Joan. DRESS IN MEDIEVAL FRANCE. Oxford, Engl.: Oxford University Press, 1952.

Complete coverage and description of French costume during
the medieval period, with some patterns and figures for reproducing the costumes plus a section of eighty-four illustrations
of primary-source examples of clothing; index and bibliography.

612 Gallois, Emile. COSTUME DE L'UNION FRANCAISE. Paris: Editions
Arc-en-Ciel, 1946.

Forty-four color paintings of costume from selected French colonies in Africa, Central America, and Asia; brief text in
French.

613 _____. COSTUMES DES PROVINCES FRANCAISES. Paris: Henry
Laurens, 1951.

Portfolio edition of survey of provincial French costumes, with
forty-eight color paintings.

614 Keim, Aline. THE COSTUMES OF FRANCE. New York: French and
European Publications, 1930.

Portfolio of sixty color plates of female costume from twenty-
four regions of France.

615 Lacroix, Paul. FRANCE IN EIGHTEENTH CENTURY: ITS INSTITUTIONS,
CUSTOMS AND COSTUMES. 1876. Reprint. New York: Frederick
Ungar Publishing Co., 1963.

Over three hundred engravings covering the social history of
the eighteenth century in France, plus a chapter on dress and
fashions.

616 Larmessin, Nicolas de. LES COSTUMES GROTESQUES ET LES METIERS
XVIIE SIECLE. Paris: Henry Veyrier, 1974.

Reproductions of seventeenth-century French plates of fantastic
costumes.

617 Lepage-Medvey. FRENCH COSTUMES. Translated by Mary Chamot.
Preface by Andre Varagnec. New York: Hyperion Press, 1939.

Forty color plates by the author of costume from various regions of France.

618 Murphy, Michelle. TWO CENTURIES OF FRENCH FASHION. New
York: Charles Scribner's Sons, 1950.

Photographs of forty-nine mannequin dolls dressed in fashions
of France from 1715 to 1906, with brief historical and descriptive notes.

619 Piton, Camille. LE COSTUME EN FRANCE DU XIII AUX XIX SIECLE. Paris: Flammarion, n.d.

Text in French but more than seven hundred valuable primary-source illustrations.

620 Rogers, Dorothy. FRENCH PROVINCIAL COSTUMES. London: Hachette, 1944.

Older source with twenty-two color photographs of French regional costumes shown on paper dolls.

621 TYPICAL REGIONAL AND PERIOD COSTUMES OF FRANCE. New York: Cultural Services of the French Embassy, 1957.

Brief, condensed textual survey of historical and major provincial costumes, illustrated with line drawings and thirty-six black-and-white photographs of costumed dolls and miniature mannequins.

622 Vernet, Horace. INCROYABLES AND MERVEILLEUSES: PARIS 1810-1818. Paris: Editions Rombaldi, 1955.

Twenty-four beautifully colored plates, with notes and text in French by Roger-Armand Weigert.

c. GERMANY, AUSTRIA, AND SWITZERLAND

623 Baud-Bovy, Daniel. PEASANT ART IN SWITZERLAND. Translated by Arthur Palliser. London: Studio, 1924.

Extensive text and numerous (431) illustrations, many in color, covering every peasant art from housing to pottery, with complete chapters on costume and textiles, accompanied by ninety primary-source illustrations of complete costumes, separate garments, accessories, needlework, and motifs.

624 Fochler, Rudolf. COSTUMES IN AUSTRIA. Munich: Verlag Welsermuehl, 1965.

Text in English, French, and German, with over fifty color photographs of excellent quality with accompanying descriptive notes for regional costume of Austria.

625 Gierl, Irmgard. PFAFFENWINKLER TRACHTENBUCH: KULTURLANDSCHAFT UND TRACHT IN WEILHEIM, MURNAU UND WERDENFELS. Weissenhorn: Anton H. Konrad Verlag, 1971.

Recent study of costume of three regions, with numerous illustrations; German text.

626 Hammerstein, Hans von. COSTUMES OF THE ALPINERS. Vienna: Herbert Reichner Verlag, 1937.

Text in German, English, and French; thirty colored and intricately detailed plates of Alpine costumes, accessories, and motifs from various regions of Austria; with descriptive notes.

627 Heierli, Julie. DIE VOLKSTRACHTEN DER SCHWEIZ. 5 vols. Zurich: Eugen Reutsch Verlag, 1922-31.

Older source with German text but numerous drawings, paintings, and photographs of every phase of Swiss costume in each region of the country.

628 Holme, Charles, ed. PEASANT ART IN AUSTRIA AND HUNGARY. London: Studio, 1911.

Many photographs and paintings covering the whole range of the subject, including costume.

629 Kresz, Maria. UNGARISCHE BAUERNTRACHTEN 1820-1867. 2 vols. Berlin: Hewschelverlag Kunst and Gesellschaft, 1957.

Descriptive text in German in volume 1 but portfolio in volume 2 of ninety-six primary-source plates, many in color, illustrating the subject excellently.

630 Pettigrew, Dora W. PEASANT COSTUME OF THE BLACK FOREST. London: Adam and Charles Black, 1937.

Condensed volume of textual description of regional costumes with numerous drawings of total costumes as well as separate drawings of garments and accessories.

631 Vincent, John Martin. COSTUME AND CONDUCT IN THE LAWS OF BASEL, BERN AND ZURICH, 1370-1800. 1935. Reprint. New York: Greenwood Press, 1969.

Very interesting survey of ordinances and sumptuary regulations concerning clothing and the areas of profanity, sabbath observances, christenings, funerals, weddings, travel, and sleigh riding; forty-seven line drawings and primary-source illustrations; bibliography; specialized study with broad reference.

d. ITALY

632 Alexander, J.J.G. ITALIAN RENAISSANCE ILLUMINATIONS. New York: George Braziller, 1977.

Thorough study of primary sources of costume in the Renaissance period, with color reproductions of forty manuscript illuminations, all containing costumed figures.

633 Birbari, Elizabeth. DRESS IN ITALIAN PAINTING, 1460-1500. London: John Murray, 1975.

Survey with many details, drawings, and patterns of Italian costume from 1460 to 1500, plus directions for tailoring and adjusting these costumes; 115 monochrome plates of Italian art important to the study of costume; index and bibliography; helpful source.

634 Calderini, Emma. IL COSTUME POPOLARE EN ITALIA [Folk costume in Italy]. 3d ed. Milan: Sperling and Kupfer, 1953.

Two hundred color paintings of regional Italian costume, with titles in English and a brief text in Italian.

635 Cappi-Bentivegna, Ferruccia. ABBIGLIAMENTO E COSTUME NELLA PITTURA ITALIANA [Clothing and costume in Italian painting]. 2 vols. Rome: Edizioni d'Arte, 1964.

Coverage in volume 1 of the Renaissance and of the baroque in volume 2; minimal text in Italian but quite an extensive collection of primary-source illustrative material carefully dated and documented with close-up detail pictures; invaluable for entire range of historical Italian costume during these two periods.

636 Gurzau, Elba Farabegoli. FOLK DANCES, COSTUMES AND CUSTOMS OF ITALY. Newark, N.J.: Folkcraft, 1969.

Four-color plates of regional costume, containing numerous drawings and diagrams of the dances with concise, descriptive notes; map.

637 Holme, Charles, ed. PEASANT ART IN ITALY. New York: Studio, 1913.

Chapter on costume with numerous illustrations.

638 Levi-Pisetzky, Rosita. STORIA DEL COSTUME IN ITALIA [History of Italian costume]. 5 vols. Milan: Instituto Editoriale Italiano, 1964.

Comprehensive treatment of Italian costume, with quite an extensive inclusion of color primary-source material covering the period from the classical era into the nineteenth century; bibliographical footnotes; major historical work.

639 Ozzola, Leandro. IL VESTIARIO ITALIANO DAL 1500 AL 1550 [Italian clothing from 1500 to 1550]. Rome: Casa Editrice Fratelli Palombi, 1939.

Italian text but 205 monochrome plates of costume from the period.

640 Vecellio, Cesare. VERCELLIO'S RENAISSANCE COSTUME BOOK. 1598. Reprint. New York: Dover Publications, 1977.

Large-format reprint of original five hundred woodcuts from 1598 edition, plus additional illustrations and new English captions, showing Italian costume of the Renaissance.

641 Vocino, Michele. STORIA DEL COSTUME: VENTI SECOLI DI VITA ITALIANA [History of costume: Twenty centuries of Italian life]. 2d ed. Rome: Librerie dello Stato, 1961.

Italian text with a very useful and extensive collection of paintings and primary sources of Italian costume, the majority in color, from antiquity to the eighteenth century; bibliography.

e. NETHERLANDS

642 A GALA DRESS ABOUT 1760. The Hague, Netherlands: Hague Museum, 1957.

Full description of a female dress of the period, with the pattern and photographs of the complete ensemble.

643 Gardilanne, Gratiane de, and Moffatt, Elizabeth Whitney. THE NATIONAL COSTUMES OF HOLLAND. London: George G. Harrap and Co., 1932.

General background introduction plus fifty detailed paintings and descriptive notes of regional Dutch costume.

644 Hijlkema, Riet. NATIONAL COSTUMES IN HOLLAND. Amsterdam: J.M. Meulenhoff, 1951.

General survey region by region, with brief descriptive notes respectively and sixty-four excellent monochrome and three color photographs.

645 Thienen, Frithjof Van. COSTUME OF THE WESTERN WORLD: THE GREAT AGE OF HOLLAND, 1600-1660. Translated by Fernand G. Reiner and Anne Cliff. London: George G. Harrap and Co., 1951.

Sixty plates of primary-source material, eight in color, representing every major Dutch portraitist of the period; photographs of some actual garments; specific notes on costume in each plate as well as a general description; short bibliography.

646 Valeton, Elsa A. DUTCH COSTUMES. Amsterdam: De Driehoek, 1974.

Excellent description of traditional costumes of Holland according to the distinctive characteristics of each of the thirty regions of the country; primary-source photographs in color and
black-and-white; bibliography; good source.

647 WOMEN'S DRESS 1800-1820. The Hague: Netherlands Museum of Costume, 1966.

English text of general costume description with twenty-six
monochrome plates of items in the collection of the museum;
pattern included for a typical fashionable dress and photographs, with notes of accessories for the dress, including fan,
gloves, stockings, stay, combs, footwear, reticule, and bon-
net.

f. SPAIN AND PORTUGAL

See also 790

648 Aguilera, Emiliano M. LOS TRAJES POPULARES DE ESPANA VISTOS
POR LOS PINTORES ESPANOLES [Civilian dress of Spain as seen by
Spanish painters]. Barcelona: Omega, 1948.

General survey of Spanish costume with reproductions of paintings, some in color, as illustrative material.

649 Amades, Juan. INDUMENTARIA TRADICIONAL CATALANA [Traditional
clothing of Catalonia]. Barcelona: La Neotipia, 1939.

Survey of the traditional regional dress of the area of Cata-
lonia.

650 Anderson, Ruth Matilda. COSTUMES PAINTED BY SOROLLA IN HIS
PROVINCES OF SPAIN. New York: Hispanic Society of America,
1957.

One hundred five illustrations and reproductions of paintings
by Sorolla, plus descriptive textual survey of Spanish costume
in nine Spanish provinces.

651 _____. GALLEGAN PROVINCES OF SPAIN: PONTEVEDRA AND LA
CORUNA. New York: Hispanic Society of America, 1939.

Numerous (682) illustrations of regional life and costume of
these two provinces of Galicia, plus descriptions and historical background.

652 _____. SPANISH COSTUME: EXTRAMADURA. New York: Hispanic Society of America, 1951.

Survey of Spanish costumes in the province of Extramadura, containing 393 monochrome illustrations.

653 Bernis Madrazo, Carmen. INDUMENTARIA ESPANOLA EN TIEMPOS DE CARLOS V [Spanish costume in the time of Charles V]. Madrid: Blass, 1962.

Spanish text but many (231) excellent monochrome illustrations of Spanish costume in the sixteenth century.

654 _____. INDUMENTARIA MEDIEVAL ESPANOLA [Spanish medieval dress]. Madrid: Instituto Diego Velazquez, 1956.

One hundred eighty-four illustrations of Spanish medieval costume; bibliography.

655 Corazzi, David, ed. ALBUM DE COSTUMES PORTUGUEZES [Album of Portugese costume]. Lisbon: Typographia Horas Romanticas, 1888.

Dated source but one of only a few of merit; forty-eight reproductions of watercolors by various artists illustrating wide range of costumes and uniforms.

656 Gallois, Emille. LE COSTUME EN ESPAGNE ET AU PORTUGAL. Paris: Henri Laurens, n.d.

Portfolio of forty-eight color plates of Spanish and Portuguese costume.

657 _____. COSTUMES ESPAGNOLS [Spanish costume]. Preface by Jacques Soustelle. New York: French and European Publications, 1939.

Portfolio of forty-eight color plates of Spanish costume.

658 Garcia Boiza, Don Antonio, and Berrueta Dominquez, Don Juan. EL TRAJE REGIONAL SALMANTINO [Regional dress of Salamanca]. Madrid: Espasa-Calpe, 1940.

Spanish text but sixty-one excellent monochrome photographs of regional costume of the area of Salamanca.

659 Gomez Tabanera, Jose Manuel. TRAJES POPULARES Y COSTUMBRES TRADICIONALES [Civilian dress and traditional customs]. Madrid: Tesor, 1950.

Survey of Spanish costume, traditional and civilian, with some color illustrations; bibliography.

660 Hispanic Society of America. COSTUME OF CANDELARIO, SALAMANCA New York: 1932.

Six color plates taken from slides of women against domestic backgrounds.

661 _____. EXTRAMADURA COSTUME: WOMEN'S FESTIVAL DRESS AT MONTEHERMOSO, CACERES. New York: 1931.

Ten plates of traditional costumes for female festival dress in the region of Caceres.

662 _____. MEN'S CAPES AND CLOAKS: LA ALBERCA, SALAMANCA. New York: 1931.

Booklet with brief descriptive notes and eleven monochrome photographs of examples of capes and cloaks from the collection of the Hispanic Society.

663 _____. WEDDING COSTUME, LA ALBERCA, SALAMANCA. New York: 1931.

Booklet of eleven monochrome photographs of the style of wedding dresses from the collection of the Hispanic Society, including brief historical background and descriptive notes.

664 _____. WOMEN'S COIFFURE: CANDELARIO, SALAMANCA. New York: 1931.

Booklet containing one folded sheet with twelve monochrome illustrations.

665 _____. WOMEN'S DRESS FOR CHURCH: CANDELARIO, SALAMANCA. New York: 1931.

Twelve monochrome illustrations in a booklet with historical and descriptive information.

666 _____. WOMEN'S JEWELRY: CANDELARIO, SALAMANCA. New York: 1931.

Booklet with one folded sheet of five illustrations, showing articles of jewelry in their actual size.

667 Hoyos Sancho, Nieves de. EL TRAJE REGIONAL [Regional costume]. 2d ed. Madrid: Publicaciones Espanolas, 1959.

Brief survey of regional Spanish costume, with selected illustrations.

668 _____. EL TRAJE REGIONAL DE GALICIA [Regional costume of Galicia]. Santiago, Spain: Compostela, 1971.

Twenty-four plates of costume of the region of Galicia; bibliography.

669 Ortiz Echague, Jose. ESPANA: TIPOS Y TRAGES [Spain: Types and dress]. 12th ed. Madrid: Mayfe, 1971.

Considerable survey with 272 monochrome and thirty-four color photographs.

670 Palencia, Isabel de. THE REGIONAL COSTUMES OF SPAIN: THEIR IMPORTANCE AS A PRIMITIVE EXPRESSION OF THE AESTHETIC IDEALS OF THE NATION. Madrid: Editorial Voluntad, 1929.

Extensive text plus 241 plates of paintings and photographs of dress from every region of the country; good source.

671 Reade, Brian. COSTUME OF THE WESTERN WORLD: THE DOMINANCE OF SPAIN, 1550-1660. London: George G. Harrap and Co., 1951.

Sixty-two primary-source plates, eight in color, with notes and descriptions of the historical development of Spanish costume; succinct text; bibliography.

672 Souza, Alberto. O TRAJO POPULAR EM PORTUGAL [Civilian costume in Portugal]. 2 vols. Lisbon: Sociedade Nacional de Tipografia, 1927.

Volume 1: XVI AND XVII CENTURIES; volume 2: XVIII AND XIX CENTURIES; combined volumes containing over six hundred illustrations, each dated, of Portuguese costume throughout the four centuries.

Chapter 4
ACCOUTREMENTS AND SPECIAL CATEGORIES
OF COSTUME

A. ACCESSORIES

See also 435, 555, 789, 889, 1503

673 Albert, Lillian Smith, and Kent, Kathryn. THE COMPLETE BUTTON
BOOK. Garden City, N.Y.: Doubleday and Co., 1949.

Very extensive illustration with some color plates of examples
of the button art.

674 Armstrong, Nancy. A COLLECTOR'S HISTORY OF FANS. New York:
Clarkson N. Potter, 1974.

Historical survey of the subject of fans with 121, mostly monochrome, photographs of examples of fans from throughout the
world.

675 Baker, Lillian. THE COLLECTORS ENCYCLOPEDIA OF HATPINS AND
HATPIN HOLDERS. Paducah, Ky.: Collector Books, 1976.

Very complete presentation of specialized topic with ample
illustration and documentation, mostly in color.

676 Beck, S. William. GLOVES, THEIR ANNUALS AND ASSOCIATIONS:
A CHAPTER OF TRADE AND SOCIAL HISTORY. 1883. Reprint. Detroit: Singing Tree Press, 1969.

Reprint of valuable source for a historical survey of the social
history of gloves throughout the centuries.

677 Blakemore, Kenneth. THE BOOK OF GOLD. New York: Stein and
Day Publishers, 1971.

Historical survey of the topic from ancient times to the modern day with coverage of the uses to which gold has been
put; its refinement processes; and the making of gold; numerous

illustrations and photographs (some in color) of accessories, crowns, and jewelry; glossary; chart of hallmarks; index and bibliography.

678 Boehn, Max von. ORNAMENTS: LACE, FANS, GLOVES, WALKING-STICKS, PARASOLS, JEWELRY AND TRINKETS. 1929. Reprint. New York: Benjamin Blom, 1970.

Extensive textual survey of accessories with historical background and development and excellent primary-source illustrations.

679 Braun-Ronsdorf, Margarete. THE HISTORY OF THE HANDKERCHIEF. Leigh-on-Sea, Engl.: F. Lewis Publishers, 1967.

Over one hundred monochrome plates of handkerchiefs from the Roman mappa to the modern version, plus excellent textual survey; bibliography.

680 Carlisle, Lilian Baker. HAT BOXES AND BANDBOXES AT SHELBURNE MUSEUM. Shelburne, Vt.: Shelburne Museum, 1960.

Specialized study of interest; well documented and illustrated; possible use to costumer on occasion.

681 Clutton, Cecil. WATCHES. New York: Viking Press, 1965.

Historical survey of timepieces and watches from 1500 to modern time, dealing with technical as well as decorative aspects; 19 color and 621 black-and-white photographs; useful source.

682 Colle, Doriece. COLLARS, STOCKS, CRAVATS: A HISTORY AND COSTUME DATING GUIDE TO CIVILIAN MEN'S NECKPIECES, 1655-1900. Emmaus, Pa.: Rodale Press, 1972.

Survey of each item in the title in both European and American styles by historical development, with concise line drawings and numerous primary-source examples; coverage of the use of colors; bibliography; extremely useful book in costuming period productions.

683 Collins, C. Cody. LOVE OF A GLOVE: THE ROMANCE, LEGENDS AND FASHION HISTORY OF GLOVES AND HOW THEY ARE MADE. New York: Fairchild Publications, 1945.

Forty-three plates in support of the textual description of the historical development of gloves; considerable section with diagrams on all phases of glove manufacture; bibliography.

684 Corson, Richard. FASHIONS IN EYEGLASSES. London: Peter Owen, 1967.

Thorough presentation of eyeglasses from their beginnings to the present, with primary-source written and visual materials; numerous line drawings arranged historically; bibliography.

685 Crawford, T.S. A HISTORY OF THE UMBRELLA. New York: Taplinger Publishing Co., 1970.

Survey of the origin and use of the umbrella and parasol in all cultures, in folklore, in literature and art, and in fashion; numerous primary-source illustrations; bibliography.

686 Curtis, Mattoon M. THE STORY OF SNUFF AND SNUFF BOXES. New York: Liveright Publishing Corp., 1935.

Survey of the development of the use of tobacco in Europe and America; historical outline of the containers for the tobacco with 118 illustrations of various types of snuff boxes; bibliography.

687 Ehwa, Carl, Jr. THE BOOK OF PIPES AND TOBACCO. New York: Random House, 1973.

Excellent chapters on historical pipes and illustrations of many examples.

688 Erickson, Joan Mowat. THE UNIVERSAL BEAD. New York: W.W. Norton and Co., 1969.

Types, uses, and symbolism of beads shown through a number of illustrations and a concise text.

689 Ertell, Viviane Beck. THE COLORFUL WORLD OF BUTTONS. Princeton, N.J.: Pyne Press, 1973.

Many color plates of buttons, arranged in historic sequence and by types.

690 Flory, M.A. A BOOK ABOUT FANS: THE HISTORY OF FANS AND FANPAINTING. 1895. Reprint. Detroit: Gale Research Co., 1974.

Interesting and thorough survey of the history of fans, with photographs and drawings of period examples.

691 Gillespie, Karen R. FASHION ACCESSORIES: A NONTEXTILE WORK MANUAL. 2d ed. New York: Prentice-Hall, 1954.

Sourcebook of general information concerning such topics as leather, shoes, gloves, handbags, furs, jewelry, and cosmetics; line drawings and diagrams; bibliography.

692 Goldring, William. THE PIPE BOOK: A HISTORY AND HOW TO.
New York: Drake Publishers, 1973.

Historical survey with good primary-source illustrative material.

693 Grass, Milton N. HISTORY OF HOSIERY FROM THE PILOI OF ANC-
IENT GREECE TO THE NYLONS OF MODERN AMERICA. New York:
Fairchild Publications, 1955.

Somewhat inclined to technical manufacturing aspects, but an
interesting historical survey with selected illustrations; useful
and informative.

694 Green, Bertha de Vere. A COLLECTOR'S GUIDE TO FANS OVER THE
AGES. London: Frederick Muller, 1975.

Extensively documented survey of the history of fans; excellent
source.

695 Guye, Samuel, and Michel, Henri. TIME AND SPACE: MEASURING
INSTRUMENTS FROM THE 15TH TO THE 19TH CENTURY. New York:
Hacker Art Books, 1971.

Survey of the developments over a 500-year period; 427 illustrations, including 20 color plates; valuable for historical timepieces and watches.

696 Harrison, Frank L., and Rimmer, Joan. EUROPEAN MUSICAL INSTRU-
MENTS. New York: W.W. Norton and Co., 1964.

Excellent survey of development of musical instruments, with
248 illustrations of their use and how to handle them; valuable
for costumer confronted with a musical instrument as part of a
costume or as an accessory.

697 Haskel, Ira J. HOISERY THRU THE YEARS. Lynn, Mass.: Carole Mail-
ing Service, 1956.

Thorough historical survey with many (124) drawings and illustrations.

698 Irwin, John. THE KASHMIR SHAWL. London: Her Majesty's Stationery
Office, 1973.

Specialized study of a particular garment-accessory with forty-
four monochrome plates, diagrams, and drawings; attention to
manufacturing processes as well.

699 _____. SHAWLS: A STUDY IN INDO-EUROPEAN INFLUENCES. London: Her Majesty's Stationery Office, 1955.

Technical treatise, particularly on the Kashmir shawl and its adoption, use, and adaptations in Europe; glossary, bibliography, and over fifty plates of primary-source examples.

700 Leary, Emmeline. FANS IN FASHION. Bradford, Engl.: Northway Printing Co., 1975.

Exhibition catalog with brief introduction to the subject of fans, with eleven monochrome photographs of various types of historical fans; short section on making and selling fans; brief bibliography.

701 Lester, Katherine Morris, and Oerke, Bess Viola. AN ILLUSTRATED HISTORY OF THOSE FRILLS AND FURBELOWS OF FASHION WHICH HAVE COME TO BE KNOWN AS: ACCESSORIES OF DRESS. Peoria, III.: Manual Arts Press, 1940.

Standard source for comprehensive treatment of the wide range of the subject; coverage of accessories arranged according to the body area with which the item would be used: accessories worn at the head, neck, shoulder and waist, feet and legs, arms and wrist, or carried or used on costume; 644 drawings by Helen Westerman and 59 plates; index and bibliography; invaluable reference.

702 Luscomb, Sally C. THE COLLECTOR'S ENCYCLOPEDIA OF BUTTONS. New York: Crown Publishers, 1967.

Illustrations of many types of buttons.

703 May Hosiery Mills. THE STORY OF HOSIERY. Burlington, N.C.: Houck, 1931.

Somewhat dated but interesting historical survey of hosiery, with many illustrations and drawings.

704 Meyer, Florence E. PINS FOR HATS AND CRAVATS WORN BY LADIES AND GENTLEMEN. Des Moines, Iowa: Wallace-Homestead, 1974.

Condensed presentation of a specialized study of stick and hat pins, with numerous color illustrations of examples.

705 Nicholls, Florence Zacharie Ellis. BUTTON HAND BOOK. Ithaca, N.Y.: Cayuga Press, 1943.

Photographs, some in color, of hundreds of buttons, arranged by type and use.

706 Peacock, P. BUTTONS FOR THE COLLECTOR. London: Newton Abbott, 1972.

General history with illustrations of buttons arranged according to material and manufacture.

707 Peltz, Leslie Ruth. FASHION ACCESSORIES. New York: Howard W. Sams and Co., 1974.

Chapters primarily from the viewpoint of the fashion world but with historical, construction, and utilization information on such accessories as jewelry, furs, hosiery, umbrellas, gloves, and handbags.

708 Percival, MacIver. THE FAN BOOK. London: T. Fisher Unwin, 1920.

Somewhat dated but still authoritative historical survey, with fifty illustrations.

709 Redfern, W.B. ROYAL AND HISTORIC GLOVES AND SHOES. London: Methuen and Co., 1904.

Dated, but yet unsurpassed study of the subject.

710 Severn, William. HAND IN GLOVE. New York: David McKay, 1965.

Entertaining survey of history of gloves, with illustrations by Vana Earle; glossary and bibliography.

711 Shackell, Dora. ACCENT ON ACCESSORIES. London: Mills and Boon, 1957.

Chapters on main types of accessories, with detailed drawings and patterns for constructing them.

712 Smith, Willard M. GLOVES: PAST AND PRESENT. New York: Imperial Engraving and Printing Co., 1918.

Interesting historical survey of the glove from antiquity but with no illustrative material, notes, or bibliography.

713 Squire, Gwen. BUTTONS: A GUIDE FOR THE COLLECTOR. London: Frederick Muller, 1972.

Guide with one hundred photographic plates, drawings, and illustrations of numbers of metal buttons in such special categories as uniforms, schools and universities, and prisons.

714 Stein, Kurt. CANES AND WALKING STICKS. York, Pa.: Liberty Cap Books, 1974.

Survey of subject from 1600 to the present with attention to special categories such as children's, sword, gun, and mechanical canes; numerous illustrations of all primary examples.

715 Wilcox, R. Turner. THE MODE IN FURS: THE HISTORY OF FURRED COSTUME OF THE WORLD FROM THE EARLIEST TIMES TO THE PRESENT. New York: Charles Scribner's Sons, 1951.

Many black-and-white drawings for illustrations of the uses of furs in garments, decorations, and accessories from the primitives to the present; short description of major uses for furs in each century; section on manufacturing with furs; glossary and bibliography.

B. DANCE WEAR

See also chapter 2, section C.

716 Bascom, Frances, and Irey, Charlotte. COSTUME CUES. Washington, D.C.: American Association for Health, Physical Education and Recreation, 1952.

Useful but brief presentation of material for basic dance costume, with illustrations and patterns for the basic dance garments.

717 Ellfeldt, Lois, and Carnes, Edwin. DANCE PRODUCTION HANDBOOK: OR LATER IS TOO LATE. Palo Alto, Calif.: National Press Books, 1971.

Outlines a total production approach for dance; chapter on costumes with attention to preplanning, designing for movement concerns, and construction techniques.

718 Joiner, Betty. COSTUMES FOR THE DANCE. New York: A.S. Barnes and Co., 1937.

Succinct treatment of use of design elements in movement and dance costumes; a chapter on construction procedures including patterns and sewing instructions; illustrated with original designs by the author; brief mention of dyeing techniques and the effects of light on costume colors.

719 Lawson, Joan, and Revitt, Peter. DRESSING FOR THE BALLET. London: Adam and Charles Black, 1958.

Invaluable study of traditional ballet and dance costume with patterns, diagrams, and instructions for constructing costumes for class and stage use; also contains a section on national costume; most valuable source.

720 Lippincott, Gertrude, ed. DANCE PRODUCTION. Washington, D.C.: American Association for Health, Physical Education and Recreation, 1956.

> Contains two pertinent sections: "Costuming the Dance" by Jane Fox and "Some Notes on Dance Costumes for the Stage" by Eileen Holding.

721 Watson, Phyllis. DESIGNED FOR APPLAUSE. Winter Park, Fla.: Performing Arts Publishers, 1972.

> Techniques for designing and costuming children's dance recitals with clear directions, helpful hints, simplified patterns, and procedural directions for a novice.

C. FASHION PLATES AND SILHOUETTES

722 Boehn, Max von. MINIATURES AND SILHOUETTES. Translated by E.K. Walker. 1928. Reprint. New York: Benjamin Blom, 1970.

> Survey of the silhouette and the miniature, with more attention to the history and application of the latter; index of artists and sitters.

723 Evans, Mary. COSTUME SILHOUETTES WITH NINETEEN ILLUSTRATIONS OF HISTORIC AND MODERN SILHOUETTES OF COSTUME. Philadelphia: J.B. Lippincott Co., 1923.

> Nineteen illustrations of silhouettes of costume from the Egyptian period to the twentieth century, showing developments in shapes and forms of historical costume; bibliography.

724 Hickman, Peggy. SILHOUETTES: A LIVING ART. New York: St. Martin's Press, 1975.

> Specialized study of the silhouette as used in many forms, with costuming being only one phase.

725 Holland, Vyvyan Beresford. HAND COLOURED FASHION PLATES, 1770 TO 1899. London: B.T. Batsford, 1955.

> Five color plates plus 129 monochrome illustrations covering the history of fashion plates; chapters on the artists and formation of a collection; lists of periodicals publishing fashion plates in each period.

726 Laver, James. FASHIONS AND FASHION PLATES 1800-1900. London: Penguin Books, 1943.

Brief survey of male and female fashion during the nineteenth century, followed by sixteen color primary-source fashion plates with descriptive notes on each.

727 Moore, Doris Langley. FASHION THROUGH FASHION PLATES. New York: Clarkson N. Potter, 1971.

Survey of fashion as seen through seventy-two color and ninety-three monochrome fashion plates arranged chronologically with accompanying descriptive notes.

728 Nevinson, John L. ORIGIN AND EARLY HISTORY OF THE FASHION PLATE. Washington, D.C.: Smithsonian Institution Press, 1967.

Amply illustrated with thirty-four plates of primary-source material; survey of history of the fashion plate from its early origin in the late fifteenth and early sixteenth centuries to its full development in the nineteenth century.

729 Wilson, Carrie. FASHIONS SINCE THEIR DEBUT. Scranton, Pa.: International Textbook Co., 1939.

Presentation of the primary female silhouette from selected costume periods from Egypt to the present, with accompanying line drawings and notes; bibliography.

730 Woodiwiss, John. BRITISH SILHOUETTES. London: Country Life, 1965.

A technical study containing costumed silhouettes (66 plates) from the origin of the practice to the present; bibliography.

D. FOOTWEAR

See also 601, 1583

731 Brooke, Iris. FOOTWEAR: A SHORT HISTORY OF EUROPEAN AND AMERICAN SHOES. New York: Theatre Arts Books, 1971.

Condensed historical survey with line drawings of various types of shoes and also of total ensembles showing correct footwear.

732 Evrard, Gwen. TWINKLETOES: FOOTGEAR TO MAKE AND WEAR. New York: Charles Scribner's Sons, 1976.

Directions, diagrams, patterns, and instructions for construction of leg wrappings, shoes, clogs, sandals, and other types of footwear.

733 Glen, Emilie. FOOTWEAR: SALESPERSON'S MANUAL AND CON-
SUMER'S GUIDE. New York: Fairchild Publications, 1948.

Practical knowledge covering such areas as materials, component parts and manufacture, styles, and proper fit of footwear;
good representation of footwear of the 1940s.

734 Hald, Margrethe. PRIMITIVE SHOES: AN ARCHAEOLOGICAL ETHNO-
LOGICAL STUDY BASED UPON SHOE FINDS FROM THE JUTLAND
PENINSULA. Copenhagen: National Museum of Denmark, 1972.

Reconstruction of basic patterns and materials from ancient
fragments of footwear.

735 Severn, William. IF THE SHOE FITS. New York: David McKay, 1964.

Popular treatment of the development of shoes and footwear,
with a glossary of footwear terminology and illustrations by
Vana Earle.

736 Thornton, John Henry, ed. TEXTBOOK OF FOOTWEAR MANUFACTURE.
London: National Trade Press, 1955.

Technical volume of selected essays on various topics of interest to the costumer concerned with footwear construction;
main sections on leather, leatherboards, footwear textiles,
rubber and synthetics, finishes, adhesives, and fasteners; glossary and bibliography; diagrams, photographs, charts, and drawings.

737 White, George M. CRAFT MANUAL OF NORTH AMERICAN INDIAN
FOOTWEAR. Ronan, Mont.: 1969.

Very valuable source for line drawings, scaled patterns, and
detailed directions for the construction of twenty-six types of
Indian footwear; basic procedures easily applied to any type
of soft leather footwear construction for any period from classical to the present.

738 Wilcox, R. Turner. THE MODE IN FOOTWEAR. New York: Charles
Scribner's Sons, 1948.

Succinct descriptive notes as well as numerous drawings of
footwear from the Egyptians to the present, with selected drawings in each period of a total costume to give the relationship
of the footwear to the costume; outline of technical aspects of
footwear manufacture.

739 Wilson, Eunice A. A HISTORY OF SHOE FASHIONS: A STUDY OF
SHOE DESIGN IN RELATION TO COSTUME FOR SHOE DESIGNERS,

PATTERN CUTTERS, MANUFACTURERS, FASHION STUDENTS AND DRESS DESIGNERS, ETC. London: Sir Isaac Pitman and Sons, 1969.

Glossary of shoe terms; historical survey of shoe fashions from the primitive to the modern man, supported by numerous and explicit drawings and photographs; drawings of costumed male and female in each costume period to show footwear in relation to the total ensemble.

740 Wohl Shoe Company. THE ROMANCE AND HISTORY OF SHOES. St. Louis: 195-?

Brief booklet with survey of historical development of boots, shoes, and other footwear, with attention to variations by countries; clear line drawings and illustrations.

741 Wright, Thomas. THE ROMANCE OF THE SHOE, BEING THE HISTORY OF SHOEMAKING IN ALL AGES AND ESPECIALLY IN ENGLAND AND SCOTLAND. London: Farncombe, 1922.

Somewhat dated survey of the development of shoemaking, with selected illustrations.

E. HEADWEAR

See also 1495, 1509

742 Amphlett, Hilda. HATS: A HISTORY OF FASHION IN HEADWEAR. Buckinghamshire, Engl.: Richard Sadler, 1974.

In-depth historical survey from the first millenium A.D. to the twentieth century, with some eight hundred drawings; attention in some centuries to military, special groups, crowns, ecclesiastical, national, and non-European headdresses; glossary.

743 Courtais, Georgine de. WOMEN'S HEADDRESS AND HAIRSTYLES IN ENGLAND: A.D. 600 TO THE PRESENT DAY. London: B.T. Batsford, 1973.

Historically arranged treatment of the entire area of female headdress, with numerous line drawings and good descriptive commentary and notes; special sections on bridal headdresses, headwear of domestic servants, and nurses caps; glossary, index, and bibliography.

744 Giafferi, Paul Louis Victor de, comp. MILLINERY IN THE FASHION HISTORY OF THE WORLD: FROM 5300 B.C. TO THE PRESENT ERA. New York: Illustrated Milliner Co., 1927.

Numerous illustrations in color of various styles of headdress
from historical periods and various nationalities.

745 Harrison, Michael. THE HISTORY OF THE HAT. London: Herbert
Jenkins, 1960.

Survey of the origin, development, uses, and significances of
headwear with 250 drawings; sections on wigs and ecclesiastical headwear; index and bibliography.

746 Kilgour, Ruth Edwards. A PAGEANT OF HATS, ANCIENT AND MOD-
ERN. New York: Robert M. McBride Co., 1958.

Descriptions and photographs of numerous hats, arranged by
continent and country.

747 Lens, Bernard. THE EXACT DRESS OF THE HEAD. London: Costume
Society, 1970.

Reprint of 1725 sourcebook of hairstyles and headwear for
women and men.

748 Lowrie, Drucella. RESTYLE YOUR HATS. New York: Thomas Y.
Crowell Co., 1952.

Somewhat dated, but useful suggestions and ideas for remaking
hats; many drawings of hat styles of the early 1950s.

749 Severn, William. HERE'S YOUR HAT. New York: David McKay, 1966.

Lighthearted popular history of hats with illustrations by Vana
Earle; glossary of millinery terms and types.

750 Stuart, Jennifer. MAKE YOUR OWN HATS. London: G. Bell and
Sons, 1968.

Practical directions for constructing twenty-five different styles
of hats with sixty-five diagrams and with illustrations.

751 Wilcox, R. Turner. THE MODE IN HATS AND HEADDRESS INCLUDING
HAIR STYLES, COSMETICS AND JEWELRY. New York: Charles Scribner's Sons, 1959.

Brief descriptions and line drawings to illustrate the historical
development of hats and other headwear; useful arrangement
and presentation of information; index and bibliography.

F. JEWELRY

See also 40, 495, 582, 666, 751, 1151, 1500

752 Aldred, Cyril. JEWELS OF THE PHARAOHS: EGYPTIAN JEWELRY OF THE DYNASTIC PERIOD. London: Frederick A. Praeger, 1971.

One hundred fifty-six excellent photographs, many in color, plus numerous line drawings, covering all facets of the subject thoroughly and authoritatively.

753 Armstrong, Nancy. JEWELLERY: AN HISTORICAL SURVEY OF BRITISH STYLES AND JEWELS. Guilford, Engl.: Lutterworth Press, 1973.

Excellent historical survey as well as an artistic assessment of British jewelry; numerous illustrations with fifty-two pages of plates, some in color; index and bibliography.

754 _____. VICTORIAN JEWELRY. New York: Macmillan Co., 1976.

Richly illustrated, partly in color, exploration of the subject.

755 Baerwald, Marcus, and Mahoney, Tom. GEMS AND JEWELRY TODAY: AN ACCOUNT OF THE ROMANCE AND VALUES OF GEMS, JEWELRY, WATCHES AND SILVERWARE. New York: Marcel Rodd Co., 1949.

Extensive coverage of the subjects in the title, with excellent color photographs especially of timepieces and brooches.

756 Benda, Klement. ORNAMENT AND JEWELLERY ACHAEOLOGICAL FINDS FROM EASTERN EUROPE. Prague, Czechoslovakia: Artia, 1967.

Numerous excellent color photographs with descriptive notes of ornaments and jewelry excavated from this geographical area; valuable depictions of ancient jewelry forms.

757 Bhushan, Jamila Brij. INDIAN JEWELLERY, ORNAMENTS AND DECORATIVE DESIGNS. 2d ed. Bombay: Taraporevala Sons and Co., 1964.

Extensive treatment of every phase of the subject, with 3 color plates, 471 line drawings, and 370 half-tone illustrations; good visual source.

758 Black, J. Anderson. THE STORY OF JEWELRY. New York: William Morrow and Co., 1974.

Illustrated completely with color plates, surveys from prehistoric time to the twentieth century, with appendixes on royal regalia and on gemstones; glossary of techniques and technical terms.

759 Bradford, Ernle. FOUR CENTURIES OF EUROPEAN JEWELLERY. Feltham, Engl.: Spring Books, 1967.

Survey of jewelry from the Italian Renaissance to the present, with illustrations and photographs of many styles and types; chapters on precious metals, precious stones, birthstones, gem-cutting, and paste; glossary, index, and selected bibliography.

760 Darling, Ada. ANTIQUE JEWELRY. Watkins Glen, N.Y.: Century House, 1953.

Survey, with section of pages from manufacturers' catalogs.

761 Davis, Mary L., and Pack, Greta. MEXICAN JEWELRY. Austin: University of Texas Press, 1973.

Only contribution to unique subject, with many photographs and drawings.

762 Desmoni, Martin J. EXHIBITION OF RENAISSANCE JEWELS SELECTED FROM THE COLLECTION OF MARTIN J. DESMONI. New York: Battista Reproductions, 1958.

Excellent monochrome and color photographs of Renaissance jewels, with descriptive notes.

763 Dickinson, Joan Younger. THE BOOK OF DIAMONDS: THEIR HISTORY AND ROMANCE FROM ANCIENT INDIA TO MODERN TIMES. New York: Crown Publishers, 1965.

Very interesting and well-illustrated survey of diamonds, their uses, significance, and history.

764 Edwards, Rod. THE TECHNIQUE OF JEWELRY. New York: Charles Scribner's Sons, 1977.

Survey of the craftsmanship of jewelry making; somewhat specialized and technical but with many photographs, illustrations, and drawings of techniques valuable for any costumer working in this area.

765 Evans, Joan. A HISTORY OF JEWELLERY, 1100-1870. Boston: Book and Art, 1970.

Historical treatment of all types of jewelry within specific historical periods, for example, early Renaissance; with numerous drawings and 190 monochrome and 12 color photographs of examples; bibliography.

766 Flower, Margaret. VICTORIAN JEWELLERY. Rev. ed. New York:
A.S. Barnes and Co., 1973.

Chronologically arranged survey from 1837 to 1901, with numerous illustrations (10 color and 118 monochrome) with descriptions of all jewelry forms including children's; information
as to how and when specific articles were worn; the most
fashionable gems and metals; list of jewelers; glossary and bibliography.

767 Fregnac, Claude. JEWELRY FROM THE RENAISSANCE TO ART NOU-
VEAU. New York: G.P. Putnam's Sons, 1965.

Survey of jewelry with many illustrations, some in color.

768 Gere, Charlotte. AMERICAN AND EUROPEAN JEWELRY, 1830-1914.
New York: Crown Publishers, 1975.

Historical survey with 228 plates, many in color, of styles,
materials, and designers of jewelry.

769 _____. VICTORIAN JEWELLERY DESIGN. London: Henry Regnery Co.,
1973.

Detailed history of the designers and their sources of inspiration; with illustrations and brief biographies of the designers
and jewelers.

770 Giltay-Nijssen, J. JEWELRY. New York: Universe Books, 1964.

Brief overview of the history of jewelry, with selected photographs and drawings.

771 Gregorietti, Guido. JEWELRY THROUGH THE AGES. New York:
American Heritage Publishing Co., 1969.

Handsome volume with many excellent color photographs.

772 Heininger, Ernest A., and Heininger, Jean. THE GREAT BOOK OF
JEWELS. Boston: New York Graphic Society, 1974.

Impressive historical study of great value for the text and especially for beautiful and numerous illustrations; chapters on
special areas, such as sacred jewels, regalia, and ceremonial
jewelry.

773 Hejj-Detari, Angela. OLD HUNGARIAN JEWELRY. Budapest: Athen-
aeum Printing House, 1965.

Historical study with fifty photographs and descriptive notes.

Accoutrements & Special Categories

774 Higgins, Reynolds A. GREEK AND ROMAN JEWELLERY. London: Methuen and Co., 1961.

Thirty-three drawings in the text plus sixty-four plates providing excellent illustration of the subject, covering all types of jewelry articles.

775 Hinks, Peter. NINETEENTH CENTURY JEWELLERY. London: Faber and Faber, 1975.

Historical treatment, with seventy-two monochrome and ten color photographs in support of text.

776 Hoffman, Herbert, and Davidson, Patricia F. GREEK GOLD: JEWELRY FROM THE AGE OF ALEXANDER. Boston: Museum of Fine Arts, 1965.

Extensive exhibition catalog with photographs of 138 examples and detailed notes on each item.

777 Hughes, Graham. THE ART OF JEWELRY. New York: Viking Press, 1972.

Historical survey of the style, the artistry, and the technique of all types of jewelry from ancient to modern times; numerous illustrations and fifty-two excellent color plates.

778 INTERNATIONAL EXHIBITION OF MODERN JEWELLERY, 1890-1961: WORSHIPFUL COMPANY OF GOLDSMITHS. Westerham, Engl.: Westerham Press, 1961.

Monochrome photographs of 101 examples of jewelry articles; with notes.

779 Janson, Dora Jane. FROM SLAVE TO SIREN: THE VICTORIAN WOMAN AND HER JEWELRY: FROM NEOCLASSIC TO ART NOUVEAU. Durham, N.C.: Duke University Museum of Art, 1971.

Exhibition catalog with 183 illustrations, color and monochrome, of all types of female jewelry during the period from cameos to Tiffany and Lalique; including background material and extensive notes on the displayed articles.

780 Jessup, Ronald. ANGLO-SAXON JEWELLERY. New York: International Publications Service, 1974.

Specialized study with descriptions and illustrations of ancient jewelry of Britain.

781 JEWELLERY OF THE ANCIENT WORLD. Toronto: Royal Ontario Museum of Archaeology, 1953.

Historical study with illustrations of jewelry items from several ancient cultures.

782 Jones, William. FINGER-RING LORE: HISTORICAL, LEGENDARY, ANECDOTAL. 1890. Reprint. Detroit: Singing Tree Press, 1968.

Historical survey of all types of rings and their uses: eccelesiastical, wedding, memorial, mortuary, token, and motto; interesting superstitions about rings; many drawings of all examples.

783 Kuzel, Vladislav. A BOOK OF JEWELRY. Prague, Czechoslovakia: Artia, 1962.

Historical survey with numerous illustrations, some in color.

784 Lesley, Parker. FABERGE: A CATALOG OF THE LILLIAN THOMAS PRATT COLLECTION OF RUSSIAN IMPERIAL JEWELS. Richmond: Virginia Museum, 1976.

Three hundred twenty-eight color photographs of examples of the noted craftsman's work: jewelry, boxes, frames, vessels, among many others.

785 _____. RENAISSANCE JEWELS AND JEWELLED OBJECTS FROM THE MELVIN GUTMAN COLLECTION. Baltimore: Museum of Art, 1968.

Illustrated exhibition catalog with numerous color and monochrome photographs of items from the collection.

786 McCarthy, James Remington. RINGS THROUGH THE AGES: AN INFORMAL HISTORY. New York: Harper and Brothers, 1945.

Informative historical survey of ring superstitions, types of rings, wedding rings, and ring craft; with only a few selected photographs; index and bibliography.

787 Maxwell-Hyslop, K.R. WESTERN ASIATIC JEWELLERY, C. 3000-612 B.C. London: Methuen and Co., 1971.

Thorough investigation into unique study, with 259 black-and-white photographs of examples.

788 MODERN JEWELRY: AN INTERNATIONAL SURVEY, 1890-1963. New York: Crown Publishers, 1963.

Survey with excellent text and 415 plates, many in color.

789 Mourey, Gabriel, and Vallance, Aymer. ART NOUVEAU JEWELLERY AND FANS. New York: Dover Publications, 1973.

Discussion of jewelry and fans arranged by country of manufacture, with 110 multifigured plates, some in color.

790 Muller, Priscilla E. JEWELS IN SPAIN, 1500-1800. New York: Hispanic Society of America, 1972.

Historical survey with many (265) illustrations and photographs
of all types of Spanish jewelry.

791 Needler, Winifred. JEWELRY OF THE ANCIENT NEAR EAST. Toronto:
Royal Ontario Museum, 1966.

Brief presentation of information chiefly on Egyptian, Mesopotamian, and Assyrian jewelry types, with fourteen photographs
and several line drawings; selected bibliography.

792 Ostier, Marianne. JEWELS AND THE WOMAN: THE ROMANCE,
MAGIC AND ART OF FEMININE ADORNMENT. New York: Horizon
Press, 1958.

Treatment of jewelry arranged by types, with sections on the
etiquette of wearing jewelry and on the care of jewels.

793 Oved, Sah. THE BOOK OF NECKLACES. London: Arthur Barker,
1953.

Sixty-two monochrome photographs of selected necklaces covering the period from the Stone Age to the modern era, with descriptive and historical material on usage, manufacture, symbolism, and materials; glossary and bibliography.

794 Sataloff, Joseph, and Richards, Alison. THE PLEASURE OF JEWELERY
AND GEMSTONES. London: Octopus Books, 1975.

Brief text of historical survey with excellent color photographs.

795 Sommer, Elyse. CONTEMPORARY COSTUME JEWELRY. New York:
Crown Publishers, 1974.

Interesting aspect of modern jewelry; illustrations.

796 Turner, Ralph. CONTEMPORARY JEWELRY: A CRITICAL ASSESSMENT,
1945-1975. New York: Van Nostrand Reinhold Co., 1976.

Many (378) photographs, colored and black and white, of
modern jewelry involving new styles, such as body jewelry;
valuable for costumers.

797 Wilkinson, Alex. ANCIENT EGYPTIAN JEWELLERY. London: Methuen
and Co., 1971.

Survey of ancient Egyptian jewelry from the predynastic period
to the end of the twenty-sixth dynasty; illustrations.

798 Willcox, Donald J. BODY JEWELRY: INTERNATIONAL PERSPECTIVES.
Chicago: Henry Regnery Co., 1973.

Works by fifty-eight craftsmen with new styles, techniques,
and materials for jewelry for the body; illustrated by monochrome and color photographs; many novel uses of jewelry for
the costumer.

799 _____. NEW DESIGN IN JEWELRY: New York: Van Nostrand Reinhold Co., 1970.

Over two hundred examples of modern jewelry from leading
world designers; excellent assessment of the position of modern
jewelry artistically.

G. JUVENILE COSTUME

See also 216, 339, 424, 453

800 Bayne-Powell, Rosamond. THE ENGLISH CHILD IN THE EIGHTEENTH
CENTURY. London: John Murray, 1939.

Dated but complete coverage of all phases of the subject,
with fifteen primary-source illustrations; list of books read and
consulted.

801 Brooke, Iris. ENGLISH CHILDREN'S COSTUME SINCE 1775. London:
Adam and Charles Black, 1930.

Historical survey with author's descriptions and drawings.

802 Buck, Anne M., and Cunnington, Phillis E. CHILDREN'S COSTUME IN
ENGLAND FROM THE 14TH TO THE END OF THE 19TH CENTURY.
New York: Barnes and Noble, 1965.

Excellent century-by-century survey of the subject based entirely on primary sources with thirty-two plates and many
drawings; bibliography; good source.

803 Collard, Ellen. FROM TODDLER TO TEENS: AN OUTLINE OF CHILD-
REN'S CLOTHING CIRCA 1780 TO 1930. Burlington, Ont.: 1973.

Overview of children's clothing in Canada during the period;
eighteen multifigured plates of drawings of juvenile garments
and accessories, with detailed descriptions and notes; six dia-

grams of patterns for children's garments; list of museums, bibliography.

804 Garland, Madge. THE CHANGING FACE OF CHILDHOOD. London: Hutchinson, 1963.

Numerous monochrome and some color illustrations and useful details of juvenile costume.

805 Jackson, Margaret. WHAT THEY WORE: A HISTORY OF CHILDREN'S DRESS. London: G. Allen and Unwin, 1936.

Somewhat dated history of children's costume, with drawings by O.H. Lister; bibliography.

806 Laver, James. CHILDREN'S FASHIONS IN THE 19TH CENTURY. London: B.T. Batsford, 1951.

Sixteen color juvenile fashion plates with background material and descriptive notes.

807 MacQuoid, Percy. CHILDREN'S COSTUME FROM THE GREAT MASTERS: XVIII AND EARLY XIX CENTURIES. London: Medici Society, 1923.

Eleven color plates with brief descriptive comment on the costume.

808 _____. FOUR HUNDRED YEARS OF CHILDREN'S COSTUME FROM THE GREAT MASTERS, 1400-1800. London: Medici Society, 1923.

Thirty-four color plates, with notes depicting the historical development of children's costume over a period of four hundred years.

809 Manchester Art Galleries. THE GALLERY OF ENGLISH COSTUME PICTURE BOOK: NUMBER SEVEN: CHILDREN'S COSTUME. Manchester: 1959.

Twenty monochrome photographs of costumes in the collection of the galleries, with a general introduction and specific descriptions of each plate.

810 Moore, Doris Langley. THE CHILD IN FASHION. London: B.T. Batsford, 1953.

Forty-nine photographs of period children's costumes dating from about 1810 to 1911; modeled by children, with author's notes and descriptions.

811 Ovenden, Graham, and Melville, Robert. VICTORIAN CHILDREN.
New York: St. Martin's Press, 1972.

One hundred forty photographs of children during the Victorian
period.

H. MAKEUP AND HAIRSTYLES

See also 30, 148, 543, 564, 664, 743, 751, 1486

812 ALBUM OF HISTORICAL COIFFURES WITH TECHNICAL DESCRIPTIONS
AND BIOGRAPHICAL DETAILS. London: R. Hovenden, 1911.

Mostly deals with eighteenth-century hairstyles.

813 Andrews, William. AT THE SIGN OF THE BARBER'S POLE: STUDIES
IN HIRSUTE HISTORY. 1904. Reprint. Detroit: Singing Tree Press,
1969.

Coverage of the entire history of masculine hair adornment and
styling, from beards through wigs to the moustache; primary-
source illustrations (27 in black and white); very interesting
and informative text.

814 Angeloglou, Maggie. A HISTORY OF MAKE-UP. New York: Macmillan Co., 1970.

Authoritative tracing of the use of adornments and makeup
from the primitives to the moderns, with good illustrations in
color and in black and white; index and bibliography.

815 Arnold, Janet. PERUKES AND PERIWIGS: A SURVEY, 1660-1740.
London: Her Majesty's Stationery Office, 1970.

Booklet of twenty-seven primary-source illustrations and photographs of actual wigs; valuable, useful study.

816 Asser, Joyce. HISTORIC HAIRDRESSING. London: Sir Isaac Pitman
and Sons, 1966.

Somewhat simplified survey, from the Egyptians to the moderns,
of hairstyles; with fifty-eight pages of illustrations by the author; glossary and index.

817 Botham, M., and Sharrad, L. MANUAL OF WIGMAKING. London:
Heinemann, 1969.

Well-illustrated and practical guide to the craft of making
wigs; glossary.

Accoutrements & Special Categories

818 Boublik, Vlastimil. ART OF MAKE-UP FOR STAGE, TELEVISION, AND FILM. New York: Pergamon Publishing Co., 1968.

   Comprehensive study of the problems of makeup in various production media; ample drawings and illustrations.

819 Brunn-Rasmussen, Ole Jens, and Petersen, Grete. MAKE-UP COSTUMES AND MASKS FOR THE STAGE. New York: Sterling Publishing Co., 1978.

   Simplified approaches, directions, diagrams, and photographs for younger readers of disguises, costume tricks, basic makeup, paper masks, and cardboard disguises; glossary; list of supplies; index.

820 Buchman, Herman. STAGE MAKEUP. New York: Watson-Guptill Publications, 1972.

   Coverage advances beyond basic makeup to deal with intricate problems clearly; excellent photographs and diagrams for beards, wigs, prostheses, black performers' makeup, and special effects; especially good sections on creating Restoration makeup, stout and lean effects; includes a course of study in makeup using the book.

821 Charles, Ann, and DeAnfrasio, Roger. THE HISTORY OF HAIR: AN ILLUSTRATED REVIEW OF HAIR FASHIONS FOR MEN THROUGHOUT THE AGES . . . PLUS A COMPLETE GUIDE TO HAIR CARE FOR MEN. New York: Bonanza Books, 1970.

   Very well illustrated historical survey with much greater emphasis on modern styles and hair care.

822 Cooley, Arnold J. THE TOILET IN ANCIENT AND MODERN TIMES WITH A REVIEW OF THE DIFFERENT THEORIES OF BEAUTY AND COPIOUS ALLIED INFORMATION SOCIAL, HYGIENIC, AND MEDICAL. 1866. Reprint. New York: Burt Franklin, 1970.

   Very interesting historical source regarding the procedures and manners of the important social practice of the toilet.

823 Cooper, Wendy. HAIR: SEX, SOCIETY, SYMBOLISM. New York: Stein and Day Publishers, 1971.

   Illustrated discussion of the facts and fictions of hair in historic and modern times.

824 Cordwell, Miriam, and Rudoy, Marion. THE COMPLETE BOOK OF HAIR STYLES, BEAUTY AND FASHION. Illustration by Lisa Cialli. New York: Crown Publishers, 1971.

Historical survey of hairdressing and practices of beauty.

825 _____. HAIR DRESSING AND FASHION: PRINCIPLES AND RELATION-
SHIPS. 5th ed. New York: Crown Publishers, 1970.

Weak on historical aspects but good coverage of modern hairstyles in photographs and diagrams.

826 Corson, Richard. FASHIONS IN HAIR: THE FIRST FIVE THOUSAND
YEARS. London: Peter Owen, 1965.

Estensive treatment of fashions in hairstyle, based on primary-
source material in the text and with 136 illustrations and 167
plates of drawings of many examples of hairstyles year by year;
also coverage of facial hair, beards, and moustaches.

827 _____. FASHIONS IN MAKEUP FROM ANCIENT TO MODERN TIMES.
New York: Universe Books, 1972.

Historical survey in twenty-two chapters of the use and result
of cosmetics, supported by a wide range and number (251) of
primary-source material; index and bibliography.

828 _____. STAGE MAKEUP. 5th ed. Englewood Cliffs, N.J.: Prentice-
Hall, 1975.

Complete treatment of all phases of makeup selection and application, including useful makeup color charts, a picture
collection, drawings of period hairstyles, and racial differences;
glossary.

829 Cox, James Stevens. HAIR AND BEAUTY SECRETS OF THE 17TH CEN-
TURY WITH A 17TH CENTURY CONVERSATION BETWEEN A PERIWIG-
MAKER AND A GENTLEMAN BUYING A WIG. Guernsey: Toucan
Press, 1971.

Interesting, brief booklet of period quotations concerning such
beauty problems as making hair grow, removing hair, and curl-
ing and dyeing hair.

830 _____, ed. THE WIGMAKERS' ART IN THE 18TH CENTURY. London:
Hairdressers' Technical Council, 1965.

Translation of 1776 treatise on the art of wigmaking, with illustrations of techniques and procedures employed.

831 _____, trans. THE ART OF THE WIGMAKER BY MONS DE GARSAULT.
London: Hairdressers' Technical Council, 1961.

Translation of one of the earliest (1767) treatises on the art
of wigmaking; original illustrations.

832 De Zemler, Charles. ONCE OVER LIGHTLY: THE STORY OF MAN AND HIS HAIR. New York: Charles De Zemler, 1939.

Interesting chapter detailing the history of barbering; valuable collection of 120 primary-source illustrations of the developments in male hairstyles; index and bibliography.

833 Frazier, Gregory, and Frazier, Beverly. THE BATH BOOK. San Francisco: Troubador Press, 1973.

Introductory historical survey and assessment of the practice of the bath in contemporary society.

834 Garland, Madge. THE CHANGING FACE OF BEAUTY: FOUR THOUSAND YEARS OF BEAUTIFUL WOMEN. New York: M. Barrows Co., 1957.

Survey of changing concepts of feminine beauty as seen through a very large number of primary-source illustrations, portraits generally, of outstanding women who were considered beautiful in their times.

835 Genders, Roy. A HISTORY OF SCENT. London: Hamish Hamilton, 1972.

Valuable survey of an interesting and unique subject, with a few selected illustrations.

836 Gunn, Fenja. THE ARTIFICIAL FACE: A HISTORY OF COSMETICS. Newton Abbot, Engl.: David and Charles, 1973.

History of cosmetics from antiquity, with century-by-century survey of ideals of beauty, moral attitudes, and social conditions; forty-two illustrations and thirty-six line drawings; bibliography.

837 Gwatkin, Nina W. YORUBA HAIRSTYLES: A SELECTION OF HAIRSTYLES IN SOUTHERN NIGERIA. Lagos, Nigeria: National Museum, 1971.

Text, photographs, diagrams, and drawings creating the distinctive hairstyles of the country.

838 Hyman, Rebecca. COMPLETE GUIDE TO WIGS AND HAIRPIECES. New York: Grosset and Dunlap, 1968.

Good, simple guide to fashion wigs and hairpieces; of use to costumers dealing with modern wigs.

839 Kehoe, Vincent, Jr. THE TECHNIQUE OF FILM AND TELEVISION MAKE-UP. New York: Communication Arts Books, 1958.

Detailed and thorough treatment of the use of makeup in specific situations of film and television, with attention to racial and national types, historical characters, fantasy figures, special effects, casting molds, and hair goods.

840 Keyes, Jean. A HISTORY OF WOMEN'S HAIRSTYLES, 1500-1965. London: Methuen and Co., 1967.

Selected line drawings showing historical development in female hairstyles, with brief commentaries; including section of accessories and jewelry for various hairstyles.

841 Lu, Steve. FACE PAINTING IN CHINESE OPERA. Singapore: M.P.H. Publications, 1968.

Short history of the development of the art of face painting, followed by eighty color illustrations of typical characters in Chinese opera and each character's particular face painting, with notes on its development and symbolism; invaluable for designing in this area.

842 Melvill, Harald. MAGIC OF MAKEUP BY THE MOST MODERN METHODS FOR STAGE AND SCREEN. New York: Theatre Arts Books, 1967.

Adequate illustration of standard techniques, with information on national characteristics and hair, among other subjects.

843 Napolitan, M. Louis. SIX THOUSAND YEARS OF HAIR STYLING. New York: Polygraphic Co., 1939.

Brief historical survey with selected illustrations.

844 Palchoudhuri, Ila. ANCIENT HAIR STYLES OF INDIA. Calcutta: Rupa, 1973.

Drawings and photographs of sixteen hairstyles, with historical and descriptive notes.

845 Perrottet, Philippe. PRACTICAL STAGE MAKE-UP. New York: Reinhold Book Corp., 1967.

Basic guide to makeup, somewhat simplified and geared more to English use; with diagrams and photographs of actors in makeup.

846 Raynes, John R. MEN'S HAIRDRESSING. London: Heinemann, 1972.

Somewhat technical, but illustration and diagrams of current styles, hairpieces, and styling procedures of value.

847 Reynolds, Reginald. BEARDS: THEIR SOCIAL STANDING, RELIGIOUS INVOLVEMENTS, DECORATIVE POSSIBILITIES, AND VALUE IN OFFENCE AND DEFENCE THROUGH THE AGES. New York: Doubleday and Co., 1949.

Readable survey of the subject, with much historical background; no illustrations.

848 Saito, R. JAPANESE COIFFURE. Translated by M.G. Mori. Tokyo: Japanese Government Railways, 1939.

Brief text with illustrations of style of Japanese hair dressings; many illustrations of costume as well.

849 Severn, William. THE LONG AND SHORT OF IT: FIVE THOUSAND YEARS OF FUN AND FURY OVER HAIR. Illustrated by Vana Earle. New York: David McKay, 1971.

Lighthearted treatment of historical developments of hairstyles illustrated with drawings by Earle, as well as many primary-source illustrations and caricatures.

850 Smith, C. Ray, ed. THE THEATRE CRAFTS BOOK OF MAKEUP, MASKS, AND WIGS. Emmaus, Pa.: Rodale Press, 1974.

Collection of articles from THEATRE CRAFTS magazine dealing primarily with the design and techniques of makeup and masks; well illustrated.

851 Strong, Roy. THE MASQUE OF BEAUTY. London: Dramrite Printers, n.d.

Exhibition catalog with portraits, some in color, illustrating concepts of period beauty in respective historical periods.

852 Terry, Ellen, and Anderson, Lynne. MAKEUP AND MASKS. New York: Richards Rosen Press, 1971.

Survey of very basic theatrical makeup; very general introduction to masks; limited number of illustrations, diagrams, and photographs, all in black and white.

853 Vail, Gilbert. A HISTORY OF COSMETICS IN AMERICA. New York: Toilet Goods Association, 1947.

Brief, unillustrated historical account of the developments in cosmetics from the American Indians to modern times.

854 Westmore, Michael G. THE ART OF THEATRICAL MAKEUP FOR STAGE AND SCREEN. New York: McGraw-Hill Book Co., 1973.

Numerous diagrams and drawings plus clear directions on a
wide variety of topics including advanced special character,
hair and wigs, prostheses, and casting and molding.

855 THE WIGMAKER IN EIGHTEENTH-CENTURY WILLIAMSBURG: AN AC-
COUNT OF HIS BARBERING, HAIRDRESSING, AND PERUKE-MAKING
SERVICES, AND SOME REMARKS ON WIGS OF VARIOUS STYLES.
Williamsburg, Va.: Colonial Williamsburg, 1921.

Interesting booklet covering the technique and styles of the
century; some illustrated materials.

856 Williams E. Neville. POWDER AND PAINT: A HISTORY OF THE ENG-
LISHWOMAN'S TOILET: ELIZABETH I-ELIZABETH II. London: Longmans,
Green and Co., 1957.

Very readable, informative, and authoritative survey drawn
from numerous primary sources and supported with plates of
cosmetic accessories: combs, mirrors, perfume bottles, and so
forth; also dealing with hairstyles and hairdressing.

857 Woodforde, John. THE STRANGE STORY OF FALSE HAIR. New York:
Drake Publishers, 1972.

Lighthearted and urbane treatment of wigs, supported with line
drawings and some primary-source material; notes and index.

858 Young, Douglas. THE ABC OF STAGE MAKE-UP FOR MEN. New York:
Samuel French, 1976.

859 _____. THE ABC OF STAGE MAKE-UP FOR WOMEN. New York:
Samuel French, 1976.

Format of looseleaf cards to describe and illustrate basic essen-
tials of makeup; coverage of selected character types.

860 Zimmerman, Ray. THE BEARD BOOK: AN IDENTIFICATION AND
MAINTENANCE MANUAL OF BEARDS AND OTHER FACE HAIR. Dan-
bury, Conn.: Rampage Press, 1974.

Practical guide for various types of beards and their styling
and care; drawings and diagrams.

I. MASKS

See also 154, 288, 289, 291, 300, 307, 309, 318, 355, 359, 360, 370, 536,
819, 850, 852

861 Baranski, Matthew. MASK MAKING: CREATIVE METHODS AND TECH-
NIQUES. Worcester, Mass.: Davis Publications, 1954.

Concise directions with illustrations for the construction of
many types of masks, from paperbag to body masks; section on
various examples of world masks; helpful source.

862 Benda, W.T. MASKS. New York: Watson-Guptill Publications, 1944.

Step-by-step instructions for making masks, plus photographs of
many types of masks and a chapter on theatrical masks.

863 Bihalji-Merin, Oto. GREAT MASKS. New York: Harry N. Abrams,
1971.

Excellently photographed, extensive collection of masks from
the primitive to the modern, with chapters on masks in ritual,
drama, humor, tragedy, war, death, labor, and art; especially
outstanding section of modern faces; very valuable source.

864 Cummings, Richard. 101 MASKS: FALSE FACES AND MAKE-UP FOR
ALL AGES, ALL OCCASIONS. New York: David McKay, 1966.

Geared for young readers, but with many techniques for making masks, from simple to complex, and with examples of many
types of character masks.

865 FACE COVERINGS. New York: Museum of Contemporary Crarts, 1970.

Many imaginative examples of uses of masks, makeup, and
hair.

866 Gregor, Joseph. MASKS OF THE WORLD: AN HISTORICAL AND
PICTORIAL SURVEY OF MANY TIMES AND LANDS. 1937. Reprint.
New York: Benjamin Blom, 1968.

Two hundred fifty-five monochrome plates not only of masks
but also of paintings and figures wearing masks; some very unusual examples such as fool sceptres and door knockers.

867 Herold, Erich. THE ART OF AFRICA: TRIBAL MASKS FROM NAPR-
STEK MUSEUM, PRAGUE. London: Paul Hamlyn, 1967.

Numerous quality photographs of many African masks; valuable
for any costumer designing in this area.

868 Hunt, Kari, and Carlson, Bernice Wells. MASKS AND MASK MAKERS.
New York: Abingdon Press, 1961.

Explanation of masks, descriptions and illustrations of many
types of specific masks as well as a useful step-by-step method,
with pictures, for making masks.

869 Kniffin, Herbert Reynolds. MASKS. Peoria, Ill.: Manual Arts Press, 1931.

History, description, and illustration of many types of masks, as well as directions for mask-making techniques, with clear diagrams and instructions.

870 Laliberte, Norman, and Mogelon, Alex. MASKS, FACE COVERINGS AND HEADGEAR. New York: Van Nostrand Reinhold Co., 1973.

Historical survey of masks and headgear, followed by contemporary photographs of the subject; valuable in giving examples of imaginative masks crafted from new and different materials.

871 Lewis, Shari, and Oppenheimer, Lillian. FOLDING PAPER MASKS. New York: E.P. Dutton Co., 1965.

Primarily for young readers, but interesting techniques for paper masks which might be of use to costumers.

872 Lommel, Andreas. MASKS: THEIR MEANING AND FUNCTION. New York: McGraw-Hill Book Co., 1972.

Extensively illustrated examination of world masks of many cultures, from Africa to Japan, and their uses from ceremonial to theatrical, with an attempt to discover meanings and functions.

873 Macgowan, Kenneth, and Rosse, Herman. MASKS AND DEMONS. London: Martin Hopkinson and Co., 1924.

Collection of monochrome photographs of world masks.

874 THE MASK: ALL PEOPLES--ALL TIMES. Antwerp, Belgium: Musee Royal des Beaux Arts, 1956.

Exhibitions catalog with many monochrome photographs of masks from various countries and historical periods.

875 Noma, Seiroku. ARTS AND CRAFTS OF JAPAN: MASKS. Rutland, Vt.: Charles E. Tuttle Co., 1957.

Concise text and plates of forty-six masks, sixteen in color.

876 Peters, Joan, and Sutcliff, Anna. CREATIVE MASKS FOR STAGE AND SCHOOL. Boston: Plays, 1975.

Illustrations of over two hundred masks, with explanations of construction techniques; many stimulating ideas for masks; useful to costume designer.

877 Powell, Doane. MASKS AND HOW TO MAKE THEM. Pelham, N.Y.: Bridgman Publishers, 1948.

Directions and diagrams for making more realistic masks.

878 Ray, Dorothy Jean. ESKIMO MASKS: ART AND CEREMONY. Seattle: University of Washington Press, 1967.

Seventy multifigured plates of photographs and drawings of masks, plus textual description of the uses and symbolism of the masks.

879 Shalleck, Jamie. MASKS. New York: Viking Press, 1973.

Well-illustrated examination of masks in three sections: decorative, protective, and professional.

880 Slade, Richard. MASKS AND HOW TO MAKE THEM. London: Faber and Faber, 1964.

Condensed treatment of techniques for making papier mache, animal, buckram, and portrait masks; with information on constructing big heads and headdresses; diagrams and photographs.

881 Snook, Barbara. MAKING MASKS FOR SCHOOL PLAYS. Boston: Plays, 1972.

Concise text and drawings of design and construction of masks.

882 Sorell, Walter. THE OTHER FACE: THE MASK IN THE ARTS. Indianapolis: Bobbs-Merrill Co., 1973.

Many illustrations (121, with 11 in color) in text covering the development of the mask and how it has been used in such areas as puppetry, theatre, dance, painting and sculpture, caricature, and death.

883 Stephens, Michael. MEXICAN FESTIVAL AND CEREMONIAL MASKS. Berkeley and Los Angeles: University of California Press, 1976.

Condensed booklet with twelve black-and-white photographs with descriptive notes; brief chapters on the history, form, materials, and uses of Mexican masks.

884 Underwood, Leon. MASKS OF WEST AFRICA. London: Alec Tiranti, 1952.

Brief introduction to the use, decoration, and construction of masks, plus forty-eight monochrome photographs of African masks.

885 Wherry, Joseph H. INDIAN MASKS AND MYTHS OF THE WEST. New York: Funk and Wagnalls Co., 1969.

Valuable photographs and descriptions of many types of masks.

J. MEN'S WEAR

See also 46, 244, 1498, 1580, 1707

886 Amies, Hardy. ABC OF MEN'S FASHIONS. London: Newnes, 1964.

Guide to terms used in men's clothing in early 1960s, with eight monochrome plates.

887 Bacharach, Bert. BOOK FOR MEN. New York: A.S. Barnes and Co., 1953.

Guidebook to male fashion and fashion practices of the period of the early 1950s.

888 Bennett-England, Rodney. DRESS OPTIONAL: THE REVOLUTION IN MENSWEAR. London: Dufour Editions, 1968.

Contemporary designs of male fashions and item-by-item treatment of latest developments in total masculine wardrobe, with numerous photographs and drawings.

889 THE BOOK OF PUBLIC SCHOOL OLD BOYS, UNIVERSITY, NAVY, ARMY, AIR FORCE, AND CLUB TIES. Introduction by James Laver. London: Seeley Service and Co., 1968.

Twenty-seven color plates of ties by category.

890 Carlson, Peter, and Wilson, William. MANSTYLE: THE GQ GUIDE TO FASHION, FITNESS, AND GROOMING. New York: Clarkson N. Potter, 1977.

Excellent illustration of contemporary male dress.

891 Cohn, Nik. TODAY THERE ARE NO GENTLEMEN: THE CHANGES IN ENGLISHMEN'S CLOTHES SINCE THE WAR. London: Weidenfeld and Nicolson, 1971.

Thirty-seven photographs illustrating points in the text about changes in male dress.

892 Eelking, Hermann Baron von. DAS BILDNIS DES ELEGANTEN MANNES: EIN ZYLINDERBREVIER VON WERTHER BIS KENNEDY. Berlin: F.A. Herbig Verlag, 1962.

Pictorial survey of male fashion; German text but helpful in
illustrating the changes.

893 Esquire Magazine. FASHIONS FOR MEN. New York: Harper and Row,
Publishers, 1966.

Survey of various options in male garments and accessories of
the 1960s; well illustrated.

894 Franzerro, Carlo Maria. BEAU BRUMMELL: HIS LIFE AND TIMES.
London: Alvin Redman, 1958.

Biographical study of fashion innovator and style setter; twenty-
one illustrations.

895 Giafferri, Paul Louis Victor de. THE HISTORY OF FRENCH MASCULINE
COSTUME. New York: Fairchild Publications, 1927.

Ten parts in portfolio edition, with each part containing eight
pages of text and ten plates, covering such topics as togas
and tunics, monastic garb, doublets and jerkins, Napoleonic
costume, and dress of the fops of the Second Empire.

896 Halls, Zillah. MEN'S COSTUME, 1580-1750. London: Her Majesty's
Stationery Office, 1970.

Catalog of male garments in the London Museum's costume collection, with a brief textual historical summary and over twenty
photographs of actual garments and costume items.

897 _____. MEN'S COSTUME, 1750-1800. London: Her Majesty's Stationery Office, 1973.

Continuation of format of entry 896; brief general description
and twenty-two monochrome plates of various male garments
and accessories from the costume collection of the London Museum.

898 Laver, James. DANDIES. London: Weidenfeld and Nicolson, 1968.

Tracing of the rise of dandyism with Brummell and its effects
on masculine attire to the New Dandyism of Carnaby Street;
well illustrated with primary material; index and bibliography.

899 Men's Wear. HISTORY OF MEN'S WEAR INDUSTRY, 1890-1950. New
York: Fairchild Publications, 1950.

Sixtieth anniversary issue of MEN'S WEAR magazine, with pictorial survey of changes in men's fashions during the period.

900 _____. SEVENTY-FIVE YEARS OF FASHION: New York: Fairchild Publications, 1965.

Decade-by-decade survey of the development of all types of male attire from 1890 to 1965 through period advertisements, drawings, and photographs, with a special feature on men's wear in the cinema.

901 Moers, Ellen. THE DANDY: BRUMMELL TO BEERBOHM. London: Secker and Warbug, 1960.

Historical survey of the Century of the Dandies, including chapters on Brummell, Bulwer, Disraeli, D'Orsay, Thackeray, Dickens, Barbey d'Aurevilly, Baudelaire, and Beerbohm; fifteen primary-source monochrome illustrations; notes and index.

902 OF MEN ONLY: A REVIEW OF MEN'S AND BOYS' FASHIONS, 1950-1975. Introduction by Elizabeth Ann Coleman. Brooklyn, N.Y.: Brooklyn Museum, 1975.

Color plates and photographs of examples of types of male garments and accessories popular during the period.

903 Price, H.P. WHEN MEN WORE MUFFS. London: J.M. Dent and Sons, 1936.

Illustrated survey of historical men's clothing.

904 Tenenbaum, Samuel. THE INCREDIBLE BEAU BRUMMELL. London: Thomas Yoseloff Publishers, 1967.

Biographical study with no illustrations.

K. MILITARIA

See also 27, 339, 341, 352, 398, 436, 457, 482, 485, 492, 495, 517, 603, 604

905 Abbott, P.E., and Tamplin, J.M.A. BRITISH GALLANTRY AWARDS. Garden City, N.Y.: Doubleday and Co., 1972.

Separate photographs, some in color, and full description of each award; index.

906 Anderson, Douglas N. SCOTS IN UNIFORM: THE MILITARY COSTUME OF SCOTLAND'S HORSE AND FOOT. Edinburgh: Holmes McDougall, 1972.

Descriptive notes of color paintings of the uniforms.

907 Angus, Ian. MEDALS AND DECORATIONS. New York: St. Martin's Press, 1973.

Broad survey with mostly black-and-white illustrations of world medals and decorations.

908 Ashdown, Charles Henry. BRITISH AND CONTINENTAL ARMS AND ARMOUR. 1909. Reprint. New York: Dover Publications, 1970.

Complete historical survey of all aspects of the subject, with many drawings and diagrams and some primary-source illustrative material.

909 _____. EUROPEAN ARMS AND ARMOUR. New York: Brussel and Brussel, 1967.

Numerous illustrations (450 engravings and 42 monochrome plates) covering the subject from prehistory to the introduction of gunpowder.

910 Barker, A.J. SOVIET ARMY UNIFORMS AND INSIGNIA, 1945-75. New York: Hippocrene Books, 1976.

Complete survey of the subject, with photographs and drawings.

911 Barnes, R. Money. THE BRITISH ARMY OF 1914: ITS HISTORY, UNIFORMS AND CONTEMPORARY CONTINENTAL ARMIES. London: Seeley Service and Co., 1968.

Survey of British army, with color plates by the author; bibliography.

912 _____. A HISTORY OF THE REGIMENTS AND UNIFORMS OF THE BRITISH ARMY. 6th ed. London: Seeley Service and Co., 1967.

Extensive text with color plates; bibliography.

913 _____. MILITARY UNIFORMS OF BRITAIN AND THE EMPIRE 1742 TO THE PRESENT TIME. London: Seeley Service and Co., 1960.

Historical survey illustrated with line drawings and color plates by the author.

914 _____. THE SOLDIERS OF LONDON. London: Seeley Service and Co., 1963.

Many color plates by the author.

915 Barnes, R. Money, et al. THE UNIFORMS AND HISTORY OF THE SCOTTISH REGIMENTS: BRITAIN, CANADA, AUSTRALIA, NEW ZEA-

Accoutrements & Special Categories

LAND, SOUTH AFRICA, 1625 TO THE PRESENT DAY. London: Seeley Service and Co., 1956.

Extensive informative textual survey with numerous illustrations, many in color.

916 Barthorp, Michael. CRIMEAN UNIFORMS: BRITISH INFANTRY. Whitstable, Engl.: Whitstable Lithographers, 1974.

Detailed text with 110 figures of primary-source material.

917 Blair, Calude. EUROPEAN AND AMERICAN ARMS, C. 1100-1850. New York: Bonanza Books, 1962.

Extensive illustration by sketches and photographs of swords and daggers, staff weapons, and projectiles.

918 _____. EUROPEAN ARMOUR CA 1066 TO CA 1700. London: B.T. Batsford, 1958.

Short historical survey with three hundred sketches and primary-source illustrations covering armor from major European countries during the period specified.

919 Bowling, A.H. SCOTTISH REGIMENTS AND UNIFORMS, 1660-1914. London: Almark, 1971.

Comprehensive textual coverage plus many line drawings and color plates.

920 Braddon, Russell. ALL THE QUEEN'S MEN: THE HOUSEHOLD CAVALRY AND THE BRIGADE OF GUARDS. New York: Hippocrene Books, 1977.

Historical survey of the origin and development of the guards from 1660 to the present, with eight color plates and numerous monochrome photographs.

921 Brosse, Jacques, and Lachouque, Henry. UNIFORMS ET COSTUMES DU 1ER EMPIRE. Paris: Bordas, 1972.

French text but extensive color plates of military and civil costume during Napoléon's First Empire.

922 Carman, William Y. BRITISH MILITARY UNIFORMS FROM CONTEMPORARY PICTURES: HENRY VIII TO THE PRESENT DAY. New York: Arco Publishing Co., 1957.

Detailed discussion of military uniforms according to the periods of the rule of the royal houses beginning with the Tudors in 1485 to the present; black-and-white and some color primary-source illustrations.

141

923 Castano, John B. THE NAVAL OFFICER'S UNIFORM GUIDE. Annapolis, Md.: Naval Institute Press, 1975.

    Rules and regulations of dress for naval officers, with illustrations.

924 Cimarelli, Aldo G. ARMS AND ARMOUR IN THE AGE OF CHIVALRY. London: Orbis Books, 1973.

    Textual survey and many (111) color photographs plus other illustrations.

925 Clammer, David. THE VICTORIAN ARMY IN PHOTOGRAPHS. New York: Hippocrene Books, 1975.

    One hundred forty-one photographs of military men and actions.

926 COLOUR GUIDE TO GERMAN ARMY UNIFORMS, 1933-1945. London: Arms and Armour Press, 1973.

    Basic guide with condensed descriptive material concerning uniforms and equipment.

927 Curtis, John Obed, and Guthman, William H. NEW ENGLAND MILITIA UNIFORMS AND ACCOUTREMENTS: A PICTORIAL SURVEY. Sturbridge, Mass.: Old Sturbridge Village Publications, 1971.

    General introduction with numerous monochrome photographs of every area, including headgear, swords, drums, belts, and equine equipment, as well as uniforms.

928 D'Ami, Rinaldo D., ed. WORLD UNIFORM IN COLOR: THE EUROPEAN NATIONS. 2 vols. London: Patrick Stephens, 1968-69.

    Survey of world uniforms country by country, with color drawings.

929 Davis, Brian L. GERMAN UNIFORMS AND INSIGNIA, 1933-1945. New York: World Publishing Co., 1972.

    Three hundred seventy-five drawings and photographs of uniforms of every rank, with descriptive notes and commentary; color charts of shoulder knots and straps and collar patches; terms for garments given in German as well as in English; bibliography.

930 Dawson, Malcolm. UNIFORMS OF THE ROYAL ARMOURED CORPS. London: Almark, 1974.

    Color paintings, line drawings, and photographs, plus descriptive text.

931 Dickens, Gerald. THE DRESS OF THE BRITISH SAILOR. London: Her Majesty's Stationery Office, 1957.

Pictorial survey of sailor uniforms from about 1300 to 1956, with general background and specific descriptive notes; depictions of badges and insignia.

932 DRESS REGULATIONS FOR THE ARMY, 1900. Newton Abbot, Engl.: David and Charles, 1970.

Very detailed document for accurate and thorough study of English army regulations in 1900.

933 Fabb, John. THE VICTORIAN AND EDWARDIAN ARMY FROM OLD PHOTOGRAPHS. London: B.T. Batsford, 1975.

Good pictorial source with 154 period photographs.

934 Fitzsimons, Bernard, ed. HERALDRY AND REGALIA OF WAR. New York: Beekman House, 1973.

One hundred sixty illustrations, mostly in color.

935 Forestier, Amedee. THE ROMAN SOLDIER: SOME ILLUSTRATIONS REPRESENTATIVE OF ROMAN MILITARY LIFE WITH SPECIAL REFERENCE TO BRITAIN. London: Adam and Charles Black, 1928.

Dated source but nevertheless valuable, with fifteen color and forty-six monochrome plates with textual notations of the whole range of ancient Roman military costume.

936 Funcken, Liliane, and Funcken, Fred. ARMS AND UNIFORMS: THE NAPOLEONIC WARS. 2 vols. London: Ward Lock and Co., 1973.

Volume 1: the French, British, Prussian and Spanish armies; volume 2: the French Garde Imperiale, the armies of the German Duchies, Switzerland, Italy, Spain, Poland, Sweden, Austria, and Russia; excellent paintings and descriptive notes in extensive text.

937 GERMAN MILITARY UNIFORMS AND INSIGNIA, 1933-1945. Old Greenwich, Conn.: WE, 1967.

Very detailed guide with monochrome paintings and drawings and charts of insignia, medals, and decorations.

938 Glover, Michael. AN ASSEMBLAGE OF INDIAN ARMY SOLDIERS AND UNIFORMS FROM THE ORIGINAL PAINTINGS BY THE LATE CHATER PAUL CHATER. London: Perpetua Press, 1973.

Forty color plates of various representative uniforms, plus detailed descriptions and smaller detail paintings; glossary and bibliography.

939 Haythornthwaite, Philip J. UNIFORMS OF THE CIVIL WAR, 1861-1865. New York: Macmillan Co., 1976.

Sixty-four color plates with descriptions, plus drawings of insignia and accessories.

940 _____. UNIFORMS OF THE NAPOLEONIC WARS IN COLOR, 1796-1814. London: Blandford Press, 1973.

Historical introduction; eighty multifigured color plates with detailed descriptive notes of the uniforms and line drawings of equipment and accessories.

941 _____. UNIFORMS OF THE RETREAT FROM MOSCOW, 1912, IN COLOR. New York: Hippocrene Books, 1976.

Sixty-four multifigured plates and numerous line drawings; historical introduction and descriptive notes.

942 _____. UNIFORMS OF WATERLOO IN COLOR, 16-18 JUNE 1815. New York: Hippocrene Books, 1974.

Color paintings and line drawings, with descriptive notes of the costumes of the armies at the Battle of Waterloo.

943 _____. WORLD UNIFORMS AND BATTLES, 1815-1850. New York: Hippocrene Books, 1976.

Detailed textual descriptions and notes for sixty-four multifigured color plates of uniforms.

944 Holding, T.H. UNIFORMS OF THE BRITISH ARMY, NAVY AND COURT. 1894. Reprint. New York: Theatre Arts Books, 1975.

Reprint of manual detailing and illustrating all aspects of most English uniforms, including some servant liveries in the last decade of the nineteenth century; sketches of details such as braid and buttons; section of patterns for reconstructing the costumes; very valuable source.

945 Howell, Edgar M. UNITED STATES ARMY HEADGEAR 1855-1902: CATALOG OF UNITED STATES ARMY UNIFORMS IN THE COLLECTIONS OF THE SMITHSONIAN INSTITUTION, II. Washington, D.C.: Smithsonian Institution Press, 1975.

Excellent historical survey, with primary-source illustrative material throughout.

946 Howell, Edgar M., and Kloster, Donald E. UNITED STATES ARMY HEADGEAR TO 1854: CATALOG OF UNITED STATES ARMY UNIFORMS IN THE COLLECTION OF THE SMITHSONIAN INSTITUTION. Washington, D.C.: Smithsonian Institution Press, 1969.

947 Jarrett, Dudley. BRITISH NAVAL DRESS. London: J.M. Dent and Sons, 1960.

> Historical survey dating from before 1748 to the modern day, with over one hundred illustrations and photographs detailing developments in British naval uniforms.

948 Johnson, David F. UNIFORM BUTTONS: AMERICAN ARMED FORCES, 1784-1948. 2 vols. Watkins Glen, N.Y.: Century House, 1948.

> Extensive information and illustration of specialized topic.

949 Kannik, Preben. MILITARY UNIFORMS IN COLOR. Edited by William Y. Carman. New York: Macmillan Co., 1968.

> Survey of military costume from the Swiss Guards to the modern, with numerous clear paintings and a textual description of each illustrated uniform.

950 Kemp, Alan. THE BRITISH ARMY IN THE AMERICAN REVOLUTION. London: Almark, 1973.

> Detailed guide to uniforms and equipment, with line drawings and eight color plates of uniforms.

951 Kemp, Peter. THE BRITISH SAILOR: A SOCIAL HISTORY OF THE LOWER DECK. London: J.M. Dent and Sons, 1970.

> Historical survey with selected primary-source illustrations; main emphasis on the text.

952 Kerrigan, Evans E. AMERICAN WAR MEDALS AND DECORATIONS. New York: Viking Press, 1964.

> Coverage of three areas: decorations, service awards, and civilian awards; descriptions, drawings, and some color photographs; bibliography.

953 Kingsland, P.W. BRITISH MILITARY UNIFORMS AND EQUIPMENT. London: Guinness Button Holdings, 1971.

> Eight of the author's paintings, plus many photographs of primary material; excellent text; four series: series 1: The Light Cavalry, 1798-1855; series 2: The Household Division, 1750-1970; series 3: The Highland Corps; and series 4: The Rifle Regiments.

Accoutrements & Special Categories

954 Kredel, Fritz, and Todd, Frederick P. SOLDIERS OF THE AMERICAN ARMY, 1775-1954. Chicago: Henry Regnery Co., 1954.

Thirty-two multifigured paintings of selected representative military uniforms from 1775 to 1954, including some women's uniforms; descriptive commentary on each uniform; bibliographical references.

955 Large, Hector. LE COSTUME MILITAIRE A TRAVERS LES AGES. 3 vols. Paris: Editions Arc-En-Ciel, 1949.

Extensive folio collection of color paintings of French military uniforms.

956 Laver, James. BRITISH MILITARY UNIFORMS. London: Penguin Books, 1948.

Brief text and twenty-four color plates of selected British military uniforms from 1742 to 1895.

957 Lawson, Cecil C.P. A HISTORY OF THE UNIFORMS OF THE BRITISH ARMY. 5 vols. 1940. Reprint. London: Kaye and Ward, 1969.

Volume 1: FROM THE BEGINNINGS TO 1760; volume 2: GEORGE I-GEORGE III; volume 3: 1760-1782; volume 4: 1797-1815; volume 5: 18TH INTO 19TH CENTURY; definitive, richly illustrated source on all aspects of British army uniforms; standard source.

958 Lefferts, Charles M. UNIFORMS OF THE AMERICAN, BRITISH, FRENCH, AND GERMAN ARMIES IN THE WAR OF THE AMERICAN REVOLUTION, 1775-1783. Edited by Alexander J. Wall. Old Greenwich, Conn.: WE, n.d.

Careful description of many uniforms and dress attire of the fighting armies in the American Revolution, with a number of paintings by the author reproduced in monochrome, unfortunately; informative text.

959 Lord, Francis A., and Wise, Arthur. UNIFORMS OF THE CIVIL WAR. New York: Thomas Yoseloff Publisher, 1970.

Primary-source photographs and some line drawings supporting discussion of uniforms of both factions in the Civil War; index and bibliography.

960 Luard, John. A HISTORY OF THE DRESS OF THE BRITISH SOLDIER FROM THE EARLIEST PERIOD TO THE PRESENT TIME. 1852. Reprint. London: Frederick Muller, 1971.

Detailed historical account, with fifty multifigured plates of
uniforms dating from 78 A.D. to 1852.

961 Martin, Paul. ARMS AND ARMOUR FROM THE 9TH TO THE 17TH CEN-
TURY. Rutland, Vt.: Charles E. Tuttle Co., 1968.

Textual survey of European armor and weaponry with 237 monochrome, 20 color plates, and 21 line drawings.

962 _____. EUROPEAN MILITARY UNIFORMS: A SHORT HISTORY. London: Spring Books, 1963.

Numerous color plates and line drawings accompanying a brief
but concise survey of the entire field of European military costume from the point at which it assumed a distinctive uniform
appearance.

963 May, R.N. THE DRESS OF NAVAL OFFICERS. London: Her Majesty's
Stationery Office, 1966.

Chronological history, with sixty-nine plates of examples of
uniforms from 1748 to 1959, including such topics as collars
and buttons; chart giving relative ranks.

964 MILITARY UNIFORMS IN AMERICA: THE ERA OF THE AMERICAN REV-
OLUTION 1755-1795. San Rafael, Calif.: Presidio Press, 1974.

Sponsored by the Company of Military Historians; detailed color
paintings (61) with concise descriptions of uniforms worn by
British regular, German, Continental, French, and American
units during the war; glossary.

965 Miller, Nathan. THE U.S. NAVY: AN ILLUSTRATED HISTORY. New
York: American Heritage Publishing Co., 1977.

Interesting text and valuable collection of numerous pictorial
sources, some in color, of the history of the navy; many excellent photographs of uniformed sailors and officers.

966 Mollo, Andrew. ARMY UNIFORMS OF WORLD WAR TWO. London:
Blandford Press, 1973.

Extensive textual descriptions of the uniforms of the armies of
all nations involved; 207 color illustrations by Malcolm McGregor
of uniforms, plus plates of helmets, weapons, and other accessories, with descriptive notes; bibliography.

967 _____. NAVAL, MARINE, AND AIR FORCE UNIFORMS OF WORLD
WAR TWO. New York: Macmillan Co., 1975.

Accoutrements & Special Categories

Extensive textual coverage with 248 color paintings, with notes, of uniforms and some weapons and accessories.

968 _____. UNIFORMS OF THE S.S. 6 vols. London: Stanwill Press, 1972.

Comprehensive study of the uniforms of all units of the German S.S.

969 Mollo, John. MILITARY FASHION: A COMPARATIVE HISTORY OF THE UNIFORMS OF THE GREAT ARMIES FROM THE 17TH CENTURY TO THE FIRST WORLD WAR. New York: G.P. Putnam's Sons, 1972.

Folio edition entirely illustrated with color plates (146) showing key points in the development of European military fashion and cross-references between the most sartorially important armies of Britain, France, Austria, Prussia, Russia, and the United States; bibliography.

970 _____. UNIFORMS OF THE AMERICAN REVOLUTION IN COLOR. New York: Macmillan Co., 1975.

Detailed text with 208 color paintings of uniforms and additional color plates of weapons, flags, ornaments, and badges.

971 _____. UNIFORMS OF THE ROYAL NAVY DURING THE NAPO-LEONIC WARS. London: Hugh Evelyn, 1965.

Series of plates by the author showing the different patterns of uniforms worn by officers of the Royal Navy during the years of the Napoleonic wars, 1793-1815, drawn in the form of silhouettes.

972 _____. UNIFORMS OF THE SEVEN YEARS WAR, 1756-1763. New York: Hippocrene Books, 1977.

General background plus description of eight specific engagements; 172 multifigured plates of uniforms of all involved major European powers, with descriptive notes of illustrated uniforms.

973 Mollo, John, and Mollo, Boris. UNIFORMS AND EQUIPMENTS OF THE LIGHT BRIGADE. London: Historical Research Unit, 1968.

Sixty-one pages of illustrations, some colored; bibliography.

974 Nelson, Henry Loomis. UNIFORMS OF THE UNITED STATES ARMY. New York: Thomas Yoseloff Publishers, 1959.

Excellent textual introduction to forty-four watercolor paintings by H.A. Ogden of uniforms dating from 1774 to 1888, with descriptive notes on each.

975 Nicholson, J.B.R. MILITARY UNIFORMS: THE SPLENDOR OF THE PAST. London: Orbis Books, 1973.

General survey with 120 color plates of uniforms from many countries and historical periods; glossary.

976 Nickel, Helmut. WARRIORS AND WORTHIES: ARMS AND ARMOR THROUGH THE AGES. New York: Atheneum, 1969.

Extensive range of authentic examples excellently photographed and with succinct descriptions.

977 Norman, Vesey. ARMS AND ARMOUR. London: Octopus Books, 1972.

More than 130 illustrations in color and black and white, with succinct text covering such topics as mail, tournaments, and weapons.

978 North, Rene. MILITARY UNIFORMS, 1686-1918. New York: Grosset and Dunlap, 1970.

Brief textual description and limited number of illustrations, though all are in color; presentation of a sampling of uniforms from every major world conflict from the Great Northern War to World War I.

979 Periocoli, Ugo. 1815: THE ARMIES AT WATERLOO. New York: Charles Scribner's Sons, 1973.

Author's research as costume designer for the film WATERLOO, with historical narrative of the battle as well as paintings of the uniforms, accessories, insignia, and weaponry of the French, Anglo-Netherlands, and Prussian armies.

980 Peterson, Harold L. THE BOOK OF THE CONTINENTAL SOLDIER BEING A COMPLEAT ACCOUNT OF THE UNIFORMS, WEAPONS, AND EQUIPMENT WITH WHICH HE LIVED AND FOUGHT. Harrisburg, Pa.: Stackpole Co., 1968.

Coverage of the total subject, with each area fully expanded and illustrated with photographs and sketches; inclusion of patterns for a few basic uniforms.

981 Preston, Antony, et al. NAVIES OF THE AMERICAN REVOLUTION. Englewood Cliffs, N.J.: Prentice-Hall, 1975.

Extensive chapter on the men in the navies; complete descriptive notes on primary-source depiction of uniforms and many color paintings of uniformed seamen; chapters on the maritime war, the ships, the weapons, and the navies.

Accoutrements & Special Categories

982 Rankin, Robert H. MILITARY HEADDRESS: A PICTORIAL HISTORY OF
MILITARY HEADGEAR FROM 1660 to 1914. New York: Hippocrene
Books, 1976.

Photographs of 230 headdresses, with complete descriptions of
each.

983 _____. UNIFORMS OF THE ARMY. New York: G.P. Putnam's Sons,
1967.

Careful historical survey of the uniforms of the army of the
United States from the Revolution to the present, with illustrative documentation; attention to female uniforms, West Point
cadet uniform, insignia, and accessories; reproductions of paintings from the U.S. Army's THE AMERICAN SOLDIER series.

984 Reid, William. ARMS THROUGH THE AGES. New York: Harper and
Row, Publishers, 1976.

Authoritative survey with many drawings and diagrams of arma-
ment, weapons, armor, and accessories.

985 Robinson, H. Russell. THE ARMOUR OF IMPERIAL ROME. New York:
Charles Scribner's Sons, 1975.

Specialized, complete study, extensively illustrated and documented (531 plates), covering all facets of the topic; index
and bibliography.

986 _____. SHORT HISTORY OF JAPANESE ARMOUR. London: Her Majesty's Stationery Office, 1965.

Brief treatment of specialized topic, but valuable for its
uniqueness.

987 Robles, Philip K. UNITED STATES MILITARY MEDALS AND RIBBONS.
Rutland, Vt.: Charles E. Tuttle Co., 1971.

Color photographs and descriptions of 139 medals and ribbons.

988 Rosignoli, Guido. ARMY BADGES AND INSIGNIA OF WORLD WAR II.
2 vols. New York: Macmillan Co., 1975.

Highly specialized material with color plates of many badges
and insignia. See also entry 989.

989 _____. ARMY BADGES AND INSIGNIA SINCE 1945. New York:
Macmillan Co., 1975.

Continuation of entry 988.

990 Saxtorph, Niels M. WARRIORS AND WEAPONS OF EARLY TIMES IN COLOR. New York: Macmillan Co., 1972.

Many color paintings (422) of military uniforms and armaments from the Egyptians (2000 B.C.) to the Europeans (1700 A.D.), with textual descriptions.

991 Smitherman, P.H. CAVALRY UNIFORMS OF THE BRITISH ARMY. London: Hugh Evelyn, 1962.

Twenty color paintings in folio edition of selected cavalry uniforms dating from 1705 to 1960, with a brief description and historical background.

992 _____. INFANTRY UNIFORMS OF THE BRITISH ARMY. 2 vols. London: Hugh Evelyn, 1971.

Folio edition with twenty color paintings and rather complete descriptive notes; volume 1: 1660-1790; and volume 2: 1790-1846.

993 _____. UNIFORMS OF THE SCOTTISH REGIMENTS. London: Hugh Evelyn, 1963.

Twenty detailed color paintings of selected uniforms from 1730 to 1959, with brief descriptions and historical background.

994 _____. UNIFORMS OF THE YEOMANRY REGIMENTS, 1783-1911. London: Hugh Evelyn, 1967.

Brief preface to twenty color paintings, and descriptive notes on each.

995 Stadden, Charles. THE LIFE GUARDS: DRESS AND APPOINTMENTS, 1660-1914. London: Almark, 1971.

Paintings, sketches, and photographs, with a condensed textual summary and descriptions.

996 Steffan, Randy. THE HORSE SOLDIER 1776-1943: THE UNITED STATES CAVALRYMAN: HIS UNIFORMS, ARMS, ACCOUTREMENTS, AND EQUIPMENTS. 4 vols. Norman: University of Oklahoma Press, 1977.

Volume 1: 1776-1850; volume 2: 1851-1880; volume 3: 1881-1916; volume 4: 1917-1943; historical survey in text, with numerous clear line drawings and sketches by the author covering all aspects of the subject; helpful color plates of uniforms; index.

997 Strachan, Hew. BRITISH MILITARY UNIFORMS, 1768-1796: THE DRESS OF THE BRITISH ARMY FROM OFFICIAL SOURCES. London: Arms and Armour Press, 1975.

Extremely detailed coverage of the uniforms of the army, general officers and staff, household cavalry, cavalry of the line, foot guards, infantry, Royal Artillery, and engineers and artificers, based upon actions of the official regulating authorities, with sixty-seven monochrome primary-source plates.

998 Tantum, William H., and Hoffschmidt, E.J. NAVY UNIFORMS, INSIGNIA AND WARSHIPS OF WW II. Old Greenwich, Conn.: WE, 1968.

Chiefly illustrated, quite complete volume covering all facets of naval forces of nations involved in World War II.

999 Taylor, Arthur. DISCOVERING FRENCH AND GERMAN MILITARY UNIFORMS. Bucks, Engl.: Shire Publications, 1974.

Condensed survey of characteristic features of each country's uniforms, with sixty-seven line drawings.

1000 Taylor, Gertrude R., and Smith, Cleveland H. UNITED STATES SERVICE SYMBOLS. New York: Duell, Sloan and Pearce, 1942.

Large amount of material although somewhat dated; many color charts; numerous drawings.

1001 Thorburn, William A. FRENCH ARMY REGIMENTS AND UNIFORMS FROM THE REVOLUTION TO 1870. Harrisburg, Pa.: Stackpole Books, 1969.

General introduction to the subject, with fifty-six monochrome and two color illustrations of uniforms, with complete descriptions.

1002 _____. UNIFORM OF THE SCOTTISH INFANTRY, 1740 TO 1900. London: Her Majesty's Stationery Office, 1970.

Thirty-three illustrations, some in color, with descriptive notes.

1003 Tily, James C. THE UNIFORMS OF THE UNITED STATES NAVY. New York: Thomas Yoseloff Publisher, 1964.

Very well documented and illustrated study with attention to insignia and accessories as well as uniforms.

1004 Todd, Frederick P. CADET GRAY: A PICTORIAL HISTORY OF LIFE AT WEST POINT AS SEEN THROUGH ITS UNIFORMS. New York: Sterling Publishing Co., 1955.

Excellent coverage in the text, drawings,and photographs showing all aspects of West Point uniform and accessories.

1005 Toman, Karel. A BOOK OF MILITARY UNIFORMS AND WEAPONS: AN ILLUSTRATED SURVEY OF MILITARY DRESS, ARMS AND PRACTICE THROUGH THE AGES. Translated by Alice Denesova. London: Paul Hamlyn and Allan Wingate, 1964.

Coverage of many lesser detailed periods, countries, and types; quite richly illustrated with 227 sketches by the author.

1006 UNIFORM REGULATIONS FOR THE ARMY OF THE UNITED STATES, 1861. Reprint. Washington, D.C.: Smithsonian Institution Press, 1961.

Reprint of 1861 publication with thirty-six official photographs of various uniforms.

1007 Warner, Richard, ed. NAPOLEON'S ENEMIES. London: Osprey Publishing Co., 1977.

Excellent pictorial record of uniforms, weaponry, and accessories of the armies of the countries opposing Napoleon.

1008 Wilkinson, Frederick J. BATTLE DRESS: A GALLERY OF MILITARY STYLE AND ORNAMENT. Garden City, N.Y.: Doubleday and Co., 1970.

Survey of military dress from ancient to modern times, with 32 color plates and 217 monochrome illustrations.

1009 _____. MILITARIA. London: Ward Lock and Co., 1969.

Valuable treatment, with numerous illustrations of military accessories, including such items as medals, helmets, and weapons; list of military museums; index and bibliography.

1010 Wilkinson-Latham, Robert. CRIMEAN UNIFORMS. Dorking, Engl.: Adlard and Con, 1973.

Seventy-five plates of primary-source material with detailed text of uniforms of the armies engaged in the Crimean War.

1011 _____. SCOTTISH MILITARY UNIFORMS. New York: Hippocrene Books, 1975.

Broad survey with fifty photographs, drawings, and paintings.

1012 Wilkinson-Latham, Robert, and Wilkinson-Latham, Christopher. CAVALRY UNIFORMS OF BRITAIN AND THE COMMONWEALTH. New York: Macmillan Co., 1970.

Survey of cavalry uniforms, with general introduction and color plates of accessories and equipment as well as uniforms.

1013 _____ . INFANTRY UNIFORMS INCLUDING ARTILLERY AND OTHER SUPPORTING CORPS OF BRITAIN AND THE COMMONWEALTH, 1855-1939, IN COLOR. New York: Macmillan Co., 1970.

> General introduction, plus detailed descriptive notes, for ninety-six multifigured plates of uniforms, weapons, accessories, and medals.

1014 _____ . INFANTRY UNIFORMS INCLUDING ARTILLERY AND OTHER SUPPORTING TROOPS OF BRITAIN AND THE COMMONWEALTH, 1742-1855, IN COLOR. New York: Macmillan Co., 1970.

> Companion volume to previous entry; detailed notes for ninety-six color multifigured plates.

1015 Windrow, Martin, ed. MEN-AT-ARMS SERIES. London: Osprey Publishing Co., 1972-77.

> Series of sixty-eight booklets dealing with military encounters in many countries and historical periods; extensive illustrative materials on uniforms, armaments, insignia, and accessories in each volume of the series; entries 1016-84 are numbers in the series:

AMERICAN SUBJECTS (see entry 1015)

1016 Katcher, Philip. THE AMERICAN INDIAN WARS, 1860-1890. 1977.

1017 _____ . THE AMERICAN PROVINCIAL CORPS. 1976.

1018 _____ . THE AMERICAN WAR, 1812-1814. 1974.

1019 _____ . THE ARMY OF NORTHERN VIRGINIA. 1976.

1020 _____ . THE ARMY OF THE POTOMAC. 1976.

1021 _____ . THE BRITISH ARMY IN NORTH AMERICA, 1775-1783. 1974.

1022 _____ . THE MEXICAN-AMERICAN WAR, 1846-1848. 1976.

1023 May, Robin. WOLFE'S ARMY. 1974.

1024 Selby, John. THE IRON BRIGADE. 1973.

1025 _____ . THE UNITED STATES CAVALRY. 1974.

1026 _____ . THE UNITED STATES MARINE CORPS. 1973.

1027 Slaughter, Frank G. THE STONEWALL BRIGADE. 1976.

1028 Windrow, Martin. MONTCALM'S ARMY. 1976.

1029 Young, Peter. GEORGE WASHINGTON'S ARMY. 1972.

BRITISH REGIMENTS (see entry 1015)

1030 Blaxland, Gregory. THE BUFFS. 1976.

1031 Carman, William Y. THE ROYAL ARTILLERY. 1976.

1032 Grant, Charles. THE BLACK WATCH. 1976.

1033 _____. COLDSTREAM GUARDS. 1976.

1034 _____. THE ROYAL SCOTS GREYS. 1976.

1035 Lawford, James. THE 30TH PUNJABIS. 1976.

1036 McClure, W. THE ARGYLL AND SUTHERLAND HIGHLANDERS. 1976.

1037 Nicholson, J.B. THE GURKHA RIFLES. 1976.

1038 Sheppard, Allan. THE CONNAUGHT RANGERS. 1976.

1039 _____. THE KING'S REGIMENT. 1976.

1040 Wilkinson-Latham, Christopher. THE ROYAL GREEN JACKETS. 1976.

1041 _____. THE SOUTH WALES BORDERERS. 1976.

MISCELLANEOUS SUBJECTS (see entry 1015)

1042 Miller, Douglas. THE LANDKNECHTS. 1976.

1043 Seaton, Albert. THE COSSACKS. 1976.

1044 Simkins, Michael. THE ROMAN ARMY FROM CAESAR TO TRAJAN. 1974.

1045 Wilkinson-Latham, Robert. THE ROYAL NAVY, 1790-1970. 1977.

1046 Windrow, Martin. THE FRENCH FOREIGN LEGION. 1973.

1047 Wise, Terence. MEDIEVAL EUROPEAN ARMIES, 1300-1500. 1976.

1048 Young, Peter. THE ARAB LEGION. 1976.

1049 _____. ENGLISH CIVIL WAR ARMIES. 1976.

Accoutrements & Special Categories

NAPOLEONIC WARS (see entry 1015)

1050 Bukhari, Emir. NAPOLEON'S CUIRASSIERS AND CARABINIERS. 1977.

1051 _____. NAPOLEON'S DRAGOONS AND LANCERS. 1976.

1052 _____. NAPOLEON'S LINE CHASSEURS. 1977.

1053 Cassin-Scott, Jack. SCANDINAVIAN ARMIES IN THE NAPOLEONIC WARS. 1976.

1054 Grant, Charles. FOOT GRENADIERS OF THE IMPERIAL GUARD. 1976.

1055 Lawford, James. WELLINGTON'S PENINSULAR ARMY. 1973.

1056 Pivka, Otto von. THE BLACK BRUNSWICKERS. 1976.

1057 _____. KING'S GERMAN LEGION. 1974.

1058 _____. NAPOLEON'S GERMAN ALLIES. 2 vols. 1976.

1059 _____. NAPOLEON'S POLISH TROOPS. 1974.

1060 _____. PORTUGUESE ARMY OF THE NAPOLEONIC WARS. 1977.

1061 _____. SPANISH ARMIES OF THE NAPOLEONIC WARS. 1976.

1062 Seaton, Albert. AUSTRO-HUNGARIAN ARMY OF THE NAPOLEONIC WARS. 1976.

1063 _____. RUSSIAN ARMY OF THE NAPOLEONIC WARS. 1973.

1064 Wilkinson-Latham, Robert. NAPOLEON'S ARTILLERY. 1976.

1065 Young, Peter. BLUECHER'S ARMY. 1973.

1066 _____. CHASSEURS OF THE GUARD. 1973.

OTHER NINETEENTH-CENTURY CAMPAIGNS (see entry 1015)

1067 McBride, Angus. THE ZULU WARS. 1976.

1068 Nicholson, J.B. BRITISH ARMY OF THE CRIMEA. 1974.

1069 Seaton, Albert. ARMY OF THE GERMAN EMPIRE, 1870-1888. 1976.

1070 _____. RUSSIAN ARMY OF THE CRIMEA. 1976.

1071 Wilkinson-Latham, Christopher. THE BOER WAR. 1977.

1072 _____. THE INDIAN MUTINY. 1977.

1073 Wilkinson-Latham, Robert. THE SUDAN CAMPAIGNS, 1881-1898. 1976.

THE SEVEN YEARS WAR (see entry 1015)

1074 May, Gerald. WOLFE'S ARMY. 1974.

1075 Seaton, Albert. THE AUSTRO-HUNGARIAN ARMY OF THE SEVEN YEARS WAR. 1976.

1076 _____. FREDERICK THE GREAT'S ARMY. 1976.

1077 Windrow, Martin. MONTCALM'S ARMY. 1976.

WORLD WAR II (see entry 1015)

1078 Seaton, Albert. THE SOVIET ARMY. 1973.

1079 Warner, Philip. THE JAPANESE ARMY OF WORLD WAR II. 1973.

1080 Windrow, Martin. LUFTWAFFE AIRBORNE AND FIELD UNITS. 1973.

1081 _____. MONTGOMERY'S DESERT ARMY. 1977.

1082 _____. THE PANZER DIVISIONS. 1973.

1083 _____. ROMMEL'S DESERT ARMY. 1976.

1084 _____. THE WAFFEN SS. 1973.

1085 Windrow, Martin, and Embleton, Gerry. MILITARY DRESS OF NORTH AMERICA, 1665-1970. New York: Charles Scribner's Sons, 1973.

> Numerous primary-source illustrative materials of uniforms, accessories, insignia, and weaponry as well as 20 color plates and 100 monochrome photographs of multifigured soldiers from various periods, with descriptive notations of each; bibliography.

1086 _____. MILITARY DRESS OF THE PENINSULAR WAR. New York: Hippocrene Books, 1974.

> Historical descriptions of uniforms plus 100 color plates of uniforms, weaponry, and accessories; bibliography.

Accoutrements & Special Categories

L. OCCUPATIONAL COSTUME INCLUDING ACADEMIC AND ECCLESIASTICAL COSTUME

See also 32, 213, 320, 339, 340, 341, 350, 398, 426, 436, 457, 469, 489, 517, 523, 742, 745, 772, 1485

1087 ACADEMIC COSTUME CODE AND CEREMONY GUIDE. Washington, D.C.: American Council on Education, 1960.

Guideline for contemporary academic costume: gowns (pattern, material, color, and trimmings); hoods (pattern, material, color, length, linings, and trimmings); and caps (material, form, color, and tassel); instruction for wearing academic costume and general color chart for academic disciplines.

1088 Blakeslee, Fred Gilbert. POLICE UNIFORMS OF THE WORLD. Norwood, Mass.: Plimpton Press, 1934.

Arranged by countries with descriptions and illustrations of police uniforms.

1089 _____. POSTAL UNIFORMS OF THE WORLD. Hollywood: Warner Publishing Co., 1937.

Specialized topic covered country by country in brief descriptive passages; lacking illustrations.

1090 _____. TRANSPORTATION UNIFORMS OF THE WORLD. Los Angeles: Murray and Gee, 1939.

Survey of transportation uniforms arranged by country.

1091 _____. UNIFORMS OF THE WORLD. New York: E.P. Dutton Co., 1929.

Careful description and illustration of military, police, civil, servant, and diplomatic costume for most major countries, with distinctions for ranks noted in color and insignia; primary-source photographs; bibliography.

1092 Boehn, Max von. POLIEZEI UND MODE. Berlin: Gersback, 1926.

German text but 124 illustrations of costume in this historical survey of police uniforms.

1093 Copeland, Peter F. WORKING DRESS IN COLONIAL AND REVOLUTIONARY AMERICA. Westport, Conn.: Greenwood Press, 1977.

Survey of working attire from 1710 to 1810, with complete text and numerous black-and-white drawings and primary-source illustrations; material arranged according to type of occupation; glossary and bibliography.

1094 Cramer, James. UNIFORMS OF THE WORLD'S POLICE WITH BRIEF DATA ON ORGANIZATION, SYSTEMS, AND WEAPONS. Springfield, Ill.: Charles C. Thomas, 1968.

Coverage of topic in countries from Abu Dhabi to Zambia, with illustrations, photographs, and descriptions of police uniforms, equipment, and accessories.

1095 Cunnington, Phillis E. COSTUME OF HOUSEHOLD SERVANTS FROM THE MIDDLE AGES TO 1900. New York: Barnes and Noble, 1974.

Excellent source with forty-eight plates, some in color, and ninety-seven drawings, plus a text with primary descriptive material; bibliography.

1096 Dearmer, Percy. THE ORNAMENTS OF THE MINISTERS. New ed. London: A.R. Mowbray and Co., 1920.

Forty-six plates and thirty-five figures plus diagrammatic sketches of garments, including primitive through modern items, usage, color significance, and ornamentation.

1097 Ditzel, Paul C. FIRE ENGINES, FIRE FIGHTERS: THE MEN, EQUIP-MENT, AND MACHINES, FROM COLONIAL DAYS TO THE PRESENT. New York: Crown Publishers, 1976.

Interesting text with many illustrations of uniformed firemen in two hundred plates, many in color.

1098 Ewing, Elizabeth. WOMEN IN UNIFORM THROUGH THE CENTURIES. Totowa, N.J.: Rowman and Littlefield, 1975.

Historical survey of female uniforms, beginning with the habits of medieval nuns and covering all other types of uniform dress in such areas as nursing, household service, military, academia, sports, industry, and civil service, with excellent illustrations; index and bibliography.

1099 Franklyn, Charles A.H. ACADEMICAL DRESS FROM THE MIDDLE AGES TO THE PRESENT DAY, INCLUDING LAMBUTH DEGREES. Lewes, Engl.: W.E. Baxter Co., 1970.

Survey of academic dress including gowns, hoods, and caps.

1100 Hargreaves-Mawdsley, W.N. A HISTORY OF ACADEMICAL DRESS IN EUROPE UNTIL THE END OF THE EIGHTEENTH CENTURY. Oxford, Engl.: Clarendon Press, 1963.

Scholarly treatment of the subject as it applies to universities in Europe, primarily those in Britain and Ireland, supported with some primary-source illustrative material.

1101 _____. A HISTORY OF LEGAL DRESS IN EUROPE UNTIL THE END OF THE EIGHTEENTH CENTURY. Oxford, Engl.: Clarendon Press, 1963.

Investigation of variations in legal dress throughout Europe, with twenty-one primary-source illustrations; glossary.

1102 Harrall, S.W. THE PICTORIAL HISTORY OF THE ROYAL CANADIAN MOUNTED POLICE. New York: McGraw-Hill Book Co., 1973.

Complete coverage of this specialized subject, with many illustrations of uniformed policemen.

1103 Haycraft, Frank W. THE DEGREES AND HOODS OF THE WORLD'S UNIVERSITIES AND COLLEGES. 4th ed. Revised and enlarged by E.W. Scobie Stringer. Cheshunt, Engl.: Cheshunt Press, 1948.

Valuable material and information as to colors, patterns, wearing procedures, degrees, and ornamentation of academic costume for major universities.

1104 Horn, Pamela. THE RISE AND FALL OF THE VICTORIAN SERVANT. Dublin: Gill and Macmillan; New York: St. Martin's Press, 1975.

Survey based on photographs and texts of period sources; excellent visual record of dress of household servants during the Victorian period; bibliography.

1105 Ireland, Marion P. TEXTILE ART IN THE CHURCH: VESTMENTS, PARA-MENTS, AND HANGINGS IN CONTEMPORARY WORSHIP, ART, AND ARCHITECTURE. Nashville, Tenn.: Abingdon Press, 1971.

Comprehensive survey of the role of textile art in the church; functions of vestments; color theory and symbolism; design principles and technique with more than three hundred illustrations (92 in color); glossary and index of denominational seals and insignia; clear drawings of vestment articles with both Western and Eastern church nomenclature; very valuable source.

1106 Lansdell, Avril. THE CLOTHES OF THE CUT: A HISTORY OF CANAL COSTUME. London: British Waterways Board, 1975.

Historical survey with numerous primary-source illustrations and sketches by the author of canal workers and inhabitants' costume, plus a general section on country and working clothes of the nineteenth century; bibliography.

1107 Lister, Margot. COSTUMES OF EVERYDAY LIFE: AN ILLUSTRATED HISTORY OF WORKING CLOTHES. Boston: Plays, 1972.

Historical survey of the subject from 900 to 1910, illustrated with 250 drawings and sketches of examples of working costume, with descriptive notes and general commentary; glossary, index, and bibliography.

1108 Lockmiller, David A. SCHOLARS ON PARADE: COLLEGES, UNIVERSITIES, COSTUMES AND DEGREES. New York: Macmillan Co.; London: Collier-Macmillan, 1969.

Historical survey of educational institutional garb with chapters on academic costumes and emblems; appendixes on colors of universities and abbreviations of degrees; selected bibliography.

1109 Macalister, R.A.S. ECCLESIASTICAL VESTMENTS: THEIR DEVELOPMENT AND HISTORY. London: Elliot Stock, 1896.

Quite dated source but one of few in the area with complete treatment and numerous drawings and descriptions; brief section on medieval university dress and its relationship to ecclesiastical dress; index and bibliography.

1110 McCarthy, Thomas Patrick. GUIDE TO THE CATHOLIC SISTERHOODS IN THE UNITED STATES. 4th ed. Washington, D.C.: Catholic University of America Press, 1958.

Information on costume of Catholic religious orders for women in the United States; illustrated.

1111 McCloud, Henry H. CLERICAL DRESS AND INSIGNIA OF THE ROMAN CATHOLIC CHURCH. Milwaukee: Bruce Publishing Co., 1948.

General chapters on ecclesiastical dress, materials, and colors, with sections on specific garments, for example, cassocks, footwear, and mozzettas; also information on accessories, thrones crosses, and ecclesiastical heraldry; line drawings and black-and-white photographs; helpful source.

1112 Mayer-Thurman, Christa C. RAIMENT FOR THE LORD'S SERVICE: A THOUSAND YEARS OF WESTERN VESTMENTS. Chicago: Art Institute, 1975.

Treatment of vestments in the Catholic, Anglican, and Protestant traditions; some patterns; historical developments, significance, and usage; extensive glossary, including technical textile terms; 186 monochrome photographs with notes; good pictorial survey.

Accoutrements & Special Categories

1113 Miller, Dwight. STREET CRIERS AND ITINERANT TRADESMEN IN
EUROPEAN PRINTS. Palo Alto, Calif.: Stanford University, 1970.

Catalog for exhibition of prints of street criers and itinerant
tradesmen by such European artists as Hogarth, Bosse, Rowland-
son, and Boucher, with historical and descriptive notes; bibliography.

1114 Nainfa, John H. COSTUME OF THE PRELATES OF THE CATHOLIC
CHURCH ACCORDING TO ROMAN ETIQUETTE. Baltimore: John
Murphy Co., 1909.

Outline of general principles followed by detailed discussion
and clear illustrations of the different parts of prelatical costume; also section on articles pertaining to prelatical dignity
such as crosses and rings; synoptic table of costumes of prelates; some color plates, brief discussion of academic dress.

1115 Norris, Herbert. CHURCH VESTMENTS: THEIR ORIGIN AND DEVEL-
OPMENT. London: J.M. Dent and Sons, 1949.

General historical background plus specific description of ecclesiastical garments and accessories, their origin, development,
and usage, with many primary-source illustrations, line drawings, and patterns for construction; 264 black-and-white illustrations and 16 color plates; index and bibliography.

1116 Pocknee, Cyril Edward. LITURIGICAL VESTURE: ITS ORIGINS AND
DEVELOPMENT. Westminster, Md.: Canterbury Press, 1961.

Clear depiction through primary-source illustration and diagram
of major vestures; several patterns.

1117 Roulin, Eugene A. VESTMENTS AND VESTURE: A MANUAL OF LI-
TURGICAL ART. London: Sands and Co.; St. Louis: B. Herder Co.,
1931.

Well-illustrated historical survey with drawings and photographs.

1118 Shaw, G.W. ACADEMICAL DRESS OF BRITISH UNIVERSITIES. Cambridge, Engl.: W. Heffer and Sons, 1966.

Complete treatment of dress on all academic levels and de-
gress, with drawings and patterns for construction.

1119 Towsen, John H. CLOWNS. New York: Hawthorn Books, 1976.

Very interesting historical survey of clowns and fools from early
periods to the modern times, with many illustrations and a separate section of color photographs of modern clowns; glossary,
index, and bibliography.

1120 Tyack, George S. HISTORIC DRESS OF THE CLERGY. London: William Andrews and Co., 1897.

Dated survey of articles of clerical costume, with historical development, descriptions, and selected illustrations.

1121 Victoria and Albert Museum. FIFTY MASTERPIECES OF TEXTILES. London: His Majesty's Stationery Office, 1951.

Booklet with several excellent photographs and descriptions of clerical costume.

1122 Welsford, Enid. THE FOOL: HIS SOCIAL AND LITERARY HISTORY. London: Faber and Faber, 1935.

Scholarly treatment of the subject of fools, with selected illustration.

1123 White, William Johnstone. WORKING CLASS COSTUME FROM SKETCHES OF CHARACTERS BY WILLIAM JOHNSTONE WHITE, 1818. Edited by Pamela Clabburn. London: Costume Society and Victoria and Albert Museum, 1971.

Collection of twenty-eight sketches showing nineteenth-century English working-class clothing, with descriptive notes.

1124 Wilson, Everett B. EARLY AMERICA AT WORK: A PICTORIAL GUIDE TO OUR VANISHING OCCUPATIONS. New York: A.S. Barnes and Co.; London: Thomas Yoseloff Publisher, 1963.

Excellent pictorial material of how people dressed when engaged in certain past occupations from servants to professionals; chapter on topical descriptive appellations for various occupations; chapters on pioneers, transportation, farm, local business, and unusual workers; helpful source.

M. REGALIA, CORONATION COSTUME, AND HERALDRY

See also 34, 50, 451, 468, 469, 470, 473, 475, 489, 758, 1336, 1392

1125 Allcock, Hubert. HERALDIC DESIGN: ITS ORIGINS, ANCIENT FORMS, AND MODERN USAGE. New York: Tudor Publishing Co., 1962.

Survey of the subject with many clearly drawn examples of heraldic badges, crests, and symbols.

1126 Boutell, Charles. BOUTELL'S HERALDRY. Rev. ed. Revised by C.W. Scott-Giles and J.P. Brooke-Little. London: Frederick Warne, 1966.

Compilation of heraldic works by Boutell published between
1863 and 1867; full coverage of the beginning, growth, and
use of heraldry, as well as other related topics: shield, tinc-
ture, lines, fields, crest, badge, mottoes, crowns, and coro-
nets; sections on knighthood orders; royal heraldry; official,
commonwealth, and foreign heraldry and flags; with 28 color
plates and 444 drawings; glossary, index, and bibliography;
useful source.

1127 Briggs, Geoffrey. NATIONAL HERALDRY OF THE WORLD. London:
J.M. Dent and Sons, 1973.

Seals and emblems in color with descriptions and historical
background of all independent states of the world as of Janu-
ary 1, 1971.

1128 Burke, John Bernard. THE GENERAL ARMORY OF ENGLAND, SCOT-
LAND, IRELAND AND WALES: COMPRISING A REGISTRY OF AMO-
RIAL BEARINGS FROM THE EARLIEST TO THE PRESENT TIME. 1884.
Reprint. Baltimore: Genealogical Press, 1969.

Background information on heraldry and armory in general;
glossary of elements and dictionary of terms and abbreviations;
general armory and the Royal Armory and Orders of Knighthood;
alphabetical listing of mottoes.

1129 Cassin-Scott, Jack, and Fabb, John. CEREMONIAL UNIFORMS OF
THE WORLD. New York: Hippocrene Books, 1973.

Eighty paintings and descriptions of ceremonial dress arranged
by country from Argentina to Yugoslavia; glossary and bibliography.

1130 Clephan, R. Coltman. THE TOURNAMENT: ITS PERIODS AND PHASES.
1919. Reprint. London: Frederick Ungar Publishing Co., 1967.

Well-documented, authoritative descriptions of the stagings,
manner, and dress of various types of tournaments, with primary-source monochrome illustrations; information on heraldry
and the regalia of the tournament.

1131 DEBRETT'S CORONATION GUIDE. London: Dean and Son, 1911.

Encyclopedia arrangement of subjects dealing with coronation
ceremonies, with many illustrations of costumes and accessories
for this occasion in addition to complete information on such
matters as processions and rank.

1132 De Le Bere, Ivan. THE QUEEN'S ORDER OF CHIVALRY. London:
Spring Books, 1964.

Quite informative study of general history of orders and such famous individual orders as Garter, Thistle, and Bath; coverage also of investitures and presentations, plus the wearing of orders; full illustration throughout.

1133 Dennys, Rodney. THE HERALDIC IMAGINATION. New York: Clarkson N. Potter, 1975.

Authoritative study of the origin, development, and uses of heraldry, with ample primary-source illustration.

1134 Fillitz, Herman. CROWN JEWELS AND ECCLESIASTICAL TREASURE CHAMBER. Translated by Geoffrey Holmes. Vienna: Kunsthistorisches Museum, 1973.

Complete description and historical background of 172 items in the collection, with 32 (8 in color) photographs of crowns, robes, portraits, and art treasures; listing of emperors of the Holy Roman Empire and houses of Habsburg and Habsburg-Lorraine.

1135 Fox-Davis, Arthur Charles. HERALDRY EXPLAINED. 1906. Reprint. Rutland, Vt.: Charles E. Tuttle Co., 1971.

Simplified explanations as to definition, component parts, uses, difference, and details of coats of arms, with 114 black-and-white drawings and sketches with descriptive notes of designs, elements, crests, and badges.

1136 Gautier, Leon. CHIVALRY. Edited by Jacques Levron. Translated by D.C. Dunning. New York: Barnes and Noble, 1965.

Introduction to origin and code of chivalry; steps to becoming a knight and training of knighthood; appendix on clothing and textiles; numerous monochrome primary-source illustrations; section on falconry.

1137 Gayre, Robert. HERALDIC CADENCY: THE DEVELOPMENT OF DIFFERENCING OF COATS OF ARMS FOR KINSMEN AND OTHER PURPOSES. London: Faber and Faber, 1961.

Historical study of which the greatest value is the number of illustrations, many in color.

1138 Grant, Francis J., ed. THE MANUAL OF HERALDRY: A CONCISE DESCRIPTION OF THE SEVERAL TERMS USED AND CONTAINING A DICTIONARY OF EVERY DESIGNATION IN THE SCIENCE. Edinburgh: John Grant, 1952.

Coverage of the origin, rights, elements, and design of coats of arms, with numerous line drawings; extensive dictionary of

heraldic terms, with illustrations; section of heraldry in connection with history, architecture, interior decoration, and
costume.

1139 Halls, Zillah. CORONATION COSTUME, 1685–1953. London: Her
Majesty's Stationery Office, 1973.

Exhibition catalog with historical survey of coronation costume
for various English kings and queens, with monochrome plates
of examples from 1821 to 1953.

1140 Hieronymussen, Paul. ORDERS AND DECORATIONS OF EUROPE IN
COLOR. New York: Macmillan Co., 1967.

Historical introduction with complete atlas of major orders and
decorations of twenty-nine European countries; illustrated with
450 color photographs, numerous line drawings, and detailed
descriptive notes.

1141 Holmes, Martin, and Sitwell, D.W. THE ENGLISH REGALIA: THEIR
HISTORY, CUSTODY AND DISPLAY. London: Her Majesty's Stationery
Office, 1972.

Detailed survey of English regalia with forty-three plates (24
in color) with a section on the history of the items of regalia
and the crown jewels.

1142 Hope, W.H. St. John. A GRAMMAR OF ENGLISH HERALDRY. 2d ed.
Revised by Anthony R. Wagner. Cambridge: Cambridge University Press,
1953.

Coverage of definition, origin, and development of heraldry
from the thirteenth through the nineteenth centuries; chapter
on heraldic nomenclature; glossary and reading list; 165 monochrome figures of badges, crests, and symbols.

1143 Jones, William. CROWN AND CORONATIONS: A HISTORY OF
REGALIA. 1902. Reprint. Detroit: Singing Tree Press, 1968.

Complete guide to the subject of coronations from the ancients
to 1900, with major emphasis on England but with limited
treatment of subject in other countries; ninety-one illustrations.

1144 Louda, Jiri. EUROPEAN CIVIC COATS OF ARMS. London: Paul
Hamlyn, 1966.

Historical origin and development of civic coats of arms, with
color examples alphabetically arranged.

Accoutrements & Special Categories

1145 Mericka, Vaclav. ORDER AND DECORATIONS. London: Paul Hamlyn, 1967.

Historical survey with section of 195 photographs, many in color, of clarity and detail showing costumes, badges, decorations, and medals.

1146 Milton, Peter. THE ENGLISH CEREMONIAL BOOK: A HISTORY OF ROBES, INSIGNIA AND CEREMONIES STILL IN USE IN ENGLAND. Newton Abbot, Engl.: David and Charles, 1972.

Very useful survey of subject with concise information regarding coronations and regalia; eight color plates and fifty-three line drawings; index and bibliography.

1147 Neubecker, Ottfried. HERALDRY: SOURCES, SYMBOLS AND MEANINGS. New York: McGraw-Hill Book Co., 1976.

Impressive volume of great importance for most aspects of heraldic design.

1148 Pakula, Marvin H. HERALDRY AND ARMOR OF THE MIDDLE AGES. New York: A.S. Barnes and Co.; London: Thomas Yoseloff Publisher, 1972.

Most complete encyclopedic treatment of the subject of heraldry in the Middle Ages: background, basic elements, crest, badges, mottoes, crowns, royal arms, ecclesiastical, civic, flags, college of arms, playing cards, tournaments, armor, and weapons, among other areas; extensive illustrations, drawings, and color paintings of crests; glossary, index, and bibliographies of heraldry, tournament, and armor; extremely useful source.

1149 Plumb, J.H. ROYAL HERITAGE: THE TREASURE OF THE BRITISH CROWN. New York: Harcourt Brace Jovanovich, 1977.

Extensively illustrated survey of collections of royalty including photographs of items of regalia and coronation.

1150 Purves, A.A. ORDERS AND DECORATIONS. London: Paul Hamlyn, 1972.

General survey and guide to orders and decorations, with color line drawings.

1151 Sitwell, H.D.W. THE CROWN JEWELS AND OTHER REGALIA IN THE TOWER OF LONDON. Edited by Clarence Winchester. London: Dropmere Press, 1953.

Eight color plates and thirty-two monochrome plates with detailed historical notes and descriptions even to the measurements; bibliography.

1152 Titman, George A., ed. DRESS AND INSIGNIA WORN AT HIS MAJESTY'S COURT. London: Harrison and Sons, 1937.

Encyclopedic coverage in minute detail of costume at court of all ranks and for all occasions, with photographs, paintings, and drawings in three sections: (1) Full Dress and Levee Dress, including Schedules of Household and Civil Uniforms; (2) Wearing of Insignia; and (3) Scale of Precedence, Court and Levee Regulations, Undress, Evening Dress, and so forth.

1153 Trendell, Herbert Arthur. DRESS WORN AT HIS MAJESTY'S COURT. London: Harrison and Sons, 1912.

Minute, complete survey of regulations for royal dress, with illustrations of costume, insignia, and accessories for all times and occasions and for all personages in attendance, from royalty to servants.

1154 Twining, Edward Francis. EUROPEAN REGALIA. London: B.T. Batsford, 1967.

Volume devoted mainly to crowns, sceptres, orbs, swords, and anointing vessels, among other items, with ninety-six multifigured plates, some in color.

1155 _____. A HISTORY OF THE CROWN JEWELS OF EUROPE. London: B.T. Batsford, 1960.

Excellent comprehensive textual survey of the histories and descriptions of crown jewels, with 230 multifigured plates illustrating the broad range of jewelry types and items from every European country.

1156 Wagner, Anthony. HERALDRY IN ENGLAND. London: Penguin Books, 1949.

Condensed introduction to the origin, development, design, and use of heraldic insignia; fifteen color plates of crests and badges and other heraldic devices.

1157 Warner, Oliver. THE CROWN JEWELS. Middlesex, Engl.: Penguin Books, 1951.

Very brief textual coverage, with sixteen color plates of paintings of the crown jewels.

1158 Werlich, Robert. ORDERS AND DECORATIONS OF ALL NATIONS: ANCIENT AND MODERN CIVIL AND MILITARY. Washington, D.C.: Quaker Press, 1965.

Country-by-country arrangement for presentation of the history; complete description and monochrome photographs of awards and decorations; several color plates; index and bibliography.

1159 Whitmore, William H. THE ELEMENTS OF HERALDRY CONTAINING AN EXPLANATION OF THE PRINCIPLES OF THE SCIENCE AND A GLOSSARY OF THE TECHNICAL TERMS EMPLOYED AND WITH AN ESSAY UPON THE USE OF COAT-ARMOR IN THE UNITED STATES. 1866. Reprint. Rutland, Vt.: Charles E. Tuttle Co., 1968.

Complete, concise discussion of the separate elements of coats of arms: shield, crest, supporters, mantling, and motto; glossary of terms and heraldic charges; discussion of heraldry in the United States; list of heraldic terms in English, French, and Latin.

N. SPECIAL OCCASION: BIRTHS, DEATHS, AND MARRIAGES

See also 321, 343, 344, 424, 438, 469, 489, 661, 663, 665

1160 Andersen, Ellen. BRUDEKJOLEN [Wedding dresses]. Copenhagen: National Museum, 1967.

Twenty-eight plates of wedding dresses.

1161 Argy, Josy, and Riches, Wendy. BRITAIN'S ROYAL BRIDES. London: St. Martin's Press, 1975.

Monochrome photographs and descriptions of seven complete royal weddings.

1162 Audiat, Pierre. VINGT-CINQ SIECLES DE MARIAGE. Paris: Hachette, 1961.

Survey of weddings through the ages, with monochrome and color plates.

1163 Carter, Charles F., ed. THE WEDDING DAY IN LITERATURE AND ART: A COLLECTION OF THE BEST DESCRIPTIONS OF WEDDINGS FROM THE WORKS OF THE WORLD'S LEADING NOVELISTS AND POETS, RICHLY ILLUSTRATED WITH REPRODUCTIONS OF FAMOUS PAINTINGS OF INCIDENTS OF THE NUPTIAL DAY. 1900. Reprint. Detroit: Singing Tree Press, 1969.

Accoutrements & Special Categories

Valuable descriptive and illustrative materials for costuming wedding scenes.

1164 Cunnington, Phillis E., and Lucas, Catherine. COSTUME FOR BIRTHS, MARRIAGES AND DEATHS. New York: Barnes and Noble, 1972.

Authoritative treatment of English costume usage in three special events from the medieval period to 1900, covering the costumes in ceremonies of both grand as well as ordinary folk; section of excellent plates of primary-source material; index and bibliography; very useful source.

1165 Deneke, Bernward. HOCHZEIT. Munich: Prestel-Verlag, 1971.

Survey of the historical development of the wedding and marriage costume and customs in Germany; 127 monochrome and color plates; bibliography.

1166 Habenstein, Robert W., and Lamers, William M. FUNERAL CUSTOMS THE WORLD OVER. Milwaukee: Bulfin Printers, 1974.

Survey of funeral procedures in all major countries and sects, with notations of customs in funerary costume where applicable.

1167 Lacey, Peter. THE WEDDING. New York: Ridge Press, 1969.

Extensive treatment of the areas of the wedding: love and courtship, the ceremony, and the celebration with historical background of the development of the practice; many primary-source illustrations, some in color; bibliography.

1168 Monsarrat, Ann. AND THE BRIDE WORE . . . : THE STORY OF THE WHITE WEDDING. New York: Dodd, Mead, and Co., 1973.

Survey of weddings and marriage customs from the Greeks to the moderns; informative, but lacking illustrative material.

1169 Murphy, Brian. THE WORLD OF WEDDINGS: AN ILLUSTRATED CELEBRATION. New York: Paddington Press, 1978.

Extensively illustrated in black-and-white and color primary-source material; historical survey in interesting and informative text from the rationale for weddings in the beginning to the present in both Western and Eastern cultures; major value to designers.

1170 TROUWEN IN HET WIT: TWEE EEUWEN BRUIDSKLEDING, 1765-1976 [Two centuries of bridal clothing]. The Hague: Nederlands Kostuummuseum, 1976.

Dutch text but valuable for twenty-two monochrome reproductions of fashion plates and original designs of wedding dresses from western Europe from 1779 to 1976.

1171 Urlin, Ethel L. A SHORT HISTORY OF MARRIAGE: MARRIAGE RITES, CUSTOMS, AND FOLKLORE IN MANY COUNTRIES AND ALL AGES. 1913. Reprint. Detroit: Singing Tree Press, 1969.

Reprint containing much information concerning the history of wedding dresses.

O. COSTUME FOR SPORTS

See also 321, 339, 343

1172 Barney, Sydney D. CLOTHES AND THE HORSE: A GUIDE TO CORRECT DRESS FOR ALL RIDING OCCASIONS. Introduction by James Laver. London: Vinton, 1953.

Illustrations of forms of equestrian costume.

1173 Campbell, Judith. ROYALTY ON HORSEBACK. Garden City, N.Y.: Doubleday and Co., 1974.

Excellent pictorial survey of developments in riding dress as displayed on royal personages.

1174 Cunnington, Phillis E., and Mansfield, Alan. ENGLISH COSTUME FOR SPORTS AND OUTDOOR RECREATION FROM THE SIXTEENTH TO THE NINETEENTH CENTURIES. New York: Barnes and Noble, 1970.

Thorough and authoritative textual discussion of twenty-one various sports and recreations, for example, cricket, tennis, hunting, cycling, skating, and picnicking, with a color frontispiece, 64 monochrome plates and 254 line drawings; some chapter bibliographies and a general bibliography; useful source.

1175 Durant, John, and Bettmann, Otto. PICTORIAL HISTORY OF AMERICAN SPORTS FROM COLONIAL TIMES TO THE PRESENT. New York: A.S. Barnes and Co., 1952.

Excellent pictorial source; survey of sportsmen in all major American sports from the seventeenth century to the twentieth century.

1176 Edey, Maitland A., ed. YESTERDAY IN SPORT. New York: Time-Life Books, 1968.

Contains many photographs of sporting history in football, baseball, racing, golf, boxing, track and field, and minor sports.

1177 Hole, Christina. ENGLISH SPORTS AND PASTIMES. Freeport, N.Y.: Books for Libraries Press, 1949.

Historical survey of a number of sports, activities, games, and diversions, with numerous primary-source illustrations; useful book.

1178 Kidwell, Claudia A. WOMEN'S BATHING AND SWIMMING COSTUME IN THE UNITED STATES. Washington, D.C.: Smithsonian Institution Press, 1968.

Eighteen illustrations and photographs from 1884 to 1930, showing full range of female bathing and swimming garments and accessories.

1179 Manchester Art Galleries. THE GALLERY OF ENGLISH COSTUME PICTURE BOOKS; VOLUME EIGHT: COSTUME FOR SPORT. Manchester: 1963.

Twenty monochrome photographs of sports costume in the collection, with a general introduction and specific descriptions of each costume shown.

1180 Paget, Guy. SPORTING PICTURES OF ENGLAND. London: Collins, 1945.

Condensed survey of major English sporting painters with examples of their work: twelve plates in color and twenty-one in black and white, dating from the seventeenth to the nineteenth centuries; depictions of costumed sportsmen.

1181 Smith, Robert A. A SOCIAL HISTORY OF THE BICYCLE: ITS EARLY LIFE AND TIMES IN AMERICA. New York: American Heritage Publishing Co., 1972.

Interesting text with many illustrations of bicycling costume.

1182 Stone, Lilly C. FOLGER BOOKS ON TUDOR AND STUART CIVILIZATION: ENGLISH SPORTS AND RECREATIONS. Charlottesville: University Press of Virginia, 1960.

Booklet with condensed treatment of major pastimes and sports of the English people in the sixteenth and seventeenth centuries; coverage of such topics as dancing, dicing, dueling, gaming, fishing, hunting, and tennis, to name a few; list for further reading.

1183 Strutt, Joseph. THE SPORTS AND PASTIMES OF THE PEOPLE OF ENGLAND FROM THE EARLIEST PERIOD, INCLUDING THE RURAL AND DOMESTIC RECREATIONS, MAY GAMES, MUMMERIES, PAGEANTS, PROCESSIONS AND POMPOUS SPECTACLES, ILLUSTRATED BY REPRODUCTIONS FROM ANCIENT PAINTINGS IN WHICH ARE REPRESENTED MOST OF THE POPULAR DIVERSIONS. 1903. Reprint. New York: Augustus M. Kelley, 1970.

Excellent source for information on manners, sports, and pastimes prior to the nineteenth century; general background introduction followed with quite specific coverage of activities of the rural gentry; of those in the rural and urban locales; and of domestic and seasonal natures; forty-one primary-source illustrations; many textual references to costume and sports accessories.

1184 Twombly, Willis. 200 YEARS OF SPORT IN AMERICA: A PAGEANT OF A NATION AT PLAY. New York: McGraw-Hill Book Co., 1976.

Excellent color photographs and paintings, plus line drawings of sports participants in America.

1185 Walker, Stella A. SPORTING ART IN ENGLAND, 1700-1900. New York: Hacker Art Books, 1972.

Survey containing a number of illustrations of people costumed for sporting activities.

P. UNDERCLOTHES AND FOUNDATION GARMENTS

See also 244, 283, 316, 438, 601

1186 Crawford, M.D.C., and Crawford, Elizabeth G. HISTORY OF LINGERIE IN PICTURES. New York: Fairchild Publications, 1952.

Brief presentation of historical lingerie with line drawings from the periods from the Egyptians to the 1940s; helpful source.

1187 Crawford, M.D.C., and Guernsey, Elizabeth A. HISTORY OF CORSETS IN PICTURES. New York: Fairchild Publications, 1951.

Brief descriptive notes with line drawings covering corsets from the time of the ancients to the 1940s; informative and helpful pictorial survey.

1188 Cunnington, C. Willet, and Cunnington, Phillis E. THE HISTORY OF UNDERCLOTHES. London: Michael Joseph, 1951.

Historical survey of the development of underclothes in light of their relationship to outer garments; period-by-period divi-

sions with succinct discussion of both male and female underclothes from the medieval period to 1939; numerous (119)
photographs of articles, drawings, and illustrations; bibliography.

1189 Ewing, Elizabeth. FASHION IN UNDERWEAR. London: B.T. Batsford,
1974.

In-depth investigation of underwear from 3000 B.C. to 1971
A.D., with line drawings and primary-source illustrative material; helpful source.

1190 Holliday, Robert Cortes. UNMENTIONABLES: FROM FIGLEAVES TO
SCANTIES. New York: Ray Long and Richard R. Smith, 1933.

Popularized treatment of the place of feminine undergarments
throughout history; lacking illustration, but some useful and
interesting information in the text.

1191 Laurent, Cecil Saint. A HISTORY OF LADIES UNDERWEAR. London:
Michael Joseph, 1968.

Complete historical survey of female underwear from the earliest times to modern times, with numerous excellent primary-
source illustrations (216 monochrome and 30 in color); bibliography.

1192 Libron, Fernand, and Clouzot, Henri. LE CORSET DANS L'ART ET LES
MOEURS DU XIIIE AU XXE SIECLE. Paris: Louis Barthou, 1933.

Survey of the corset and all its aspects from the thirteenth
to the twentieth centuries, with eighty-five monochrome and
color plates and some line drawings; bibliography.

1193 Morel, Juliette. LINGERIE PARISIENNE. London: Academy Editions;
New York: St. Martin's Press, 1976.

Brief text and pictorial survey of fashionable lingerie in Paris
in the 1920s, as illustrated partly in color in period drawings,
advertisements, and in primary-source photographs.

1194 Pearce, Arthur W. THE FUTURE OUT OF THE PAST: AN ILLUSTRATED
HISTORY OF THE WARNER BROTHERS COMPANY ON ITS 90TH ANNI-
VERSARY. Hartford: Connecticut Printers, 1964.

Not specifically about costume as such, but valuable for illustrations of developments in corsets and undergarments as shown
in reproductions of advertisements.

Accoutrements & Special Categories

1195 Reyburn, Wallace. BUST-UP. London: Macdonald, 1971.

Illustrated with photographs and sketches showing the development of the brassiere.

1196 Rothacker, Nanette. THE UNDIES BOOK. New York: Charles Scribner's Sons, 1976.

Construction guide for modern lingerie, with patterns, drawings, instructions, and diagrams.

1197 Warren, Helen. CORSETS: SALESPERSON'S MANUAL AND CONSUMER'S GUIDE. New York: Fairchild Publications, 1949.

Not geared primarily for costume designers but good information on measuring and fitting the corset; line drawings of style of corsets in the 1940s.

1198 Waugh, Norah. CORSETS AND CRINOLINES. New York: Theatre Arts Books, 1954.

Excellent historical account with primary-source illustration; detailed patterns; contemporary references covering the subject in three time periods: to 1670; 1670-1900; and 1900-1925; notes in appendixes on construction techniques, supports, and whalebone; glossary.

1199 Zilliancus, Benedict. THE CORSET. Helsinki: Frenckellska Tryckeri Ab, 1963.

Historical survey of the corset, with interesting and numerous illustrations.

Chapter 5

THEATRICAL AND HISTORICAL MOVEMENT AND DANCE

See also 29, 295, 382, 481, 535, 537, 549, 551, 592, 636, 1330

1200 Alberts, David. PANTOMIME: ELEMENTS AND EXERCISES. Lawrence:
University Press of Kansas, 1971.

> Presentation in part 1 of the elements of essence and illusion,
> with presentation in part 2 of exercises for body, face, hands,
> and illusory exercises; presentation in part 3 of mime and pan-
> tomime; bibliography; good movement exercise source.

1201 Alford, Violet, ed. HANDBOOKS OF EUROPEAN NATIONAL DANCES.
London: Max Parrish, 1948-59.

> Series of ten volumes; presentation in volume of brief histori-
> cal background, concise directions for selected national dances,
> and four color illustrations of pairs of costumed dancers; ap-
> propriate music also; map and bibliography with each volume in
> in series; individual titles are given in entries 1202-11.

1202 Armstrong, Lucille. DANCES OF PORTUGAL. 1948.

1203 _____. DANCES OF SPAIN. 2 vols. 1951.

1204 Fyfe, Agnes. DANCES OF GERMANY. 1951.

1205 Grindea, Miron, and Grindea, Carola. DANCES OF RUMANIA. 1952.

1206 Katsarova, Raina. DANCES OF BULGARIA. 1951.

1207 Lubinova, Mila. DANCES OF CZECHOSLOVAKIA. 1959.

1208 Marcel-Dubois, Claudie, and Alford, Violet. DANCES OF FRANCE.
1950.

1209 Pinon, Roger, and Jamar, Henri. DANCES OF BELGIUM. 1953.

1210 Semb, Klara. DANCES OF NORWAY. 1951.

1211 Wolska, Helen. DANCES OF POLAND. 1952.

1212 Angelo, Domenico. THE SCHOOL OF FENCING: HUNGARIAN AND HIGHLAND BROADSWORDS. New York: Land's End Press, 1971.

> Reprint of three period fencing manuals with drawings and dia-
> grams of period fencing movements.

1213 Arbeau, Thoinot. ORCHESOGRAPHY. Translated by Mary Stewart Evans. New York: Dover Publications, 1967.

> Newest translation and most accurate edition with a Labanota-
> tion section added for easier use of this sixteenth-century guide
> to dances of the day (basse, pavan, galliard, etc.); also per-
> iod mores, deportment, and movement; excellent source for
> actor as well as dancer.

1214 _____. ORCHESOGRAPHY: A TREATISE IN THE FORM OF A DIA-
LOGUE WHEREBY ALL MANNER OF PERSONS MAY EASILY ACQUIRE AND PRACTICE HONOURABLE EXERCISE OF DANCING. Translated by Cyril W. Beaumont. London: C.W. Beaumont, 1925.

> Valuable sixteenth-century guide to dances of the day; also a
> guide to period movement and deportment.

1215 Aubert, Charles. THE ART OF PANTOMIME. Translated by Edith Sears. 1927. Reprint. New York: Benjamin Blom, 1970.

> Excellent drawings and diagrams illustrating the techniques and
> exercises for expressive use of body, hands, and face.

1216 Barlanghy, Istvan. MIME: TRAINING AND EXERCISES. Translated by Hugo Kerey. Edited by Cyril W. Beaumont. London: Imperial Society of Teachers of Dancing, 1967.

> Treatment of mime in four groups: subjective, objective, ideo-
> logical, and impersonal; directions and diagrams for numerous
> mime exercises and studies.

1217 Bartal, Lea, and Ne'eman, Nira. MOVEMENT AWARENESS AND CREA-
TIVITY. New York: Harper and Row, Publishers, 1975.

> Short, scientific introduction; body awareness; sensory percep-
> tion; use of imagination; structural lessons; children's exercises;
> and an experimental three-year course in movement, planned
> for a drama school.

1218 Beaumont, Cyril W. A BIBLIOGRAPHY OF DANCING. London: Dancing Times, 1929.

Alphabetical listing with subject index of books in the British Museum Library in the subject area.

1219 Breckinrdige, Scott D. SWORD PLAY. New York: A.S. Barnes and Co., 1941.

Somewhat simplified introduction to sword play based on the French school of the foil; appropriate diagrams and instructions.

1220 Burgess, Hovey. CIRCUS TECHNIQUES: JUGGLING, EQUILIBRISTICS, VAULTING. New York: Drama Book, 1976.

Almost three hundred monochrome photographs accompanying comprehensive survey of the union of physicality and theatricality in application of special circus techniques as an aid to theatrical movement and physical aspects of comedy.

1221 Caballero Bonald, Jose M. ANDALUSIAN DANCES. Translated by Charles David Ley. Barcelona: Editorial Noguer, 1959.

Succinct survey with a chapter on theatrical dances, plus sixty-six monochrome photographs of costumed dancers.

1222 Chisman, Isabel, and Raven-Hart, Hester Emilie. MANNERS AND MOVEMENTS IN COSTUME PLAYS. Boston: Walter H. Baker, Co.; London: H.F.W. Deane and Sons, n.d.

Very useful guidebook dealing with historical and theatrical deportment, manners, dances, weapons, and ceremonial functions from ancient through modern times.

1223 Dickens, Guillermina. THE TRADITIONAL DANCES OF LATIN AMERICA, DANCES OF MEXICO. Edited by W.O. Galbraith. London: Max Parrish, 1954.

Brief treatment of representative national dances of Mexico, with four plates of color paintings of costumed dancers; appropriate music; bibliography.

1224 Dolmetsch, Mabel. DANCES OF ENGLAND AND FRANCE FROM 1450 TO 1600 WITH THEIR MUSIC AND AUTHENTIC MANNER OF PERFORMANCE. London: Routledge and Paul, 1949.

Invaluable book for period dancing and movement; clear directions, appropriate music, helpful diagrams and illustrations for such dances as the basse, measure, galliard, allemande, and others.

1225 _____. DANCES OF SPAIN AND ITALY FROM 1400 TO 1600. London: Routledge and Paul, 1954.

Excellent historical survey plus directions to perform the dances with diagrams and illustrations.

1226 Duggan, Anne Schley, et al. THE FOLK DANCE LIBRARY. 5 vols. New York: A.S. Barnes and Co., 1948.

All volumes illustrated with monochrome and color plates with appropriate music; clear descriptions and illustrations for performing the dances; map and bibliography at the end of each volume: volume 1: THE TEACHING OF FOLK DANCE; volume 2: FOLK DANCES OF SCANDINAVIA; volume 3: FOLK DANCES OF EUROPEAN COUNTRIES; volume 4: FOLK DANCE OF THE BRITISH ISLES; volume 5: FOLK DANCES OF THE UNITED STATES AND MEXICO.

1227 Enters, Angna. ON MIME. Middletown, Conn.: Wesleyan University Press, 1965.

Full explanation for author's personal approach to mime through the use of images.

1228 Fallon, Dennis J., and Kuchenmeister, Sue Ann. THE ART OF BALLROOM DANCE. Minneapolis: Burgess Publishing Co., 1977.

Simple and advanced steps for popular ballroom dances, including the waltz, tango, and polka; with photographs, diagrams, and brief historical backgrounds.

1229 Flett, J.F., and Flett, T.M. TRADITIONAL DANCING IN SCOTLAND. Nashville: Vanderbilt University Press, 1966.

Well-illustrated diagrams in support of concise historical survey and modern approach to performing the dances.

1230 Franks, A.H. SOCIAL DANCE: A SHORT HISTORY. London: Routledge and Kegan Paul, 1963.

Historical survey from the fifteenth to the twentieth centuries, with illustrative material; valuable source for information on social dance and period movement.

1231 Gordon, Gilbert. STAGE FIGHTS: A SIMPLE HANDBOOK OF TECHNIQUES. London: J. Garnet Miller, 1973.

Condensed treatment with a useful chapter on the use of costumes and accessories in fights.

1232 Green, Ruth M. THE WEARING OF COSTUME: THE CHANGING TECHNIQUES OF WEARING CLOTHES AND HOW TO MOVE IN THEM FROM ROMAN BRITAIN TO THE SECOND WORLD WAR. London: Sir Isaac Pitman, 1966.

> Thorough investigation of problems of movement in period costume with chapters on long skirts, cloaks, and shoes; historical survey of solutions to movement problems within each century; line drawings.

1233 Hobbs, William. STAGE FIGHTS, SWORDS, FIREARMS, FISTICUFFS AND SLAPSTICK. New York: Theatre Arts Books, 1967.

> Succinct presentation of author's ideas and directions to enable less experienced personnel to stage a more convincing professional stage encounter; useful diagrams, system of movement notation for a duel; section of pictures of professional stage fights and drawings of historic weaponry; index and list of suppliers.

1234 Horst, Louis. PRE-CLASSIC DANCE FORMS. 1937. Reprint. New York: Kamin Dance Publications, 1953.

> Guide to development of historical court dances, for example, pavane, galliard, and sarabande, with suggested music and authentic dance steps; appropriate primary-source illustrations.

1235 Howard, Guy. TECHNIQUE OF BALLROOM DANCING. Brighton, Engl.: International Dance Teachers' Association, 1976.

> General introduction and explanation of notation system, with complete choreographic charts for such dances as the waltz, quickstep, fox trot, and tango.

1236 Humphrey, Doris. THE ART OF MAKING DANCES. New York: Grove Press, 1959.

> An introductory choreography and dance movement text with clear drawings and diagrams to enforce the points of the text.

1237 Hunt, Douglas, and Hunt, Kari. PANTOMIME: THE SILENT THEATRE. New York: Atheneum, 1964.

> Short history of the art of pantomime from the ancients to the moderns, with selected primary-source illustrations.

1238 Ivanova, Anna. THE DANCE IN SPAIN. New York: Frederick A. Praeger, 1970.

> Historical survey with extensive chapter on theatrical dancing; seventy-one period and contemporary illustrations of dancers.

1239 Lloyd, Albert L. THE TRADITIONAL DANCES OF LATIN AMERICA: DANCES OF ARGENTINA. Edited by W.O. Galbraith. London: Max Parrish, 1960.

> Brief treatment of representative national dances of the country, with four plates of color paintings of costumed dancers; appropriate music; bibliography.

1240 Katz, Albert M. STAGE VIOLENCE. New York: Richards Rosen Press, 1976.

> Presentation with clear diagrams and photographs of basic tenets of stage fighting but also exploration of often ignored or neglected areas, such as knife handling, martial arts, and firearms; also attention to creating appropriate character-oriented violence.

1241 Kennedy, Douglas. ENGLAND'S DANCES: FOLK-DANCING TO-DAY AND YESTERDAY. London: G. Bell and Sons, 1949.

> Historical survey of the development from primitive to regularized forms of folk dancing in England, with twenty illustrations; two musical scores for the Morris; particular emphasis on the Morris dance.

1242 _____. ENGLISH FOLK DANCING TODAY AND YESTERDAY. London: G. Bell and Sons, 1964.

> Historical survey and descriptions of popular folk dances of England through the ages, with chapters on the Morris and Sword dances and a section of eighteen monochrome plates of costumed dancers.

1243 King, Nancy. THEATRE MOVEMENT: THE ACTOR AND HIS SPACE. New York: Drama Book, 1971.

> Exploration of physical conditioning and nonverbal communication enabling an actor to physically express first himself and then a specific characterization; number of individual exercises suggested.

1244 Kipnis, Claude. THE MIME BOOK. New York: Harper and Row, Publishers, 1974.

> Mime exercise book in format of flip pages illustrating techniques and exercises with a sense of movement.

1245 Kirstein, Lincoln. THE BOOK OF DANCE: A SHORT HISTORY OF CLASSIC THEATRICAL DANCING. Garden City, N.Y.: Garden City Publishing Co., 1942.

Excellent textual survey of theatrical dance from early origins to modern forms, with a section of 123 illustrations; bibliography.

1246 Kline, Peter, and Meadors, Nancy. PHYSICAL MOVEMENT FOR THE THEATRE. New York: Richards Rosen Press, 1971.

Exploration of theories and practices of stage movement, with an exercise guide and illustrations.

1247 Laban, Rudolf. THE MASTERY OF MOVEMENT. 3d ed. Revised by Lisa Ullmann. Boston: Plays, 1971.

Originally entitled THE MASTERY OF MOVEMENT ON THE STAGE: moving from analysis of simple and complex body movements through the significance of movement into mime and ending with a study of movement for individual characters for group scenes.

1248 Lambranzi, Gregorio. NEW AND CURIOUS SCHOOL OF THEATRICAL DANCING: WITH ALL THE ORIGINAL PLATES BY JOHANN GEORG PUSCHNER. Translated by Derra de Moroda. Edited by Cyril W. Beaumont. 1928. Reprint. New York: Dance Horizons, 1972.

Brief introduction and many plates showing various positions in performing certain dances; valuable for illustration of period movement and dance steps and positions.

1249 Lawler, Lillian B. THE DANCE IN ANCIENT GREECE. Middletown, Conn.: Wesleyan University Press, 1964.

Historical and descriptive survey of various types of ancient Greek dance; Cretan, Mycenean, Animal, Theatrical, Festival, and Professional, with a number (61) of primary-source illustrations; bibliographical references.

1250 _____. THE DANCE OF THE ANCIENT GREEK THEATRE. Iowa City: University of Iowa Press, 1964.

Coverage of dance in dithyrambs, tragedy, comedy, and satyr plays; no illustrations; bibliographical footnotes.

1251 Lawson, Joan. EUROPEAN FOLK DANCE: ITS NATIONAL AND MUSICAL CHARACTERISTICS. London: Sir Isacc Pitman and Sons, 1964.

Valuable chapters on the development and influence of costume on the dances, as well as drawings of dancers in native folk costumes; coverage of the characteristic dances of the Turki-Tartans, Greeks, Slavs, Alpines, Teutons, Celts, Finno-Ugrians, Latins, and Basques.

1252 _____. MIME: THE THEORY AND PRACTICE OF EXPRESSIVE GES-
TURE WITH A DESCRIPTION OF ITS HISTORICAL DEVELOPMENT.
London: Sir Isaac Pitman and Sons, 1957.

One hundred illustrations by Peter Revitt in support of discussion of technique and development; interesting treatment of
gesture in terms of emotion, occupation, and character.

1253 Martin, Gyorgy. HUNGARIAN FOLK DANCES. Translated by Rudolf
Fisher. Budapest: Corvina Press, 1974.

Textual description and survey with sixteen color and thirty-
eight monochrome photographs of folk dancing illustrating wide
range of costumed dancers.

1254 Martin, John Joseph. THE DANCE: THE STORY OF THE DANCE TOLD
IN PICTURES AND TEXT. New York: Tudor Publishing Co., 1946.

Extensive pictorial coverage of many forms of dance from primitive to modern.

1255 Noverre, Jean Georges. LETTERS ON DANCING AND BALLETS. Translated by Cyril W. Beaumont. London: C.W. Beaumont, 1951.

Much information on contemporary dance, styles, manners,
costumes, masks, theatres, and opera in the eighteenth century; with selected illustrations.

1256 Oxenford, Lyn. DESIGN FOR MOVEMENT: A TEXTBOOK ON STAGE
MOVEMENT. New York: Theatre Arts Books, 1952.

Deals with individual and group, period and modern dancing
and acting movement.

1257 _____. PLAYING PERIOD PLAYS. London: J. Garnet Miller, 1958.

Excellent discussions in each of four chronologically arranged
historical sections of period movement, for example, effects of
costume, manners, dances and music; practice scenes for each
section; line drawings; numerous lists of plays and sources with
each section; very useful source.

1258 Palffy-Alpar, Julius. SWORD AND MASQUE. Philadelphia: F.A.
Davis Co., 1967.

Two sections, "History of Fencing" and "Theatrical Fencing,"
valuable in area of movement; photographs, diagrams, and
sample fencing scenes from several plays.

1259 Penrod, James. MOVEMENT FOR THE PERFORMING ARTIST. Palo
Alto, Calif.: National Press Books, 1974.

Identification, mastery, and application of movement to the
development of a theatrical role; chapter on correct movement
in historic periods and costume in terms of characteristic body
movement, period props, and dance; bibliography.

1260 Pisk, Litz. THE ACTOR AND HIS BODY. New York: Theatre Art
Books, 1976.

Exercises for the actor's movement with stylized diagrams and
a supplement of X-rays showing movement patterns.

1261 Playford, John. THE ENGLISH DANCING MASTER: OR, PLAINE AND
EASIE RULES FOR THE DANCING OF COUNTRY DANCES, WITH THE
TUNE OF EACH DANCE. 1651. Reprint. New York: Dance Horizons,
1933.

Directions and music for period country dances.

1262 Rameau, Pierre. THE DANCING MASTER. Translated by Cyril W.
Beaumont. New York: Dance Horizons, 1970.

Standard work on technique of eighteenth-century dancing,
providing a guide of current social etiquette, fashionable
dances, various steps and arm movements, and, most impor-
tantly, explanation of how to execute the steps; illustrated
with engraved plates.

1263 Richardson, Philip John S. THE SOCIAL DANCES OF THE NINETEENTH
CENTURY IN ENGLAND. London: Herbert Jenkins, 1960.

Complete survey of the subject with attention to such dances
as the waltz, quadrille, polka, and cotillion; section on
changes in costume and its relationship to dance during the
century; nineteen primary-source illustrations.

1264 Seyler, Athene, and Haggard, Stephen. THE CRAFT OF COMEDY.
New York: Theatre Arts Books, 1957.

Helpful essay on period acting involving the use of fans,
handling of skirts and trains, and the wearing of corsets.

1265 Sharp, Cecil J., and Macilwaine, Herbert C. THE MORRIS BOOK
WITH A DESCRIPTION OF DANCES AS PERFORMED BY THE MORRIS
MEN OF ENGLAND. London: Novello, 1912.

Historical development of the dance and music, plus directions
and diagrams for performance of the Morris.

1266 Sharp, Cecil J., and Oppe, A.P. THE DANCE: AN HISTORICAL SUR-
VEY OF DANCING IN EUROPE. London: Halton and Truscott, 1924.

Somewhat dated but valuable concise treatment accompanied
by four color and seventy-five monochrome plates of primary-
source material of costumed performers.

1267 Shepard, Richmond. MIME: THE TECHNIQUE OF SILENCE. New
York: Drama Book, 1971.

A brief historical survey of mime followed by thirty lessons in
mime and movement.

1268 Slade, Peter. NATURAL DANCE: DEVELOPMENTAL MOVEMENT AND
GUIDED ACTION. London: Hodder and Stoughton, 1977.

Outline for development of natural improvised dance through
polished improvisation to dance drama and then on to a professional level.

1269 Taubert, K.H. HOEFISCHE TAENZE. Mainz, Germany: B. Schott's
Soehne, 1968.

Valuable source, despite German text, for period choreography; with diagrams and illustrations that can be followed without much difficulty.

1270 Terrone, Leonardo, F. RIGHT AND LEFT HAND FENCING: New York:
Dodd, Mead and Co., 1959.

Fencing manual with clear illustrative line drawings.

1271 Viski, Karoly. HUNGARIAN DANCES. London: Simpkin Marshall,
1937.

Descriptions and directions for performing traditional national
dances; section on appropriate costumes.

1272 Wise, Arthur. WEAPONS IN THE THEATRE. New York: Barnes and
Noble, 1968.

Manual for the staging and directing of stage violence; presentation of a notation system for theatrical fights; consideration
of fights in various historical periods from ancients to the
eighteenth century; sample application of theories to fight
scenes from several dramas: JULIUS CAESAR, ROMEO AND
JULIET, and CYRANO DE BERGERAC.

1273 Wood, Melusine. ADVANCED HISTORICAL DANCES. London: C.W.
Beaumont, 1960.

Continuation of presentation of period dances with well-chosen
illustrations, accompanying music, concise directions, and
clear diagrams primarily for eighteenth-century dances.

1274 _____. MORE HISTORICAL DANCES COMPRISING THE TECHNICAL PART OF THE ELEMENTARY SYLLABUS AND THE INTERMEDIATE SYLLABUS, THE LATTER SECTION INCLUDING SUCH DANCES AS APPERTAIN BUT NOT PREVIOUSLY DESCRIBED. London: C.W. Beaumont, 1956.

> Particularly helpful sections, with diagrams, on medieval deportment and period honors, plus directions on elementary and advanced technical preparations for such dances as the cascarda, branle, pavana, and mattei.

1275 _____. SOME HISTORICAL DANCES (TWELFTH TO NINETEENTH CENTURY): THEIR MANNER OF PERFORMANCE AND THEIR PLACE IN THE SOCIAL LIFE OF THE TIME. London: C.W. Beaumont, 1952.

> Clear presentation of major dances by century, with period music and primary-source illustrations; very valuable source for information on dances that can easily be adapted for theatrical use.

1276 Zarina, Xenia. CLASSIC DANCES OF THE ORIENT. New York: Crown Publishers, 1967.

> Presentation of the history, character, training, costume, mask, technique exercises, and performances of selected dances of India, Thailand, Cambodia, Java, Bali, and Japan; with many illustrations and photographs; glossary, index, and bibliography.

Chapter 6
MANNERS, MODES, AND CUSTOMS

See also 486, 489, 531, 615, 636

1277 Adburgham, Alison. A PUNCH HISTORY OF MANNERS AND MODES, 1841-1940. London: Hutchison of London, 1961.

Excerpts from PUNCH greatly enhanced by numerous illustrations and cartoons covering the range of Victorian life, customs, and behavior.

1278 _____. VIEW OF FASHION. London: G. Allen and Unwin, 1966.

Interesting collection of comment and criticism, mostly from PUNCH and the GUARDIAN, reflecting changes in manners and customs of fashion of the decades of the 1950s and early 1960s.

1279 Bott, Alan John. THIS WAS ENGLAND: MANNERS AND CUSTOMS OF THE ANCIENT VICTORIANS: A SURVEY IN PICTURES AND TEXT OF THEIR HISTORY, MORALS, WARS, INVENTIONS, SPORTS, HEROES, AND SOCIAL AND SEXUAL DISTINCTIONS BETWEEN 1870 AND 1900. Garden City, N.Y.: Doubleday, Doran and Co., 1931.

Titled OUR FATHERS in English publications; extensive illustrative material on a wide range of subjects as title indicates.

1280 Bott, Alan John, and Clephane, Irene. OUR MOTHERS: A CAVALCADE IN PICTURES, QUOTATION AND DESCRIPTION OF LATE VICTORIAN WOMEN, 1870-1900. 1932. Reprint. New York: Benjamin Blom, 1969.

Well-illustrated survey of feminine attitudes, manners, and behavior during the late Victorian period.

1281 Brooke, Iris. PLEASURES OF THE PAST: A LIGHT-HEARTED COMMENTARY ON THE ENJOYMENTS OF PAST GENERATIONS. London: Odhams Press, 1955.

Survey covering such topics as eating, dressing, and dancing; illustrated with seventeen line drawings by the author.

1282 Cable, Mary. AMERICAN MANNERS AND MORALS: A PICTURE HISTORY OF HOW WE BEHAVED AND MISBEHAVED. New York: American Heritage Publishing Co., 1969.

Extensive volume with numerous illustrations, many in color, of American behavior.

1283 Camden, Carroll. THE ELIZABETHAN WOMAN. London: Cleaver-Hume; New York: Elsevier Press, 1952.

Scholarly work with a number of illustrations from period sources; composed of chapters on cosmetics, clothing, and marriage, among others; a wide view of the total feminine manners of the Elizabethan woman; bibliography.

1284 Christian, Roy. OLD ENGLISH CUSTOMS. New York: Drake Publishers, 1973.

Well-illustrated survey of customs, with chapters on traditional dances and folk drama as well as on general manners and customs; bibliography.

1285 Churchill, Allen. THE UPPER CRUST: AN INFORMAL HISTORY OF NEW YORK'S HIGHEST SOCIETY. Englewood Cliffs, N.J.: Prentice-Hall, 1970.

Readable study of all facets of manners and customs throughout history in New York, with many primary-source photographs and other illustrative materials; bibliography.

1286 Cohn, David L. THE GOOD OLD DAYS: A HISTORY OF AMERICAN MORALS AND MANNERS AS SEEN THROUGH THE SEARS, ROEBUCK, CATALOGS, 1905 TO PRESENT. New York: Simon and Schuster, 1940.

Chapters on male and female fashions with selected primary-source photographs, advertisements, and commentary.

1287 Cosman, Madeleine Pelner. FABULOUS FEASTS: MEDIEVAL COOKERY AND CEREMONY. New York: George Braziller, 1976.

Extensively illustrated discussion of medieval manners and customs concerned with food and eating; interesting and useful source; bibliography.

1288 Crewe, Quentin. THE FRONTIERS OF PRIVILEGE: A CENTURY OF SOCIAL CONFLICT AS REFLECTED IN THE QUEEN. London: Collins, 1961.

Collection of material taken from the magazine as a reflection of manners and mores of the upper level of British society from the Victorians to the moderns; with much primary-source illustrative material on fashions, customs, personalities, behavior, and so forth.

1289 Delgado, Alan. VICTORIAN ENTERTAINMENT. Newton Abbot, Engl.: David and Charles, 1971.

Survey of the history of popular pastimes, manners, and customs of the Victorian period, with many primary-source illustrations; bibliography.

1290 Ditchfield, Peter H. OLD ENGLISH CUSTOMS EXTANT AT THE PRESENT TIME: AN ACCOUNT OF LOCAL OBSERVANCES, FESTIVAL CUSTOMS, AND ANCIENT CEREMONIES YET SURVIVING IN GREAT BRITAIN. 1896. Reprint. Detroit: Singing Tree Press, 1968.

Rather complete coverage of the subject but unfortunately lacking illustrative material; bibliographical footnotes.

1291 Drake-Carnell, F.J. OLD ENGLISH CUSTOMS AND CEREMONIES. London: B.T. Batsford; New York: Charles Scribner's Sons, 1938.

First-hand description with excellent photographs, some in color, of many old holiday customs still observed in modern England.

1292 Du Boulay, F.R.H. AN AGE OF AMBITION: ENGLISH SOCIETY IN THE LATE MIDDLE AGES. New York: Viking Press, 1970.

English manners and life; numerous illustrations; bibliography.

1293 Dunbar, Janet. THE EARLY VICTORIAN WOMAN: SOME ASPECTS OF HER LIFE, 1837-1857. London: George G. Harrap and Co., 1953.

Excellent survey of manners and modes in a specific period, with a chapter on fashion; illustrated with primary-source material; bibliography.

1294 Earle, Alice Morse. CUSTOMS AND FASHIONS IN OLD NEW ENGLAND. 1893. Reprint. Detroit: Singing Tree Press, 1968.

Social history of New England dealing with numerous topics covering martial, religious, domestic, literary, fashion, medicinal, and funeral customs; no illustrations.

1295 Erlanger, Philippe. THE AGE OF COURTS AND KINGS: MANNERS AND MORALS, 1558-1715. New York: Harper and Row, Publishers, 1967.

Discussion of manners and morals in Spain, France, Italy,
England, Germany, and the Low Countries during the period;
ninety-six pages of primary-source illustrations.

1296 George, Mary Dorothy. HOGARTH TO CRUIKSHANK: SOCIAL CHANGE
IN GRAPHIC SATIRE. London: Penguin Books, 1967.

Extremely large number (201) of period prints showing developments in every phase of manners, customs, and costumes of
the period; bibliographical references.

1297 Gloag, John. GEORGIAN GRACE: A SOCIAL HISTORY OF DESIGN
FROM 1160 TO 1830. London: Spring Books, 1967.

Extensive volume with coverage of entire range of social history of the broad Georgian period, including fashions, manners,
mores, and customs in a number of social areas; numerous primary-source illustrations; bibliographies.

1298 _____. VICTORIAN COMFORT: A SOCIAL HISTORY OF DESIGN
FROM 1830-1900. New York: St. Martin's Press, 1973.

Manners and customs of the Victorians: at home, travel,
dress, pleasure, morality, and death; thorough survey of their
likes and dislikes, all based on period illustrations, narrative,
and description.

1299 Hogg, Garry. CUSTOMS AND TRADITIONS OF ENGLAND. Newton
Abbot, Engl.: David and Charles, 1971.

Many excellent photographs and descriptions of the customs
and traditions of various geographical locations in England;
map and bibliography.

1300 Hole, Christina. ENGLISH HOME-LIFE, 1500-1800. London: B.T.
Batsford, 1949.

Amply illustrated coverage of the subject drawn from period
sources on such subjects as housing, dress, disease, recreations, and religions; index and bibliography.

1301 _____. ENGLISH TRADITIONAL CUSTOMS. London: B.T. Batsford,
1975.

Survey of manners and customs associated with holidays, social
occasions, and special events; interesting and useful source;
bibliography.

1302 Hunt, Cecil. BRITISH CUSTOMS AND CEREMONIES: WHEN, WHERE,
AND WHY: AN INFORMATIVE GUIDE. London: Ernest Benn, 1954.

Alphabetically arranged listing of various traditional ceremonies, events, celebrations, and festivals, for example, Ascot, Chester Miracle Plays, May Day, and Twelfth Night; with background of development of the customs, mode of celebration, and any special features; handy reference guide; no illustrations.

1303 Ickis, Marguerite. THE BOOK OF FESTIVALS AND HOLIDAYS THE WORLD OVER. New York: Dodd, Mead and Co., 1970.

Particular attention to nationalistic festivals and celebration variations from country to country.

1304 Jahn, Raymond. CONCISE DICTIONARY OF HOLIDAYS. New York: Philosophical Library, 1958.

Attention to holidays and customs of celebration, including notes on costume, with selected illustrations.

1305 James, Edwin O. SEASONAL FEASTS AND FESTIVALS. New York: Barnes and Noble, 1961.

Historical survey of feasts and festivals, primarily English, from prehistory to some modern celebrations; bibliographies.

1306 Laver, James. THE AGE OF ILLUSION: MANNERS AND MORALS, 1750-1848. New York: David McKay, 1972.

Very well illustrated survey of the dominant morals and mores and behavioral factors of the period in many areas, from religion to romanticism; extensive bibliography.

1307 _____. BETWEEN THE WARS. London: Vista Books, 1961.

Continuation of English social history, with particular attention to manners and fashions; in chronological sequence after VICTORIAN VISTA and EDWARDIAN PROMENADE (see entries 1311 and 1308.)

1308 _____. EDWARDIAN PROMENADE. Boston: Houghton Mifflin Co., 1958.

Textual survey of social history of the period; period illustrations; chronologically follows VICTORIAN VISTA (see entry 1311).

1309 _____. MANNERS AND MORALS IN THE AGE OF OPTIMISM, 1848-1914. New York: Harper and Row, Publishers, 1966.

Manners, Modes, and Customs

Detailed study of manners and mores of the period, with
ninety-six pages of illustrations; coverage of such topics as
social conditions, education, prostitution, religion, social
pastimes, art, and war; extensive bibliography.

1310 _____. VICTORIAN VISTA. London: Hulton Press, 1954.

Interesting textual examination of Victorian social history including manners, customs, and fashions, with contemporary
literary quotations and period illustrations.

1311 _____, ed. MEMORABLE BALLS. London: Derek Verschoyle, 1954.

Collection of complete descriptions of eleven historic balls
from Le Bal des Ardents in 1393 to the Poiret Ball in 1910;
valuable as far as insight into dress, dance, manners, and behavior at elegant entertainments during history.

1312 Lindsay, Jack. THE ANCIENT WORLD: MANNERS AND MORALS.
New York: G.P. Putnam's Sons, 1968.

Beginning with Minoans, discussion of the manner of life for
the ancients through the Byzantines, with selected illustrations;
list of important dates and bibliography.

1313 Masson, Georgina. COURTESANS OF THE ITALIAN RENAISSANCE.
New York: St. Martin's Press, 1975.

Interesting specialized study of manners and modes of a dra-
matically important social class, with a useful collection of
primary-source illustrative material; bibliography.

1314 Maurice, Arthur Bartlett, and Cooper, Frederick Taber. HISTORY OF
THE NINETEENTH CENTURY IN CARICATURE. 1904. Reprint. New
York: Cooper Square, 1970.

Very fascinating and informative social history as seen by the
perceptive eyes of the caricaturists; many period illustrations.

1315 Percival, Rachel, and Percival, Allen. THE COURT OF ELIZABETH THE
FIRST. London: Stainer and Bell, 1976.

Generously illustrated history of the part played by performing
arts (music, dance, and theatre) in Elizabeth's court specifically
and Elizabethan society generally.

1316 Rust, Frances. DANCE IN SOCIETY: AN ANALYSIS OF THE RELATION-
SHIP BETWEEN THE SOCIAL DANCE AND SOCIETY IN ENGLAND
FROM THE MIDDLE AGES TO THE PRESENT DAY. London: Routledge
and Kegan Paul, 1969.

Primarily a sociohistorical study of dance for recreation and pleasure in the framework of period manners, with a few monochrome illustrations; bibliography.

1317 Spicer, Dorothy Gladys. THE BOOK OF FESTIVALS. New York: Woman's Press, 1947.

Descriptions of festivals and customs; arranged by country.

1318 _____. FESTIVALS OF WESTERN EUROPE. New York: H.W. Wilson Co., 1958.

Survey of festivals by countries of Western Europe; bibliography.

1319 _____. YEARBOOK OF ENGLISH FESTIVALS. New York: H.W. Wilson Co., 1954.

Month-by-month description of English celebrations with customs pertaining to costume where applicable.

1320 Stenton, Doris Mary. THE ENGLISH WOMAN IN HISTORY. New York: Macmillan Co.; London: Allen and Unwin, 1957.

Survey of the English female from the Anglo-Saxons to the late Victorians, through selected specific women but with limited illustrative material.

1321 Swenson, Evelyn. VICTORIANA AMERICANA. Milwaukee: Greatlakes Living Press, 1976.

Well-illustrated survey of American Victorian life, manners, customs, and fashions.

1322 Symonds, Emily Morse [George Paston]. SOCIAL CARICATURE IN THE 18TH CENTURY. 1905. Reprint. New York: Benjamin Blom, 1968.

Manners, customs, and fashion as objects of the caricaturists; seen in numerous excellent primary-source illustrations and a very informative text.

1323 Thiselton-Dyer, T.F. BRITISH POPULAR CUSTOMS, PRESENT AND PAST: ILLUSTRATING THE SOCIAL AND DOMESTIC MANNERS OF THE PEOPLE: ARRANGED ACCORDING TO THE CALENDAR OF THE YEAR. 1876. Reprint. Detroit: Singing Tree Press, 1968.

Valuable study of observances of holidays, showing significance regional differences and specific significance of costumes in conjunction with the celebration.

1324 Tunis, Edwin. COLONIAL LIVING. Cleveland: World Publishing Co., 1957.

Valuable for number and clarity of author's drawings; succinct descriptions of all aspects of life in the colonies in sixteenth, seventeenth, and eighteenth centuries, including clothing, manners, and customs.

1325 Turberville, Arthur Stanley. ENGLISH MEN AND MANNERS IN THE 18TH CENTURY: AN ILLUSTRATIVE NARRATIVE. New York: Oxford University Press, 1957.

Generously illustrated social history with general background information, plus chapters on specific types such as artists, dramatists, and military men; bibliography.

1326 Tweedsmuir, Susan. THE EDWARDIAN LADY. London: Gerald Duckworth, 1966.

Very personal view of the life and times of an upper-class woman during the first decade of the twentieth century; chapters on London, the theatre, the fashions, and pastimes; selected black-and-white photographs; valuable for female manners and sentiments during the period.

1327 Vogue Magazine. THE WORLD IN VOGUE. New York: Viking Press, 1963.

Extensive social history of the period from 1893 to 1963 as reflected in the noted fashion magazine; all period illustrations, many in color.

1328 Wagner, Leopold. MANNERS, CUSTOMS AND OBSERVANCES: THEIR ORIGIN AND SIGNIFICATION. 1894. Reprint. Detroit: Gale Research Co., 1968.

Valuable guide to costume usage in connection with customary ceremonial activities in royalty, ecclesiastical, military, parliamentary, social, marital, funerary, and holiday areas.

1329 Wald, Carol, and Papachristou, Judith. MYTH AMERICA: PICTURING WOMEN 1865-1945. New York: Random House, 1975.

The American female as depicted in advertising media in the areas of childhood, sports, work, marriage, and the home; extensive illustrations, many in color.

1330 Wildeblood, Joan, and Brinson, Peter. THE POLITE WORLD: A GUIDE TO ENGLISH MANNERS AND DEPORTMENT FROM THE 13TH TO THE 19TH CENTURY. Oxford, Engl.: Oxford University Press, 1965.

Excellent study of the ideals of feminine decorum and the environment; and, lastly, the achievement of movement, manners, and etiquette: managing trains, walking, curtsying, and so forth; great value to the costumer for text and selected illustrations as well; bibliographic footnotes.

1331 Wilson, Everett B. AMERICA'S VANISHING FOLKWAYS. New York: A.S. Barnes and Co., 1965.

Pictorial and textual description of many customs, manners, and modes of previous decades in the United States, covering such areas as recreation, social pastimes, and business and personal lives.

1332 Withington, Robert. ENGLISH PAGEANTRY: AN HISTORICAL OUTLINE. 1918. Reprint. New York: Benjamin Blom, 1963.

Well-documented, mostly from period sources, description of various ceremonies, including mumming, processions, minstrels, tournaments, pageants, masques, and entries; with a few illustrations and sketches; bibliography.

1333 Worsley-Gough, Barbara. FASHIONS IN LONDON. The Londoner's Library. London: Allan Wingate, 1952.

Survey with illustrations of many practices, entertainments, and institutions which dictated London manners in the last century, such as fashions, housing, shops, and hotels.

Chapter 7
SELECTED ILLUSTRATED SOCIAL HISTORY

1334 Amory, Cleveland, and Bradless, Frederic, eds. VANITY FAIR: SELEC-
TIONS FROM AMERICA'S MOST MEMORABLE MAGAZINE: A CAVAL-
CADE OF THE 1920'S AND 1930'S. New York: Viking Press, 1960.

Very well illustrated social history of the two decades as reflected in material from the magazine.

1335 Bagley, John J. LIFE IN MEDIEVAL ENGLAND. New York: G.P.
Putnam's Sons, 1960.

Social history covering full range of medieval life in England;
numerous illustrations.

1336 Barber, Richard W. THE KNIGHT AND CHIVALRY. Totowa, N.J.:
Rowman and L ttlefield, 1975.

Study of the subject of chivalry and knighthood; eight color
and twenty-six monochrome illustrations; bibliography.

1337 Barrett, Marvin. THE JAZZ AGE. New York: G.P. Putnam's Sons,
1959.

Social history of the 1920s, generally based on the television
program of the same name by the National Broadcasting Company; numerous photographs and pictorial materials; bibliography.

1338 Bentley, Nicolas. THE VICTORIAN SCENE: A PICTURE BOOK OF THE
PERIOD, 1837-1901. New York: Spring Books, 1968.

Thoroughly and extensively illustrated social history with coverage of such areas as home life, food and eating, clothing,
education, religion, labor, travel, and pastimes; many color
illustrations.

Selected Illustrated Social History

1339 Bishop, Morris. THE HORIZON BOOK OF THE MIDDLE AGES. Norman Kotker, editor-in-charge. New York: American Heritage Publishing Co., 1968.

Extensive pictorial social history with excellent text and primary-source illustrations, many in color.

1340 Bonney, Mabel Therese. REMEMBER WHEN: A PICTORIAL CHRONICLE OF THE TURN OF THE CENTURY AND OF THE DAYS KNOWN AS EDWARDIAN. New York: Coward-McCann, 1933.

Older book but excellent photographic record of the period.

1341 Brander, Michael. THE VICTORIAN GENTLEMAN. London: Gordon Cremonesi, 1975.

Discussion of dominant influences on men during the period from 1830 to 1901; coverage of such areas as childhood, education, tastes and manners, morality, travel and sports and pastimes; chronological chart of major historical events; well illustrated with period sources; index and bibliography.

1342 Briggs, Asa, ed. THE NINETEENTH CENTURY: THE CONTRADICTIONS OF PROGRESS. New York: McGraw-Hill Book Co., 1970.

Extensively illustrated survey of the century.

1343 Brosse, Jacques, et al. 100,000 YEARS OF DAILY LIFE: A VISUAL HISTORY. Translated by Anne Carter. New York: Golden Press, 1961.

Extensive coverage of daily life and social history through visual materials, many in color.

1344 Casson, Lionel. THE HORIZON BOOK OF DAILY LIFE IN ANCIENT EGYPT. New York: American Heritage Publishing Co., 1975.

Excellent pictorial survey of the important facets of daily life of the ancient Egyptians; bibliography.

1345 _____. THE HORIZON BOOK OF DAILY LIFE IN ANCIENT ROME. New York: American Heritage Publishing Co., 1975.

Continuation of format of previous entry with numerous primary-source illustrations; bibliography.

1346 Chastel, Andre. THE AGE OF HUMANISM: EUROPE, 1480-1530. Translated by Katherine M. Delavenay and E.M. Gwyer. New York: McGraw-Hill Book Co., 1963.

Extensive social history with monochrome and color illustrations; three sections of history, cultural concerns, and art and poetry.

1347 Cobban, Alfred, et al. THE EIGHTEENTH CENTURY: EUROPE IN THE AGE OF ENLIGHTENMENT. New York: McGraw-Hill Book Co., 1969.

Expansive pictorial social history covering such topics as government, technology, architecture, art, and music; 589 illustrations, 173 in color; maps and bibliography.

1348 Davidson, Marshall. LIFE IN AMERICA. 2 vols. Boston: Houghton Mifflin Co., 1951.

Richly illustrated social history in cooperation with the Metropolitan Museum of Art; bibliography.

1349 Dickens, Arthur G., ed. THE COURTS OF EUROPE: POLITICS, PATRONAGE AND ROYALTY, 1400-1800. New York: McGraw-Hill Book Co., 1977.

Collected essays on various facets of the period's social history with 342 illustrations, 63 in color, covering such areas and rulers as Lorenzo de Medici, Francis I, the Tudors, Philip IV of Spain, Louis XIV, Peter the Great, and Louis XV; bibliography.

1350 Dodd, A.H. ELIZABETHAN ENGLAND. London: B.T. Batsford; New York: G.P. Putnam's Sons, 1973.

Excellently illustrated with some color plates; social history with chapters covering the range of Elizabethan life: country, town, home life, church, education, arts, pastimes, and travel; bibliography.

1351 Dutton, Ralph. ENGLISH COURT LIFE FROM HENRY VII TO GEORGE II. London: B.T. Batsford, 1963.

Valuable, concise treatment of court life, with well-chosen primary-source illustrations.

1352 Evans, Joan. THE VICTORIANS. Cambridge: Cambridge University Press, 1966.

Pictorial social history of the period shown through quotations from period novels and 102 primary-source illustrations.

1353 Ford, Colin, ed. AN EARLY VICTORIAN ALBUM: THE PHOTOGRAPHIC MASTERPIECES (1843-1847) OF DAVID OCTAVIUS HILL AND ROBERT ADAMSON. New York: Alfred A. Knopf, 1976.

Excellent reproduction of photographs that capture representative history of the period.

Selected Illustrated Social History

1354 _____. HAPPY AND GLORIOUS: 130 YEARS OF ROYAL PHOTO-
GRAPHS. New York: Macmillan Co., 1977.

The reflections of the times from Queen Victoria to Queen
Elizabeth II as seen in photographs of the royalty.

1355 Foss, Michael. CHIVALRY. New York: David McKay, 1975.

Extensive illustrations in color and black and white of the entire medieval period and the age of chivalry; coverage of the
Crusades, tournaments, and daily life, among other topics.

1356 Gies, Joseph, and Gies, Frances. LIFE IN A MEDIEVAL CASTLE.
New York: Thomas Y. Crowell Co., 1974.

Complete and well-documented coverage in entries 1356 and
1357 which are complementary; concerning social history of
the entire period; containing illustrations, drawings, and photographs; bibliography in both.

1357 _____. LIFE IN A MEDIEVAL CITY. New York: Apollo, 1973.

1358 Gosling, Nigel. NADAR. New York: Alfred A. Knopf, 1976.

The panorama of nineteenth-century Parisian life presented
through 359 period photographs.

1359 Hart, Roger. ENGLISH LIFE IN CHAUCER'S DAY. New York: G.P.
Putnam's Sons, 1973.

1360 _____. ENGLISH LIFE IN THE EIGHTEENTH CENTURY. New York:
G.P. Putnam's Sons, 1970.

1361 _____. ENGLISH LIFE IN THE NINETEENTH CENTURY. New York:
G.P. Putnam's Sons, 1971.

1362 _____. ENGLISH LIFE IN THE SEVENTEENTH CENTURY. New York:
G.P. Putnam's Sons, 1971.

1363 _____. ENGLISH LIFE IN TUDOR TIMES. New York: G.P. Putnam's
Sons, 1972.

In entries 1359-63, presentation of extensive and well-illustrated social history of England from 1485 through the nineteenth
century; primary-source illustrative materials, many in color,
throughout; helpful appendixes, for example, a Tudor cost-of-
living equivalency table and chronological charts and time-
tables; bibliography in each volume; helpful books.

1364 Harthan, John. THE BOOK OF HOURS. New York: Thomas Y. Crowell Co., 1977.

Historical survey of evolution, contents, decorations, and social aspects of the form, including color illustrations from thirty-four different sources.

1365 Hartley, Dorothy, and Elliott, Margaret M. LIFE AND WORK OF THE PEOPLE OF ENGLAND: A PICTORIAL RECORD FROM CONTEMPORARY SOURCES. New York: G.P. Putnam's Sons, 1926.

Somewhat dated source but valuable for contents of a number of plates of the entire range of life, with a chapter devoted to clothing and fashion.

1366 Hay, Denys, ed. THE AGE OF THE RENAISSANCE. New York: McGraw-Hill Book Co., 1967.

Valuable source for both text and 600 illustrations: 180 in color, plus 420 drawings and other pictorial sources.

1367 Herold, J. Christopher. THE HORIZON BOOK OF THE AGE OF NAPOLEON. New York: American Heritage Publishing Co., 1963.

Extensive pictorial guide to the period.

1368 Hibbert, Christopher. THE HORIZON BOOK OF DAILY LIFE IN VICTORIAN ENGLAND. New York: American Heritage Publishing Co., 1975.

Not as expansive as some social histories, but good pictorial sources.

1369 Horst, Horst P. SALUTE TO THE THIRTIES. New York: Viking Press, 1971.

Social history of the decade of the 1930s as seen through the photographs of Horst.

1370 Jarrett, Derek. ENGLAND IN THE AGE OF HOGARTH. New York: Viking Press, 1974.

Well-illustrated social history seen through the artist and his work.

1371 Jenkins, Alan. THE THIRTIES. New York: Stein and Day Publishers, 1976.

Social history with numerous photographs and other primary-source illustrations of every aspect of the decade from fashion to war; index and bibliography.

1372 _____. THE TWENTIES. New York: Universe Books, 1974.

> Extensive pictorial social history of the decade, with chapters
> on manners, fashions, dancing, sports, and entertainments; in-
> dex and bibliography.

1373 Jensen, Oliver, et al. AMERICAN ALBUM. New York: American
Heritage Publishing Co., 1968.

> Collection of black-and-white photographs of American life
> from 1839 to 1915, divided into sections on rural America,
> the big city, and the pursuit of happiness, among many.

1374 Josephy, Alvin M., Jr., ed. THE HORIZON HISTORY OF AFRICA.
New York: American Heritage Publishing Co., 1971.

> Single-volume survey of the whole continent, with good pri-
> mary-source illustrative material.

1375 Kinross, John Patrick Douglas Balfour. THE WINDSOR YEARS: THE
LIFE OF EDWARD, AS PRINCE OF WALES, KING, AND DUKE OF
WINDSOR. New York: Viking Press, 1967.

> Excellent reflection of the times and styles of the upper class
> as seen through a photographic record of the life of the influ-
> ential Edward.

1376 Lichten, Frances. DECORATIVE ART OF VICTORIA'S ERA. New York:
Charles Scribner's Sons, 1950.

> Well-documented and illustrated social history.

1377 Lofts, Norah. QUEENS OF ENGLAND. Garden City, N.Y.: Doubleday and Co., 1977.

> Social history through biographies of queens; illustrated.

1378 Lucie-Smith, Edward, and Dars, Celestine. HOW THE RICH LIVED: THE
PAINTER AS WITNESS, 1870-1914. New York: Paddington Press, 1976.

> Color and monochrome reproductions of artists' renderings of
> social life.

1379 Margetson, Stella. LEISURE AND PLEASURE IN THE NINETEENTH CEN-
TURY. New York: Coward-McCann, 1969.

> Well-illustrated social history emphasizing the pastimes of the
> century.

1380 ____. THE LONG PARTY: HIGH SOCIETY IN THE TWENTIES AND THIRTIES. Farnborough, Engl.: Saxon House, 1974.

Well-illustrated social history of the twenty-year period.

1381 Marshall, Rosalind K. THE DAYS OF DUCHESS ANNE: LIFE IN THE HOUSEHOLD OF THE DUCHESS OF HAMILTON 1656-1716. London: Collins, 1973.

One of few illustrated sources of social history of this period.

1382 Mee, Charles L., Jr. THE HORIZON BOOK OF DAILY LIFE IN REN-AISSANCE ITALY. New York: American Heritage Publishing Co., 1975.

Emphasis on illustrative materials rather than on text; bibliography.

1383 Nicoll, Allardyce. THE ELIZABETHANS. Cambridge: Cambridge University Press, 1957.

Four hundred twenty-one monochrome primary-source plates and photographs covering the range of social history of this important period.

1384 Partridge, Bellamy, and Bettmann, Otto. AS WE WERE: FAMILY LIFE IN AMERICA, 1850-1900, IN PICTURES AND TEXT. New York: McGraw-Hill Book Co., 1946.

Older source but well illustrated with primary-source material.

1385 Pearsall, Ronald. EDWARDIAN LIFE AND LEISURE. Newton Abbot, Engl.: David and Charles, 1973.

Social history with numerous photographs and drawings from the period; bibliography.

1386 Plumb, J.H. THE HORIZON BOOK OF THE RENAISSANCE. Edited by Richard M. Ketchum. New York: American Heritage Publishing Co., 1961.

Series of essays covering some aspects of the period's social history: the arts, cities, and women, among many; excellent primary-source illustrative materials, many in color; bibliography.

1387 Priestly, John B. THE EDWARDIANS. New York: Harper and Row, Publishers, 1970.

Extensive pictorial social history of period from 1901 to 1914, with many illustrations, some of fashions and their influences; bibliography.

1388 _____. THE ENGLISH. New York: Viking Press, 1973.

Extensive treatment and numerous illustrations of the basic English character.

1389 _____. VICTORIA'S HEYDAY. New York: Harper and Row, Publishers, 1972.

Pictorial record of the decade of 1850-59; bibliography.

1390 Quennell, Peter. VICTORIAN PANORAMA: A SURVEY OF LIFE AND FASHION FROM CONTEMPORARY PHOTOGRAPHS. New York: Charles Scribner's Sons; London: B.T. Batsford, 1937.

Survey of Victorian scene with 154 photographs and many sketches and drawings; a chapter on fashions.

1391 Reader, William Joseph. VICTORIAN ENGLAND. London: B.T. Batsford; New York: G.P. Putnam's Sons, 1973.

Pictorial social history with numerous black-and-white and some color illustrations; coverage of such areas as the setting, the gentry, the rural class, the urban class, and the towns; detailed survey of the life of the middle class; bibliography.

1392 Rudorff, Raymond. KNIGHTS AND THE AGE OF CHIVALRY. New York: Viking Press, 1974.

Historical survey with numerous monochrome illustrations and twenty-four color plates.

1393 Sansom, William. VICTORIAN LIFE IN PHOTOGRAPHS. London: Thames and Hudson, 1974.

One hundred eight-one period photographs.

1394 Schneider, Pierre. THE WORLD OF WATTEAU 1684-1721. New York: Time-Life Books, 1967.

Social history of the times; work and life of famous artist; many color reproductions of paintings and portraits.

1395 Simpson, Jeffrey. THE AMERICAN FAMILY: A HISTORY IN PHOTO-GRAPHS. New York: Viking Press, 1976.

Photographic record of the American family's development during the last century.

1396 Smith, Lacey Baldwin. THE HORIZON BOOK OF THE ELIZABETHAN WORLD. New York: American Heritage Publishing Co., 1967.

Best single pictorial and textual social history of the period.

1397 Stryker, Emerson, and Wood, Nancy. IN THIS PROUD LAND: AMER-
ICA 1935-1943 AS SEEN IN THE FSA PHOTOGRAPHS. Greenwich,
Conn.: New York Graphic Society, 1973.

Excellent photographic record of the period.

1398 Thomas, Alan. TIME IN A FRAME: PHOTOGRAPHY AND THE NINE-
TEENTH CENTURY MIND. New York: Schocken Books, 1977.

One hundred forty-seven period photographs recording the panorama of the century with many examples of dress, manners,
customs, and mores; bibliography.

1399 Trevor-Roper, Hugh, et al. THE AGE OF EXPANSION: EUROPE AND
THE WORLD, 1559-1660. New York: McGraw-Hill Book Co., 1968.

Extensive social history with chapters on each European country during the period; 604 illustrations (185 in color), 419 other
illustrative items; bibliography.

1400 Unstead, R.J. THE THIRTIES: AN ILLUSTRATED HISTORY IN COLOUR,
1930-1939. London: Macdonald, 1974.

Brief textual survey with major emphasis on primary-source pictorial materials; bibliography.

1401 _____. THE TWENTIES: AN ILLUSTRATED HISTORY IN COLOUR,
1919-1929. London: Macdonald, 1973.

Condensed text and extensive illustrations, many in color;
bibliography.

1402 Veronesi, Guilia. STYLE AND DESIGN, 1909-1929. New York:
George Braziller, 1968.

Excellent survey of social history of the period as seen in the
artists of the day and the artistic trends; 246 monochrome illustrations and 10 color plates.

1403 Williams, E. Neville. LIFE IN GEORGIAN ENGLAND. New York:
G.P. Putnam's Sons, 1962.

Generously illustrated with primary-source material; general descriptions and then discussion of all three social classes' social
life.

1404 Winston, Clare, and Winston, Richard. THE HORIZON BOOK OF DAILY
LIFE IN THE MIDDLE AGES. New York: American Heritage Publishing
Co., 1975.

Excellent pictorial social history.

1405 Wood, Christopher. VICTORIAN PANORAMA: PAINTINGS OF VIC-
TORIAN LIFE. London: Faber and Faber, 1976.

Pictorial social history with 261 color monochrome plates of
paintings of all aspects of Victorian life.

Chapter 8
COSTUME DESIGN

See also 45, 47

1406 Anderson, Donald M. ELEMENTS OF DESIGN. New York: Holt, Rinehart and Winston, 1961.

   Treatment of basic design elements: fundamentals, sources, symbolism, and functions.

1407 Barton, Lucy. APPRECIATING COSTUME. Boston: Walter H. Baker Co., 1969.

   Guide to various problems and consideration for the costume designer in essay form; general bibliography.

1408 _____. COSTUME BY YOU: EIGHT ESSAYS FROM EXPERIENCE. Boston: Walter H. Baker Co., 1940.

   Costumer's personal recollections and suggestions for future costumers in the areas of design and construction.

1409 Birren, Faber. COLOR: A SURVEY IN WORDS AND PICTURES FROM ANCIENT MYSTICISM TO MODERN SCIENCE. New Hyde Park, N.Y: University Books, 1963.

   Comprehensive survey of color, dealing with such areas as color theroy, symbolism, historical uses, and preferences.

1410 _____. COLOR, FORM AND SPACE. New York: Reinhold Book Corp., 1961.

   Discussion of perception of forms in space, relationship of color and form, and organization and control; bibliography.

1411 _____. COLOR IN YOUR WORLD. New York: Collier; London: Collier-Macmillan, 1962.

Interrelation of color preference and personality as an insight to psychological uses of color in design; symbolism and traditions of color usage.

1412 _____. COLOR PERCEPTION IN ART. New York: Van Nostrand Reinhold Co., 1976.

Background to twentieth-century color expression, visual phenomena, and illusions; perceptions of color and twelve full-color studies; listing of Birren's major books; annotated bibliography.

1413 _____. CREATIVE COLOR. New York: Reinhold Publishing Co., 1961.

Complete survey of color and its properties; many color illustrations; chapters on color terms, organization, mixture, value, luminosity, highlights and shadows, and palettes; bibliography; very useful source.

1414 _____. HISTORY OF COLOR IN PAINTING: WITH NEW PRINCIPLES OF COLOR EXPRESSION. New York: Reinhold Publishing Co., 1965.

Extensive survey of historical artists and art movements and their use of color; analysis of color usage today and in the future; thirty-two color plates and many monochrome illustrations; bibliography.

1415 _____, ed. A GRAMMAR OF COLOR. New York: Van Nostrand Reinhold Co., 1969.

Introduction to and explanation of the Munsell color system.

1416 Bossert, Helmuth T. AN ENCYCLOPEDIA OF COLOUR DECORATION FROM THE EARLIEST TIMES TO THE MIDDLE OF THE XIXTH CENTURY. London: Victor Gollancz, 1928.

Explanatory text and 225 color plates of samples of colors and decorations arranged by major countries.

1417 Bradley, Carolyn C. COSTUME DESIGN: AN INTRODUCTORY OUTLINE WITH AIDS FOR STUDENTS AND TEACHERS. Scranton, Pa.: International Textbook Co., 1954.

Inclusion of more material for fashion design than costume design but with much material common to both areas and with some attention to historical background and concerns.

1418 Brockman, Helen L. THE THEORY OF FASHION DESIGN. New York: John Wiley and Sons, 1965.

Geared to fashion world but useful information for costume designer in dual focus of book: fashion influences and techniques of design.

1419 Brogden, Joanne. FASHION DESIGN. London: Studio Publications, 1971.

Introduction to practical aspects of fashion design with a chapter of biographies of famous designers.

1420 Burris-Meyer, Elizabeth. HISTORICAL COLOR GUIDE: PRIMITIVE TO MODERN TIMES WITH THIRTY PLATES IN COLOR. New York: W. Helburn, 1938.

Helpful in costume designer's selection of appropriate colors in a particular historical period; chart for assistance in mixing historical colors.

1421 _____. THIS IS FASHION. New York: Harper and Brothers, 1943.

Usable and informative source containing historical material with valuable sections on artistic qualities of costume throughout history in regard to specific colors and shapes; chapters on accessories, fabrics, and cosmetics and coiffures; material easily found due to outline form of presentation.

1422 Chuse, Anne R. COSTUME DESIGN. Pelham, N.Y.: Bridgeman Publishers, 1943.

Century-by-century historical arrangement of costume, with brief descriptions of the design and large line drawings.

1423 Corey, Irene. THE MASK OF REALITY: AN APPROACH TO DESIGN FOR THE THEATRE. Anchorage, Ky.: Anchorage Press, 1968.

A design text which emphasizes techniques and processes, particularly those of the author; many illustrations of new techniques in the areas of costume and makeup.

1424 Dobkin, Alexander. PRINCIPLES OF FIGURE DRAWING. New York: World Publishing Co., 1960.

Excellent guide to anatomical studies, with drawings by famous artists used as examples.

1425 Doten, Hazel R., and Boulard, Constance. COSTUME DRAWING. 2d ed. London: Sir Isaac Pitman and Sons, 1956.

Very brief and basic introduction to technique of drawing costumes, historical and modern.

1426 _____. FASHION DRAWING: HOW TO DO IT. New York: Harper and Brothers, 1939.

Somewhat geared to fashion illustrator but much useful information for costume designer: figure drawing, clothing detail illustration, historic costume, rendering techniques, color, fabric designing, and a glossary.

1427 Ein, Claudia. HOW TO DESIGN YOUR OWN CLOTHES AND MAKE YOUR OWN PATTERNS. Garden City, N.Y.: Doubleday and Co., 1975.

Use of basic sloper method to create endless fashions with concise directions, clear illustrations, and diagrams.

1428 Ellsworth, Evelyn Peters. TEXTILES AND COSTUME DESIGN. San Francisco: Paul Elder and Co., 1917.

Somewhat dated but valuable study of the relationship between textiles and costume in historical periods.

1429 Gatto, Joseph A. ELEMENTS OF DESIGN: COLOR AND VALUE. Worcester, Mass.: Davis Press, 1974.

Well-illustrated condensed textual discussion of the characteristics, uses, and properties of both color and value.

1430 Graves, Maitland. THE ART OF COLOR AND DESIGN. 2d ed. New York: McGraw-Hill Book Co., 1951.

Standard text covering extensively the elements and principles of design; analysis of each design element with questions and exercises for each chapter; glossary.

1431 Green, Joyce Mary Conyngham. PERIOD COSTUMES AND SETTINGS FOR THE SMALL STAGE. London: George G. Harrap and Co., 1939.

Brief, simplified explanation for designing historical costumes; selected illustrations.

1432 Guptill, Arthur L. COLOR IN SKETCHING AND RENDERING. New York: Reinhold Publishing Co., 1935.

Somewhat older source but excellent presentation of color theory and technique; full coverage of media, equipment, paper; exercises in texturing, sketching, and composition; many illustrations in color.

1433 Hardy, Kay. COSTUME DESIGN. New York: McGraw-Hill Book Co., 1948.

Full treatment of major aspects of costume design; good chapter on procedures and techniques of drawing the human figure.

1434 Hogarth, Burne. DYNAMIC FIGURE DRAWING. New York: Watson-Guptill Publications, 1970.

Guide for sketching the human form in movement.

1435 Ireland, Patrick John. DRAWING AND DESIGNING MENSWEAR. New York: John Wiley and Sons, 1976.

Even though geared to fashion market, general procedures and techniques applicable to modern and period costume sketching.

1436 _____. FASHION DESIGN DRAWING. 2d ed. New York: John Wiley and Sons, 1975.

Geared to fashion illustrator but some helpful information on techniques for costume designer.

1437 Itten, Johannes. THE ART OF COLOR: THE SUBJECTIVE EXPERIENCE AND OBJECTIVE RATIONALE OF COLOR. New York: Reinhold Book Corp., 1961.

Extensive investigation of the entire range of color, with excellent illustrative color materials; chapters on color contrasts, mixing, harmony, form, and spatial effects; many color reproductions of historic artists' works for illustrative purposes.

1438 _____. DESIGN AND FORM: THE BASIC COURSE AT THE BAUHAUS AND LATER. Rev. ed. New York: Van Nostrand Reinhold Co., 1975.

Design text with chapters on contrast, color theory, materials and textures, form, rhythm, expressive forms, and subjective forms; many illustrations, some in color.

1439 Jacobson, Egbert. BASIC COLOR: AN INTERPRETATION OF THE OSTWALD COLOR SYSTEM. Chicago: Paul Theobald, 1948.

Complete technical description with color charts and diagrams for a full understanding of the Ostwald system.

1440 Kawashima, Masaaki. FUNDAMENTALS OF MEN'S FASHION DESIGN. New York: Charles Scribner's Sons, 1975.

Variations of general design, basic techniques, equipment, and measurements for the male figure.

1441 Loomis, Andrew. FIGURE DRAWING FOR ALL IT'S WORTH. New York: Viking Press, 1971.

Basic figure drawing book.

1442 Maier, Manfred. BASIC PRINCIPLES OF DESIGN: THE FOUNDATION PROGRAM AT THE SCHOOL OF DESIGN, BASEL, SWITZERLAND. 4 vols. New York: Van Nostrand Reinhold Co., 1977.

Well-illustrated color and monochrome coverage of basic design principles through extensive presentation of examples and exercises, including sections on material studies and textile design.

1443 Mortimer-Dunn, Gloria. FASHION DESIGN. Adelaide, Australia: Rigby, 1972.

Some consideration of historical costume and presentation of design elements, but primarily geared to fashion design.

1444 Naylor, Brenda. THE TECHNIQUE OF DRESS DESIGN. London: B.T. Batsford, 1966.

Coverage primarily of contemporary fashion, but good presentation of basic design elements and some concern with costume since 1916.

1445 Parker, Xenia Ley. DESIGNING FOR CRAFTS. New York: Charles Scribner's Sons, 1974.

Source of many new ideas for designers; translations of one art form to another; many illustrations.

1446 Paterek, Josephine. COSTUMING FOR THE THEATRE. New York: Crown Publishers, 1959.

Basic introductory overview of the costume design process with attention to analysis, historical period concerns, elements of design, workshop, and construction techniques.

1447 Pepin, Harriet. FUNDAMENTALS OF APPAREL DESIGN. New York: Funk and Wagnalls Co., 1948.

Careful consideration and explanation of design elements and principles.

1448 Prisk, Berneice, and Byers, Jack A. THE THEATRE STUDENT: COSTUMING. New York: Richards Rosen Press, 1970.

Basic introduction to technical costuming process, with attention to design, planning, construction, and the production aspects on a somewhat simplified and general level.

1449 Reed, Walt. THE FIGURE: AN ARTIST'S APPROACH TO DRAWING AND CONSTRUCTION. New York: Watson-Guptill Publications, 1976.

Elementary to advanced techniques of figure drawing of use to costume designer.

1450 Russell, Douglas A. STAGE COSTUME DESIGN: THEORY, TECHNIQUE AND STYLE. New York: Appleton-Century-Crofts, 1973.

Extensive introduction to the study of costume design with coverage of theory and technique, including the costume sketch, analysis, elements and principles of design and characterization, color, fabric, patterns, ornamentation, accessories, and production organization in part 1; coverage in part 2 of style in historical plays from the ancients to the moderns; survey in part 3 in outline form of history of Western costume; a few color plates and many monochrome illustrations and line drawings; sources of theatrical supplies; index and bibliography.

1451 _____. THEATRICAL STYLE: A VISUAL APPROACH TO THE THEATRE. Palo Alto, Calif.: Mayfield, 1976.

Not specifically dealing with costume but theatrical design generally; survey of art, culture, and dramatic and theatrical developments of major historical periods.

1452 Sloan, Eunice Moore. ILLUSTRATING FASHION. New York: Harper and Row, Publishers, 1968.

Detailed treatment with emphasis on fashion but with many techniques useful to costumer.

1453 Smith, C. Ray, ed. THE THEATRE CRAFTS BOOK OF COSTUMES. Emmaus, Pa.: Rodale Press, 1973.

Collection of essays and illustrations from THEATRE CRAFTS magazine dealing primarily with the design of costume for the modern theatre.

1454 Traphagen, Ethel. COSTUME DESIGN AND ILLUSTRATION. New York: John Wiley and Sons, 1932.

Dated and somewhat superficial in attempting to cover a wide range of topics from design methodology to historic costume.

1455 Volland, Virginia. DESIGNING WOMAN: THE ART AND PRACTICE OF THEATRICAL COSTUME DESIGN. Garden City, N.Y.: Doubleday and Co., 1966.

Personal experiences of costume designer covering the preproduction as well as the performance aspects of theatrical costume design.

1456 Westerman, Maxine. ELEMENTARY FASHION DESIGN AND TRADE SKETCHING. New York: Fairchild Publications, 1973.

Illustrations by the author; geared more for fashion designer but clear presentation of basic elements and principles; unit on sources of inspiration for design dealing with historical sources and trimmings.

1457 Zaidenberg, Arthur. HOW TO DRAW PERIOD COSTUMES. New York: Abelard-Schuman, 1966.

Steps for imposing period costumes on several standard basic poses of a human figure form; useful to young or beginning student.

1458 Zinkeisen, Doris. DESIGNING FOR THE STAGE. London: Studio Publications, 1945.

Condensed treatment of simplified approaches to both scenic and costume design, with brief chapters on historic costume, group costumes, construction, wigs and headwear, and footwear, including a number of designs and photographs of complete costumes.

1459 Zirner, Laura. COSTUMING FOR THE MODERN STAGE. Urbana: University of Illinois Press, 1957.

Simplified introduction to theatrical costuming process, with selected photographs and line drawings.

Chapter 9
ORNAMENTATION AND SYMBOLS

See also 49, 354, 355, 357, 360, 393, 394, 399, 412, 418, 419, 525, 527, 556, 564

1460 Alexander, Mary Jean. HANDBOOK OF DECORATIVE DESIGN AND ORNAMENT. New York: Tudor Publishing Co., 1965.

Basic design principles, plus many examples of decoration and ornamentation from historical periods.

1461 Binder, Pearl. MAGIC SYMBOLS OF THE WORLD. New York: Paul Hamlyn, 1972.

Extensively illustrated survey of magic signs and symbols and their meanings.

1462 Blanc, Charles. ART IN ORNAMENT AND DRESS. 1877. Reprint. Detroit: Gale Research Co., 1971.

Study of the artistic principles of ornamentation in dress and accessories with several period illustrations.

1463 Bossert, Helmuth T. ORNAMENT IN APPLIED ART: 122 COLOR PLATES REPRODUCING OVER 2000 DECORATIVE MOTIVES FROM THE ARTS OF ASIA, PRIMITIVE EUROPE, NORTH, CENTRAL, AND SOUTH AMERICA, AFRICA, OCEANIA, AND FROM THE PEASANT ARTS OF EUROPE. New York: E. Weyhe, 1924.

Presentation in color plates of numerous decorative motifs taken from costume articles and accessories the world over.

1464 Brod, Fritzi. DECORATIVE DESIGN. New York: Sir Isaac Pitman and Sons, 1949.

Suggestions of various types of ornament and design for particular uses.

1465 Coffin, Harry B. DESIGNS, BORDERS, BACKGROUNDS, TINTS AND PATTERNS. New York: Thomas Y. Crowell Co., 1951.

> Presentation of many examples of motifs useful to the costumer.

1466 Estrin, Michael. 2,000 DESIGNS, FORMS AND ORNAMENTS: AN ALBUM THAT REPRESENTS THE ENTIRE RANGE OF ORNAMENT FROM PREHISTORIC TIMES UNTIL THE PRESENT. New York: William Penn Publishing Co., 1947.

> Survey, including sections on costume, as well as on accessories and other examples of sources of decorative motifs; no text but numerous examples.

1467 Evans, Joan. PATTERN: A STUDY OF ORNAMENT IN WESTERN EUROPE FROM 1180 TO 1900. 2 vols. 1931. Reprint. New York: Hacker Art Books, 1975.

> Authoritative study of historical pattern; quite thoroughly documented and illustrated with 435 primary-source plates; chronological arrangement of dominant influences and resultant patterns and ornaments and motifs of historical stylistic periods; basic for understanding of artistic movements which ultimately affected the design of costume.

1468 Griesbach, C.B. HISTORIC ORNAMENT: A PICTORIAL ARCHIVE. New York: Dover Publications, 1975.

> Nine hundred examples of decoration and ornaments from ancient Egypt to 1800, featuring some from textile designs and accessories.

1469 Justema, William. THE PLEASURE OF PATTERN. New York: Reinhold Book Corp., 1968.

> Coverage of pattern in general and in particular; eight lessons in using design elements in pattern making; extensive array of monochrome plates of historic and contemporary patterns; annotated bibliography.

1470 Koch, Rudolf. THE BOOK OF SIGNS: 493 SYMBOLS USED FROM EARLIEST TIMES TO THE MIDDLE AGES BY PRIMITIVE PEOPLES AND EARLY CHRISTIANS. 1930. Reprint. New York: Dover Publications, n.d.

> Contains drawings and explanations of numerous symbols useful for costume design.

1471 Lehner, Ernst. THE PICTURE BOOK OF SYMBOLS. New York: William Penn Publishing Co., 1956.

Drawings and descriptions with meanings for twenty-nine subject divisions of signs, for example, astronomy, magic, mythol-
ogy.

1472 Meyer, Franz Sales. HANDBOOK OF ORNAMENT: A GRAMMAR OF
ART INDUSTRIAL AND ARCHITECTURAL DESIGNING IN ALL ITS
BRANCHES FOR PRACTICAL AS WELL AS THEORETICAL USE. 1892.
Reprint. New York: Dover Publications, 1957.

Numerous (3,002) illustrations of decorations and ornamenta-
tions useful to costumer, as in religious articles, heraldry,
jewelry, and other accessories.

1473 Shaw, Henry. THE ENCYCLOPEDIA OF ORNAMENT. 1842. Reprint.
New York: St. Martin's Press, 1974.

Complete reprint of historical ornament sourcebook.

1474 Smeets, Rene. SIGNS, SYMBOLS AND ORNAMENTS. New York:
Van Nostrand Reinhold Co., 1975.

Fully illustrated survey of development of geometric and natural motifs as pattern and decoration.

1475 Vilimkova, M. EGYPTIAN ORNAMENT. London: Allen Wingate,
1963.

Three hundred forty-three color examples of Egyptian decorative motifs.

1476 Wedd, J.A. Dunkin. SOURCES OF DESIGN: PATTERN AND TEXTURE.
New York: Studio Publications, 1956.

Treatment and discussion of two elements of design often overlooked.

Chapter 10

COSTUME CONSTRUCTION TECHNIQUES
AND PATTERN SOURCES

See also 26, 28, 42, 57, 201, 206, 212, 240, 254, 263, 287, 316, 317, 323, 326, 330, 344, 353, 358, 369, 374, 408, 411, 418, 419, 424, 425, 457, 527, 559, 568, 569, 642, 647, 716, 717, 718, 719, 721, 803, 1196, 1198, 1448

1477 Armes, Alice. ENGLISH SMOCKS WITH DIRECTIONS FOR MAKING THEM. Leicester, Engl.: Dryad Press, 1961.

> Descriptions, decorative motifs, patterns, and construction directions for English smocks.

1478 Arnold, Janet. PATTERNS OF FASHION: ENGLISHWOMEN'S DRESSES AND THEIR CONSTRUCTION, C. 1660-1860. London: Wace and Co., 1964.

1479 _____. PATTERNS OF FASHION: ENGLISHWOMEN'S DRESSES AND THEIR CONSTRUCTION, C. 1860-1940. London: Wace and Co., 1966.

> Indispensable guidebooks to costume and construction techniques with at least forty drawings and patterns for dresses from the periods specified; detailed sketches; guides for cutting and enlarging patterns which are reproduced on graphed paper; section on period techniques of dressmaking; pictorial outline of costume, model doll construction; reading lists and list of primary-source depositories and museums; invaluable sources.

1480 Bane, Allyne. CREATIVE CLOTHING CONSTRUCTION. 2d ed. New York: McGraw-Hill Book Co., 1966.

> Comprehensive survey of basic sewing techniques with clear instructions, diagrams, and drawings.

1481 _____. TAILORING. 3d ed. New York: McGraw-Hill Book Co., 1974.

Comprehensive guide to tailoring techniques, with many diagrams and clear instructions; chapters on equipment, fabric selection, pattern selection and alteration, muslin copy, and
special problems in tailoring.

1482 Barton, Lucy. COSTUMING THE BIBLICAL PLAY. Boston: Walter H.
Baker Co., 1962.

Condensed survey of most facets of the subject of biblical costume, including construction procedures, materials, and draping techniques, with clear drawings and directions.

1483 Barton, Lucy, and Edson, Doris. PERIOD PATTERNS. Boston: Walter
H. Baker, Co., 1942.

Forty plates giving patterns, sewing directions, and construction guides for selected costumes dating from 1575 to 1911;
photographs included of most of the completed garments; instructions for enlarging and reading the patterns; very useful
source.

1484 Baverstock, Doreen M. STAGE COSTUME CONSTRUCTION. Los Angeles:
Lyman House, 1939.

Instructions for drafting a fitted bodice and period variations;
supplementary bibliography.

1485 Beese, Pat. EMBROIDERY FOR THE CHURCH. Newton Centre, Mass.:
Charles T. Branford, 1975.

Historical background of church vestments, plus new techniques
and materials for adaptations of period styles; directions, diagrams, and illustrations.

1486 Berk, Barbara. FIRST BOOK OF STAGE COSTUME AND MAKE-UP.
New York: Franklin Watts, 1954.

Suggestions for simplified costume; helpful to a youthful reader.

1487 Boyes, Janet. MAKING PAPER COSTUMES. Boston: Plays, 1973.

Instructions for making, decorating, and fireproofing paper costumes for both youths and adults; clear directions and photographs; many creative ideas for a costumer.

1488 Bress, Helene. THE MACRAME BOOK. New York: Charles Scribner's
Sons, 1972.

Beginning instructions, plus design ideas for use of technique;
many drawings, clear instructions, and photographs; list of suppliers; bibliography.

1489 Brooke, Iris. MEDIEVAL THEATRE COSTUME: A PRACTICAL GUIDE
TO THE CONSTRUCTION OF GARMENTS. London: Adam and Charles
Black, 1969.

Background introduction with coverage of wardrobe and sixteen
diagrammatic patterns for constructing the garments; chapters
on religious drama, heraldry, headwear and footwear, armor,
masks and wings, and dress of the royalty; many line drawings.

1490 Bryson, Nicholas L. THERMOPLASTIC SCENERY FOR THE THEATRE:
VOLUME I--VACUUM FORMING. New York: Drama Book, 1972.

Introduction to new technique, with some usefulness to theatrical costumers especially in the areas of armor and accessories,
chapters on general considerations, tools and equipment, fabrication processes, and the vacuum forming machine; clear directions and numerous drawings, diagrams, and photographs.

1491 Burnham, Dorothy K. CUT MY COTE. Toronto: Royal Ontario Museum, 1973.

Interesting study of the relationship of loom width to intrica-
cies of garments' cut, including twenty-nine patterns of shirts
and coats from many countries and time periods.

1492 Chernoff, Goldie Taub. EASY COSTUMES YOU DON'T HAVE TO SEW.
New York: Four Winds, 1975.

Instructions and illustrations for easily constructed costumes
which do not require sewing: sack; bag; sandwich board, and
carton; sections on hats and disguises.

1493 Clark, Winifred. DRESSMAKING TECHNIQUES FOR TRADE STUDENTS.
New York: Drake Publishers, 1970.

Practical lessons and techniques in construction with instructions and diagrams; glossary of terms and specifications of suggested supplies and equipment.

1494 Collard, Eileen. THE CUT OF WOMEN'S 19TH CENTURY DRESS. 2
vols. Toronto: Custume Society of Ontario, 1972, 1973.

Volume title: (1) THE VERTICAL EPOCH, 1800-1821; and (2)
ROMANCE AND SENTIMENT, 1822-1839; each containing
brief notes on the background of the dress, with primary textual documentation and a few line drawings; several patterns
of basic dress fashions of each period.

1495 Collins, Wanda Summers. THE COMPLETE BOOK OF HOME MILLINERY.
New York: Funk and Wagnalls Co., 1951.

One of the few books in the subject area; specific and general construction techniques applicable to costume millinery work; treatment of all types and styles of headwear.

1496 Crane, Nancy. THE INSTRUCTOR HANDBOOK SERIES: CREATIVE COSTUMES FOR THE CLASSROOM. Dansville, N.Y.: F.A. Owen Publishing Co., 1960.

Simplified directions and diagrams for construction of basic children's costumes, for example, animals, flowers, fairies, and national and historical garments.

1497 Crider, James R. COSTUMING WITH BASICS AND SEPARATES. New Haven, Conn.: Whitlock's, 1954.

Directions for basic bodice and skirt pattern variations to create period costumes; directions, diagrams, and photographs.

1498 Croonborg, Frederick T. THE BLUE BOOK OF MEN'S TAILORING: THEATRICAL COSTUMEMAKER'S PATTERN BOOK FOR EDWARDIAN MEN'S COSTUMES. New York: Van Nostrand Reinhold Co., 1977.

Excellent reissue of costumer's practical tailoring systems, measurements, pattern drafts, primary illustrations for many styles and physical variations; includes not only civilian dress but military, livery, sporting, civil service, and clerical garments; excellent source.

1499 Cummings, Richard. ONE HUNDRED AND ONE COSTUMES FOR ALL AGES, ALL OCCASIONS. New York: David McKay, 1970.

Introductory book for juvenile costumes mainly; numerous diagrams, simplified patterns, and drawings, with some creative suggestions.

1500 Davies, Natalie. BEADS AS JEWELRY. Radnor, Pa.: Chilton Book Co.k 1975.

Very interesting source with directions and diagrams for over fifty projects for jewelry accessories and costumes, using new techniques and ideas.

1501 Dendel, Esther Warner. AFRICAN FABRIC CRAFTS: SOURCES OF AFRICAN DESIGN AND TECHNIQUES. New York: Taplinger Publishing Co., 1974.

Chapters on techniques of applique, embroidery, dyeing, looping, braiding, and ethnic costume, with many photographs and diagrams of costumes and accessories; bibliography.

1502 Elicker, Virginia Wilk. BIBLICAL COSTUMES FOR CHURCH AND SCHOOL. New York: A.S. Barnes and Co., 1953.

> Simplified but practical and useful approaches to biblical costumes, with appropriate drawings and a few simplified patterns.

1503 Emlyn-Jones, Gwen. MAKE YOUR OWN GLOVES. New York: Charles Scribner's Sons, 1974.

> Brief historical background; complete directions for all types of gloves and mittens made of many materials from leather to fabric; pattern section of twelve patterns each in ladies' and gentlemen's sizes; suppliers list and bibliography.

1504 Etheridge, Ken. STAGE COSTUME FOR THE AMATEUR. Edinburgh: Albyn Press, 1947.

> Very simplified attempt to cover historical dress; with some patterns and diagrams.

1505 Evans, Mary. DRAPING AND DRESS DESIGN. Ann Arbor, Mich.: Edwards Brothers, 1941.

> Detailed directions for usable draping method, with a chapter devoted to each segment of a garment; drawings and diagrams.

1506 _____. HOW TO MAKE HISTORIC AMERICAN COSTUMES. New York: A.S. Barnes and Co., 1942.

> Beginning with Indians through the Civil War, somewhat simplified patterns and instructions for some historical costumes and accessories.

1507 Evans, R.K. DRESS: THE EVOLUTION OF CUT AND ITS EFFECT ON MODERN DESIGN. London: Faber and Faber, 1939.

> Simplified guide to construction of period costumes, with attention to the evolution from older construction methods to more modern techniques; numerous illustrations and diagrams.

1508 Fernald, Mary, and Shenton, Eileen. COSTUME DESIGN AND MAKING: A PRACTICAL HANDBOOK. 2d ed. New York: Theatre Arts Books, 1967.

> Intended as a guide for construction of period costumes, with a brief historical section followed by simplified patterns and sewing directions.

1509 Frager, Dorothy. CLOTH HATS, BAGS 'N BAGGAGE. Radnor, Pa.: Chilton Book Co., 1978.

Almost fifty-page section dealing with patterns, directions, photographs, and diagrams for constructing many modern hat styles; glossary of terms and list of suppliers.

1510 Geen, Michael. THEATRICAL COSTUME AND THE AMATEUR STAGE. Boston: Plays, 1968.

Simplified approaches to constructing and altering stage costumes, with a brief guide to historical costume; simplified patterns, diagrams, and drawings.

1511 Greenhowe, Jean. COSTUMES FOR NURSERY TALE CHARACTERS. Boston: Plays, 1976.

Simplified approach to nineteen costumes for nursery tale characters, with simple patterns and easy-to-follow instructions.

1512 _____. STAGE COSTUME FOR GIRLS. Boston: Plays, 1975.

Simplified directions, patterns, diagrams, and photographs for making fourteen girls' costumes ranging from Grecian to Victorian styles.

1513 Handford, Jack. PROFESSIONAL PATTERNMAKING FOR DESIGNERS OF WOMEN'S WEAR. Los Angeles: Handford Enterprises, 1974.

Thorough and extensive treatment of pattern drafting for women's wear, with concise directions and diagrams.

1514 Harmand, Adrien. JEANNE D' ARC: SES COSTUMES, SON ARMURE. Paris: Librarie Ernest Leroux, 1929.

French text, but widest range of available patterns from the period; numerous illustrations.

1515 Hartley, Dorothy. MEDIAEVAL COSTUME AND LIFE: A REVIEW OF THEIR SOCIAL ASPECTS ARRANGED UNDER VARIOUS CLASSES AND WORKERS WITH INSTRUCTIONS FOR MAKING NUMEROUS TYPES OF DRESS. New York: Charles Scribner's Sons; London: B.T. Batsford, 1931.

Topically arranged and informative volume covering a wide range of costume-related items; primary-source illustrations plus clear drawings and diagrams for further clarification or construction; photographs of constructed garments.

1516 Healy, Daty. DRESS THE SHOW: A BASIC COSTUME BOOK. New York: Row, Peterson Co., 1948.

Simplified approach with emphasis on costumes for children and fantasy; clear patterns and drawings.

1517 Hill, Margot Hamilton, and Bucknell, Peter A. THE EVOLUTION OF
FASHION: PATTERN AND CUT FROM 1066 TO 1930. London: B.T.
Batsford, 1967.

Coverage of historical development in English costume patterns
and construction; fifty-six sections dating from William I to
George V; each section with a typical male and female costume, with somewhat simplified patterns for each garment item
and with limited notes on patterns and construction; each garment pictured in a black-and-white drawing; bibliography; useful source.

1518 Hillhouse, Marion S., and Mansfield, Evelyn A. DRESS DESIGN--
DRAPING AND FLAT PATTERN MAKING. New York: Houghton Mifflin
Co., 1948.

Older text but coverage of two primary techniques of pattern
making with diagrams and instructions for garments of the
1940s.

1519 Hollen, Norma R. FLAT PATTERN METHODS WITH SELECTED SEWING
SUGGESTIONS. Minneapolis: Burgess Publishing Co., 1961.

Detailed textbook in construction techniques and procedures
with clear, explicit directions, diagrams, and drawings.

1520 Hughes, Talbot. DRESS DESIGN: AN ACCOUNT OF COSTUME FOR
ARTISTS AND DRESSMAKERS. London: Sir Isaac Pitman and Sons, 1932.

Numerous secondary-source line drawings and sixty-eight general period patterns with vague scale and no directions.

1521 Ives, Suzy. CREATING CHILDREN'S COSTUMES FROM PAPER AND
CARD. New York: Taplinger Publishing Co., 1973.

Imaginative and interesting usage of available materials for
simple, effective costumes; presentation of techniques with
application for more serious costumes.

1522 Jackson, Sheila. SIMPLE STAGE COSTUMES AND HOW TO MAKE
THEM. New York: Watson-Guptill Publications, 1968.

Basic introduction to theatrical costume construction on a very
elementary level.

1523 Jaffe, Holde, and Relis, Nurie. DRAPING FOR FASHION DESIGN.
Reston, Va.: Reston Publishing Co., 1975.

Presentation of muslin draping method of pattern making; pro-
gression from basic patterns to more detailed processes, with

clear direction and over four hundred excellent drawings; additional chapters on draping in finished fabric and dart elimination.

1524 Jorgensen, Kirsten T. MAKING LEATHER CLOTHES. New York: Van Nostrand Reinhold Co., 1972.

Directions and patterns with special instructions for constructing garments and accessories from leather.

1525 Kawashima, Masaaki. FUNDAMENTALS OF MEN'S FASHION DESIGN: A GUIDE TO TAILORED CLOTHES. New York: Fairchild Publications, 1974.

Directions, drawings, and patterns of tailoring techniques for male garments.

1526 Kelly, Francis M., and Schwabe, Randolph. HISTORIC COSTUME: A CHRONICLE OF FASHION IN WESTERN EUROPE, 1490-1790. 2d ed. New York: Charles Scribner's Sons; London: B.T. Batsford, 1929.

Historical survey of costume, with twelve selected period patterns for construction of garments.

1527 Kopp, Ernestine, et al. HOW TO DRAFT BASIC PATTERNS. New York: Fairchild Publications, 1968.

Basic approach to principles and instruction for drafting basic slopers, with detailed directions and diagrams.

1528 Krevitsky, Nik, and Ericson, Lois. SHAPED WEAVING: MAKING GARMENTS AND ACCESSORIES WITH SIMPLE NEEDLE AND FINGER WEAVING TECHNIQUES. New York: Van Nostrand Reinhold Co., 1974.

Photographs, diagrams, and instructions for a method of weaving; ideas useful for costume garments and accessories; part 1 on technique and part 2 on examples such as collars, sleeves, jewelry, ties, and belts.

1529 Lambourne, Norah. DRESSING THE PLAY. New York: Studio Publications, 1953.

Simplified guide to construction of costumes, with brief attention to a number of areas: accessories, sources, masks, and wardrobe; bibliography.

1530 Laury, Jean Ray, and Aiken, Joyce. CREATING BODY COVERINGS. New York: Van Nostrand Reinhold Co., 1973.

Interesting, well-illustrated volume with many new ideas and techniques applicable to costumes in the areas of embroidery, applique, dyeing, patchwork, and leather, as well as separate garments.

1531 Lawson, Donna. IF YOU CAN'T GO NAKED HERE ARE CLOTHES TO SEW FAST. New York: Grosset and Dunlap, 1973.

Basic sewing tools and equipment; instant patterns; diagrams and directions for mostly draped and/or tied garments, many of regional origin, such as Nigerian knotted skirt, Samoan fantasy dress, and Thai panung; interesting exploration of possibilities for costumes.

1532 Leeming, Joseph. THE COSTUME BOOK. New York: J.B. Lippincott Co., 1938.

Brief directions on construction of simplified costumes, including storybook, historic, and national examples.

1533 Leloir, M. Maurice. HISTORIE DU COSTUME DE L'ANTIQUITE A 1914. Paris: H. Ernest, 19-- .

Intended as a multivolume publication but only volumes 8-12 published; inclusion of patterns with detail and refinement in cut.

1534 Ley, Sandra. AMERICA'S SEWING BOOK. New York: Charles Scribner's Sons, 1972.

Coverage of aspects of sewing from basic patterns to slipcovers, with clear directions and drawings.

1535 Link, Nelle Weymouth. PRECISION DRAPING: A SIMPLE METHOD FOR DEVELOPING DESIGNING TALENT. New York: Funk and Wagnalls Co., 1948.

Concise and clear directions and diagrams for techniques of costume pattern making and design.

1536 _____. STITCHING FOR STYLE: FABRIC MANIPULATION FOR SELF TRIM. New York: Liveright Publishing Corp., 1948.

Unique volume with concise directions and clear illustrations for creating thirty decorative fabric motifs and trims.

1537 Lobley, Priscilla. MAKING CHILDREN'S COSTUMES. New York: Taplinger Publishing Co., 1972.

Patterns and diagrams for construction of children's costumes in a very simplified manner.

Costume Construction and Patterns

1538 McCunn, Donald H. HOW TO MAKE SEWING PATTERNS. San Francisco: Design Enterprises, 1977.

> Concise directions with many illustrations and photographs for drafting individual pattern pieces; sections on creating basic patterns, pattern alteration techniques, designing garments, fabric, the dress form, and altering commercial patterns.

1539 _____. HOW TO MAKE YOUR OWN SEWING PATTERNS. New York: Galahad Books, 1973.

> Pattern drafting and construction techniques for the theatrical costumer.

1540 Margolis, Adele P. DESIGN YOUR OWN DRESS PATTERNS: A PRIMER IN PATTERN MAKING FOR WOMEN WHO LIKE TO SEW. Garden City, N.Y.: Doubleday and Co., 1971.

> Complete presentation of all facets of pattern making for contemporary fashions, with clear directions and diagrams; unique chapter on the use of remnants.

1541 _____. HOW TO MAKE CLOTHES THAT FIT AND FLATTER. Garden City, N.Y.: Doubleday and Co., 1969.

> General guide to fitting with useful chapters on use of a basic pattern, dress forms, and a muslin trial garment.

1542 Mooi, Hetty. CREATIVE WORK WITH TEXTILES. New York: Van Nostrand Reinhold Co., 1975.

> Coverage of the subject from basic qualities of materials and stitches to advanced techniques, designs, three-dimensional shapes, and unusual materials and items such as parasols; bibliography.

1543 Mori, Maria. BASIC PATTERN CUTTING. New York: Taplinger Publishing Co., 1970.

> System of pattern adaptation from basic blocks or pattern pieces clear directions and diagrams.

1544 Morris, Ben, and Morris, Elizabeth. MAKING CLOTHES IN LEATHER. New York: Taplinger Publishing Co., 1975.

> Clear directions, patterns, diagrams, and photographic aids for constructing leather clothing, including decorative techniques and accessories; glossary of leather terms and list of suppliers.

1545 Moulton, Bertha. GARMENT-CUTTING AND TAILORING FOR STUDENTS. New York: Theatre Arts Books, 1968.

Thorough, detailed, extensively diagramed instructional book for student tailors and costumers.

1546 _____. SIMPLIFIED TAILORING. New York: Theatre Arts Books, 1968.

Well-illustrated guidebook devoted exclusively to tailoring techniques, particularly for the theatrical costumer.

1547 Nordquist, Barbara. THE COMPLETE GUIDE TO PATTERNMAKING. New York: Drake Publishers, 1974.

Coverage of basics of pattern design, plus alterations of shapes and sizes, with many diagrams and directions.

1548 Palmer, Cherie. THE PERFECT FIT. New York: Charles Scribner's Sons, 1975.

Directions and diagrams for charting and finishing knitted and crocheted garments.

1549 Parish, Peggy. COSTUMES TO MAKE. New York: Macmillan Co., London: Collier-Macmillan, 1970.

Simple patterns and directions for children's costumes from other countries, holidays, and storybook characters.

1550 Parker, Xenia Ley. WORKING WITH LEATHER: HOW TO MAKE LEATHER CLOTHING AND ACCESSORIES. New York: Charles Scribner's Sons, 1972.

Directions, patterns, and diagrams for working with leather.

1551 Peters, Joan, and Sutcliffe, Anna. MAKING COSTUMES FOR SCHOOL PLAYS. Boston: Plays, 1977.

Basic information for young people in making simple costumes; materials, styles, patterns, cutting and sewing, altering, and accessories; list of inexpensive materials to use for costumes.

1552 A PORTFOLIO OF FOLK COSTUME PATTERNS. 2 vols. Sante Fe, N. Mex.: Museum of International Folk Art, 1971.

Two volumes or portfolios of separate sheets containing general construction information, patterns for thirty-two garments from such countries as North Africa, Norway, Croatia, and Japan; suggested embroidery designs; valuable source.

1553 Poulin, Clarence. TAILORING SUITS THE PROFESSIONAL WAY. Peoria, Ill.: Charles A. Bennet Co., 1973.

Basic text covering areas such as supplies and equipment,
hand-sewing techniques; pressing; materials, sections on pattern drafting, coat, vest, trouser, and skirt making with clear
instructions, patterns, diagrams, and photographs; glossary.

1554 Prisk, Berneice. STAGE COSTUME HANDBOOK. New York: Harper
and Row, Publishers, 1966.

Condensed guide with line drawings to simplified historical,
national, and traditional costumes in part 1; general instructions and patterns for costume construction in part 2; bibliography.

1555 Purdy, Susan. COSTUMES FOR YOU TO MAKE. New York: J.B.
Lippincott Co., 1971.

Intended primarily for young readers but contains many simplified and practical ideas and suggestions, with diagrams and
patterns for use in making all types of costumes and accessories
for many theatrical productions, especially children's theatre
and/or fantasy costumes.

1556 Rhinehart, Jane. HOW TO MAKE MEN'S CLOTHES. Garden City,
N.Y.: Doubleday and Co., 1975.

Clear step-by-step directions and over two hundred illustrations
and drawings for beginning construction techniques for male
garments.

1557 Roberts, Edmund B. FUNDAMENTALS OF MEN'S FASHION DESIGN:
A GUIDE TO CASUAL CLOTHES. New York: Fairchild Publications,
1975.

Extensive volume with numerous diagrams and clear instructions
for designing men's casual wear.

1558 Robinson, Julian. INSTANT DRESSMAKING: THREE-IN-ONE GUIDE.
London: Bodley Head, 1973.

Condensed and concise directions and drawings of construction
techniques, with two supplements: dress design ideas and
fashion detailing; general index helpful and necessary due to
confusing printing arrangement.

1559 Rojinskii, Lillian. SEVENTEENTH CENTURY COSTUME. London: Sir
Isaac Pitman and Sons, 1952.

Brief, condensed descriptions, line drawings, and rather complete patterns for ten period costumes from 1603 to 1702; patterns in standardized size; treatment of accessories and hairstyles.

1560 Romaniuk, Anna, and Knight, J. PANTS: HOW TO DO YOUR OWN MEASURING, PATTERN MAKING, FABRIC SELECTION, CUTTING FOR THE PERFECT FIT. New York: Crown Publishers, 1974.

Study of specialized area with clear instructions and diagrams for drafting, cutting, and sewing pants; helpful guide to fitting procedures.

1561 Russell, Elizabeth. ADAPTABLE STAGE COSTUME FOR WOMEN: A HUNDRED-IN-ONE COSTUMES DESIGNED BY ELIZABETH RUSSELL. New York: Theatre Arts Books, 1974.

Economical, simplified methods of adapting female period costumes from a basic gown and basic bodice and skirt with patterns, instructions, and diagrams; some historical background.

1562 Schwebke, Phyllis W., and Dorfmeister, Margary. SEWING WITH THE NEW KNITS: TODAY'S TECHNIQUES FOR TODAY'S NEW FABRICS. New York: Macmillan Co.; London: Collier-Macmillan, 1975.

Valuable guide to general techniques in working with knits; clear drawings and concise instruction; chapters on special areas such as lingerie, swimwear, and menswear; appendix on the history of knits.

1563 Schwebke, Phyllis W., and Krohn, Margaret. HOW TO SEW LEATHER, SUEDE, FUR. Rev. ed. New York: Macmillan Co., 1970.

Many useful hints and procedures with diagrams for construction with these materials.

1564 Shaw, William Harlan. BASIC PATTERN DRAFTING FOR THE THEATRICAL COSTUME DESIGNER. New York: Drama Book, 1974.

Handbook in drafting eleven basic templates or slopers from which unlimited adaptations are possible for period theatrical costume patterns; ten specific examples of adaptations for period costumes given.

1565 Shelden, Martha Gene. DESIGN THROUGH DRAPING. 2d ed. Minneapolis: Burgress Publishing Co., 1974.

Complete explanation of the techniques of draping with charts, drawings, diagrams, and directions; useful chapter on constructing a dress form.

1566 Smolensky, Sheila. COSTUMING FOR CHILDREN'S THEATRE. Denver: Pioneer, 1977.

Booklet with simplified approaches from basic measurements to different pattern types; line drawings, bibliography.

1567 Snook, Barbara. COSTUMES FOR CHILDREN. Newton Centre, Mass.: Charles T. Branford, 1969.

Directions for a number of simplified juvenile costumes.

1568 Sommer, Elyse, and Sommer, Mike. A NEW LOOK AT FELT: APPLI-QUE, STITCHERY AND SCULPTURE. New York: Crown Publishers, 1975.

Guidebook to new ideas and techniques for working with felt; index and bibliography.

1569 _____. WEARABLE CRAFTS: CREATING CLOTHING, BODY ADORN-MENTS, AND JEWELRY FROM FABRICS AND FIBERS. New York: Crown Publishers, 1976.

Presentation of new ideas in designing and constructing garments and accessories; many illustrations, bibliography.

1570 Sommer, Joellen, and Sommer, Elyse. SEW YOUR OWN ACCESSORIES. New York: Pocket Books, 1973.

Listing of materials, instructions for sewing accessories such as belts, jewelry, handbags.

1571 Stahl, Leroy. THE SIMPLIFIED STAGECRAFT MANUAL. Minneapolis: T.S. Denison and Co., 1962.

Five chapters dealing with elementary costume design and construction, with simplified patterns for selected historical patterns.

1572 Sweat, Lynn. COSTUMES TO MAKE. New York: Macmillan Co., 1970.

Simplified diagrams, patterns, and instructions for children's costumes.

1573 Tanous, Helen Nicol. DESIGNING DRESS PATTERNS. 3d ed. Peoria, Ill.: Charles A. Bennett Co., 1971.

Clear directions and easy-to-use diagrams helpful for costume patterns and construction.

1574 Taylor, Gertrude. AMERICA'S KNITTING BOOK. Rev. ed. New York: Charles Scribner's Sons, 1974.

Encyclopedic instructions, patterns, diagrams, and one hundred photographs; details on equipment and materials; useful chapter on knitting with sequins, beads, and ribbon; best for reference source.

1575 Tilke, Max. COSTUME PATTERNS AND DESIGNS: A SURVEY OF COSTUMES PATTERNS AND DESIGNS FOR ALL PERIODS AND NATIONS FROM ANTIQUITY TO MODERN TIMES. New York: Frederick A. Praeger, 1957.

One hundred twenty-eight plates, mostly color, covering costume patterns and designs, including basic garments, accessories, colors, and motifs; generally presented in a form for easy reproduction; some patterns and construction details.

1576 Tompkins, Julia. EASY-TO-MAKE COSTUME FOR STAGE AND SCHOOL. Boston: Plays, 1976.

Attempts to reduce complexities of costume and accessories from various historical periods through simplified patterns, drawings, and instructions.

1577 _____. STAGE COSTUMES AND HOW TO MAKE THEM. London: Sir Isaac Pitman and Sons, 1969.

Somewhat simplified approach including descriptions, patterns, and instructions for period costumes for the theatre.

1578 Tuit, Ann. HOW TO FIT CLOTHES. New York: Drake Publishers, 1972.

Explanations of "reasons for" and "methods of correcting" common defects in fitting ladies' garments; divisions according to areas of garments; explicit directions; black-and-white illustrations and drawings; useful source.

1579 _____. INTRODUCING PATTERN CUTTING. London: Heinemann Educational Books, 1974.

Technical treatment covering separate components of a total pattern, with clear directions and ample diagrams.

1580 Waugh, Norah. THE CUT OF MEN'S CLOTHES, 1600-1900. New York: Theatre Arts Books, 1964.

Survey of men's clothing as seen through period tailoring manuals literary and pictorial references, and cutting diagrams; twenty-nine plates, forty-two patterns, and twenty-seven tailor's patterns; sections of garments for special occasions and purposes; directions for period tailoring techniques; lists of artists and engravers; materials and decorations; listing of museums with costume collections; bibliography; very valuable source.

1581 _____. THE CUT OF WOMEN'S CLOTHES, 1600-1930. London: Faber and Faber, 1968.

> Detailed, technical survey of women's clothes enriched with quotations and illustrations from period sources; seventy-five patterns with sketches of completed garments; fifty-four tailors' patterns; seventy-one plates; notes on the cutting diagrams; glossary of materials; bibliography; indispensable source.

1582 Whife, A.A. DESIGNING AND CUTTING LADIES' GARMENTS. London: Tailor and Cutter, n.d.

> Presentation of basic principles in a concise manner, with patterns and instructions.

1583 Willcox, Donald J. MODERN LEATHER DESIGN. New York: Watson-Guptill Publications, 1969.

> Extensive coverage of all phases of leather work including tools and equipment, procedures, leather and its properties and care; garments and accessories; with explicit instructions, diagrams, drawings, and photographs; excellent chapters on footwear and sandals; list of suppliers; bibliography.

1584 Williams, Helen W. THE BASIC PATTERN: THE MAGIC TOOL. Ames: Iowa State University Press, 1973.

> Approach to drafting and adjusting and then adapting a basic muslin pattern step by step, with instructions and diagrams.

1585 Wilson, Violet I. THE JOY OF SEWING. New York: Charles Scribner's Sons, 1973.

> General introduction and guide to simple as well as more advanced practices in sewing; well-illustrated directions.

1586 _____. SEWING WITHOUT TEARS. New York: Charles Scribner's Sons, 1972.

> Complete guide with clear instructions and drawings for dressmakers; additional chapters on fibers, fabric construction, and identification.

1587 Woman's Institute of Domestic Arts and Sciences. DESIGNING BY DRAPING: DRAPING METHODS, DESIGNING TECHNIQUES. New York: International Educational Publishing Co., 1948.

> Clear, logical presentation with numerous drawings of a simplified draping process.

1588 Wright, Marion Logan. BIBLICAL COSTUME WITH ADAPTATIONS FOR USE IN PLAYS. London: Society for Promoting Christian Knowledge, 1936.

Four sections of description of all types of costumes; patterns for garments and accessories of the Palestines, Romans, and Old Testament figures; bibliographies.

1589 Young, Agnes Brooke. STAGE COSTUMING. New York: Macmillan Co., 1927.

Dated text but twenty-two patterns for historic costumes; sketches of completed garment but no sewing instructions or directions.

Chapter 11

TEXTILE HISTORY AND CONSERVATION

See also 39, 52, 53, 67, 307, 422, 501, 525, 538, 543, 562, 594, 1542

1590 Bendure, Zelma, and Pfeiffer, Gladys. AMERICA'S FABRICS: ORIGIN AND HISTORY, MANUFACTURE, CHARACTERISTICS AND USES. New York: Macmillan Co., 1946.

Informative source with valuable chapter on individual fabrics with summary of fiber, construction, characteristics, and uses, plus a close-up monochrome photograph of each for easy recognition.

1591 Bunt, Cyril G.E., ed. THE WORLD'S HERITAGE OF WOVEN FABRICS. Leigh-on-Sea, Engl.: F. Lewis Publishers, 1955-69.

Series of fourteen guides to woven fabrics of the world; each volume with brief historical background; usually around fifty monochrome plates of fabrics. See items 1592-1605 for individual titles.

1592 Bolingbroke, Judith. CAROLIAN FABRICS. 1969.

1593 _____. WILLIAM AND MARY FABRICS. 1969.

1594 Bunt, Cyril G.E. BYZANTINE FABRICS. 1967.

1595 _____. CHINESE FABRICS. 1961.

1596 _____. FLORENTINE FABRICS. 1962.

1597 _____. HISPANO-MORESQUE FABRICS. 1966.

1598 _____. PERSIAN FABRICS. 1963.

1599 _____. SICILIAN AND LUCCHESE FABRICS. 1961

1600 _____. THE SILKS OF LYONS. 1960.

1601 _____. SPANISH SILKS. 1965.

1602 _____. TUDOR AND STUART FABRICS. 1961.

1603 _____. VENETIAN FABRICS. 1959.

1604 Henere, Enrique. SPANISH TEXTILES. 1955.

1605 Van Stan, Ina. THE FABRICS OF PERU. 1966.

1606 Bunt, Cyril G.E., and Rose, Ernest A. TWO CENTURIES OF ENGLISH CHINTZ 1750-1950 AS EXEMPLIFIED BY THE PRODUCTIONS OF STEAD, McALPIN AND COMPANY. Leigh-on-Sea, Engl.: F. Lewis Publishers, 1957.

> Textual survey of English chintz with seventy-six black-and-white plates of examples; useful for suggestions of chintz patterns for costumes.

1607 Crown, Fenja. THE FABRIC BOOK FOR PEOPLE WHO SEW. New York: Grosset and Dunlap, 1973.

> Survey of current popular fabrics arranged by fibers with special chapters on fake furs, stretch fabrics, special finishes, and linings and interfacings; glossaries and wholesale resources in each chapter; drawings and diagrams and twenty-one color plates.

1608 Digby, G.W. ELIZABETHAN EMBROIDERY. London: Faber and Faber, 1963.

> Numerous monochrome photographs of examples of embroidered garments and accessories; one section on special embroideries and techniques for dress.

1609 Emery, Irene. THE PRIMARY STRUCTURE OF FABRICS: AN ILLUSTRATED CLASSIFICATION. Washington, D.C.: Textile Museum, 1966.

> Numerous monochrome plates and diagrams in technical study of structure of fabrics; bibliography.

1610 Fennelly, Catherine. TEXTILES IN NEW ENGLAND, 1790-1840. Sturbridge, Mass.: Old Sturbridge Village, 1961.

> Photographs of many specimans with some taken from garments.

1611 Finch, Karen, and Putnam, Greta. CARING FOR TEXTILES. New York: Watson-Guptill Publications, 1977.

Unique sourcebook with sections on display, protection, storage, cleaning, restoration, and conservation of period costumes; list of equipment, stocklists, and glossary; very valuable for costumers with an interest in or collection of period clothing.

1612 Hollen, Norma R., and Saddler, Jane. TEXTILES. 3d ed. New York: Macmillan Co., 1968.

Introductory text to study of textiles in regard to concepts, principles, and facts about fibers, yarns, construction, finishes, and color, with numerous monochrome illustrations and drawings; glossary.

1613 Irwin, John, and Brett, K.B. ORIGINS OF CHINTZ. London: Her Majesty's Stationery Office, 1970.

Descriptive catalog of painted cotton chintz in the Victoria and Albert Museum and the Royal Ontario Museum, with 158 monochrome plates, some of chintz as used for clothing.

1614 Jones, Mary Eirwen. THE ROMANCE OF LACE. New York: Staples Press, 1951.

Well-illustrated discussion of historical lace by geographical regions.

1615 Kendrick, A.F. ENGLISH DECORATIVE FABRICS OF THE SIXTEENTH TO EIGHTEENTH CENTURIES. Essex, Engl.: F. Lewis Publishers, 1934.

Somewhat dated textual survey with more than sixty black-and-white illustrations of examples of fabrics from an important period for costumers; some illustrations of clothing and accessories.

1616 Kleeberg, Irene Cumming, ed. THE BUTTERICK FABRIC HANDBOOK: A CONSUMER'S GUIDE TO FABRICS FOR CLOTHING AND HOME FURNISHINGS. New York: Butterick, 1975.

Quick reference guide to purchasing and selecting fabric with information on fibers; care and cleaning of fur and leather; width conversions and stretch gauge; over fifteen hundred definitions in dictionary section of pronunciation, properties, fiber, manufacture, and usage for modern fabrics.

1617 Leene, Jentina, ed. TEXTILE CONSERVATION. Washington, D.C.: Smithsonian Institution Press, 1972.

Collection of essays of a technical nature with chapters on costumes and accessory conservation.

1618 Mayer, Christa C. MASTERPIECES OF WESTERN TEXTILES FROM THE ART INSTITUTE OF CHICAGO. Chicago: Art Institute, 1969.

Exhibition catalog with 172 plates (9 in color) of examples of textiles, including costumes and accessories dating from 100 A.D. to 1925, with descriptive notes; glossary and selected bibliography.

1619 Meulen-Nulle, L.W. van der. LACE. New York: Universe Books, 1964.

Concise introduction to design and technical finish of various types of lace, illustrated by forty-eight selected primary-source plates and numerous line drawings.

1620 Miller, Edward. TEXTILES: PROPERTIES AND BEHAVIOUR. New York: Theatre Arts Books, 1975.

Guidebook to many textiles and their characteristics and features.

1621 Montgomery, Florence M. PRINTED TEXTILES: ENGLISH AND AMERI-CAN COTTONS AND LINENS, 1700-1850. London: Thames and Hudson: New York: Viking Press, 1970.

Historical treatment and numerous figures (428) of period textiles for interior decoration as well as for costume.

1622 Nylander, Jane C. FABRICS FOR HISTORIC BUILDINGS. Washington, D.C.: Preservation Press, 1977.

Not intended for costume usage but nevertheless a very useful condensed survey of historic fabrics; glossary of historic fabric terms; sources of supply of fabrics with period design; many illustrations; of considerable use to costumer of period plays.

1623 Pettit, Florence H. AMERICA'S INDIGO BLUES: RESIST-PRINTED AND DYED TEXTILES OF THE EIGHTEENTH CENTURY. New York: Hastings House, 1974.

Interesting technical study with 106 photographs, 8 color plates, and 44 drawings, many of historic patterned textiles of the eighteenth century; glossary and bibliography.

1624 _____. AMERICA'S PRINTED AND PAINTED FABRICS, 1600-1900: ALL THE WAYS THERE ARE TO PRINT UPON TEXTILES; A MOST COMPLETE

HISTORY OF WORLD FABRIC PRINTS: ALL ABOUT THE PRINTERS AND
PATTERNS OF AMERICAN AND OTHER THINGS THAT WENT ON FROM
1600 TO 1900. New York: Hastings House, 1970.

> Interesting and valuable source that does what the subtitle
> says.

1625 Pfannschmidt, Ernst-Eric. TWENTIETH CENTURY LACE. New York:
Charles Scribner's Sons, 1975.

> Illustrations and survey of modern lace in Europe and the
> United States; generally dealing with more traditional styles
> but some modern and highly imaginative uses of lace tech-
> niques of value to designers in areas of materials, motifs, tech-
> niques, garments, and accessories.

1626 Preston, Paula Simpson. PRINTED COTTONS AT OLD STURBRIDGE
VILLAGE. Sturbridge, Mass.: Old Sturbridge Village, 1969.

> Booklet with more than thirty plates of characteristic textiles,
> some as used for costumes.

1627 Seagroatt, Margaret. A BASIC TEXTILE BOOK. New York: Van Nostrand Reinhold Co., 1975.

> Condensed treatment of areas of fibers, spinning, and weaving,
> with a good chapter on dyes and dyeing techniques; fully il-
> lustrated; lists of suppliers; bibliography.

1628 SURVEY OF WORLD TEXTILES. Leigh-on-Sea; Engl.: F. Lewis Publishers, 1951-63.

> Series of nineteen guidebooks to textiles of various countries
> of the world; all with general background including mono-
> chrome plates of examples of historical and modern fabrics in-
> digenous to the country. See entries 1629-47 for individual
> titles.

1629 Colombo, Ruggero. ITALIAN TEXTILES. 1953.

1330 DUTCH TEXTILES. In collaboration with INTERNATIONAL TEXTILES.
1960.

1631 Engelstad, Helen. NORWEGIAN TEXTILES. 1952.

1632 Ferriere, Maud Trube. SWISS TEXTILES. 1953.

1633 Frankl, Paul T. AMERICAN TEXTILES. 1954.

1634 Gabor, Magda. HUNGARIAN TEXTILES. 1961.

1635 Geliazkova, Nevena. BULGARIAN TEXTILES. 1958.

1636 Henere, Enrique. SPANISH TEXTILES. 1955.

1637 Leprade, M.D. de. FRENCH TEXTILES. 1955.

1638 Lewis, Frank. BRITISH TEXTILES. 1951.

1639 _____. CZECHOSLOVAK TEXTILES. 1962.

1640 Link, Pablo. SOUTH AMERICAN TEXTILES. 1957.

1641 Neppert-Boehland, Maria. GERMAN TEXTILES. 1955.

1642 Nomachi, Katsutoshi. JAPANESE TEXTILES. 1958.

1643 Rasmussen, Steen Eiler. DANISH TEXTILES. 1956.

1644 Saarto, Martha. FINNISH TEXTILES. 1954.

1645 Stellwag-Clarion, Fritz. AUSTRIAN TEXTILES. 1960.

1646 Thompson, John Henry. CANADIAN TEXTILES. 1963.

1647 Wollin, Nils G. SWEDISH TEXTILES. 1951.

1648 Thornton, Peter. BAROQUE AND ROCOCO SILKS. London: Faber and Faber, 1965.

> Numerous plates, some in color, and interesting text, covering baroque and rococo silks.

1649 Victoria and Albert Museum. EUROPEAN PRINTED TEXTILES. London: His Majesty's Stationery Office, 1949.

> Sixty-three plates of historical textiles from about 1480 to 1920, with brief textual comments.

1650 Volbach, W. Fritz. EARLY DECORATIVE TEXTILES. London: Paul Hamlyn, 1969.

> Brief introduction plus seventy-one color illustrations of early textiles, many from dated garments with descriptions.

1651 Walkley, Christina, and Foster, Vanda. CRINOLINES AND CRIMPING IRONS: VICTORIAN CLOTHES HOW THEY WERE CLEANED AND CARED FOR. London: Peter Owen, 1978.

> Unusual book on the care and cleaning of clothing in the Victorian period, with illustrations and information from contemporary recipes and household hints in magazines of the day.

1652 Wardle, Patricia. VICTORIAN LACE. New York: Frederick A. Praeger, 1969.

Detailed study with eighty-two plates showing types of lace and costumes and accessories incorporating lace.

1653 Weibel, Adele Coulin. TWO THOUSAND YEARS OF TEXTILES: THE FIGURED TEXTILES OF EUROPE AND THE NEAR EAST. New York: Pantheon Books, 1952. Reprint. New York: Hacker Art Books, 1972.

General introduction plus 331 plates, some color, of examples with very detailed descriptive notes; bibliography.

Chapter 12

TEXTILE DECORATION:
DYEING, PAINTING, AND PRINTING

See also 485, 1627

1654 Axford, Lavonne Brady. WEAVING, SPINNING, DYEING. Spare Time
Guides: Information Sources for Hobbies and Recreations, no. 7. Little-
ton, Colo.: Libraries Unlimited, 1975.

> Over four hundred entries with notations of various sources of
> information, instruction, supplies, and techniques for three
> specified crafts; list of periodicals; list of publishers; index.

1655 Belfer, Nancy. DESIGNING IN BATIK AND TIE DYE. Worcester,
Mass.: Davis Press, 1972.

> Guide to various techniques in creating with batik and tie
> dyeing; directions and illustrations for procedures.

1656 Bronson, J., and Bronson, R. EARLY AMERICAN WEAVING AND DYE-
ING. 1819. Reprint. New York: Dover Publications, 1977.

> Practical and historical guide to hand weaving and dye for-
> mulas with a new introduction, glossary of terms, and a table
> of chemicals with early and current names and formulas.

1657 Brunello, Franco. THE ART OF DYEING IN THE HISTORY OF MAN-
KIND. Vincenza, Italy: Neri Pozza, 1973.

> Authoritative historical survey with 178 black-and-white and
> 7 color illustrations.

1658 Bystrom, Ellen. CREATING WITH BATIK. New York: Van Nostrand
Reinhold Co., 1972.

> Especially clear line drawings and directions plus photographs
> for guide to basic technique and advanced variations; guide
> for blending dyes; list of suppliers.

1659 _____. PRINTING ON FABRIC: BASIC TECHNIQUES. New York: Van Nostrand Reinhold Co., 1967.

Step-by-step instructions with diagrams and photographs.

1660 Deyrup, Astrith. GETTING STARTED IN BATIK. New York: Macmillan Co.; London: Collier-Macmillan, 1971.

Introduction to basic procedures and simplified projects with black-and-white and color photographs; glossary; lists of suppliers; bibliography.

1661 Erickson, Janet. BLOCK PRINTING ON TEXTILES: A COMPLETE GUIDE. New York: Watson-Guptill Publications, 1961.

Clear directions, diagrams, and photographs for a concise introduction to the technique.

1662 Gonsalves, Alyson Smith, ed. CLOTHING DECORATION. Menlo Park, Calif.: Lane Publishing Co., 1977.

Coverage of areas of embroidery, applique, dyes, and paints; basic patterns for decoration; silk screening; decorative stitches; concise directions, diagrams; list of supplies; bibliography.

1663 Haywood, Hilary. ENJOYING DYES: HOW TO PATTERN YOUR OWN FABRICS. New York: Drake Publishers, 1975.

Simple directions and clear diagrams of use to any costumer.

1664 Kafka, Francis J. THE HAND DECORATION OF FABRICS. Bloomington, Ill.: McKnight and McKnight Publishing Co., 1959.

Guide to such techniques as hand stenciling, batik, tie dyeing, linoleum block printing, freehand painting, and silk screening, with clear directions and illustrations; chapters on color and color mixing of dyes and caring for decorated fabrics; list of suppliers.

1665 Krevitsky, Nik. BATIK: ART AND CRAFT. New York: Reinhold Publishing Corp., 1964.

Coverage of traditional and contemporary batik techniques, with directions and photographs; pictorial gallery of examples.

1666 Larsen, Jack Lenor. THE DYER'S ART: IKAT, BATIK, PLANGI. New York: Van Nostrand Reinhold Co., 1976.

Impressive volume richly illustrated with many examples of costumes, plus technical coverage of techniques of great value to the costumer.

1667 Monk, Kathleen. FUN WITH FABRIC: PRINTING. New York: Taplinger Publishing Co., 1969.

> Explanation of different printing techniques with directions, diagrams, and photographs.

1668 Proud, Nora. INTRODUCING TEXTILE PRINTING. New York: Watson-Guptill Publications, 1968.

> Basic techniques and suggested designs with photographs and drawings.

1669 _____. TEXTILE DYEING AND PRINTING SIMPLIFIED. New York: Arco Publishing Co., 1974.

> Simplified directions and illustration of techniques of tie dyeing, resist dyeing, block and screen printing, discharge, painting, trailing, spraying, and rolling; guide to dyes and suppliers; very useful source.

1670 Russ, Stephen. FABRIC PRINTING BY HAND. New York: Watson-Guptill Publications, 1965.

> Complete guide to major fabric printing processes: silk screen, block, batik, tie dyeing, and starch resist, as well as painting and drawing with step-by-step directions, recipes, formulas; color and black-and-white illustrations; directory of suppliers; bibliography.

1671 Samuel, Evelyn. INTRODUCING BATIK. London: B.T. Batsford; New York: Watson-Guptill Publications, 1968.

> Complete guide to techniques and variations from basic equipment to design sources; numerous photographs; list of suppliers; bibliography.

1672 Stein, Vivian. BATIK AS A HOBBY. New York: Sterling Publishing Co., 1969.

> Introduction to basic beginning techniques with clear directions and illustrations.

Chapter 13

FASHION DESIGNERS AND THE FASHION WORLD

See also 66, 1421

1673 Amies, Hardy. JUST SO FAR. London: Collins, 1954.

> Autobiography of the fashion designer Hardy Amies and an account of the founding of the couture house.

1674 Baillen, Claude. CHANEL SOLITAIRE. Translated by Barbara Bray. New York: New York Times Book Co., 1974.

> Biography of the famous designer with a retrospective photographic record of her designs.

1675 Battersby, Martin. ART DECO FASHION: FRENCH DESIGNERS, 1908-1925. New York: St. Martin's Press, 1974.

> Richly illustrated with ninety-seven color and monochrome plates; survey of the great French couturiers of this most important period.

1676 Bertin, Celia. PARIS A LA MODE: A VOYAGE OF DISCOVERY. Translated by Majorie Deans. London: Victor Gollancz, 1956.

> Author's recollections of Parisian fashion operations plus chapters on individual well-known designers: Chanel, Schiuparelli, Lanvin, Dior, Balenciaga, among others.

1677 Brooklyn Museum. THE HOUSE OF WORTH. Brooklyn: 1962.

> Exhibition catalog with monochrome photographs of twenty gowns designed by Worth.

1678 Chase, Edna Woolman, and Chase, Ilka. ALWAYS IN VOGUE. London: Victor Gollancz, 1954.

Recollections by former editor of the magazine, illustrated with photographs and drawings from VOGUE.

1679 Dior, Christian. CHRISTIAN DIOR AND I. Translated by Antonia Fraser. New York: E.P. Dutton Co., 1957.

Autobiography of designer with twenty black-and-white photographs, some showing his designs.

1680 Fairchild, John. THE FASHIONABLE SAVAGES. New York: Doubleday and Co., 1965.

The world of fashion from the viewpoint of the publisher of WOMEN'S WEAR DAILY.

1681 Greer, Howard. DESIGNING MALE. London: Robert Hale, 1952.

Autobiography of the fashion designer; with illustrations.

1682 Hartnell, Norman. SILVER AND GOLD. London: Sir Isaac Pitman and Sons, 1956.

Autobiography of designer and his work in the twentieth century in fashion and in theatre and foremost as a designer of fashions for royalty, including his designs and illustrations of gowns worn by Elizabeth II and her entourage at her wedding and coronation and numerous other functions.

1683 HAUTE COUTURE: NOTES ON DESIGNERS AND THEIR CLOTHES IN THE COLLECTIONS OF THE ROYAL ONTARIO MUSEUM. Toronto: Royal Ontario Museum, 1969.

Guide to the foremost fashion designers with biographies, addresses, awards, and photographs of their most distinctive creations; some attention to theatrical designers also.

1684 Latour, Anny. KINGS OF FASHION. Translated by Mervyn Savill. London: Weidenfeld and Nicolson, 1958.

Traces the emergence of the fashion designer, the couturier, from a position of oblivion in historical periods to a position of prominence in contemporary society; many photographs of fashion designers and their designs.

1685 Lee, Sarah Tomelin, ed. AMERICAN FASHION: THE LIFE AND LINES OF ADRIAN, MAINBOCHER, McCARDELL, NORELL, TRIGERE. New York: Fashion Institute of Technology, 1975.

Extensive retrospective textual and pictorial survey of American fashion in the twentieth century through the lives and work of these five prominent designers; bibliography.

1686 Levin, Phyllis Lee. THE WHEELS OF FASHION. Garden City, N.Y.: Doubleday and Co., 1965.

Inside story of fashion world and its designers, with thirty-seven black-and-white photographs.

1687 Lynam, Ruth, ed. COUTURE: AN ILLUSTRATED HISTORY OF THE GREAT PARIS DESIGNERS AND THEIR CREATIONS. New York: Doubleday and Co., 1972.

Development of couture in 1900 to the present, with textual and illustrative coverage of every important French designer.

1688 Metropolitan Museum of Art. Costume Institute. THE 10S THE 20S, THE 30S: INVENTIVE CLOTHES, 1909-1939. New York: 1973.

Exhibition catalog demonstrating unique fashion changes that occurred between 1909 and 1939 as seen in the works of five fashion designers: Poiret, Vionnet, Callot, Chanel, and Schiaparelli; monochrome photographs of garments and drawings; biographical sketches of the designers.

1689 Picken, Mary Brooks, and Miller, Dora Loues. DRESSMAKERS OF FRANCE: THE WHO, HOW AND WHY OF THE FRENCH COUTURE. New York: Harper and Brothers, 1956.

Guidebook to the world of French fashion and fashion designers through alphabetically arranged biographies; some material on theatrical designers as well as French fashion and millinery designers from the past.

1690 Poiret, Paul. KING OF FASHION: THE AUTOBIOGRAPHY OF PAUL POIRET. Translated by Stephen Haden Guest. Philadelphia: J.B. Lippincott Co., 1931.

Designer's reminiscences about a life in fashion, with sixteen photographs.

1691 Quant, Mary. QUANT BY QUANT. New York: G.P. Putnam's Sons, 1966.

Designer's recollections, with photographs of some of her sketches and fashions.

1692 Saunders, Edith. THE AGE OF WORTH: COUTURIER TO EMPRESS EUGENIE. Bloomington: Indiana University Press, 1955.

Biography of the English designer, Charles Frederick Worth, who dominated Parisian fashion in the nineteenth century; also the social history of period; nine photographs, including two of his sketches; index and bibliography.

1693 Schiaparelli, Elsa. SHOCKING LIFE. New York: E.P. Dutton Co., 1954.

> Autobiography of the famous designer, with selected illustrations of her creations.

1694 Tirtoff, Romain de [Erte]. ERTE FASHIONS. London: Academy Editions; New York: St. Martin's Press, 1972.

> Historical survey of fashion by Erte; chapters on accessories and jewelry; chronology of designer's life and work, both in couture and theatre.

1695 Vecchio, Walter, and Riley, Robert. THE FASHION MAKERS: A PHO-TOGRAPHIC RECORD. New York: Crown Publishers, 1968.

> Many black-and-white photographs of all facets of the fashion industry, including designers, construction, and showings.

1696 Watkins, Josephine Ellis, comp. FAIRCHILD'S WHO'S WHO IN FASH-ION. New York: Fairchild Publications, 1975.

> Alphabetically arranged listing of famous designers, living and dead, primarily in the world of fashion but with some entries for theatrical costumers.

1697 White, Palmer. POIRET. New York: Clarkson N. Potter, 1973.

> Biography of twentieth-century French designer, with a chapter devoted to his theatrical designs and with several photographs and designs; bibliography.

1698 THE WORLD OF BALENCIAGA. New York: Metropolitan Museum of Art, 1973.

> Exhibition catalog of designs and photographs of creations by the famous designer.

1699 Worth, Jean Philippe. A CENTURY OF FASHION. Translated by Ruth Scott Miller. Boston: Little, Brown, 1928.

> Account of leading couturier's and his father's influence upon fashion, with numerous photographs of designs and patrons.

Chapter 14

THEORY AND PSYCHOLOGY OF FASHION

AND COSTUME

1700 Adams, J. Donald. NAKED WE CAME: A MORE OR LESS LIGHT-
HEARTED LOOK AT THE PAST, PRESENT, AND FUTURE OF CLOTHES.
New York: Holt, Rinehart and Winston, 1967.

> Examination of the reasons for clothes and fashions with many
> monochrome illustrations; humorous presentation of material.

1701 Anspach, Karlyne. THE WHY OF FASHION. Ames: Iowa State University Press, 1967.

> Three sections dealing with the social need, the economic
> good, and the reflections of American life in fashion; biblio-
> graphical references in notes.

1702 Ballard, Bettina. IN MY FASHION. New York: David McKay, 1960.

> Psychology of fashion through the designers, well-dressed
> women, and the motivators.

1703 Beaton, Cecil. THE GLASS OF FASHION. Garden City, N.Y.:
Doubleday and Co., 1954.

> One designer's personal survey of fashion, particularly in the
> twentieth century, with his personal theories and conclusions
> on the whole subject.

1704 Bell, Quentin. ON HUMAN FINERY. 2d ed. New York: Schocken
Books, 1976.

> Illustrated examination of the theories of fashion and clothing.

1705 Bender, Marilyn. THE BEAUTIFUL PEOPLE. New York: Coward-
McCann, 1967.

> Viewpoints on theories and practices of modern fashion and its
> designers with selected black-and-white photographs of fashions
> of the 1960s.

1706 Binder, Pearl. MUFFS AND MORALS. New York: William Morrow and Co., 1954?

Psychohistorical survey of topics concerning fashion, for example, foundation garments, wigs, and accessories; well-illustrated with eighty-three line drawings and eleven plates in half-tone of primary-source material.

1707 _____. THE PEACOCK'S TAIL. London: George G. Harrap and Co., 1958.

Sociohistorical study of the reasons for the drabness of male attire resulting from men's discarding art and embracing science; 204 illustrations.

1708 Brenninkmeyer, Ingrid. THE SOCIOLOGY OF FASHION. Paris: Librarie du Recueil Sirey; Koeln-Opladen: Westdeutscher Verlag, 1963.

Interesting, scholarly investigation of the nature, origin, diffusion, and social structure of fashion as a reflection of culture; interesting theories of the cycle of fashion and the relationship of regional, court, and bourgeois fashion; bibliography.

1709 Craig, Hazel Thompson. CLOTHING: A COMPREHENSIVE STUDY. Philadelphia: J.B. Lippincott Co., 1973.

Extensive treatment of clothing; origin and development of fashion; sociology and psychology of clothing; selection and construction of clothing; glossary.

1710 Cunnington, C. Willett. THE ART OF ENGLISH COSTUME. London: Collins, 1948.

Critical study and analysis of dress from the fifteenth century to the present, with chapters on symbolism, sources, principles, color, material, and movement, among others; forty-eight monochrome plates and four in color.

1711 _____. FEMININE ATTITUDES IN THE NINETEENTH CENTURY. New York: Macmillan Co., 1936.

Study of female manners and attitudes, decade by decade, with a few illustrations.

1712 _____. THE PERFECT LADY. London: Max Parrish; New York: Chanticleer Press, 1948.

Survey of feminine attire, manners, customs, and use of dress, among other areas, from 1815 to 1914; with forty-six line drawings and sixteen color photographs.

1713 _____. WHY WOMEN WEAR CLOTHES. London: Faber and Faber, 1941.

> Exploration of theories of costume and fashion, with an interesting chapter on the influence of sport on dress.

1714 Flugel, John Carl. THE PSYCHOLOGY OF CLOTHES. London: Hogarth Press, 1966.

> Psychological investigation of such theories of clothes as decoration, modesty, sexual differences, and the future of dress, among many topics; selected photographs and illustrative materials; bibliography.

1715 Garland, Madge. THE CHANGING FORM OF FASHION. New York: Frederick A. Praeger, 1970.

> Psychological study of human attempts to alter the shape of the body through fashion whims; with eighty-six illustrations.

1716 Gurel, Lois M., and Beeson, Mariaime S. DIMENSIONS OF DRESS AND ADORNMENT: A BOOK OF READINGS. Dubuque, Iowa: Kendall-Hunt, 1975.

> Collection of interesting essays dealing with the areas of anthropological perspectives on dress and adornment; historical influences on costume; clothing behavior; and the economics of apparel.

1717 Hall, Carrie A. FROM HOOPSKIRTS TO NUDITY: A REVIEW OF THE FOLLIES AND FOIBLES OF FASHION, 1866-1936. Caldwell, Idaho: Caxton Printers, 1946.

> Survey of fashionable oddities during the period from 1866 to 1936, including hoops, bustles, various sleeves and accessories; with many monochrome illustrations; bibliography.

1718 Harris, Christie, and Johnston, Moira. FIGLEAFING THROUGH HISTORY: THE DYNAMICS OF DRESS. New York: Atheneum, 1971.

> Historical survey of the psychology of dress with a number of illustrations and drawings; bibliography.

1719 Horn, Marilyn J. THE SECOND SKIN: AN INTERDISCIPLINARY STUDY OF CLOTHING. 2d ed. Boston: Houghton Mifflin Co., 1975.

> Technical investigation of such aspects of clothing as cultural interrelationships; human behavior, aesthetics; economy and consumption; many illustrations, charts, drawings, graphs, all presented against a historical background; bibliographical references.

1720 Koenig, Rene. A LA MODE: ON THE SOCIAL PSYCHOLOGY OF FASHION. Translated by F. Bradley. New York: Seabury Press, 1974.

>   Examination of the common facets of all fashions throughout history; bibliography.

1721 _____. THE RESTLESS IMAGE: A SOCIOLOGY OF FASHION. Translated by F. Bradley. London: G. Allen and Unwin, 1973.

>   Psychological study of common features of fashion throughout history.

1722 Langer, Lawrence. THE IMPORTANCE OF WEARING CLOTHES. Introduction by James Laver. New York: Hastings House, 1959.

>   Presentation of author's theories of dress and fashion; monochrome plates and photographs.

1723 Latzke, Alpha, and Hostetter, Helen P. THE WIDE WORLD OF CLOTHING: ECONOMICS, SOCIAL SIGNIFICANCE, SELECTION. New York: Ronald Press, 1968.

>   Chapters on the rationale of clothing uses: individual influences on dress and modesty; the cultural role of clothing; primary source illustrations, charts, diagrams, and drawings; glossary.

1724 Laver, James. DRESS: HOW AND WHY FASHIONS IN MEN'S AND WOMEN'S CLOTHES HAVE CHANGED DURING THE PAST FEW HUNDRED YEARS. 2d ed. London: John Murray, 1966.

>   Well-illustrated study of reasons behind shifts of fashion; presentation of Laver's principles of attraction, hierarchy, and utility.

1725 _____. MODESTY IN DRESS: AN INQUIRY INTO THE FUNDAMENTALS OF FASHION. Boston: Houghton Mifflin Co., 1969.

>   Complete discussion into costume theories with numerous illustrations; chapters on military dress, sport attire, and children's wear; bibliography.

1726 _____. STYLE IN COSTUME. London: Oxford University Press, 1949.

>   Brief study of the relationship of architecture and furnishings to costume; selected illustrations.

1727 McJimsey, Harriet T. ART AND FASHION IN CLOTHING SELECTION. 2d ed. Ames: Iowa State University Press, 1973.

Early chapters dealing with theories of fashion and clothing funds.

1728 Mead, Sidney M. TRADITIONAL MAORI CLOTHING: A STUDY OF TECHNOLOGICAL AND FUNCTIONAL CHANGE. Wellington, New Zealand: A.H. and A.W. Reed, 1969.

More of a sociological study but with many photographs of native textiles and costume; basic understanding of the development of clothing.

1729 Newton, Stella Mary. HEALTH, ART AND REASON: DRESS REFORMERS OF THE NINETEENTH CENTURY. London: John Murray, 1974.

Unique approach to psychology and motivation of clothing changes as seen through dress reformers; sixty-six monochrome illustrations; index and bibliography.

1730 O'Connor, K. THE ANTHROPOLOGY OF FASHION. New York: McGraw-Hill Book Co., 1974.

Theories of fashion that man has been culturally conditioned and psychologically determined by what he wears.

1731 Richardson, Jane, and Kroeber, A.L. THREE CENTURIES OF WOMEN'S FASHIONS: A QUANTITATIVE ANALYSIS. Berkeley and Los Angeles: University of California Press, 1940.

Analytical study defining stylistic fashion changes in objectives and quantitative terms.

1732 Roach, Mary Ellen, and Eicher, Joanne Bubolz. THE VISIBLE SELF: PERSPECTIVE ON DRESS. Englewood Cliffs, N.J.: Prentice-Hall, 1973.

General introduction to the study of dress, with more specialized section on the body and dress; clothing as an art; dress and society; numerous monochrome illustrations; bibliographical notes.

1733 _____, eds. DRESS, ADORNMENT AND THE SOCIAL ORDER. New York: John Wiley and Sons, 1965.

Collections of essays in six sections: study of dress; dress and adornment; cultural patterns of dress and adornment; social organization and dress; dress and the individual; and stability and change in patterns of dress; annotated bibliography.

1734 Rosencranz, Mary Lou. CLOTHING CONCEPTS: A SOCIAL-PSYCHOLOGICAL APPROACH. New York: Macmillan Co., 1972.

Coverage of the symbolic implications of clothing; illustrated with selected line drawings.

1735 Rudofsky, Bernard. THE UNFASHIONABLE HUMAN BODY. Garden City, N.Y.: Doubleday and Co., 1974.

Exploration of the need for dress and the constantly occurring changes in fashion and the standards of fashion; numerous monochrome illustrations.

1736 Ryan, Mary Shaw. CLOTHING: A STUDY IN HUMAN BEHAVIOR. New York: Holt, Rinehart and Winston, 1966.

Survey of social psychological factors related to clothing; bibliographies.

1737 Taylor, John. IT'S A SMALL, MEDIUM AND OUTSIZE WORLD. New York: World Publishing Co., 1966.

Casually written and illustrated examination of various theories of fashion and dress.

AUTHOR INDEX

This index contains the names of all authors, editors, and compilers cited in this text. It is alphabetized letter by letter. Numbers refer to entry numbers.

A

Abbate, Francesco 288
Abbott, P.E. 905
Abrahams, Ethel 420
Adams, J. Donald 1700
Adburgham, Alison 1277-78
Adrian, Rupert 381
Aguilera, Emiliano M. 648
Aiken, Joyce 1530
Albert, Lillian Smith 673
Alberts, David 1200
Alberu de Villava, Helena 382
Aldred, Cyril 752
Alexander, J.J.G. 632
Alexander, Mary Jean 1460
Alexandre, Arsene 156
Alford, Violet 1201, 1208
Allcock, Hubert 1125
Allen, Agnes 194
Alyoshina, T.S. 499
Amades, Juan 649
Ambrose, Kay 535
Amies, Hardy 886, 1673
Amory, Cleveland 1334
Amphlett, Hilda 742
Andersen, Ellen 570-71, 1160
Anderson, Donald M. 1406
Anderson, Douglas N. 906
Anderson, Jack 157
Anderson, Lynne 852
Anderson, Ruth Matilda 650-52

Ando, Tsuro 138
Andrews, William 813
Angelo, Domenico 1212
Angeloglou, Maggie 814
Angus, Ian 907
Anspach, Karlyne 1701
Anthony, Gordon 158
Anthony, Ilid 479
Anthony, Pegaret 3
Applebaum, Stanley 73
Appleton, Leroy H. 354-55
Arbeau, Thoinot 1213-14
Aretz, Gertrude 195
Argenti, Philip O. 500
Argy, Josy 1161
Arlington, Lewis C. 139
Armes, Alice 1477
Armstrong, Lucille 1202-3
Armstrong, Nancy 674, 753-54
Arneberg, Halfdan 572
Arno-Berg, Inga 573
Arnold, Janet 3, 53, 815, 1478-79
Ashdown, Charles Henry 908-9
Ashdown, Emily Jessie 426
Asser, Joyce 816
Astroem, Paul 415
Aubert, Charles 1215
Axford, Lavonne Brady 1654
Ayer, Jacqueline 536

Author Index

B

Bacharach, Bert 887
Baerwald, Marcus 755
Bagley, John J. 1335
Bahti, Tom 356
Baillen, Claude 1674
Bain, Robert 480
Baker, Blanch M. 4-5
Baker, Lillian 675
Baker, William Henry 23
Bakst, Leon 160
Ballard, Bettina 1702
Banateanu, T. 501
Bane, Allyne 1480-81
Baranski, Matthew 861
Barber, Richard W. 1336
Barbier, George 74
Barfoot, Audrey 196, 427
Barker, A.J. 910
Barlanghy, Istvan 1216
Barnes, R. Money 911-15
Barney, Sydney D. 1172
Barrett, Marvin 1337
Barsis, Max 197
Bartal, Lea 1217
Barthorp, Michael 916
Barton, Lucy 198, 1407-8, 1482-83
Bascom, Frances 716
Batterberry, Ariane 199
Batterberry, Michael 199
Battersby, Martin 269-70, 1675
Baud-Bovy, Daniel 623
Baverstock, Doreen M. 1484
Bayne-Powell, Rosamond 800
Baynes, Pauline 259
Beaton, Cecil 200, 1703
Beaumont, Cyril W. 75, 161-63, 1218
Beck, S. William 676
Beese, Pat 1485
Beeson, Mariaime S. 1716
Belfer, Nancy 1655
Bell, John 76
Bell, Quentin 1704
Benda, Klement 756
Benda, W.T. 862
Bender, Marilyn 1705
Bendure, Zelma 1590
Benitez, Jose R. 383

Bennett, H. 54
Bennett-England, Rodney 888
Bentley, Nicolas 1338
Berk, Barbara 1486
Bernis, Madrazo Carmen 653-54
Bernolles, Jacques 289
Bernstein, Aline 201
Berrueta Dominquez, Don Juan 658
Bertin, Celia 1676
Bettmann, Otto 1175, 1384
Bhavnani, Enakshi 537
Bhushan, Jamila Brij 538, 757
Bigelow, Marybelle S. 202
Bihalji-Merin, Oto 863
Binder, Pearl 1461, 1706-7
Birbari, Elizabeth 633
Birmingham, Frederic A. 24
Birren, Faber 1409-15
Bishop, Morris 1339
Black, J. Anderson 228, 758
Blair, Claude 917-18
Blake, Lois 481
Blakemore, Kenneth 677
Blakeslee, Fred Gilbert 539, 1088-91
Blanc, Charles 1462
Bland, Alexander 164
Blaxland, Gregory 1030
Blum, Andre 605-6
Blum, Stella 312
Boegel, Jozsef 77
Boehn, Max von 78, 203-4, 678, 722, 1092
Bogatyrev, Petr G. 502
Bolingbroke, Judith 1592-93
Bonfante, Larissa 411
Bonney, Mabel Therese 1340
Bossert, Helmuth Theodor 412, 595, 1416, 1463
Boster, Joan 290
Botham, M. 817
Bott, Alan John 1279-80
Boublik, Vlastimil 818
Boucher, Francois 205
Boulard, Constance 1425-26
Boutell, Charles 1126
Bowling, A.H. 919
Bowman, Ned Allen 55
Boyd, Margaret A. 56
Boyes, Janet 1487
Braddon, Russell 920

Bradfield, Nancy 206, 428
Bradford, Ernle 759
Bradless, Frederic 1344
Bradley, Carolyn C. 1417
Bradley, Carolyn Gertrude 207
Bradshaw, Angela 208
Brander, Michael 1341
Braun-Ronsdorf, Margarete 210, 607, 679
Breckinridge, Scott D. 1219
Brenninkmeyer, Ingrid 1708
Bress, Helene 1488
Brett, K.B. 313-14, 1613
Briggs, Asa 1342
Briggs, Frederico Guilherme 384
Briggs, Geoffrey 1127
Brinson, Peter 1340
Broby-Johansen, R. 211
Brockman, Helen L. 1418
Brod, Fritzi 1464
Brogden, Joanne 1419
Broholm, Hans Christian 413
Brondsted, Johannes 574
Bronson, J. 1656
Bronson, R. 1656
Brooke, Iris 79, 212, 429-34, 596, 731, 801, 1281, 1489
Brosse, Jacques 303, 921, 1343
Bruhn, Wolfgang 213
Brunello, Franco 1657
Brunn-Rasmussen, Ole Jens 819
Bryson, Nicholas L. 1490
Buchman, Herman 820
Buck, Anne M. 435, 802
Buckle, Richard 165-66
Bucknell, Peter A. 1517
Buell, William Ackerman 80
Bukhari, Emir 1050-52
Bullard, Daphne 57
Bunt, Cyril G.E. 1591-1603, 1606
Burdick, Elizabeth B. 81
Burgess, Hovey 1220
Burke, John Bernard 1128
Burnham, Dorothy K. 1491
Burris-Meyer, Elizabeth 214, 1420
Burshears, J.F. 366
Burston, W.H. 6
Busfield, Roger M., Jr. 2
Bustros, Evelyne 540
Button, Jeanne 215

Byers, Jack A. 1448
Bystrom, Ellen 1658-59

C

Caballero Bonald, Jose M. 1221
Cabasino, Salvatore 82
Cable, Mary 1282
Calasibetta, Charlotte Mankey 25
Calderini, Emma 634
Camden, Carroll 1283
Cammann, Schuyler 541
Campbell, Archibald 482
Campbell, Judith 1173
Capon, Edmund 542
Cappi-Bentivegna, Ferruccia 635
Carbone, Linda 26
Carlisle, Lilian Baker 680
Carlson, Bernice Wells 868
Carlson, Peter 890
Carman, W.Y. 27, 922, 1031
Carnes, Edwin 717
Carrillo y Gariel, Abelardo 385-86
Carter, Charles F. 1163
Carter, Ernestine 271-72
Cassin-Scott, Jack 216, 1053, 1129
Casson, Lionel 1344-45
Castano, John B. 923
Caulfield, S.F.A. 28
Chalif, Louis Harvey 503
Chambers, Bernice G. 1421
Chandra, Moti 543
Charles, Ann 821
Chase, Edna Woolman 1678
Chase, Ilka 1678
Chastel, Andre 1346
Chernoff, Goldie Taub 1492
Chierichetti, David 189
Chisman, Isabel 1222
Chotek, Karel 504
Christian, Roy 1284
Churchill, Allen 1285
Chuse, Anne R. 1422
Cimarelli, Aldo G. 924
Clammer, David 925
Clark, Winifred 1493
Clarke, Mary 29, 167-68
Clephan, R. Coltman 1130
Clephane, Irene 1280
Clinch, George 436

Author Index

Clouzot, Henri 1192
Clutton, Cecil 681
Cobban, Alfred 1347
Coffin, Harry B. 1465
Cohn, David L. 1286
Cohn, Nik 891
Colas, Rene 8
Cole, Herbert 291
Coleman, Elizabeth Ann 217
Colin, Paul 58
Collard, Eileen 316-17, 803, 1494
Colle, Doriece 682
Collie, George 483
Collier, John 357
Collins, C. Cody 683
Collins, Henry B. 318
Collins, Wanda S. 1495
Colombo, Ruggero 1629
Conn, Richard 358
Connat, Madeline 608
Contini, Mila 218
Cook, Dorothy E. 17
Cooke, Patricia Gerrard 437
Cooley, Arnold J. 822
Cooper, Douglas 83
Cooper, Frederick Taber 1314
Cooper, Wendy 823
Copeland, Peter F. 1093
Corazzi, David 655
Cordry, Donald Bush 387-88
Cordry, Dorothy M. 387-88
Cordwell, Miriam 824-25
Corey, Irene 1423
Corson, Richard 684, 826-28
Cosman, Madeleine Pelmer 1287
Courtais, Georgine de 743
Covarrubias, Luis 389
Cox, James Stevens 30, 829-31
Crabb, Michael 181
Craig, Hazel Thompson 1709
Cramer, James 1094
Crane, Nancy 1496
Crawford, Elizabeth G. 1186
Crawford, M.D.C. 219, 1186-87
Crawford, T.S. 685
Crewe, Quentin 1288
Crider, James R. 1497
Crisp, Clement 167-68, 170
Crookshank, Anne 484
Croonborg, Frederick T. 1498

Crown, Fenja 1607
Cummings, Richard 864, 1499
Cunnington, C. Willett 31, 439-46, 1188, 1710-13
Cunnington, Phillis 441-48, 467, 802, 1095, 1164, 1174, 1188
Curtis, John Obed 927
Curtis, Mattoon M. 686

D

D'Allemagne, Henry Rene 610
Damase, Jacques 85
D'Ami, Rinaldo 928
Dar, Shiv Nath 544
Darling, Ada 760
Dars, Celestine 1383
D'Assailly, Gisele 220
Davenport, Milia 221
Davidson, Marshall 1348
Davidson, Patricia F. 776
Davis, Brian L. 929
Davis, Mary L. 761
Davis, Natalie 1500
Dawson, Malcolm 930
DeAnfrasio, Roger 821
Dearmer, Percy 1096
De La Bere, Ivan 1132
De La Iglesia, Maria Elena 59
DeLange, Jacqueline 300
Delgado, Alan 1289
Demidov, Alexander 171
Dendel, Esther Warner 1501
Deneke, Bernward 1165
Denlinger, Donald M. 319
Dennys, Rodney 1133
De Palavecion, Maria Delia Millan 390
DeQuincey, Thomas 505
Desmoni, Martin J. 762
Deyrup, Astrith 1660
De Zemler, Charles 832
D'Harnoncourt, Rene 361
Dickason, Olive Patricia 359
Dickens, Arthur G. 1349
Dickens, Gerald 931
Dickens, Guillermina 1223
Dickinson, Joan Younger 763
Digby, G.W. 1608
Dines, Glen 320

264

Dior, Christian 1679
Disher, M. Willson 86
Ditchfield, Peter H. 1290
Ditzel, Paul C. 1097
Dobkin, Alexander 1424
Dockstader, Frederick J. 360
Dodd, A.H. 1350
Doerner, Gerd 391
Doeser, Linda 173
Dolmetsch, Mabel 1224-25
Dominic, Zoe 174
Dongerkery, Kamala S. 545
Dorfmeister, Margery 1562
Dorner, Jane 222, 273-74
Doten, Hazel R. 1425-26
Douglas, Frederic H. 361
Downs, Harold 32
Drake-Carnell, F.J. 1291
DuBoulay, F.R.H. 1292
Duchartre, Pierre Louis 87
Duggan, Anne Schley 1226
Dunbar, Janet 1293
Dunbar, John Telfer 485, 494-95
Dunham, Lydia Roberts 60
Durant, John 1175
Du Solier, Wilfrido 392
Dutton, Ralph 1351

E

Earle, Alice Morse 321, 1294
Echeverria, Salvador 406
Edey, Maitland A. 1176
Edson, Doris 1483
Edwards, Anne 449
Edwards, Rod 764
Eelking, Baron von 892
Ehwa, Carl, Jr. 687
Eicher, Joanna Bubolz 9, 1732-33
Ein, Claudia 1427
Ekstrand, Gudrun 575
Elicker, Virginia Wilk 1502
Ellfeldt, Lois 717
Elliott, Margaret M. 1373
Ellis, M. 486
Ellsworth, Evelyn Peters 1428
Embleton, Gerry 1085-86
Emery, Irene 1609
Emlyn-Jones, Gwen 1503
Enachescu-Cantemir, Alexandrina 506

Enciso, Jorge 393
Engelstad, Helen 1631
Enters, Angna 1227
Erickson, Janet 1661
Ericson, Lois 1528
Erikson, Joan Mowat 688
Erlanger, Philippe 1295
Ernst, Earle 141
Erte 133, 1694
Ertell, Viviane Beck 689
Espinosa, Carmen 322
Estrin, Michael 1466
Etheridge, Ken 487, 1504
Evans, Joan 611, 765, 1352, 1467
Evans, Lady 420
Evans, Mary 223, 723, 1505-6
Evans, R.K. 1507
Evrard, Gwen 732
Ewers, John Canfield 362
Ewing, Elizabeth 275, 1098, 1189

F

Fabb, John 933, 1129
Fabre, Maurice 224
Fabri, Charles Louis 546
Fagg, William Buller 292
Fairchild, John 1680
Fairholt, F.W. 33, 450
Fairservis, Walter A., Jr. 547
Fallon, Dennis J. 1228
Fennelly, Catherine 324, 1610
Fernald, Helen E. 548
Fernald, Mary 1508
Ferriere, Maud Trube 1632
Fife, Austin 325
Filene, Adele 10
Fillitz, Herman 1134
Finch, Karen 1611
Fischel, Max 204
Fitzsimons, Bernard 934
Fletcher, Marion 225-26
Flett, J.F. 1229
Flett, T.M. 1229
Flory, M.A. 690
Flower, C. 488
Flower, Margaret 766
Flugel, John Carl 1714
Flynn, Dorris 549
Fochler, Rudolf 624

Author Index

Fol, Alexander 414
Ford, Colin 1353-54
Forestier, Amedee 935
Foss, Michael 1355
Foster, Vanda 1651
Fox, Lilla M. 489, 508, 597-98
Fox-Davis, Arthur Charles 1135
Frankl, Paul T. 1633
Franklyn, Charles A.H. 1099
Franklyn, Julian 34
Franks, A.H. 1230
Franzerro, Carlo Maria 894
Fraser, Antonia 451
Frazier, Beverly 833
Frazier, Gregory 833
Fregnac, Claude 767
Fulop-Miller, Rene 88
Funcken, Fred 936
Funcken, Liliane 936
Fundabunk, Emma Lila 363
Fyfe, Agnes 1204

G

Gabor, Magda 1634
Gaborjan, Alice 509
Galbraith, W.O. 1223, 1239
Gale, William 46
Gallois, Emile 550, 612-13, 656-57
Garcia Boiza, Don Antonio 658
Gardi, Rene 293-94
Gardilanne, Gratiane de 643
Gargi, Balwant 142-43
Garland, Madge 228, 276, 804, 834, 1715
Gatto, Joseph A. 1429
Gautier, Leon 1136
Gayre, Robert 1137
Geen, Michael 1510
Gehret, Ellen J. 326
Geliazkova, Nevena 1635
Genauer, Emily 89
Genders, Roy 835
George, Mary Dorothy 1296
Gere, Charlotte 768-69
Gernsheim, Alison 229
Gervers-Molnar, Veronika 510
Ghurye, G.S. 551-52
Giafferri, Paul Louis Victor de 230, 744, 895

Gibbs-Smith, Charles J. 452
Gibson, Mary 453
Gierl, Irmgard 625
Gies, Frances 1356-57
Gies, Joseph 1356-57
Gilbert, John 231
Gilbert, John Selwyn 174
Gillespie, Karen R. 691
Giltay-Nijssen, L. 770
Ginsburg, Madeline 61, 277
Gjessing, Gjertrud 576
Gjessing, Gutorm 576
Glassman, Judith 62-63
Glen, Emilie 733
Gloag, John 1297-98
Glover, Michael 938
Gold, Annalee 278
Goldring, William 692
Gomez Tabanera, Jose Manuel 659
Gonsalves, Alyson Smith 1662
Goodman, Frances Schaill 394
Gordon, Gilbert 1231
Gorer, Geoffrey 295
Gorsline, Douglas 232
Gosling, Nigel 1358
Grange, Richard M.D. 490
Grant, Charles 1032-34, 1054
Grant, Francis J. 1138
Grass, Milton N. 693
Graves, Maitland 1430
Green, Bertha De Vere 694
Green, C.W. 6
Green, Joyce M. Conyngham 1431
Green, Ruth M. 234, 1232
Greenhowe, Jean 1511-12
Greer, Howard 1681
Gregor, Joseph 88, 866
Gregorietti, Guido 771
Griesbach, C.B. 1468
Grindea, Carola 1205
Grindea, Miron 1205
Gudjonsson, Elsa E. 577
Guernsey, Elizabeth A. 1187
Gullberg, Elsa 415
Gummere, Amelia Mott 327
Gunji, Masakatsu 144
Gunn, Fenja 836
Gunsaulus, H.C. 553
Guptill, Arthur L. 1432
Gurel, Lois M. 1716

Gurzau, Elba Farabegoli 636
Guthman, William H. 927
Guye, Samuel 695
Gwatkin, Nina W. 837

H

Habenstein, Robert W. 1166
Haggard, Stephen 1264
Hainaux, Rene 90-93
Haire, Frances Hamilton 328
Hald, Margrete 413, 734
Hall, Carrie A. 1717
Halls, Zillah 454-55, 896-97, 1139
Halouze, Edouard 395
Hammerstein, Hans von 626
Handford, Jack 1513
Hansen, Henny Harald 235, 554
Hardy, Kay 1433
Hargreaves-Mawdsley, W.N. 1100-1101
Harmand, Adrien 1514
Harrall, S.W. 1102
Harris, Christie 1718
Harrison, Frank L. 696
Harrison, Michael 745
Hart, Roger 1359-63
Harthan, John 1364
Hartley, Dorothy 1365, 1515
Hartmann, Rudolf 94
Hartnell, Norman 236, 1682
Hashimoto, Sumiko 555
Haskell, Ira J. 697
Haskins, Sam 296
Hassrick, Peter 329
Hauglid, Roar 579
Hawley, W.M. 556
Hay, Denys 1366
Hayashi, Tadaichi 557
Haycraft, Frank W. 1103
Haythornthwaite, Philip J. 939-43
Haywood, Hilary 1663
Hazelius-Berg, Gunnel 573, 580
Healy, Daty 1516
Heierli, Julie 627
Heininger, Ernest A. 772
Heininger, Jean 772
Hejj-Detari, Angela 773
Henere, Enrique 1604, 1636
Herold, Erich 867

Herold, J. Christopher 1367
Hesketh, Christian 491
Hibbert, Christopher 95, 1368
Hickmann, Peggy 724
Hicks, Majorie 330
Hieronymussen, Paul 1140
Higgins, Reynolds A. 774
Hijlkema, Riet 644
Hiler, Hilaire 11, 416
Hiler, Meyer 11
Hill, Margot Hamilton 601, 1517
Hillhouse, Marion S. 1518
Hinks, Peter 775
Hobbs, William 1233
Hoellrigl, Joseph 511
Hoffman, Herbert 776
Hoffschmidt, E.J. 998
Hofsinde, Robert 364
Hogarth, Burne 1434
Hogg, Garry 1299
Hoggett, Chris 64
Holden, Angus 456
Holding, T.H. 944
Hole, Christina 1177, 1300-1301
Hollen, Norma R. 1519, 1612
Holliday, Robert Cortes 1190
Holme, Charles 512, 581, 628, 637
Holmes, M.R. 96
Holmes, Martin 1141
Hope, Thomas 417
Hope, W.H. St. John 1142
Hopper, Janice H. 396
Horan, James D. 331, 365
Horn, Marilyn J. 1719
Horn, Pamela 1104
Hornblower, Florence S. 418
Horst, Horst P. 1369
Horst, Louis 1234
Hostetler, John A. 332-33
Ilustetter, Helen P. 1723
Hougen, Bjorn 582
Houston, Mary G. 418-19, 457
Howard, Guy 1235
Howell, Edgar M. 945-46
Howell, Georgina 279
Hoyos Sancho, Nieves de 667-68
Hubbard, Margaret 513
Huenefeld, Irene Pennington 65
Hughes, Graham 777
Hughes, Talbot 1520

Author Index

Humphrey, Doris 1236
Hunt, Cecil 1302
Hunt, Douglas 1237
Hunt, Kari 868, 1237
Hunt, W. Ben 366
Hunter, Frederick J. 12
Huntingford, G.W.B. 297
Hurry, Leslie 175
Hutchinson, Robin 493
Hyman, Rebecca 838
Hyobu, Nishimura 558

I

Ickis, Marguerite 1303
Inder, P.M. 458
Innes, R.A. 559
Innes, Thomas 492
Ireland, Marion P. 1105
Ireland, Patrick John 1435-36
Irey, Charlotte 716
Ironside, Janey 35
Irwin, John 698-99, 1613
Itten, Johannes 1437-38
Ivanova, Anna 1238
Ives, Suzy 1521

J

Jackson, Margaret 805
Jackson, Sheila 1522
Jacobson, Egbert 1439
Jacopetti, Alexandra 334
Jaffe, Hilde 1523
Jahn, Raymond 1304
Jamar, Henri 1209
James, Edwin O. 1305
Janosa, Lajos 78
Janson, Dora Jane 779
Jarrett, Derek 1370
Jarrett, Dudley 947
Jefferson, Louise E. 298
Jenkins, Alan 1371-72
Jensen, Oliver 1373
Jessup, Ronald 780
Johnson, Alfred Edwin 176
Johnson, David F. 948
Johnson, Marie 420
Johnston, Moira 1718
Joiner, Betty 718

Jones, Inigo 97
Jones, Mary Eirwen 1614
Jones, William 782, 1143
Jorgensen, Kirsten T. 1524
Josephy, Alvin M., Jr. 368, 1374
Juliao, Carlos 397
Justema, William 1469

K

Kafka, Francis J. 1664
Kahan, Gerald 98
Kahlenberg, Mary Hunt 237
Kannik, Preben 949
Katcher, Philip 1016-22
Katsarova, Raina 1206
Katz, Albert M. 1240
Kawashima, Masaaki 1440, 1525
Kawatake, Shigetoshi 145
Kehoe, Vincent, Jr. 839
Keim, Aline 614
Kelly, Francis M. 99, 238, 1526
Kemp, Alan 950
Kemp, Peter 951
Kemper, Rachel H. 239
Kendrick, A.F. 1615
Kennedy, Douglas 1241-42
Kent, Kathryn 673
Kerr, Rose Netzorg 246, 335
Kerrigan, Evans E. 952
Keyes, Jean 840
Kidwell, Claudia A. 336, 1178
Kilgour, Ruth Edwards 746
King, Nancy 1243
Kingsland, P.W. 953
Kinross, John P.D.B. 1375
Kipnis, Claude 1244
Kirstein, Lincoln 177-78, 1245
Klapthor, Margaret Brown 337
Kleeberg, Irene Cumming 1616
Klein, Ruth 36
Klepper, Erhard 245, 421
Kline, Peter 1246
Kloster, Donald E. 946
Kniffin, Herbert Reynolds 869
Knight, J. 1560
Koch, Ronald P. 369
Koch, Rudolf 1470
Kochno, Boris 179

Koehler, Carl 240
Koenig, Rene 1720-21
Kok, Annette 485
Komisarjevsky, Theodore 100-101
Kopp, Ernestine 1527
Kredel, Fritz 954
Kresz, Maria 629
Krevitsky, Nik 1528, 1665
Kroeber, A.L. 1731
Krohn, Margaret 1563
Kuchenmeister, Sue Ann 1228
Kunciov, Robert 338
Kuzel, Vladislav 783
Kybalova, Ludmilla 37
Kyerematen, A.A.Y. 299

L

Laban, Rudolf 1247
Lacey, Peter 1167
Lachouque, Henry 921
Lacroix, Paul 615
Laliberte, Norman 870
La Mar, Virginia 459
Lamb, Ruth S. 102
Lambert, Eleanor 66
Lambourne, Norah 1529
Lambranzi, Gregorio 1248
Lamers, William M. 1166
Langner, Lawrence 1722
Lansdell, Avril 1106
Large, Hector 955
Larmessin, Nicolas de 616
Larsen, Jack Lenor 1666
Latour, Anny 1684
Latzke, Alpha 1723
Laurent, Cecil Saint 1191
Laury, Jean Ray 1530
Laver, James 13, 103-4, 127, 241-45, 280, 421, 434, 460-65, 726, 806, 898, 956, 1306-11, 1724-26
Lawford, James 1035, 1055
Lawler, Lillian B. 1249-50
Lawson, Cecil C.P. 957
Lawson, Donna 1531
Lawson, Joan 719, 1251-52
Leary, Emmeline 700
Lee, Sarah Tomelin 1685
Leeming, Joseph 1532

Leene, Jentina 1617
Leese, Elizabeth 190
Lefferts, Charles M. 958
Lehner, Ernst 1471
Leiris, Michel 300
Leloir, Maurice 38, 1533
Lens, Bernard 747
Lepage-Medvey 515, 617
Leprade, M.D. de 1637
Lesley, Parker 784-85
Lessing, Alice 281
Lester, Katherine Morris 246, 701
Levin, Phyllis Lee 1686
Levinson, Andre 180
Levi-Pisetzky, Rosita 638
Levy, June Rosine 14
Lewis, Frank 1638-39
Lewis, Shari 871
Ley, Sandra 247, 1534
Libron, Fernand 1192
Lichten, Frances 1376
Linati, Claudio 398
Lindsay, Jack 1312
Link, Nelle Weymouth 1535-36
Link, Pablo 1640
Linthicum, M. Channing 105
Lipperheide, Franz Joseph 15
Lippincott, Gertrude 720
Lippmann, Deborah 58
Lister, Margot 248-49, 1107
Lloyd, Albert L. 1239
Lobley, Priscilla 1537
Lockmiller, David A. 1108
Lofts, Norah 1377
Lommel, Andreas 872
Loomis, Andrew 1441
Lord, Francis A. 959
Louda, Jiri 1144
Louden, Adelaide Bolton 250
Louden, Norman P. 250
Lowrie, Drucella 748
Lu, Steve 841
Luard, John 960
Lubell, Cecil 67
Lubinova, Mila 1207
Lucas, Catherine 1164
Lucie-Smith, Edward 1378
Luscomb, Sally C. 702
Lutz, Henry F. 422
Lyford, Carrie Alberta 371-73
Lynam, Ruth 1687

Author Index

M

Macalister, R.A.S. 1109
McBride, Angus 1067
McCarthy, James Remington 786
McCarthy, Thomas Patrick 1110
McClellan, Elisabeth 339
McClintock, H.F. 493-94
McCloud, Dwight 1111
McClure, W. 1036
McConathy, Dale 191
McCracken, Harold 340
McCunn, Donald H. 1538-39
Macgowan, Kenneth 873
Macilwaine, Herbert C. 1265
McJimsey, Harriet T. 1727
Mackerras, Colin 146
Mackey, Margaret Gilbert 341
MacQuoid, Percy 807-8
Madhloom, T.A. 423
Mahoney, Tom 755
Maier, Manfred 1442
Mallath, Regine 251
Mander, Raymond 106-11
Mann, Kathleen 599
Mansfield, Alan 467, 1174
Mansfield, Evelyn A. 1518
Marazov, Ivan 414
Marcel-Dubois, Claudie 1208
Maresova, Sylva 112
Margetson, Stella 1379-80
Margolis, Adele P. 1540-41
Markov, Jozef 516
Marks, Stephen S. 39
Marshall, Herbert 113
Marshall, Rosalind K. 1381
Martin, Gyorgy 1253
Martin, John Joseph 1254
Martin, Paul 961-62
Mason, Anita 40
Mason, Bernard S. 374
Mason, Georgina 1313
Maurice, Arthur Bartlett 1314
May, Gerald 1074
May, R.N. 963
May, Robin 1023
Mayer, L.A. 517
Mayer-Thurman, Christa C. 1112, 1618
Maxwell, Stuart 495

Maxwell-Hyslop, K.R. 787
Mead, Sidney M. 1728
Meadors, Nancy 1246
Mee, Charles L., Jr. 1382
Mellencamp, Emma Hirsch 115
Melnitz, William W. 1
Melvill, Harald 842
Melville, Robert 811
Mericka, Vaclav 1145
Merida, Carlos 399
Messel, Oliver 116
Meulen-Nulle, L.W. van der 1619
Meyer, Florence E. 704
Meyer, Franz Sales 1472
Meyers, Charles L. 16
Michel, Henri 695
Milbern, Gwendolyn 342
Miller, Dora Loues 1689
Miller, Douglas 1042
Miller, Dwight 1113
Miller, Edward 1620
Miller, Nathan 965
Mills, Betty J. 343
Milton, Peter 1146
Minnich, Helen Benton 561
Mitchenson, Joe 108-11
Moers, Ellen 901
Moffatt, Elizabeth Whitney 643
Mogelon, Alex 870
Molinari, Cesare 117
Mollo, Andrew 966-68
Mollo, Boris 973
Mollo, John 969-73
Moncrieff, M.C. Scott 468
Monk, Kathleen 1667
Monro, Isabel 17
Monsarrat, Ann 1168
Montgomery, Elizabeth 118
Montgomery, Florence M. 1621
Mooi, Hetty 1542
Moore, Doris Langley 253, 727, 810
Morel, Juliette 1193
Mori, Maria 1543
Morris, Ben 1544
Morris, Elizabeth 1544
Morrison, R. Boyd 128
Morse, H.K. 469
Mortimer-Dunn, Gloria 1443
Motley 118
Moulton, Bertha 1545-46

Mourey, Gabriel 789
Moussinac, Leon 119
Muller, Priscilla E. 790
Munksgaard, E. 583
Murphy, Brian 1169
Murphy, Michelle 618

N

Nainfa, John H. 1114
Nakamura, Yasuo 147
Napolitan, M. Louis 843
Naylor, Brenda 1444
Needler, Winifred 791
Ne'eman, Nira 1217
Nelson, Henry Loomis 974
Neppert-Boehland, Maria 1641
Neubecker, Ottfried 1147
Nevinson, John L. 728
Newton, Stella Mary 120, 1729
Nicholls, Florence Z.E. 705
Nicholson, J.B.R. 975, 1037, 1068
Nickel, Helmut 976
Nicoll, Allardyce 121, 1383
Noma, Seiroku 562, 875
Nomachi, Katsutoshi 1642
Nordquist, Barbara 302, 1547
Norlund, Poul 584
Norman, Vesey 977
Norris, Herbert 600, 1115
North, Rene 978
Noverre, Jean Georges 1255
Nylander, Jane C. 1622
Nylen, Anna-Maja 585-86

O

Oakes, Alma 601
O'Conner, K. 1730
Oerke, Bess Viola 701
Oman, Julia Trevelyan 474
Onassis, Jacqueline 518
Oppe, A.P. 1266
Oppenheimer, Lillian 871
Oprescu, George 519
Oreglia, Giacomo 122
Orgel, Stephen 123
Ormond, Richard 470
Ortiz Echague, Jose 669
Osborne, Harold 41

Osborne, Lilly de Jongh 400, 407
Ostier, Marianne 792
Oved, Sah 793
Ovenden, Graham 811
Oxenford, Lyn 1256-57
Oxenham, Andrew 181
Ozzola, Leandro 639

P

Pack, Greta 761
Paget, Guy 1180
Pakula, Marvin H. 1148
Palchoudhuri, Ila 844
Palencia, Isabel de 670
Palffy-Alpar, Julius 1258
Palmer, Cherie 1548
Palotay, Gertrude de 520
Papachristou, Judith 1339
Parker, Xenia Ley 1445, 1550
Parmelin, Helene 124
Parrish, Peggy 1549
Partridge, Bellamy 1384
Paterek, Josephine 1446
Paulme, Denise 303
Payne, Blanche 254
Payne, Charles 182
Peacock, John 283
Peacock, P. 706
Pearce, Arthur W. 1194
Pearsall, Ronald 1385
Pe-Chin, Chang 148
Peck, Esther 513
Peltz, Leslie Ruth 707
Penrod, James 1259
Penzer, Norman H. 521
Pepin, Harriet 1447
Percival, Allen 1315
Percival, MacIver 708
Percival, Rachel 1315
Pericoli, Ugo 979
Perlberg, H.C. 522
Perrottet, Philippe 845
Peters, Joan 876, 1551
Petersen, Grete 819
Peterson, Harold L. 980
Pettigrew, Dora W. 630
Pettit, Florence H. 1623-24
Pfannschmidt, Ernst-Eric 1625
Pfeiffer, Gladys 1590

Philp, Richard 183
Picken, Mary Brooks 42-43, 1689
Pinon, Roger 1209
Pisk, Litz 1260
Piton, Camille 619
Pivka, Otto von 1056-61
Planche, James Robinson 44
Plath, Iona 587
Playford, John 1261
Plumb, J.H. 1149, 1386
Pocknee, Cyril Edward 1116
Poiret, Paul 1690
Poulin, Clarence 1553
Powell, Doane 877
Preston, Antony 981
Preston, Paula Simpson 1626
Price, H.P. 903
Prideaux, Tom 125
Priest, Alan 563
Priestley, John B. 1387-89
Primmer, Kathleen 588
Pringle, Patrick 255
Prisk, Berneice 1448, 1554
Proud, Nora 1668-69
Purdy, Susan 1555
Purves, A.A. 1150
Putnam, Greta 1611
Pylkkanen, Riitta 589-90

Q

Quant, Mary 1691
Quennell, Peter 1390
Quick, John 45

R

Rameau, Pierre 1262
Rankin, Robert H. 982-83
Rasmussen, Steen Eiler 1643
Raven-Hart, Hester Emilie 1222
Ray, Dorothy Jean 878
Raynes, John R. 846
Reade, Brian 184, 671
Reader, William Joseph 1391
Redfern, W.B. 709
Reed, Walt 1449
Reid, William 984
Relis, Nurie 1523
Revitt, Peter 719

Reyburn, Wallace 1195
Reyes, Roman B. 401
Reynolds, Graham 471
Reynolds, Reginald 847
Ricciardi, Mirella 304
Richards, Alison 794
Richardson, Jane 1731
Richardson, Philip John S. 1263
Riches, Wendy 1161
Riefenstahl, Leni 305-6
Riley, Robert 1695
Rimmer, Joan 696
Rinehart, Jane 1556
Rischbieter, Henning 126
Roach, Mary Ellen 1732-33
Roberts, Edmund B. 1557
Robinson, H. Russell 985-86
Robinson, Julian 284-85, 1558
Robles, Philip K. 987
Roediger, Virginia M. 375
Rogers, Dorothy 620
Rojinskii, Lillian 1559
Romanink, Anna 1560
Rose, Ernest A. 1606
Rosencranz, Mary Lou 1734
Rosignoli, Guido 988-89
Rosse, Herman 873
Rothacker, Nanette 1196
Roulin, Eugene A. 1117
Rubens, Alfred 523
Rudofsky, Bernard 1735
Rudorff, Raymond 1392
Rudoy, Marion 824-25
Russ, Stephen 1670
Russell, Douglas A. 1450-51
Russell, Elizabeth 1561
Rust, Frances 1316
Ryan, Mary Shaw 1736

S

Saarto, Martha 1644
Saddler, Jane 1612
Sahay, Sachidanand 564
Saito, R. 848
Samuel, Evelyn 1671
Sansom, William 1393
Sataloff, Joseph 794
Saunders, Edith 1692
Saward, B.C. 28

Saxtorph, Niels M. 990
Sbarge, Stephen 215
Scarlett, James D. 496
Schiaparelli, Elsa 1693
Schneider, Pierre 1394
Schoeffler, O.E. 46
Schroeder, Joseph J., Jr. 345
Schwabe, Randolph 238, 1526
Schwebke, Phyllis W. 1562-63
Scott, Adolphe Clarence 149, 565
Seagrott, Margaret 1627
Seaton, Albert 1043, 1062-63,
    1069-70, 1075-76, 1078
Selbie, Robert 256
Selby, John 1024-26
Sellner, Eudora 346
Semb, Klara 1210
Settle, Alison 472
Severa, Joan 347
Severn, William 710, 735, 749,
    849
Seyler, Athene 1264
Shackell, Dora 711
Shalleck, Jamie 879
Sharaff, Irene 193
Sharp, Cecil J. 1265-66
Sharrad, L. 817
Shaver, Ruth M. 150
Shaw, G.W. 1118
Shaw, Henry 1473
Shaw, William Harlan 1564
Shelden, Martha Gene 1565
Shenton, Eileen 1508
Shepard, Richmond 1267
Sheppard, Allan 1038-39
Sheppard, Mubin 566
Sheringham, George 127-28
Shover, Edna Mann 47
Sichel, Marion 257
Sieber, Roy 307
Silvester, Hans 402
Simkins, Michael 1044
Simon, Bernard 68
Simonson, Lee 101
Simpson, Jeffrey 1395
Sitwell, H.D.W. 1141, 1151
Slade, Peter 1268
Slade, Richard 880
Slaughter, Frank G. 1027
Sloane, Eunice Moore 1452

Smeets, Rene 1474
Smith, C. Ray 850, 1453
Smith, Cleveland H. 1000
Smith, Lacey Baldwin 1396
Smith, Robert A. 1181
Smith, Willard M. 712
Smitherman, P.H. 991-94
Smolensky, Sheila 1566
Snook, Barbara 881, 1567
Snow, Lois Wheeler 151
Snowden, James 19
Sobic, Ierina 525
Sommer, Elyse 795, 1568-70
Sommer, Joellen 1570
Sommer, Mike 1568-69
Sooy, Louise Pickney 341
Sorell, Walter 882
Sotkova, Blazena 526
Souza, Alberto 672
Spencer, Charles 129-30, 186-87
Spicer, Dorothy Gladys 403, 1317-
    19
Squire, Geoffrey 258-59
Squire, Gwen 713
Sronkova, Olga 260, 602
Stadden, Charles 995
Stafford, Maureen 49
Stahl, Leroy 1571
Stavridi, Margaret 261
Steffan, Randy 996
Stein, Kurt 714
Stein, Vivian 1672
Stellwag-Clarion, Fritz 1645
Stenton, Doris Mary 1320
Stephens, Michael 883
Stephenson, Lois 20
Stephenson, Richard 20
Stewart, Janice S. 591
Stibbert, Frederic 603
Stirling, Matthew W. 376
Stone, Lilly C. 1182
Strachan, Hew 997
Strathern, Andrew 567
Strathern, Marilyn 567
Strong, Roy 123, 131-32, 473-74,
    851
Strutt, Joseph 475, 1183
Stryker, Emerson 1397
Stuart, Jennifer 750
Sutcliff, Anna 876, 1551

Sweat, Lynn 1572
Swenson, Evelyn 1321
Symonds, Emily Morse 1322

T

Tamplin, J.M.A. 905
Tanner, John 34
Tanous, Helen Nicol 1573
Tantum, William H. 998
Taubert, K.H. 1269
Taylor, Arthur 999
Taylor, Gertrude 1574
Taylor, Gertrude R. 1000
Taylor, John 1737
Telford, Alexander Alan 497
Tenenbaum, Samuel 904
Terrone, Leonardo F. 1270
Terry, Ellen 852
Thienen, Frithjof Van 645
Thiselton-Dyer, T.F. 1323
Thomas, Alan 1398
Thompson, John Henry 1646
Thompson, Judy 377
Thorburn, William A. 1001-2
Thornton, John Henry 736
Thornton, Peter 1648
Thorpe, Edward 170
Tilke, Max 213, 527, 568, 1575
Tily, James C. 1003
Tirtoff, Romain de 133, 1694
Titman, George A. 1152
Todd, Frederick P. 954, 1004
Togi, Masataro 152
Toita, Yasuji 153
Toman, Karel 1005
Tompkins, Julia 1576-77
Torrens, Deborah 287
Torres Mendez, Ramon 405
Towsen, John H. 1119
Traetteberg, Gunor Ingstad 593
Trahey, Jane 348
Traphagen, Ethel 1454
Trendall, Arthur Dale 135
Trendell, Herbert Arthur 1153
Trevor-Roper, Hugh 1399
Troster, Frantisek 134
Truett, Randle Bond 349
Tuchelt, Klaus Franz 528
Tuit, Ann 1578-79

Tunis, Edwin 1324
Turbeville, Arthur Stanley 1325
Turner, Ralph 796
Tweedsmuir, Susan 1326
Twining, Edward Francis 1154-55
Twombly, Willis 1184
Tyler, Ron 350
Tyack, George S. 1120
Tyrrell, Barbara Harcourt 308

U

Uden, Grant 50
Underhill, Ruth Murray 378
Underwood, Leon 884
Unstead, R.J. 1400-1401
Urlin, Ethel L. 1171

V

Vail, Gilbert 853
Valdiosera, Ramon 406
Valeton, Elsa A. 646
Vallance, Aymer 789
Van Stan, Ina 1605
Vaughan, David 29
Vecchio, Walter 1695
Vecellio, Cesare 640
Veleva, Maria 529
Vernet, Horace 622
Veronesi, Giulia 1402
Vertes, Marcel 262
Vilimkova, M. 1475
Vilppula, Hilkka 594
Vincent, John Martin 631
Viski, Karoly 531-32, 1271
Vlahovic, Mitar S. 533
Vocino, Michele 641
Volbach, W. Fritz 1650
Volland, Virginia 1455
Vollmer, John E. 569
Vreeland, Diana 191

W

Wagner, Anthony 1156
Wagner, Eduard 604
Wagner, Leopold 1328
Wald, Carol 1329
Walker, Stella A. 1185

Walkley, Christina 1651
Walkup, Fairfax Proudfit 263
Wardle, Patricia 1652
Ware, Dore 49
Wark, R. 476
Warner, James A. 319
Warner, Oliver 1157
Warner, Philip 1079
Warner, Richard 1007
Warren, Helen 1197
Warwick, Edward 351
Wassing, Rene S. 309
Watkins, Josephine Ellis 1696
Watson, Phyllis 721
Waugh, Norah 1198, 1580-81
Webster, Thomas B.L. 135
Wedd, J.A. Dunkin 1476
Weibel, Adele Coulin 1653
Weintraub, Stanley 136
Welsford, Enid 1122
Werlich, Robert 1158
Westerman, Maxine 1456
Westmore, Michael G. 854
Wherry, Joseph H. 885
Whife, A.A. 1582
White, George M. 737
White, Palmer 1697
White, William Johnstone 1123
Whiteford, Andrew Hunter 379
Whitmore, William H. 1159
Whitney, Mary 183
Wilcox, R. Turner 51, 264-65, 352, 715, 738, 751
Wildeblood, Joan 1330
Wilkerson, Marjorie 266
Wilkinson, Alex 797
Wilkinson, Frederick J. 1008-9
Wilkinson-Latham, Christopher 1012-14, 1040-41, 1071-72
Wilkinson-Latham, Robert 1010-14, 1045, 1064, 1073
Willcox, Donald J. 798-99, 1583
Willett, Frank 310
Williams, E. Neville 856, 1403
Williams, Helen W. 1584
Wilson, Anne 498
Wilson, Carrie 729
Wilson, Eunice A. 739
Wilson, Everett B. 1124, 1331
Wilson, Lillian M. 424-25
Wilson, Violet I. 1585-86

Wilson, William 890
Windrow, Martin 1015, 1028, 1046, 1077, 1080-86
Wingate, Isabel E. 52
Winston, Clare 1404
Winston, Richard 1404
Winter, Marian Hannah 188
Wise, Arthur 959, 1272
Wise, Terence 1047
Wissler, Clark 380
Withington, Robert 1332
Witt, C. 54
Wlock, Violet 71
Wollin, Nils G. 1647
Wolska, Helen 1211
Wood, Christopher 1405
Wood, Josephine 407
Wood, Melusine 1273-75
Wood, Nancy 1399
Woodforde, John 857
Woodiwiss, John 730
Worrell, Estelle Ansley 353
Worsley-Gough, Barbara 1333
Worth, Jean Philippe 1699
Wright, Marion Logan 1588
Wright, Thomas 741

Y

Yarwood, Doreen 267, 477-78
Yoshinobu, Tokugawa 154
Young, Agnes Brooks 268, 1589
Young, Douglas 858-59
Young, Peter 1029, 1048-49, 1065-66

Z

Zaidenberg, Arthur 1457
Zarate, Dora P. 408
Zarate, Manuel F. 408
Zarina, Xenia 1276
Zderciuc, Boris 534
Zechlin, Ruth 72
Zeh, Gisela 137
Zilliacus, Benedict 1199
Zimmerman, Ray 860
Zimmern, Nathalie 409
Zinkeisen, Doris 1458
Zirner, Laura 1459
Zung, Cecilia Sieu-Ling 155

TITLE INDEX

This index includes the titles of all books cited in this text. It is alphabetized letter by letter. Numbers refer to entry numbers.

A

Abbigliamento e Costume 635
ABC of Men's Fashions 886
ABC of Stage Make-Up for Men, The 858
ABC of Stage Make-Up for Women, The 859
Academical Dress 1099
Academical Dress of British Universities 1118
Academic Costume Code, An 1087
Accent on Accessories 711
Accessories du Costume, Les 610
Accessories of Dress 701
Actor and His Body, The 1260
Adaptable Stage Costume for Women 1561
Advanced Historical Dances 1273
African Art 300
African Art: An Introduction 310
African Art: Its Background 309
African Art and Oceanic Art 288
African Arts of Transformation 291
African Crafts and Craftsmen 293
African Dances 295
African Dress 9
African Elegance 290
African Fabric Crafts 1501
African Image 296
African Textiles 307

African Traditional Garb 14
Age of Ambition, An 1292
Age of Courts and Kings, The 1295
Age of Expansion, The 1399
Age of Humanism, The 1346
Age of Illusion, The 1306
Age of the Renaissance, The 1366
Age of Worth, The 1692
Ages of Elegance 220
A la Mode: On the Social Psychology of Fashion 1720
Album de Costumes Portuguezes 655
Album of Historical Coiffures 812
All the Queen's Men 920
Always in Vogue 1678
American Album 1373
American and European Jewelry 768
American Ballet Theatre 182
American Costume Book, The 328
American Costumes 346
American Cowboy, The 340
American Family, The 1395
American Fashion 1685
American Heritage Book of Indians, The 368
American Indian Beadwork 366
American Indian Design and Decoration 354
American Indian Wars, The 1016
American Mail Order Fashions 311
American Manners and Morals 1282

Title Index

American Provincial Corps 1017
American Textiles 1633
American War, The 1018
American War Medals and Decorations 952
America's Fabrics 1590
America's Indigo Blues 1623
America's Knitting Book 1574
America's Printed and Painted Fabrics 1624
America's Sewing Book 1534
America's Vanishing Folkways 1331
Amish Life 332
Anatomy of Costume, The 256
Ancient Egyptian, Assyrian, and Persian Costumes 418
Ancient Egyptian Jewellery 797
Ancient Greek, Roman and Byzantine Costume 419
Ancient Greek Dress 410
Ancient Greek Dress: A New Illustrated Edition 420
Ancient Hair Styles of India 844
Ancient Mexican Costume 392
Ancient World, The 1312
Andalusian Dances 1221
And the Bride Wore . . . 1168
Anglo-Saxon Jewellery 780
Anthropology of Fashion, The 1730
Antique Jewelry 760
Appreciating Costume 1407
Arab Legion, The 1048
Argyll and Sutherland Highlanders, The 1036
Armour of Imperial Rome, The 985
Arms and Armour 977
Arms and Armour from the 9th to the 17th Century 961
Arms and Armour in the Age of Chivalry 924
Arms and Uniforms 936
Arms through the Ages 984
Army Badges and Insignia of World War II 988
Army Badges and Insignia since 1945 989
Army of Northern Virginia, The 1019
Army of the German Empire 1069
Army of the Potomac, The 1020
Army Uniforms of World War II 966

Art and Fashion 262
Art and Fashion in Clothing Selection 1727
Art and the Stage 126
Art Deco Fashion 1675
Artificial Face, The 836
Art in Costume Design 47
Art in Ornament and Dress 1462
Artists' and Illustrators' Encyclopedia 45
Art Nouveau Jewellery 789
Art of Africa: Tribal Masks 867
Art of Ballroom Dance, The 1228
Art of Color, The 1437
Art of Color and Design, The 1430
Art of Dyeing, The 1657
Art of English Costume, The 1710
Art of Jewelry, The 777
Art of Make-Up for Stage, Television and Film 818
Art of Making Dances, The 1236
Art of Pantomime, The 1215
Art of Theatrical Makeup, The 854
Art of the Wigmaker, The 831
Arts and Crafts of Japan: Masks 875
Arts of Man: Costume 241
Assemblage of Indian Army Soldiers and Uniforms, An 938
As We Were 1384
At the Sign of the Barber's Pole 813
Aubrey Beardsley 136
Austrian Textiles 1645
Austro-Hungarian Army of the Napoleonic Wars 1062
Austro-Hungarian Army of the Seven Years War, The 1075

B

Bakst 159
Bakst: The Story of the Artist's Life 180
Ballet: An Illustrated History 167
Ballet and Dance 173
Ballet Design Past and Present 161
Ballet Designs and Illustrations 184
Barokin Pukumuoti Suomessa 589
Baroque and Rococo Silks 1648
Basic Color 1439
Basic Pattern, The 1584

Basic Pattern Cutting 1543
Basic Pattern Drafting 1564
Basic Principles of Design 1442
Basic Textile Book, A 1627
Bath Book, The 833
Batik 1665
Batik as a Hobby 1672
Battle Dress 1008
Bayreuther Buehnenkosteum, Das 137
Beads as Jewelry 1500
Beard Book, The 860
Beards 847
Beau Brummell 894
Beautiful People, The 1705
Between the Wars 1307
Bharatanatya and Its Costume 551
Biblical Costume 1588
Biblical Costumes for Church and
    School 1502
Bibliographie Generale du Costume 7
Bibliography of Colonial Costume 16
Bibliography of Costume 11
Bibliography on Costume 10
Bibliography of Dancing, A 1218
Bildnis des Eleganten Mannes, Das
    892
Black Brunswickers, The 1056
Blackfeet Crafts 362
Black Watch, The 1032
Block Printing on Textiles 1661
Blue Book of Men's Tailoring, The
    1498
Bluecher's Army 1065
Body and Clothes 211
Body Jewelry 798
Boer War, The 1071
Book about Fans, A 690
Book for Men 887
Book of Costume, The 221
Book of Diamonds, The 763
Book of Festivals, The 1317
Book of Festivals and Holidays, The
    1303
Book of Gold, The 677
Book of Hours, The 1364
Book of Indian-Crafts and Costumes
    374
Book of Jewelry, A 783
Book of Military Uniforms and Weapons,
    A 1005

Book of Necklaces, The 793
Book of Pipes and Tobacco, The 687
Book of Public School Old Boys,
    University, Navy, Army, Air Force,
    and Club Ties, The 889
Book of Signs, The 1470
Book of the Continental Soldier, The
    980
Book of the Dance, The 1245
Boutell's Heraldry 1126
Britain's Royal Brides 1161
British and Continental Arms and
    Armour 908
British Army in North America, The
    1022
British Army in the American
    Revolution, The 950
British Army of 1914, The 911
British Army of the Crimea 1068
British Costume during XIX Centuries
    426
British Customs and Ceremonies 1302
British Gallantry Awards 905
British Military Uniforms 956
British Military Uniforms and Equip-
    ment 953
British Military Uniforms from Con-
    temporary Pictures 922
British Military Uniforms 1768-1796
    997
British Naval Dress 947
British Popular Customs 1323
British Sailor, The 951
British Silhouettes 730
British Textiles 1638
Broadway and Hollywood 193
Brudekjolen 1160
Buffs, The 1030
Buhnenkostum, Das 78
Bulgarian National Attire 529
Bulgarian Textiles 1635
Bunraku 138
Bust-Up 1195
Butterick Fabric Handbook, The 1616
Button Hand Book 705
Buttons 713
Buttons for the Collector 706
Buyo 144
Byzantine Fabrics 1594

Title Index

C

Cadet Gray 1004
Canadian Textiles 1646
Canes and Walking Sticks 714
Caring for Textiles 1611
Carolian Fabrics 1592
Catalogue of the Costume Collection 57
Cavalry Uniforms of Britain 1012
Cavalry Uniforms of the British Army 991
Cecil Beaton Stage and Film Designs 129
Century of Fashion, A 1699
Ceremonial Costumes of the Pueblo Indians 375
Ceremonial Uniforms of the World 1129
Chagall at the "Met" 89
Chanel Solitaire 1674
Changing Face of Beauty, The 834
Changing Face of Childhood, The 804
Changing Fashions 217
Changing Form of Fashion, The 1715
Changing World of Fashion, The 271
Chasseurs of the Guard 1066
Child in Fashion, The 810
Children's Costume 807
Children's Costume in England 802
Children's Fashions in the 19th Century 806
China on Stage 151
China's Dragon Robes 541
Chinese Costume in Transition 565
Chinese Court Costumes 548
Chinese Court Robes 542
Chinese Drama, The 139
Chinese Fabrics 1595
Chinese Folk Design 556
Chinese Opera and Painted Face 148
Chinese Opera Costumes 140
Chinese Theatre in Modern Times, The 146
Chivalry (Foss) 1355
Chivalry (Gautier) 1136
Christian Dior and I 1679
Chronology of Neo-Assyrian Art, The 423
Church Vestments 1115

Cinq Peintres et le Theatre 124
Circus Techniques 1220
City of New York Golden Anniversary of Fashion 315
Civil and Military Clothing in Europe 603
Clans, Septs and Regiments of the Scottish Highlands 492
Clans and Tartans of Scotland 480
Classical Dances and Costumes of India 535
Classical Dances of the Orient 1276
Classical Theatre of China, The 149
Clerical Dress and Insignia of the Roman Catholic Church 1111
Clothes 266
Clothes and the Horse 1172
Clothes of the Cut, The 1106
Cloth Hats, Bags 'n Baggage 1509
Clothing 1736
Clothing: A Comprehensive Study 1709
Clothing Concepts 1734
Clothing Decoration 1662
Clothing for Ladies and Gentlemen 330
Clothing in English Canada 316
Clothing of the Ancient Romans 424
Clowns 1119
Clowns and Pantomimes 86
Coldstream Guards 1033
Collars, Stocks, Cravats 682
Collection of Costumes, The 71
Collector's Encyclopedia of Buttons, The 702
Collectors Encyclopedia of Hatpins, The 675
Collector's Guide to Fans, A 694
Collector's History of Fans, A 674
Colonial Living 1324
Color 1409
Color, Form and Space 1410
Color and Design 1421
Colorful World of Ballet, The 170
Color in Sketching and Rendering 1432
Color in Your World 1411
Color Perception in Art 1412
Colourful World of Buttons, The 689
Colour Guide to German Army Uniforms 926

Commedia Dell' Arte, The 122
Common Man through the Centuries, The 197
Complete Book of Hairstyles, Beauty and Fashion, The 824
Complete Book of Handcrafts 72
Complete Book of Home Millinery, The 1495
Complete Button Book, The 673
Complete Guide to Patternmaking, The 1547
Complete Guide to Wigs and Hair-pieces 838
Complete View of the Dress and Habits of the People of England, A 475
Concise Dictionary of Holidays 1304
Concise History of Costume, A 242
Connaught Rangers, The 1038
Contemporary Costume Jewelry 795
Contemporary Jewelry 796
Contemporary Stage Design U.S.A. 81
Coronation Costume 1139
Corset, The 1199
Corset Dans l'Art, Le 1192
Corsets 1197
Corsets and Crinolines 1198
Cossacks, The 1043
Costume 243
Costume: A General Bibliography 3
Costume: A List of Books 8
Costume: An Illustrated Survey 248
Costume and Conduct in the Laws of Basel, Bern and Zurich 631
Costume and Fashion 600
Costume and Fashion in Color 216
Costume and Fashion in Colour 234
Costume Book, The 1532
Costume Collection 60
Costume Cues 716
Costume Design (Chuse) 1422
Costume Design (Hardy) 1433
Costume Design: An Introductory Outline 1417
Costume Design and Illustration 1454
Costume Design and Making 1508
Costume Design in the Movies 190
Costume Drawings 1425
Costume en Espagne et au Portugal, Le 656

Costume en France, Le 619
Costume for Births, Marriages and Deaths 1164
Costume Illustration: The Nineteenth Century 460
Costume Illustration: The Seventeenth and Eighteenth Centuries 461
Costume in Antiquity 421
Costume in Detail 206
Costume Index 17
Costume in England 450
Costume in Greek Classic Drama 79
Costume in Pictures 458
Costume in the Drama of Shakespeare 105
Costume in the Theatre 103
Costume Militaire, Le 955
Costume of Candelario, Salamanca 660
Costume of Household Servants 1095
Costume of the Prelates of the Catholic Church 1114
Costume of the Theatre, The 100
Costume of the Western World: Early Bourbon 605
Costume of the Western World: Early Tudor 462
Costume of the Western World: Elizabethan and Jacobean 471
Costume of the Western World: The Dominance of Spain 671
Costume of the Western World: The Great Age of Holland 645
Costume of the Western World: The Last Valois 606
Costume on the Stage 134
Costume Patterns and Designs 1575
Costume Popolare en Italia, II 634
Costume Reference 257
Costumes, Textiles, Cosmetics and Coiffure in Ancient and Mediaeval India 543
Costumes and Curtains from the Diaghilev and De Basil Ballets 169
Costumes and Customs of the British Isles 489
Costumes and Ornaments 525
Costumes and Style 235
Costumes and Textiles of India, The 538

Costumes and Textiles of the Aztec Indians 387

Costumes by You 1408

Costumes de l'Union Francaise 612

Costumes des Provinces Francaises 613

Costumes Espagnols 657

Costumes for Children 1567

Costumes for Nursery Tale Characters 1511

Costumes for the Dance 718

Costumes for You to Make 1555

Costumes Francais Du XVIII Siecle 609

Costumes from the Forbidden City 563

Costumes Grotesques et les Metiers, Les 616

Costume Silhouettes 723

Costumes in Austria 624

Costumes in Shakespeare's Play of the Winters Tale 84

Costumes Japonais et Indonesiens 550

Costumes of Chios, The 500

Costumes of Eastern Europe, The 527

Costumes of Everyday Life 1107

Costumes of France, The 614

Costumes of India 549

Costumes of India and Pakistan 544

Costumes of South America 395

Costumes of the Bronze Age in Denmark 413

Costumes of the East 547

Costumes of the Greeks and Romans 417

Costumes of the Nineteenth Century 447

Costumes of the Welsh People 479

Costumes of Upper Burma and the Shan States 559

Costumes Painted by Sorolla 650

Costumes to Make (Parish) 1549

Costumes to Make (Sweat) 1572

Costume throughout the Ages 223

Costume through the Ages 245

Costuming for Children's Theatre 1566

Costuming for the Modern Stage 1459

Costuming for the Theatre 1446

Costuming the Biblical Play 1482

Costuming with Basics and Separates 1497

Country Garb in Early New England 324

Courtesans of the Italian Renaissance 1313

Court of Elizabeth the First, The 1315

Courts of Europe, The 1349

Couture 1687

Cowboy, The 350

Craft Manual of North American Indian Footwear 737

Craft of Comedy, The 1264

Crafts of the Ojibewa, The 371

Craft Sources 58

Creating Body Coverings 1530

Creating Children's Costumes 1521

Creating with Batik 1658

Creative Clothing Construction 1480

Creative Color 1413

Creative Costumes for the Classroom 1496

Creative Masks for Stage and School 876

Creative West African Fashion 302

Creative Work with Textiles 1542

Crimean Uniforms: British Artillery 1010

Crimean Uniforms: British Infantry 916

Crinolines and Crimping Irons 1651

Crown Jewels, The 1157

Crown Jewels and Ecclesiastical Treasure Chamber 1134

Crown Jewels and Other Regalia 1151

Crowns and Coronations 1143

Cuadros de Costumbres 405

Customs and Fashions in Old New England 1294

Customs and Traditions of England 1299

Cut My Cote 1491

Cut of Men's Clothes, The 1580

Cut of Women's Clothes, The 1581

Cut of Women's 19th Century Dress 1494

Cyclopaedia of Costume, A 44

Czechoslovak Textiles 1639

Czech Stage Costumes 112

D

Dance 157

Dance: An Historical Survey of Dancing in Europe, The 1266
Dance: The Story of the Dance Told in Pictures and Text, The 1254
Dance in Ancient Greece, The 1249
Dance in India, The 537
Dance in Society 1316
Dance in Spain, The 1238
Dance of the Ancient Greek Theatre, The 1250
Dance Production 720
Dance Production Handbook 717
Dances of Belgium 1209
Dances of Bulgaria 1206
Dances of Czechoslovakia 1207
Dances of England and France 1224
Dances of France 1208
Dances of Germany 1204
Dances of Norway 1210
Dances of Poland 1211
Dances of Portugal 1202
Dances of Rumania 1205
Dances of Spain 1203
Dances of Spain and Italy 1225
Dance Today in Canada 181
Dancing Master, The 1262
Dandies 898
Dandy, The 901
Danish Folk Costumes 570
Danish Textiles 1643
Danseur 183
Days of Duchess Anne, The 1381
Debrett's Coronation Guide 1131
Decorative Art of Leon Bakst, The 156
Decorative Art of Victoria's Era 1376
Decorative Arts of Africa, The 298
Decorative Arts of Sweden, The 587
Decorative Design 1464
Decorative Thirties, The 269
Decorative Twenties, The 270
Degrees and Hoods of the World's Universities and Colleges, The 1103
Design and Form 1438
Designed for Applause 721
Design for Ballet 168
Design for Movement 1256
Design for the Ballet 162
Designing and Cutting Ladies' Garments 1582
Designing and Making Stage Costumes 118
Designing by Draping 1587
Designing Dress Patterns 1573
Designing for Crafts 1445
Designing for the Stage 1458
Designing in Batik and Tie Dye 1655
Designing Male 1681
Designing Woman 1455
Design in the Theatre 127
Design Motifs of Ancient Mexico 393
Designs, Borders, Backgrounds, Tints and Patterns 1465
Designs by Inigo Jones 97
Designs of Leon Bakst, The 160
Diaghilev and Russian Stage Designers 172
Diaghilev and the Ballets Russes 179
Dictionnaire du Costume 38
Dictionary of Chivalry, A 50
Dictionary of Costume, The 51
Dictionary of English Costume, A 31
Dictionary of Men's Wear, A 23
Dictionary of Military Uniform, A 27
Dictionary of Needlework, The 28
Dictionary of Sewing Terminology 26
Dimensions of Dress and Adornment 1716
Discovering Costume 196
Discovering French and German Military Uniforms 999
Drama: Its Costume and Decor 104
Drama Bibliography 12
Dramatic Bibliography 4
Dramatic Character Plates 76
Draping and Dress Design 1505
Draping for Fashion Design 1523
Drawing and Designing Menswear 1435
Dress 1723
Dress, Adornment and the Social Order 1733
Dress: The Evolution of Cut 1507
Dress and Insignia Worn at His Majesty's Court 1152
Dress and Society 258
Dress and Undress 212
Dress Clothing of the Plains Indians 369
Dress Design 1520

Dress Design--Draping and Flat Pattern Making 1518
Dressing for the Ballet 719
Dressing the Part 263
Dressing the Play 1529
Dress in Italian Painting 633
Dress in Medieval France 611
Dressmakers of France 1689
Dressmaking Techniques for Trade Students 1493
Dress of Naval Officers, The 963
Dress of the British Sailor, The 931
Dress Optional 888
Dress Regulations for the Army 932
Dress the Show 1516
Dress Worn at His Majesty's Court 1153
Duck and Cabbage Tree 488
Dutch Costumes 646
Dutch Textiles 1630
Dyer's Art, The 1666
Dynamic Figure Drawing 1434

E

Early America at Work 1124
Early American Costume 353
Early American Dress 351
Early American Weaving and Dyeing 1656
Early California Costumes 341
Early Clothing in Southern Ontario 317
Early Decorative Textiles 1650
Early Victorian Album, An 1353
Early Victorian Woman, The 1293
Eastern Costume 539
Easy Costumes You Don't Have to Sew 1492
Easy-to-Make Costumes for Stage and School 1576
Ecclesiastical Vestments 1109
Edwardian Lady, The 1326
Edwardian Life and Leisure 1385
Edwardian Promenade 1308
Edwardians, The 1387
Egyptian Ornament 1475
1815: The Armies at Waterloo 979
Eighteenth Century, The 1347
18th Century Women's Costume 54

Elegant Modes in the Nineteenth Century 456
Elegant Woman, The 195
Elementary Fashion Design and Trade Sketching 1456
Elements of Design 1406
Elements of Design: Color and Value 1429
Elements of Heraldry, The 1159
Elizabethan Embroidery 1608
Elizabethan England 1350
Elizabethan Pageantry 469
Elizabethans, The 1383
Elizabethan Woman, The 1283
Elizabeth I.R.: Her Face and Costumes 474
Embroidery for the Church 1485
Embroidery of Mexico and Guatemala, The 394
Encyclopaedia Dictionary of Heraldry 34
Encyclopedia of Colour Decoration, An 1416
Encyclopedia of Dance and Ballet, The 29
Encyclopedia of Ornament, The 1473
Encyclopedia of Textiles 22
England in the Age of Hogarth 1370
England's Dances 1241
English, The 1388
English Ceremonial Book, The 1146
English Child in the Eighteenth Century, The 800
English Children's Costume 801
English Civil War Armies 1049
English Costume 434
English Costume: Its History and Its Design 437
English Costume for Sports and Outdoor Recreation 1174
English Costume from Prehistoric Times to the End of the 18th Century 436
English Costume from the Second Century B.C. to 1967 477
English Costume in the Age of Elizabeth 429
English Costume of the Early Middle Ages 430
English Costume of the Eighteenth Century 463

English Costume of the Later Middle Ages 431
English Costume of the Nineteenth Century 464
English Costume of the Seventeenth Century 432
English Court Life from Henry VII to George II 1351
English Dancing Master, The 1261
English Decorative Fabrics 1615
English Dress in the Age of Shakespeare 459
English Fashion 472
English Folk Dancing 1242
English Home-Life 1300
English Life in Chaucer's Day 1359
English Life in the Eighteenth Century 1360
English Life in the Nineteenth Century 1361
English Life in the Seventeenth Century 1362
English Life in Tudor Times 1363
English Men and Manners in the 18th Century 1325
English Pageantry 1332
English Regalia, The 1141
English Sports and Pastimes 1177
English Sports and Recreations 1182
English Smocks with Directions for Making Them 1477
English Traditional Customs 1301
English Woman in History, The 1320
English Women's Clothing in the Nineteenth Century 439
English Women's Clothing in the Present Century 440
Enjoying Dyes 1663
Erte 130
Erte Fashions 1694
Eskimo Masks 878
Espana: Tipos y Trajes 669
Esquire Fashion Guide for All Occasions 24
Esquire's Encyclopedia of 20th Century Men's Fashions 46
Etruscan Dress 411
European and American Arms 917
European Armour 918
European Arms and Armour 909

European Civic Coats of Arms 1144
European Costume 267
European Folk Dance 1251
European Folk Dress 19
European Military Uniforms 962
European Musical Instruments 696
European Printed Textiles 1649
European Regalia 1154
Everyday Costume in Britain 427
Evolution of Fashion, The 1517
Exact Dress of the Head 747
Exhibition of Renaissance Jewels 762
Exhibition of Victorian and Edwardian Dresses 252
Extramadura Costume 661

F

Faberge 784
Fabric and Fashion 237
Fabric Book for People Who Sew, The 1607
Fabric Printing by Hand 1670
Fabrics for Historic Buildings 1622
Fabrics of Peru, The 1605
Fabulous Feasts 1287
Face Coverings 865
Face of Monarchy, The 470
Face Painting in Chinese Opera 841
Fairchild's Dictionary of Fashion 25
Fairchild's Dictionary of Textiles (Marks) 39
Fairchild's Dictionary of Textiles (Wingate) 52
Fairchild's Who's Who in Fashion 1696
Fan Book, The 708
Fans in Fashion 700
Far North, The 318
Fashion (Garland) 276
Fashion (Pringle) 255
Fashion: An Anthology 200
Fashion: An Anthology by Cecil Beaton 277
Fashion, 1900-1939 286
Fashion: The Changing Shape 222
Fashionable Lady in the 19th Century, The 452
Fashionable Savages, The 1680
Fashion Accessories 707

Title Index

Fashion Accessories: A Nontextile Work Manual 691
Fashion Alphabet, A 35
Fashion and Reality 229
Fashion Design (Brogden) 1419
Fashion Design (Mortimer-Dunn) 1443
Fashion Design Drawing 1436
Fashion Dictionary 42
Fashion Drawing 1426
Fashion for Everyone 247
Fashion from Ancient Egypt to the Present Day 218
Fashion Illustrated 287
Fashion in History 202
Fashion in the Forties 284
Fashion in the Forties and Fifties 273
Fashion in the Twenties and Thirties 274
Fashion in Underwear 1189
Fashion Makers, The 1695
Fashions and Fashion Plates 726
Fashions for Men 893
Fashions in Eyeglasses 684
Fashions in Hair 826
Fashions in London 1333
Fashions in Makeup 827
Fashion Sketchbook 283
Fashions of the Seventies 323
Fashions since Their Debut 729
Fashions through the Centuries 260
Fashion through Fashion Plates 727
Female Costume in the 19th Century 225
Female Portrait in Russian Art, The 507
Feminine Attitudes in the Nineteenth Century 1711
Festival Designs by Inigo Jones 131
Festivals of Western Europe 1318
Fifty Masterpieces of Textiles 1121
Figleafing through History 1718
Figure, The 1449
Figure Drawing for All It's Worth 1441
Figurino Nel Teatro, Il 82
Finger-Ring Lore 782
Finnish Textiles 1644
Fire Engines, Fire Fighters 1097
First Book of Stage Costume and Make-Up 1486

First Ladies Hall, The 337
First Ladies in Fashion, The 349
Five Centuries of American Costume 352
Five Centuries of Ballet Design 163
Flashes of Fashion 343
Flat Pattern Methods 1519
Florentine Fabrics 1596
Folding Paper Masks 871
Folies du Music-Hall, Les 85
Folk and Festival Costume of the World 264
Folk Art in Rumania 534
Folk Art of Asia, Africa and the Americas 412
Folk Art of Europe 595
Folk Art of Mexico 391
Folk Arts of Norway, The 591
Folk Costume of Eastern Europe 508
Folk Costume of Southern Europe 597
Folk Costumes 501
Folk Costumes and Textiles 594
Folk Costumes in Denmark 571
Folk Costumes of Norway 593
Folk Costumes of Sweden 573
Folk Costumes of Western Europe 598
Folk Dance Library 1226
Folk Dances, Costumes and Customs of Italy 636
Folk Dances and Mexican Costumes 382
Folk Theater of India 142
Fool, The 1122
Foot Grenadiers of the Imperial Guard 1054
Footwear: A Short History of European and American Shoes 731
Footwear: Salesperson's Manual and Costumer's Guide 733
Forms upon the Frontier 325
Four Centuries of European Jewellery 759
Four Hundred Years of Children's Costume 808
France in the Eighteenth Century 615
Frederick Ashton 174
Frederick the Great's Army 1076
French Army Regiments and Uniforms 1001
French Costumes 617

French Foreign Legion, The 1046
French Provincial Costumes 620
French Textiles 1637
From Hoopskirts to Nudity 1717
From Nudity to Raiment 416
From Slave to Siren 779
From Toddler to Teens 803
Frontiers of Privilege, The 1288
Functions of Folk Costume in Moravian
  Slovak 502
Fundamentals of Apparel Design 1447
Fundamentals of Men's Fashion Design
  1440
Fundamentals of Men's Fashion Design:
  A Guide to Casual Clothes 1557
Fundamentals of Men's Fashion Design:
  A Guide to Tailored Clothes 1525
Funeral Customs the World Over 1166
Fun with Fabric 1667
Future Out of the Past, The 1194

G

Gagaku 152
Gala Dress about 1760, A 642
Galla of Ethiopia, The 297
Gallegan Provinces of Spain 651
Gallery of English Costume, The 466
Gallery of English Costume: Children's
  Costume, The 809
Gallery of English Costume: Costume
  for Sport, The 1179
Gallery of Fashion 227
Garment-Cutting and Tailoring for
  Students 1545
Gems and Jewelry Today 755
General Armory of England, Scotland,
  Ireland, and Wales, The 1128
Gentle People, The 319
George Washington's Army 1029
Georgian Grace 1297
German Military Uniforms and Insignia
  937
German Textiles 1641
German Uniforms and Insignia 929
Getting Started in Batik 1660
Gilbert and Sullivan and Their
  Victorian World 95
Glass of Fashion, The 1703
Glass of Fashion, 1830-1930, The 347

Glossary of Costume, A 33
Gloves 712
Gloves, Their Annuals and Associations
  676
Golden Age of Style, The 285
Golden Guide: North American
  Indian Arts 379
Good Old Days, The 1286
Gothic Woman's Fashion 602
Grammar of Color, A 1415
Grammar of English Heraldry, A 1142
Great American West, The 331
Great Book of Jewels, The 772
Great Costumes 1550-1950 233
Great Masks 863
Greek and Roman Jewellery 774
Greek Gold 776
Guide to the Catholic Sisterhoods
  1110
Guide to the Collection of Costumes
  69
Gurkha Rifles, The 1037

H

Hair 823
Hair and Beauty Secrets of the 17th
  Century 829
Hair Dressing and Fashion 825
Hamlets of the Theatre, The 80
Hamlet through the Ages 106
Handbook for History Teachers 6
Handbook of Costume, A 53
Handbook of Decorative Design and
  Ornament 1460
Handbook of English Costume in the
  Eighteenth Century 441
Handbook of English Costume in the
  Nineteenth Century 442
Handbook of English Costume in the
  Seventeenth Century 443
Handbook of English Costume in the
  Sixteenth Century 444
Handbook of English Costume in the
  Twentieth Century 467
Handbook of English Medieval
  Costume 445
Handbook of Ornament 1472
Handbook of Technical Practice for
  the Performing Arts 55

Title Index

Handbooks of European National Dances 1201
Hand Coloured Fashion Plates 725
Handcraft in Sweden 578
Hand Decoration of Fabrics, The 1664
Hand in Glove 710
Happy and Glorious 1354
Harem, The 521
Hat Boxes and Bandboxes 680
Hats 742
Haute Couture 1683
Health, Art and Reason 1729
Heraldic Cadency 1137
Heraldic Design 1125
Heraldic Imagination, The 1133
Heraldry 1147
Heraldry and Armor of the Middle Ages 1148
Heraldry and Regalia of War 934
Heraldry Explained 1135
Heraldry in England 1156
Here's Your Hat 749
Highland Dress 483
Highland Dress, Arms and Ornament 482
High Victorian Costume 438
Hispano-Moresque Fabrics 1597
Historical Color Guide 1420
Historical Costumes of England 428
Historical Russian Costumes 522
Historic Costume 246
Historic Costume: A Chronicle of Fashion 1526
Historic Costume Designs 251
Historic Costume for the Stage 198
Historic Costume in Pictures 209
Historic Costume through the Ages 250
Historic Dress of the Clergy 1120
Historic Hairdressing 816
Historic Hungarian Costumes 511
Historic Ornament 1468
Historie du Costume 1533
History and Annotated Bibliography of Skating, A 20
History of Academical Dress in Europe, A 1100
History of American Costume 339
History of Color in Painting 1414
History of Corsets in Pictures 1187

History of Cosmetics in America, A 853
History of Costume 261
History of Costume, A 240
History of Costume: In Slides, Notes, and Commentaries, A 215
History of Costume from the Ancient Egyptians to the Twentieth Century 254
History of Costume in the West, A 205
History of English Costume, A 433
History of Fashion 224
History of Fashion, A 228
History of Feminine Costume of the World, The 230
History of French Masculine Costume, The 895
History of Hair, The 821
History of Harlequin, The 75
History of Highland Dress 485
History of Hosiery 693
History of Indian Dress, A 546
History of Jewellery, A 765
History of Jewish Costume, A 523
History of Ladies Underwear, A 1191
History of Legal Dress in Europe, A 1101
History of Lingerie in Pictures 1186
History of Makeup, A 814
History of Men's Wear Industry 899
History of Russian Costume 499
History of Scent, A 835
History of Shoe Fashions, A 739
History of the Crown Jewels of Europe, A 1155
History of the Dress of the British Soldier, A 960
History of the Handkerchief, The 679
History of the Hat, The 745
History of the Nineteenth Century in Caricature 1314
History of the Regiments and Uniforms of the British Army, A 912
History of the Umbrella, A 685
History of the Uniforms of the British Army, A 957
History of Twentieth Century Fashion 275
History of Underclothes, The 1188

History of Women's Hairstyles, A 840
Hochzeit 1165
Hoefische Taenze 1269
Hogarth to Cruikshank 1296
Hollywood Costume Design 189
Hollywood Costume Design: Glamour, Glitter, Romance 191
Horizon Book of Daily Life in Ancient Egypt, The 1344
Horizon Book of Daily Life in Ancient Rome, The 1345
Horizon Book of Daily Life in Renaissance Italy, The 1382
Horizon Book of Daily Life in the Middle Ages, The 1404
Horizon Book of Daily Life in Victorian England, The 1368
Horizon Book of the Age of Napoleon, The 1367
Horizon Book of the Elizabethan World, The 1396
Horizon Book of the Middle Ages, The 1339
Horizon Book of the Renaissance, The 1386
Horizon History of Africa, The 1374
Horse Soldier, The 997
Hosiery thru the Years 697
House of Worth, The 1677
How the Rich Lived 1378
How to Design Your Own Clothes 1427
How to Draft Basic Patterns 1527
How to Draw Period Costumes 1457
How to Fit Clothes 1578
How to Make Clothes That Fit and Flatter 1541
How to Make Historic American Costumes 1506
How to Make Men's Clothes 1556
How to Make Sewing Patterns 1538
How to Make Your Own Sewing Patterns 1539
How to Sew Leather, Suede, Fur 1563
Hungarian Dances 1271
Hungarian Decorative Folk Art 514
Hungarian Folk Costumes 520
Hungarian Folk Dances 1253
Hungarian Peasant Costumes 509
Hungarian Peasant Customs 531

Hungarian Szur, The 510
Hungarian Textiles 1634

I

If the Shoe Fits 735
If You Can't Go Naked Here Are Clothes to Sew Fast 1531
Illustrated Dictionary of Hairdressing and Wigmaking, An 30
Illustrated Dictionary of Jewellery, An 40
Illustrated Dictionary of Ornament, An 49
Illustrating Fashion 1452
Illustrations of Greek Drama 135
Importance of Wearing Clothes, The 1722
Incredible Beau Brummell, The 904
Incroyables and Merveilleuses 622
Indian Art in America 360
Indian Art of the Americas 355
Indian Art of the United States 361
Indian Arts in Canada 359
Indian Costume 552
Indian Costume, Coiffure and Ornament 564
Indian Costumes 364
Indian Costumes in the United States 380
Indian Costumes of Guatemala 407
Indian Crafts of Guatemala and El Salvador 400
Indian Jewellery, Ornaments and Decorative Designs 757
Indian Masks and Myths of the West 885
Indian Mutiny, The 1072
Indian Sari, The 545
Indians of Brazil in the Twentieth Century 396
Indigenous African Architecture 294
Indumentaria Colonial 386
Indumentaria Espanola 653
Indumentaria Medieval Espanola 654
Indumentaria Tradicional Catalona 649
Infantry Uniforms including Artillery and Other Supporting Corps of Britain and the Commonwealth 1855-1939 1013

Infantry Uniforms including Artillery and Other Supporting Troops of Britain and the Commonwealth 1742-1855 1014
Infantry Uniforms of the British Army 992
Inigo Jones 123
In My Fashion 1702
In Search of Diaghilev 165
Instant Dressmaking 1558
International Directory of Historical Clothing 65
International Exhibition of Modern Jewellery 778
In the Presence of the Dragon Throne 569
In the Russian Style 518
In This Proud Land 1397
Introducing Batik 1671
Introducing Pattern Cutting 1579
Introducing Textile Printing 1668
Introduction to American Indian Art 367
Introduction to Peruvian Costume 409
Introduction to Southwestern Indian Arts and Crafts, An 356
In Vogue 279
Irish Portraits 484
Iron Brigade, The 1024
Iroquois Crafts 372
Isaac Cruikshank's Drawings for Drolls 476
Italian Comedy, The 87
Italian Renaissance Illuminations 632
Italian Textiles 1629
It's a Small, Medium and Outsize World 1737

J

Jacques Callot 98
Japanese Accessories 555
Japanese Army of World War II 1079
Japanese Coiffure 848
Japanese Costume 553
Japanese Costume and Textile Arts 562
Japanese Costume and the Makers of Its Elegant Tradition 561
Japanese Textiles 1642
Japanese Women's Costumes 557
Jazz Age, The 1337

Jeanne d' Arc 1514
Jewellery 753
Jewellery of the Ancient World 781
Jewelry 770
Jewelry from the Renaissance to Art Nouveau 767
Jewelry of the Ancient Near East 791
Jewelry through the Ages 771
Jewels and the Woman 792
Jewels in Spain 790
Jewels of the Pharaohs 752
Joy of Sewing, The 1585
Just So Far 1673

K

Kabuki 145
Kabuki: The Popular Theatre 153
Kabuki Costume 150
Kabuki Theatre, The 141
Karl X Gustavus Draekter 575
Kashmir Shawl, The 698
Katalog der Freiherrlich von Lipper-heide'schen Kosteumbibliothek 15
King of Fashion 1690
Kings and Queens of England 468
King's German Legion 1057
Kings of Fashion 1684
King's Regiment, The 1039
Knight and Chivalry, The 1336
Knights and the Age of Chivalry 1392
'Ksan 370

L

Lace 1619
Lady of Fashion 226
Landknechts, The 1042
Language of Fashion, The 43
Lappedrakten 576
Last of the Nuba, The 305
Latin American Costumes 403
Lebanese and Syrian Costumes 540
Leisure and Pleasure in the Nineteenth Century 1379
Lembranac Do Brasil 384
Leon Bakst 186
Letters on Dancing and Ballets 1256
Lexikon der Mode 36
Life and Work of the People of England 1365
Life Guards, The 995

Life in a Medieval Castle 1356
Life in a Medieval City 1357
Life in America 1348
Life in Georgian England 1403
Life in Medieval England 1335
Lingerie Parisienne 1193
Literature of Fashion, The 13
Liturgical Vesture 1116
Lives of the Kings and Queens of
   England, The 451
Living Arts of Nigeria, The 292
Long and Short of It, The 849
Long Party, The 1380
Love of a Glove 683
Luftwaffe Airborne and Field Units
   1080

M

McKenney-Hall Portrait Gallery of
   American Indians, The 365
Macrame Book, The 1488
Magic of Makeup 842
Magic Symbols of the World 1461
Mail-Order Crafts Catalogue, The 56
Makeup and Masks 852
Make-Up, Costumes and Masks for the
   Stage 819
Make Your Own Gloves 1503
Make Your Own Hats 750
Making Children's Costumes 1537
Making Clothes in Leather 1544
Making Costumes for School Plays
   1551
Making Leather Clothes 1524
Making Masks for School Plays 881
Making Paper Costumes 1487
Malaysians 560
Mamluk Costume 517
Manners, Customs and Observances
   1328
Manners and Morals in the Age of
   Optimism 1309
Manners and Movements in Costume
   Plays 1222
Manstyle 890
Manual of Heraldry, The 1138
Manual of Wigmaking 817
Mask, The 874
Mask Making 861

Mask of Reality, The 1423
Masks (Benda) 862
Masks (Kniffin) 869
Masks (Shalleck) 879
Masks, Face Coverings and Headgear
   870
Masks: Their Meaning and Function
   872
Masks and Demons 873
Masks and How to Make Them
   (Powell) 877
Masks and How to Make Them (Slade)
   880
Masks and Mask Makers 868
Masks of the World 866
Masks of West Africa 884
Masque of Beauty, The 851
Masterpieces of Western Textiles
   1618
Masterpieces of Women's Costume 201
Mastery of Movement, The 1247
Max Reinhardt 114
Medals and Decorations 907
Mediaeval Costume and Life 1515
Medieval and Tudor Costume 448
Medieval Costume, Armour and
   Weapons 604
Medieval Costume in England and
   France 457
Medieval European Armies 1047
Medieval Theatre Costume 1489
Memorable Balls 1311
Men-at-Arms Series 1015
Mennonite Life 333
Men's Capes and Cloaks 662
Men's Costume 1580-1750 896
Men's Costume 1750-1800 897
Men's Hairdressing 846
Merveilleuses, Des 607
Mexican-American War, The 1022
Mexican Costume 399
Mexican Costumes and Customs 381
Mexican Festival and Ceremonial
   Masks 883
Mexican Indian Costumes 388
Mexican Jewelry 761
Mexican Native Costumes 389
Migration Style in Norway, The 582
Militaria 1009
Military Dress of North America 1085

Title Index

Military Dress of the Peninsular War 1086
Military Fashion 969
Military Headdress 982
Military Uniforms 975
Military Uniforms, 1686-1918 978
Military Uniforms in America 964
Military Uniforms in Color 949
Military Uniforms of Britain and the Empire 913
Millinery in the Fashion History of the World 744
Mime 1252
Mime: The Technique of Silence 1267
Mime: Training and Exercises 1216
Mime Book, The 1244
Miniatures and Silhouettes 722
Mirror Mirror 199
Mirror of Fashion 210
Modedraekter 580
Mode in Costume, The 265
Mode in Footwear, The 738
Mode in Furs, The 715
Mode in Hats and Headdress, The 751
Modern Ballet Design 166
Modern Jewelry 788
Modern Leather Design 1583
Modes and Manners 203
Modes and Manners of the Nineteenth Century 204
Modes des Annees Folles 282
Modes 1785-89 608
Modesty in Dress 1724
Modesty to Mod 344
Mongol Costumes 554
Montcalm's Army 1028
Montcalm's Army: The Seven Years War 1077
Montgomery's Desert Army 1081
More Historical Dances 1274
Morris Book, The 1265
Movement and Metaphor 177
Movement Awareness and Creativity 1217
Movement for the Performing Artist 1259
Mr. Godey's Ladies 338
Muffs and Morals 1706
Musical Comedy 108
Myth America 1329

N

Nadar 1358
Naked We Came 1700
Napoleon's Artillery 1064
Napoleon's Cuirassiers and Carabiniers 1050
Napoleon's Dragoons and Lancers 1051
Napoleon's Enemies 1007
Napoleon's German Allies 1058
Napoleon's Line Chasseurs 1052
Napoleon's Polish Troops 1059
National Costume of Women in Iceland, The 577
National Costumes 515
National Costumes in Holland 644
National Costumes of Czechoslovakia 526
National Costumes of Holland, The 643
National Costumes of Serbia 533
National Costumes of the Slavic Peoples 513
National Costumes of the World 231
National Geographic on Indians of the Americas 376
National Guide to Craft Supplies 62
National Heraldry of the World 1127
Native Art of Norway 579
Native Funk and Flash 334
Natural Dance 1268
Naval, Marine and Air Force Uniforms of World War II 967
Naval Officer's Uniform Guide, The 923
Navies of the American Revolution 981
Navy Uniforms, Insignia and Warships of World War II 998
New and Curious School of Theatrical Dancing 1248
New Catalogue of Catalogues, The 59
New Design in Jewelry 799
New England Militia Uniforms and Accoutrements 927
New Look at Felt, A 1568
New Movement in the Theatre, The 119
New York City Ballet, The 178

New York Guide to Craft Supplies 63
Nigeria in Costume 301
Nineteenth Century, The 1342
Nineteenth Century Jewellery 775
Noh 147
Norwegian Peasant Art 572
Norwegian Textiles 1631
Nureyev Image, The 164

O

Observer's Book of European Costume, The 259
Of Men Only 902
Old English Customs 1284
Old English Customs and Ceremonies 1291
Old English Customs Extant at the Present Time 1290
Old Highland Dress and Tartans 493
Old Hungarian Jewelry 773
Old Irish and Highland Dress 494
Oldtidsdragter 583
Once Over Lightly 832
One Hundred and One Costumes for All Ages, All Occasions 1499
101 Masks 864
100,000 Years of Daily Life 1343
100 Years of Costumes in America 335
100 Years of the American Female from Harper's Bazaar 348
One World of Fashion 219
On Human Finery 1704
On Mime 1227
Opera 94
Orchesography 1213
Orchesography: A Treatise in the Form of a Dialogue 1214
Orders and Decorations (Mericka) 1145
Orders and Decorations (Purves) 1150
Orders and Decorations of All Nations 1158
Orders and Decorations of Europe in Color 1140
Oriental Costume 536
Oriental Costumes 568
Origin and Early History of the Fashion Plate 728

Origin and History of "La Pollera" 401
Origins of Chintz 1613
Ornament and Jewellery 756
Ornament in Applied Art 1463
Ornaments 678
Ornaments of the Ministers, The 1096
Other Face, The 882
Our Mothers 1280
Outline of English Costume 478
Oxford Companion to the Decorative Arts, The 41

P

Pageant of Hats, A 746
Panoply of Ghana 299
Pantomime 109
Pantomime: Elements and Exercises 1200
Pantomime: The Silent Theatre 1237
Pants 1560
Panzer Divisions, The 1082
Paris a la Mode 1676
Parures Africaines 303
Pattern 1467
Patterns and Ceremonials of the Indians of the Southwest 357
Patterns of Fashion, 1860-1940 1478
Patterns of Fashion, 1660-1860 1479
Peacock's Tail, The 1707
Peasant Art in Austria and Hungary 628
Peasant Art in Italy 637
Peasant Art in Roumania 519
Peasant Art in Russia 512
Peasant Art in Sweden, Lapland and Iceland 581
Peasant Art in Switzerland 623
Peasant Costume in Europe 599
Peasant Costume of the Black Forest 630
People of Kau, The 306
Perfect Fit, The 1548
Perfect Lady, The 1712
Period Costume 453
Period Costumes and Settings for the Small Stage 1431
Period Patterns 1483
Permanence de la Parure et du Masque Africains 289

Persian Fabrics 1598
Perukes and Periwigs 815
Pfaffenwinkler Trachtenbuch 625
Physical Movement for the Theatre 1246
Picasso Theatre 83
Pictorial Encyclopedia of Fashion, The 37
Pictorial History of American Sports 1175
Pictorial History of Costume, A 213
Pictorial History of the Royal Canadian Mounted Police, The 1102
Pictorial History of the Russian Theatre, The 113
Picture Book of Symbols, The 1471
Picture History of English Costume, A 446
Picture History of the British Theatre, A 110
Pins for Hats and Cravats 704
Pipe Book, The 692
Playing Period Plays 1257
Pleasure of Jewelry and Gemstones, The 794
Pleasures of Pattern, The 1469
Pleasures of the Past 1281
Poiret 1697
Police Uniforms of the World 1088
Polite World, The 1330
Polizei und Mode 1092
Pollera Panamena, La 408
Popular Arts of the Hungarians of Transylvania 532
Popular Culture and Costume in Czecho-Slovakia 504
Popular Roumanian Dress 506
Portfolio of Folk Costume Patterns, A 1552
Portraits of Queen Elizabeth I 473
Portuguese Army of the Napoleonic Wars 1060
Postal Uniforms of the World 1089
Powder and Paint 856
Practical Stage Make-Up 845
Precision Draping 1535
Pre-Classic Dance Forms 1234
Preliminary Study of Traditional Kutchin Clothing in Museums 377
Pre-Romantic Ballet, The 188

Primary Structures of Fabrics, The 1609
Primitive Shoes 734
Principles of Figure Drawing 1424
Printed Cottons at Old Sturbridge Village 1626
Printed Textiles 1621
Printing on Fabric 1659
Professional Patternmaking 1513
Psychology of Clothes, The 1714
Pueblo Crafts 378
Punch History of Manners and Modes, A 1277

Q

Quaker, The 327
Quant by Quant 1691
Queen's Clothes, The 449
Queens of England 1377
Queen's Orders of Chivalry, The 1132
Quill and Beadwork of the Western Sioux 373

R

Raiment for the Lord's Service 1112
Reading and Reference List on Costume, A 18
Recurring Cycles of Fashion 268
Regional Costumes of Spain, The 670
Remember When 1340
Renaissance Classical Costume 115
Renaissance Jewels and Jewelled Objects 785
Renaissance Theatre Costume 120
Restless Image, The 1721
Restyle Your Hats 748
Revue 111
Right and Left Hand Fencing 1270
Rings through the Ages 786
Riscos Illuminados 397
Rise and Fall of the Victorian Servant, The 1104
Robes of Thespis 128
Robes of White Shell and Sunrise 358
Roman Army from Caesar to Trajan, The 1044
Romance and History of Shoes, The 740

Romance of Lace, The 1614
Romance of the Shoe, The 741
Roman Soldier, The 935
Romantic and Glamorous Hollywood
    Design 192
Roman Toga, The 425
Rommel's Desert Army 1083
Route of the Incas, The 402
Royal and Historic Gloves and Shoes
    709
Royal Artillery, The 1031
Royal Courts of Fashion 236
Royal Green Jackets, The 1040
Royal Heritage 1149
Royal Navy, The 1045
Royal Scots Greys 1034
Royalty on Horseback 1173
Rural Costume 601
Rural Pennsylvania Clothing 326
Russian Army of the Crimea 1070
Russian Army of the Napoleonic Wars
    1063
Russian Ballet, The 176
Russian Ballet Past and Present, The
    171
Russian Festivals and Costumes 503
Russian Stage and Costume Designs
    185
Russian Theatre, The 88
Russkii Kostium 524

S

Saatylaispuke Suomessa Vanhemmalla
    590
Sadler's Wells Ballet, The 158
Salute to the Thirties 1369
Scandinavian Armies in the Napoleon-
    ic Wars 1053
Scandinavian Peasant Costume 588
Scenes from the Nineteenth Century
    Stage 73
Scenographia Hungarica 77
Scholars on Parade 1108
School of Fencing, The 1212
Scots in Uniform 906
Scottish Costume 495
Scottish Military Uniforms 1011
Scottish Regiments and Uniforms 919
Sculpture of Style, The 70

Seasonal Feasts and Festivals 1305
Second Skin, The 1719
Secrets of the Chinese Drama 155
Self-Decoration in Mount Hagen 567
Settings and Costumes for Sadler's
    Wells Ballets 175
Settings and Costumes of the Modern
    Stage 101
Seventeenth Century Costume 1559
75 Years of Fashion 278
Seventy-Five Years of Fashion 900
Sewing without Tears 1586
Sewing with the New Knits 1562
Sew Your Own Accessories 1570
Shaker Clothing 342
Shakespearian Costume for Stage and
    Screen 99
Shaped Weaving 1528
Shawls 699
Shawls, Crinolines, Filigree 322
Shocking Life 1693
Short History of Costume and Armour,
    A 238
Short History of Japanese Armour 986
Short History of Marriage, A 1171
Short History of the Scottish Dress
    490
Sibylles Modelexikon 48
Sicilian and Lucchese Fabrics 1599
Signs, Symbols and Ornaments 1474
Silhouettes 724
Silks of Lyons, The 1600
Silver and Gold 1682
Simon's Directory 68
Simple Stage Costumes and How to
    Make Them 1522
Simplified Stagecraft Manual, The
    1571
Simplified Tailoring 1546
Six Thousand Years of Hair Styling
    843
Sixty Years of Fashion 281
Slovak National Dress, The 516
Social Caricature in the 18th Century
    1322
Social Dance 1230
Social Dances of the Nineteenth
    Century in England, The 1263
Social History of the Bicycle, A 1181
Sociology of Fashion, The 1708

Soldiers of London, The 914
Soldiers of the American Army 954
Some Historical Dances 1275
Sources of Design 1476
South American Textiles 1640
Southeastern Indians 363
South Wales Borderers, The 1041
Soviet Army, The 1078
Soviet Army Uniforms and Insignia 910
Spanish Armies of the Napoleonic Wars 1061
Spanish Costume 652
Spanish Silks 1601
Spanish Textiles 1604, 1636
Spare Time Guides 1659
Splendor at Court 132
Sporting Art in England 1185
Sporting Pictures of England 1180
Sports and Pastimes of the People of England, The 1183
Stage Costume 249
Stage Costume and Accessories 96
Stage Costume Construction 1484
Stage Costume Design 1450
Stage Costume for the Amateur 1504
Stage Costume Handbook 1554
Stage Costumes and How to Make Them 1577
Stage Costumes for Girls 1512
Stage Costuming 1589
Stage Crafts 64
Stage Designs and Costumes by Oliver Messel 116
Stage Design throughout the World 1970-75 93
Stage Design throughout the World since 1950 91
Stage Design throughout the World since 1960 90
Stage Design throughout the World since 1935 92
Stage Fights 1231
Stage Fights, Swords, Firearms, Fisticuffs and Slapstick 1233
Stage Makeup (Buchman) 820
Stage Makeup (Corson) 828
Stage Violence 1240
Stitching for Style 1536
Stonewall Brigade, The 1027

Storia del Costume 20
Storia del Costume in Italia 638
Story of Clothes, The 194
Story of Hosiery, The 703
Story of Jewelry, The 758
Story of Snuff and Snuff Boxes, The 686
Strange Story of False Hair, The 857
Street Criers and Itinerant Tradesmen 1113
Style and Design 1402
Style in Costume 172
Sudan Campaigns, The 1073
Suiting Everyone 336
Sun, Sand and Steel 320
Survey of World Textiles 1628
Swedish Folk Dances 592
Swedish Handcraft 585
Swedish Peasant Costumes 586
Swedish Textiles 1647
Swiss Textiles 1632
Sword and Masque 1258
Sword Play 1219

T

Tagasode 558
Tailoring 1481
Tailoring Suits the Professional Way 1553
Taman Indera 566
Tartans 491
Tartans of Scotland 496
Taste and Fashion 244
Technique of Ballroom Dancing 1235
Technique of Dress Design, The 1444
Technique of Film and Television Make-Up, The 839
Technique of Jewelry, The 764
10s, the 20s, the 30s, The 1688
Textbook of Footwear Manufacture 736
Textile Art in the Church 1105
Textile Collections of the World 7
Textile Conservation 1617
Textile Dyeing and Printing Simplified 1669
Textiles 1612
Textiles: Properties and Behaviour 1620

Textiles and Costume Design 1428
Textiles and Costumes among the
    Peoples of the Ancient Near East
    422
Textiles in New England 1610
Theatre and Allied Arts 5
Theatre and Stage 32
Theatre Arts Publications, 1953-57 2
Theatre Arts Publications, 1947-52 1
Theatre Crafts Book of Costumes, The
    1453
Theatre Crafts Book of Make-Up,
    Masks and Wigs, The 850
Theatre in India 143
Theatre Movement 1243
Theatre Student: Costuming, The
    1448
Theatre through the Ages 117
Theatrical Companion to Shaw 107
Theatrical Costume and the Amateur
    Stage 1510
Theatrical Style 1451
Theory of Fashion Design, The 1418
Thermoplastic Scenery for the Theatre
    1490
Things I Remember 133
Thirties, The 1371
Thirties: An Illustrated History in
    Colour, 1930-1939, The 1400
30th Punjabis, The 1035
This Is Fashion 214
This Was England 1279
Thrace and the Thracians 414
Thread of Ariadne, The 415
Three Centuries of Women's Dress
    Fashions 1731
Time and Space 695
Time in a Frame 1398
Today There Are No Gentlemen 891
Toilet in Ancient and Modern Times,
    The 822
Toilette of the Hebrew Lady 505
Tokugawa Collection, The 154
Tournament, The 1130
Trachten der Alpenlander 626
Traditional Dances of Latin America,
    The 1239
Traditional Dances of Latin America:
    Dances of Mexico 1223
Traditional Dancing in Scotland 1229

Traditional Maori Clothing 1728
Traje en la Nueva Espana, El 385
Traje Regional, El 667
Traje Regional de Galicia, El 668
Traje Regional Salmantino, El 658
Trajes Civiles, Militares y Religiosos
    de Mexico 398
Trajes Populares de Espana, Los 648
Trajes Populares y Costumbres Tradi-
    cionales 659
Trajes Tipicos de Guatemala 404
Traje y el Adorno en Mexico, El
    383
Trajo Popular em Portugal, O 672
Tribal Peoples of Southern Africa 308
Tudor and Stuart Fabrics 1602
Turkische Gewander 528
Twelve Mexican Native Costumes 406
Twenties, The 1372
Twenties: An Illustrated History in
    Colour, 1919-1929, The 1401
20th Century Fashion 272
Twentieth Century Lace 1625
Twinkletoes 732
Two Centuries of Costume in America
    321
Two Centuries of English Chintz 1606
Two Centuries of French Fashion 618
200 Years of Sport in America 1184
2,000 Designs, Forms and Ornaments
    1466
Two Thousand Years of Textiles 1653
Transportation Uniforms of the World
    1090
Trouwen in Het Wit 1170
Typical Regional and Period Costumes
    of France 621

U

Undies Book, The 1196
Unfashionable Human Body, The 1735
Ungarische Bauerntrachten 629
Uniform Buttons 948
Uniformes et Costumes du 1er Empire
    921
Uniform of the Scottish Infantry 1002
Uniform Regulation for the Army of
    the United States 1006
Uniforms and Equipment of the Light
    Brigade 973

Uniforms and History of the Scottish Regiments, The   915
Uniforms of the American, British, French and German Armies in the War of the American Revolution   958
Uniforms of the American Revolution   970
Uniforms of the Army   983
Uniforms of the British Army, Navy and Court   944
Uniforms of the Civil War   959
Uniforms of the Civil War, 1861–65   939
Uniforms of the Napoleonic Wars   940
Uniforms of the Retreat from Moscow   941
Uniforms of the Royal Armoured Corps   930
Uniforms of the Royal Navy during the Napoleonic Wars   971
Uniforms of the Scottish Regiments   993
Uniforms of the Seven Years War   972
Uniforms of the SS   968
Uniforms of the United States Army   974
Uniforms of the United States Navy, The   1003
Uniforms of the World   1091
Uniforms of the World's Police   1094
Uniforms of the Yeomanry Regiments   994
Uniforms of Waterloo   942
United States Army Headgear, 1855–1902   945
United States Army Headgear to 1854   946
United States Cavalry, The   1025
United States Marine Corps, The   1026
United States Military Medals and Ribbons   987
United States Navy, The   965
United States Service Symbols   1000
Universal Bead, The   688
Unmentionables   1190
Upper Crust, The   1285

V

Vanishing Africa   304
Vanity Fair   1334
Vecellio's Renaissance Costume Book   640
Venetian Fabrics   1603
Vestiario Italiano, II   639
Vestimenta Argentina   390
Vestments and Vesture   1117
Victoria and Albert Museum: The Costume Court   61
Victoriana   465
Victoriana Americana   1321
Victorian and Edwardian Army, The   933
Victorian Army, The   925
Victorian Children   811
Victorian Costume and Costume Accessories   435
Victorian Comfort   1298
Victorian Fashions and Costumes   312
Victorian England   1391
Victorian Entertainment   1289
Victorian Gentleman, The   1341
Victorian Jewellery   766
Victorian Jewellery Design   769
Victorian Jewelry   754
Victorian Lace   1652
Victorian Life in Photographs   1393
Victorian Panorama: A Survey of Life and Fashion from Contemporary Photographs   1390
Victorian Panorama: Paintings of Victorian Life   1405
Victorians, The   1352
Victorian Scene, The   1338
Victorian Vista   1310
Victoria's Heyday   1389
View of Fashion   1278
Vikings, The   574
Viking Settlers in Greenland   584
Village Arts of Romania   530
Vingt–Cinq Costumes Pour le Theatre   74
Vingt–Cinq Siecles de Mariage   1162
Visible Self, The   1732
Volkstrachten der Schweiz, Die   627

W

Waffen SS, The 1084
Warriors and Weapons of Early Times 990
Warriors and Worthies 976
Watches 681
Way West, The 329
Weapons in the Theatre 1272
Wearable Crafts 1569
Wearing of Costume, The 1232
Wedding, The 1167
Wedding Costume 663
Wedding Day in Literature, The 1163
Wellington's Peninsular Army 1055
Welsh Costume 487
Welsh Costume and Customs 486
Welsh Folk Dance and Costume 481
Western Asiatic Jewellery 787
Western European Costume 596
Western Reserve Historical Society 21
Western World Costume 207
What People Wore 232
What They Wore 805
Wheels of Fashion, The 1686
When Men Wore Muffs 903
Why of Fashion, The 1701
Why Women Wear Clothes 1713
Wide World of Clothing, The 1723
Wigmaker in Eighteenth Century Williamsburg, The 855
Wigmaker's Art, The 830
William and Mary Fabrics 1593
Windsor Years, The 1375
Wolfe's Army 1023
Wolfe's Army: The Seven Years War 1074
Woman in Fashion, The 253
Women in Uniform 1098
Women's Bathing and Swimming Costume in the United States 1178
Women's Clothing in the 19th Century 498
Women's Coiffure 664

Women's Costume in Early Ontario 313
Women's Costume in Ontario 314
Women's Costumes, 1750-1800 454
Women's Costumes, 1600-1750 455
Women's Dress 647
Women's Dress for Church 665
Women's Dress in the Jazz Age 280
Women's Headdress and Hairstyles in England 743
Women's Jewelry 666
Wonderful World of Ladies' Fashion, The 345
Working Class Costume 1123
Working Dress in Colonial and Revolutionary America 1093
Working with Leather 1550
World Costumes 208
World in Vogue, The 1327
World of Balenciaga, The 1698
World of Culture: Costume 239
World of Fashion 66
World of Harlequin, The 121
World of Romanian Theatre, The 102
World of Serge Diaghilev, The 187
World of Watteau, The 1394
World of Weddings, The 1169
World's Heritage of Woven Fabrics, The 1591
World Theatre in Pictures 125
World Uniform in Color 928
World Uniforms and Battles 943

Y

Yearbook of English Festivals 1319
Yesterday in Sport 1176
Yesterday's Dress 497
Yoruba Hairstyles 837

Z

Zulu Wars, The 1067

SUBJECT INDEX

This index is alphabetized letter by letter. Numbers refer to entry numbers.

A

Academic costume 1087, 1099,
   1100, 1103, 1108, 1118
Accessories 677–78, 688, 691,
   701, 707, 711, 715, 1570
   buttons 673, 689, 702, 705,
      706, 713, 948
   canes 714
   eyeglasses 684
   fans 674, 690, 694, 700, 708,
      789
   gloves 676, 683, 709, 710,
      712, 1503, 1509
   handkerchiefs 679
   hat boxes 680
   hatpins 675, 704
   hosiery 693, 697, 703
   musical instruments 696
   neckwear 682, 889
   pipes 687, 692
   shawls 698, 699
   snuff and snuff boxes 686
   umbrellas 685
   watches and timepieces 681, 695,
      755
Adrian 1685
African costume 9, 14, 288–310,
   867, 884, 1374, 1501
African hairstyles 837
American Ballet Theatre 182
Amies, Hardy 1673
Amish costume 319, 326, 332

Ancient costume 412, 416, 418,
   421–23, 781, 791, 797
   Denmark 413
   Etrusca 411
   Greece and Rome 410, 415,
      417, 419, 420, 424, 425,
      774, 776, 935, 985, 1044
   Thrace 414
Argentine costume 390
Arms and armor 238, 604, 908,
   909, 917–18, 924, 961,
   976–77, 984–86, 1005,
   1148. See also Heraldry and
   chivalry
Ashton, Frederick 174
Australian costume 488
Austrian costume 624, 626, 628
Aztec costume 387

B

Bakst, Leon 156, 159–60, 180,
   186
Balenciaga 1698
Bathing costume, U.S. 1178
Bayreuth costumes 137
Beadwork, American Indian 366,
   373
Beardsley, Aubrey 136
Beaton, Cecil 129
Bertain, Celia 1676
Bicycle costume, U.S. 1181
Birth and death costume 1164, 1166

Subject Index

Blackfeet costume 362
British Commonwealth costume 489
  Australia 488
  Ireland 484, 494, 498
  Scotland 480, 482-83, 485,
    490-96
  South Africa 497
  Wales 479, 481, 486-87
Brazilian costume 384, 396-97
British costume 426-28, 433-34,
    436-37, 446, 450-51, 453,
    458, 468, 470, 472, 475,
    477-78
  tenth-fifteenth centuries 430-31,
    445, 448, 457
  sixteenth century 429, 444, 454,
    459, 462, 469, 471, 473-
    74
  seventeenth century 432, 443,
    455, 461
  eighteenth century 441, 454-55,
    461, 463, 476
  nineteenth century 435, 438-39,
    442, 447, 452, 456, 460,
    464-66
  twentieth century 440, 449, 466-
    67
Brummell, Beau 894, 904
Bulgarian costume 529
Bunraku 138
Burmese costume 559
Buttons 673, 689, 702, 705-6, 713,
    948
Buyo 144

C

Callot, Jacques 98
Canadian costume 313-14, 316-17,
    323, 344, 359, 370
Canes 714
Central and South American costume
    395, 403, 405
  Argentina 390
  Aztec 387
  Brazil 384, 396-97
  El Salvador 400
  Guatemala 394, 400, 404, 407
  Inca 402
  Mexico 381-83, 385-89, 391-94,
    398-99, 406, 761, 883,
    1223
  Panama 401, 408
  Peru 409
Ceremonial costume 1129, 1131,
    1134, 1143, 1154-55
Chagall, Marc 89
Chanel, Coco 1674
Chinese costume 541-42, 548,
    556-65, 569
Chinese opera costume 140, 148,
    841
Chinese stage costume 139, 146,
    149, 151, 155
Chios costume 500
Circus technique 1220
Clowns and fools 86, 1119, 1122
Color, historical 1409, 1414,
    1420
Color and color theory 1411-13,
    1415-16, 1421, 1430,
    1432, 1437, 1439
Commedia dell arte 75, 121-22
Coronation costume, England 1139,
    1141, 1146, 1149, 1151-
    53, 1157
Corsets 1187, 1192, 1197-99. See
    also Undergarments
Costume appreciation 1407-8
Costume bibliography 1-5, 7-8,
    10-13, 15, 17-18, 21
Costume collections 54, 57, 60-61,
    65, 67, 69, 70-71, 1683
Costume dictionaries 25-28, 31,
    33-38, 48, 51
Costume encyclopedias 32, 44
Costume for Hamlet 80, 106
Costume for the cinema 189-93
Costume history, general 194-268
Court costume, England 944, 1161
Crafts and supplies 56, 58-59,
    62-63, 68, 72
Czechoslovakian costume 504, 526
Czechoslovakian stage costume 112

D

Dance, ballroom and social 1228,
    1230, 1235
Dance, period 1213-14, 1224-25,
    1234, 1245, 1248, 1255-57,

1261-63, 1265, 1269, 1273-75. See also Dance, ballroom and social
Dance and costume
Africa 295
Ancient Greece 1249-50
Andalusia 1221
Argentina 1239
Belgium 1209
Bulgaria 1206
Canada 181
Czechoslovakia 1207
England 1224, 1241-42, 1261, 1263, 1265, 1316
Europe 1201, 1226, 1251, 1266
France 1208, 1224
Germany 1204
Hungary 1253, 1271
India 535, 537, 551
Italy 636, 1225, 1233
Latin America 382, 1223, 1226
Norway 1210
Orient 1276
Poland 1211
Portugal 1202
Romania 1205
Scotland 1229
Spain 1203, 1221, 1225, 1238
Sweden 592
Wales 481
Dance bibliography 1218
Dance costume 29, 157, 161-63, 166-68, 170, 173, 177, 183-84, 188, 716-21
Dance in Canada 181
Dancewear. See Dance costume
Dandies 894, 898, 901, 904
Danish costume 413, 570-71, 583, 590, 1160
Decorative arts 41
Design, costume and fashion 45, 47, 55, 1417-23, 1427-28, 1431, 1433, 1435, 1440, 1443-51, 1453-56, 1458-59, 1505
Design elements 1406, 1410, 1429-30, 1438, 1442. See also Color and color theory
Diaghilev, Serge 165, 169, 172, 179, 187
Dior, Christian 1679

Draping technique 1505, 1518, 1523, 1535, 1565, 1587
Drawing technique 1424-26, 1434-36, 1441, 1449, 1452, 1454, 1456-57
Dutch costume 642-47
Dyeing, batik and printing 1654-72

E

Eastern European costume 508, 513, 515-16, 525, 527, 756
Bulgaria 529
Chios 500
Czechoslovakia 504, 526
Hebrew 505, 523
Hungary 509-11, 514, 520, 531-32, 628, 773
Mamluk 517
Moravian Slovakia 502
Romania 501, 506, 519, 530, 534
Russia 499, 503, 507, 512, 518, 522, 524
Serbia 533
Turkey 521, 528
Ecclesiastical costume 1096, 1105, 1109-12, 1114-17, 1120-21
El Salvadorian costume 400
Entertainments, Victorian 1289
Equestrian costume 1172-73
Erte. See Tirtoff, Romain de Erte
Eskimo costume 318, 878
Etruscan costume 411
Eyeglasses 684

F

Faberge, Carl 784
Fans 674, 690, 694, 700, 708, 789
Fashion designers 66, 1673-99
Fashion dictionary 42-43
Fashion plates 725-29
Feasts 1287, 1305
Fencing and swordplay 1212, 1219, 1234, 1258, 1270, 1272
Festivals and holidays 1302-5, 1311, 1317-19, 1328, 1332
Finnish costume 589, 594

Subject Index

Footwear 731-41
French costume 605-22, 895

G

Gagaku 152
Garment patterns and construction 64,
        1427, 1477, 1484-87, 1493,
        1496-97, 1499, 1502, 1504-
        5, 1508, 1510-13, 1516,
        1520, 1522, 1528-29, 1531-
        32, 1534, 1536-37, 1541-
        42, 1548-49, 1551-52,
        1554-58, 1561-62, 1566-72,
        1576-78, 1585-86, 1588-89
    Africa 1501
    cote 1491
    nontextile materials 1487, 1490,
        1492, 1496, 1500, 1521,
        1524, 1530, 1544, 1550,
        1563, 1583
    period 26, 28, 118, 1477-79,
        1482-84, 1489, 1491, 1494,
        1498, 1506-7, 1514-15,
        1517, 1526, 1533, 1559,
        1575, 1580-81
    smocks 1477
    See also Pattern making and cutting;
        Tailoring
German costume 625, 629-30
Gilbert and Sullivan 95
Gloves 676, 683, 709-10, 712,
        1503
    construction of 1503
Greek and Roman costume 410, 415,
        417, 419-20, 424-25, 774,
        776, 935, 985, 1044
Greek drama costumes 79, 135
Greer, Howard 1681
Guatemalan costume 394, 400, 404,
        407

H

Hairstyles 30, 664, 743, 751, 812-
        13, 815-16, 821, 823-26,
        829, 832, 837, 840, 843-
        44, 846-49, 860
    India 543, 564
Handkerchiefs 679

Harlequin 75, 121. See also Com-
        media dell arte
Hartnell, Norman 1682
Hat boxes 680
Hatpins 675, 704
Hats. See Headwear
Headwear 742-51, 870, 1495,
        1509
Hebrew costume 505, 523
Heraldry and chivalry 34, 50, 924,
        934, 1125-30, 1132-33,
        1135-38, 1142, 1144,
        1147-48, 1156, 1159,
        1336, 1355, 1392
Holidays. See Festivals and holidays
Hosiery 693, 697, 703
Household servants' costume 1095,
        1104
Hungarian costume 509-11, 514,
        520, 531-32, 628, 773
Hungarian stage costume 77

I

Icelandic costume 577
Incan costume 402
Indian costumes 535, 537-38,
        543-46, 549, 551-52,
        564, 566, 757, 844
Indian stage costume 142-43
Irish costume 484, 494, 498
Iroquois costume 372
Italian costume 632-41
Italian stage costume 82, 87

J

Japanese and Indonesian costume
        550, 553, 555, 557-58,
        561-62, 848, 875, 986
Jewelry 40, 751, 753, 755-56,
        758-60, 763-65, 767-68,
        771-72, 775, 777-78,
        783-84, 787-88, 792,
        794-96, 798-99
    ancient 781, 791
    Anglo-Saxon 780
    Egypt 752, 797
    Greece and Rome 774, 776
    Hungary 773

India 757
Mexico 761
necklaces 793
Renaissance 762, 785
rings 782, 786
Spain 666, 790
Victorian 754, 766, 769, 779, 789
Jones, Inigo 97, 123, 131
Juvenile costume 800-811

K

Kabuki costume 141, 145, 150, 153
Knitting, stitching, and weaving technique 1485, 1488, 1528, 1530, 1536, 1542, 1548, 1574, 1608, 1614, 1619, 1625, 1652, 1654, 1656, 1662, 1664

L

Lace 1614, 1619, 1625, 1652
Lebanese and Syrian costume 540
Legal costume 1101
Lingerie 1186, 1189, 1191, 1193, 1195-96. See also Undergarments

M

McCardell, Claire 1685
Macrame 1488. See also Knitting, stitching, and weaving technique
Mainbocher 1685
Makeup 148, 814, 818-20, 822, 827-28, 833-36, 839, 841-42, 845, 850-54, 856, 858-59, 864, 1486
Malaysian costume 560, 567
Mamluk costume 517
Manners and customs 1295, 1297-98, 1306-12, 1314, 1322, 1327-28
England 1277-78, 1280-81, 1285, 1288, 1291-92, 1296, 1299-1301, 1315-16, 1323, 1325, 1330, 1332-33

female 1283, 1293, 1313, 1320, 1326, 1329
United States 1279, 1282, 1284, 1286, 1294, 1321, 1324, 1329, 1331
See also Entertainments, Victorian; Feasts
Masks 819, 850, 852, 861-85
Mennonite costume 333
Men's wear 23-24, 46, 886-904, 1707
Messel, Oliver 116
Mexican costume 381-83, 385-89, 391-94, 398-99, 406, 761, 883, 1223
Military costume 27, 603, 916, 928, 936, 940-43, 949, 955, 958, 962, 966-67, 969, 972, 975, 978-79, 990, 1005, 1007-9, 1015, 1042-43, 1047-48, 1067, 1071-77, 1079, 1086. See also Naval costume
ancient 935, 1044
England and British Commonwealth 906, 911-16, 919-20, 922, 925, 930, 932-33, 938, 944, 950, 953, 956-57, 960, 973, 991, 993-96, 998, 1002, 1010-14, 1030-41, 1049, 1055, 1068, 1074, 1076, 1081
France 921, 999, 1001, 1046, 1050-66
Germany 926, 929, 937, 968, 999, 1058, 1069, 1080, 1082-84
headdress 982
medals and awards 905, 907, 934, 952, 987-89, 1000
Russian 910, 1063, 1070, 1076, 1078
Scotland 906, 915, 919, 994, 1002, 1011
United States 927, 939, 945-46, 948, 954, 959, 964, 970, 974, 980, 983, 997, 1004, 1006, 1016-29, 1085
Millinery. See Headwear
Millinery technique 748, 750, 1495, 1509

Subject Index

Mime 1216, 1227, 1244, 1253, 1267. See also Pantomime
Miniatures 722
Mongol costume 554
Moravian Slovakian costume 502
Movement technique, dance and theatrical 1217, 1232, 1236, 1243, 1245-48, 1254-57, 1259-60, 1268
    period theatrical 1222, 1232, 1257, 1264
Musical comedy costume 108
Musical instruments 696
Music hall costume 85, 111

N

National costume 164, 231. See also individual countries
Naval costume
    England 931, 944, 947, 951, 963, 971, 1045
    United States 923, 965, 981, 998, 1003
    See also Military costume
Necklaces 793
Neckwear 682, 889
New York City Ballet 178
Noh 147, 154
Norelle, Norman 1685
North American Indian costume 354-80, 737, 885
    Blackfeet 362
    Eskimo 318, 878
    Iroquois 372
    Ojibewa 371
    Pueblo 378
Norwegian costume 572, 576, 579, 582, 591, 593
Nureyev, Rudolf 164

O

Occupational costume 1091, 1093, 1107, 1113, 1123-24. See also specific professions
Ojibewa costume 371
Opera costume 94
Orders and decorations 1140, 1145, 1150, 1158

Oriental costume 536, 539, 547, 568
    Burma 559
    China 541-42, 548, 556, 565
    India 535, 537-38, 545-46, 549, 551-52, 564, 566, 757, 844
    Japan and Indonesia 550, 553, 555, 557-58, 561-62, 848, 875, 986
    Lebanon and Syria 540
    Malaysia 560, 567
    Mongol 554
    Pakistan 544
    Tibet 563
Ornament
    Egyptian 1475
    guide and handbooks 49, 1460-69, 1472-74. See also Signs and symbols

P

Pakistani costume 544
Panamanian costume 401, 408
Pantomime 109, 1200, 1215, 1237. See also Mime
Pattern making and cutting 1518-19, 1527, 1538-41, 1543, 1545, 1547, 1560, 1564, 1573, 1579, 1582, 1584. See also Garment patterns and construction
Period dances 1213-14, 1223-24, 1235, 1245, 1248, 1254-57, 1261-63, 1265, 1269, 1273-75
Peruvian costume 409
Picasso, Pablo 83
Pipes 687, 692
Poiret, Paul 1690, 1697
Police and firemen uniforms 1088, 1092, 1094, 1097, 1102
Portuguese costume 655-56, 672
Postal service uniforms 1089
Psychology of dress and fashion 1700-1737
Pueblo costume 378
PUNCH (magazine) 1277

Q

Quaker costume 327
Quant, Mary 1691

R

Reinhardt, Max 114
Renaissance stage costume 115, 120, 132
Rings 782, 786
Romanian costume 501, 506, 519, 530, 534
Romanian stage costume 102
Royal Canadian Mounted Police 1102
Russian ballet design 171, 176, 185
Russian costume 499, 503, 507, 512, 518, 522, 524
Russian stage costume 88, 113

S

Sadler's Wells Ballet 158, 175
Sari 545
Scandinavian costume 581, 588
Denmark 570-71, 583, 590, 1160
Finland 589, 594
Iceland 577
Norway 572, 576, 579, 582, 591, 593
Sweden 573, 575, 578, 580, 585-87, 592
Viking 574, 584
Schiaparelli, Elsa 1693
Scottish costume 480, 482-83, 485, 490-96
Serbian costume 533
Shaker costume 342
Shakespearian stage costume 84, 99, 105
Sharaff, Irene 193
Shaw, George B. 107
Shawls 698-99
Signs and symbols 1461, 1470-71, 1474. See also Ornament
Silhouettes 722-24, 730
Skating costume 20
Snuff and snuff boxes 686
Social history 6, 1343
ancient 1344-45

tenth-fifteenth centuries 1336, 1339, 1355-57, 1366, 1382, 1392, 1404
sixteenth-eighteenth centuries 1346-47, 1349, 1367, 1382, 1386, 1394, 1396, 1399
nineteenth century 1338, 1341-42, 1352-53, 1358, 1367, 1378-79, 1393, 1398
England 1365, 1377, 1388
tenth-fifteenth centuries 1335, 1359, 1363-64
sixteenth-nineteenth centuries 1350-51, 1354, 1360-63, 1368, 1370, 1376, 1381, 1383, 1389-91, 1403, 1405
twentieth century 1354, 1375, 1385, 1387, 1400-1402
United States 1348, 1395
nineteenth century 1353, 1373, 1378, 1384
twentieth century 1334, 1337, 1340, 1369, 1371-73, 1380, 1397, 1400-1402
See also Manners and customs
South African costume 497
Spanish costume 648-71, 790
Sports costume 20, 1176
England 1174, 1177-78, 1180, 1182-83, 1185
United States 1175, 1184
See also specific sports
Stage combat 1231, 1233, 1240
Stitching technique. See Knitting, stitching, and weaving technique
Swedish costume 573, 575, 578, 580, 585-87, 592
Swiss costume 623, 627, 631

T

Tailoring 1481, 1498, 1525, 1545-46, 1553. See also Garment patterns and construction
Textiles 53, 1591, 1607, 1609, 1612-13, 1616, 1618, 1620-22, 1627-28, 1648-50, 1653

Africa 307
Balkan countries 1634-35, 1639
Byzantine 1594
Canada 1646
England 1592-93, 1602, 1606,
    1608, 1615, 1621, 1638
France 1600, 1637
Germany, Switzerland, and
    Austria 1632, 1641, 1645
India 538, 543
Italy and Sicily 1596, 1599,
    1603, 1629
Japan and China 562, 1595, 1642
Netherlands 1630
Persia 1598
Scandinavia 594, 1631, 1643-44,
    1647
South America 1605, 1640
Spain 1597, 1601, 1604, 1636
United States 1590, 1610, 1621,
    1623-24, 1626, 1633
Textile care and preservation 1611,
    1617, 1651
Textile encyclopedias and dictionaries
    21-22, 39, 52
Theatrical costume, general 73-74,
    76-78, 81, 90-93, 96,
    100-101, 103-4, 110,
    117-19, 124-28, 134
Thracian costume 414
Tibetan costume 563
Tirtoff, Romain de Erte 130, 133,
    1694
Transportational service uniforms
    1090, 1106
Trigere, Pauline 1685
Turkish costume 521, 528
Twentieth-century costume 269-87,
    1688

U

Umbrellas 685

Undergarments 1186-99
Uniforms for women 1098
U.S. costume 16, 311-12, 315,
    321, 324-25, 328, 330,
    334-39, 343, 345-49, 351-
    53
  Amish 319, 326, 332
  Mennonite 333
  Quaker 327
  Shaker 342
  Western 320, 322, 329, 331,
    340-41, 350

V

VANITY FAIR Magazine 1334
Viking costume 574, 584
VOGUE Magazine 279, 1327, 1678

W

Watches and timepieces 681, 695,
    755
Weaving technique. See Knitting,
    stitching, and weaving tech-
    nique
Wedding costume 1160-65, 1167-71
Welsh costume 479, 481, 486-87
Western European costume 19, 595-
    604, 1515
  Austria 624, 626, 628
  France 605-22, 895, 1514
  Germany 625, 629-30
  Italy 623-41
  Netherlands 642-47
  Portugal 655-56, 672
  Spain 648-54, 656-71, 790
  Switzerland 623, 627, 631
Wigs and Wigmaking 815, 817,
    830-31, 838, 850, 855,
    857. See also Hairstyles
THE WINTER'S TALE 84
Worth, House of 1677, 1692, 1699